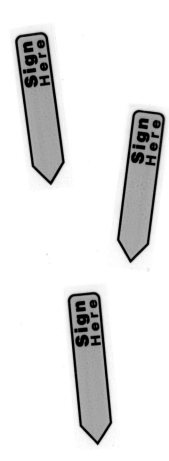

MUSEUMS *of* Southeast Asia

IOLA LENZI

MUSEUMS *of* Southeast Asia

ARCHIPELAGO PRESS

The publisher would like to thank
SG Private Banking (Asia Pacific)
for their generous support.

Editors
Marilyn Seow
Laura Jeanne Gobal

Assistant Editors
Pasha Siraj
Malcolm Tay

Museums Coordinator
Gwenaëlle Solignac

Designer
Annie Teo

Production Manager
Sin Kam Cheong

Sales and Marketing Director
Antoine Monod

Every effort has been made to ensure the accuracy of the information in
this book at the time of going to press. The publisher cannot be held
responsible for any inaccuracies and omissions. Readers are advised to
call the various institutions, if appropriate, to verify details.

Published by
Archipelago Press
an imprint of
Editions Didier Millet
121 Telok Ayer Street, #03-01
Singapore 068590

www.edmbooks.com

Printed in Singapore

ISBN 981-4068-96-9

FRONT COVER | **Sandstone figure of Shiva and Uma** | *Prasat Banteay Srei* | *Late 10th century* | *H: 64.8 cm* | *National Museum of Cambodia, Phnom Penh*
P. 2 | **Façade** | *Asian Civilisations Museum (Empress Place), Singapore*
P. 3 | **Celadon elephant** | *Sawankhalok* | *Sukhothai period, 14th–15th century* | *H: 20 cm* | *National Museum Bangkok, Thailand*
P. 5 | **Brass plated Turkoman pectoral piece** | *Turkmenistan, Central Asia* | *20th century* | *30 x 20 cm* | *Islamic Arts Museum, Kuala Lumpur, Malaysia*
P. 6 | **Detail of a stone figure of Prajnaparamita** | *Malang, East Java* | *13th century* | *H: 126 cm* | *National Museum, Jakarta, Indonesia*
P. 8 | **Jayavarman VII** | *Carved sandstone* | *Angkor Thom* | *Bayon style, late 12th–early 13th century* | *H: 136 cm* | *National Museum of Cambodia, Phnom Penh*
P. 10 | **Scene from the Vessantara Jataka** | *Pigment on cloth* | *19th century* | *51 x 60.8 cm* | *Jim Thompson House, Bangkok, Thailand*
P. 206 | **Detail of the Tra Kieu pedestal** | *Sandstone* | *Tra Kieu style, 10th century* | *H: 43 cm, B: 175 cm* | *Museum of Cham Sculpture, Danang, Vietnam*
BACK COVER | **Interior view of the dome** | *Singapore History Museum*

INTRODUCTION 9
MAP 11

BRUNEI 12

Bandar Seri Begawan
• Brunei Museum 14

CAMBODIA 18

Phnom Penh
• National Museum of Cambodia 20
• The Royal Palace's Silver Pagoda 25
• Tuol Sleng Genocide Museum 26

INDONESIA 28

Bali (Bedulu)
• Purbakala Archaelogical Museum 30

Bali (Sanur)
• Le Mayeur Museum 31

Bali (Denpasar)
• Museum Bali 32

Bali (Semarapura / Klungkung)
• Museum Semarajaya and Kertha Gosa 34

Bali (Ubud)
• A. Blanco Renaissance Museum 35
• Agung Rai Museum of Art 36
• Museum Puri Lukisan 38
• Neka Art Museum 40

Java (Ambarawa)
• Ambarawa Railway Museum 42

Java (Jakarta)
• Jakarta History Museum 43
• National Museum 44

Java (Sumedang)
• Museum Prabu Geusan Ulun 49

Java (Yogyakarta)
• Museum Seni Lukis Affandi 50
• Ullen Sentalu Museum 51

Contents

LAOS 52

Luang Prabang
- Luang Prabang National Museum 54

Pakse
- Champasak Provincial Museum 56

Vientiane
- Lao National Museum 57

MALAYSIA 58

Kuala Lumpur
- Islamic Arts Museum Malaysia 60
- Maybank Numismatic Museum 65
- National Art Gallery 66
- National History Museum 68
- National Museum 70
- Orang Asli Museum 72
- Petronas Gallery (Galeri Petronas) 73
- Royal Malaysian Police Museum 74

Labuan
- Labuan Maritime Museum 75

Kuching
- Sarawak State Museum 76

Melaka
- Baba Nyonya Heritage Museum 78
- Melaka Sultanate Palace Museum 79

Penang
- Museum and Art Gallery, Penang 80

Taiping
- Perak State Museum 82

MYANMAR 84

Yangon
- National Museum of Myanmar 86

THE PHILIPPINES 90

Cebu City
- University of San Carlos Museum 92

Metro Manila (Makati City)
- Ayala Museum 93

Metro Manila (Manila)
- Bahay Tsinoy: Museum of Chinese in Philippine Life 94
- Metropolitan Museum of Manila 96
- Museo Pambata 99
- Museum of Philippine Political History 100
- National Museum of the Philippines 102
- University of Santo Tomas Museum of Arts and Sciences 104

Metro Manila (Pasay City)
- Cultural Center of the Philippines 106

Metro Manila (Pasig City)
- Lopez Memorial Museum 108

Metro Manila (Quezon City)
- Ateneo Art Gallery 110
- Jorge B. Vargas Museum and Filipiniana Research Center 112

SINGAPORE 114

- Asian Civilisations Museum (Armenian Street) 116
- Asian Civilisations Museum (Empress Place) 118
- The Changi Museum 123
- Raffles Hotel Museum 124
- Singapore Art Museum 126
- Singapore History Museum 130
- Singapore Philatelic Museum 134

THAILAND 136

Bangkok
- Jim Thompson House 138
- National Art Gallery 143
- National Museum Bangkok 144
- Prasart Museum 148
- The Siam Society and Kamthieng House Museum 150
- Suan Pakkad Palace Museum 152
- Vimanmek Mansion Museum 154

Chiang Mai
- Chiang Mai National Museum 156
- Tribal Museum 159

Nakhon Si Thammarat
- Nakhon Si Thammarat National Museum 160

Pathum Thani
- National Science Museum 162

VIETNAM 164

Danang
- Museum of Cham Sculpture 166

Hanoi
- Contemporary Arts Centre 171
- Hoa Lo Prison Museum 172
- Ho Chi Minh Museum 173
- National Museum of Vietnamese History 174
- Vietnam Fine Arts Museum 176
- Vietnam Museum of Ethnology 180

Ho Chi Minh City
- The Museum of Vietnamese History 182

Hoi An
- Museum of Sa Huynh Culture 184
- Museum of Trade Ceramics 185

Hue
- Hue Museum of Royal Fine Arts 186

OTHER SPACES 188

GLOSSARY 196
BIBLIOGRAPHY 198
PICTURE CREDITS 199
INDEX 200
ACKNOWLEDGEMENTS 205

Introduction

Assembling the museums of Southeast Asia together for study seems at first glance rather contrived, an exercise appealing to the practical dictates of travel rather than any art historical or historical imperatives. And yet, as a group these institutions convincingly challenge the still conventional notion of Southeast Asia as a cultural extension of China and India. Further, if these museums are fascinating for what they display, they are equally interesting for the genealogy of their creation, many of which are comparable. Whether recently conceived or initiated by the colonisers, the museums of Southeast Asia reach out well beyond the world of objects to link the past art of man to his ambitions for the future.

Southeast Asia as a unified body is a relatively modern concept. It was outsiders who were keener, initially, on establishing a commonality amongst its peoples. The great European colonising surges of the 19th century did much to bring disparate populations—some perennially at war—with their differing languages, religions and cultures together under a single administrative mantle.

Most Europeans, ignorant of the lands they had vanquished, thought of Southeast Asia as provinces of China and India, its civilisations mere cultural appendages. Yet some, economic conquerors though they were, recognised the significance of indigenous culture and sought to preserve it by researching and displaying its material manifestation. Thus, the museum, an invention of the European enlightenment of the late 18th century, was introduced to Southeast Asia. Sir Stamford Raffles, the Batavian Society, the 'White Rajahs' of Sarawak, and the French in Indochina played their part in establishing a methodology of conservation and public display that would benefit local audiences then and today.

If some of Southeast Asia's great museums were established by the colonial administrations, many more were not. The more recently formed collections have been the effort of local patrons or governments acting in the name of their peoples. And though national identity, culture and politics can be an unsavoury mix, the better museums of Southeast Asia achieve an honourable balance between these competing strands, avoiding the overtly propagandistic.

But whether old or new, the museums of Southeast Asia are often outstanding because the art they champion is outstanding. And along with the ancient religious sites of Southeast Asia, it is the region's museums that above all must refute the still commonly held notion that Southeast Asian art and culture derive from the master cultures of China and India. Indeed, much of Southeast Asia's art—beautiful and original—

has been demonstrated to have sprung from local sources, onto which were juxtaposed localised references to the world religions of Asia. This layering of the indigenous with the extraneous created sophisticated and wholly individual cultures.

If the breathtaking archaeological sites of Southeast Asia provide material evidence of its artistic grandeur, its museums, the work of modern men, make the necessary theoretical connections between art and history, intelligently exploiting new scholarship of the last decades.

The people of Southeast Asia have only lately come to refer to themselves as 'Southeast Asians'—their sense of geographical and political fraternity non-existent as recently as a century ago, their political reality not much older than ASEAN (Association of Southeast Asian Nations). But as nationhood and a regional identity have emerged, so too a new sense of cultural affirmation is reflected in the proliferation of new museums as well as in the refurbishment of the old.

For museums offer sure tools of cultural empowerment. Museums as varied as the peoples and cultures they illuminate have sprung up in all parts presenting a local view of art, society and history. The wide variety of institutions present in this book attests not only to Southeast Asia's broad cultural spectrum, but also to the innumerable approaches to cultural presentation. For if museums project indigenous realities outward to visiting foreigners, more importantly, they speak to locals, serving to interpret culture, society and history as these evolve.

The museums of Southeast Asia are an exciting and challenging bunch. Many tell much of place but, in their thoughtful approach, also make intellectual demands of the visitors. New or old, as the region's societies grow and communicate beyond borders, ancient art is taught to speak to 21st-century audiences while new museums on a wealth of topics are created, reflecting 21st-century knowledge and interests.

And if Southeast Asia has been busy creating new museums, it has been equally occupied making new art to place inside them. For if there is anything as exciting as the ancient art of the region, it is the expression of its living artists. With wit, innovation and sophistication, their work probes the shifting ground of old societies facing new realities. Though at this time there are few art institutions in Southeast Asia representing the current, the pace of progress suggests a bevy of contemporary art museums a decade from now. Southeast Asia, already gloriously endowed, has much to look forward to.

Iola Lenzi
September 2004

Museums of Southeast Asia

MYANMAR
(Burma)

• HANOI

• Luang Prabang

LAOS

Chiang Mai •

• VIENTIANE

GON •

Sukhothai •

• Ban Chiang

• Hue
• Danang
• Hoi An

THAILAND

Ayutthaya •

Pathum Thani •

BANGKOK •

• Pakse

VIETNAM

• Angkor

CAMBODIA

PHNOM PENH •

• Ho Chi Minh City

L U Z O N

• MANILA

• Cebu

A m a n
S e a

• Nakhon Si Thammarat

South China Sea

THE PHILIPPINES

M I N D A N A

MALAYSIA

Penang •

• Taiping

• KUALA LUMPUR

Melaka •

SINGAPORE

Labuan •

BRUNEI

• BANDAR SERI BEGAWAN

M A L A Y S I A

Kuching •

B O R N E O

S
U
M
A
T
R
A

I N D O N E S I A

• JAKARTA

Sumedang •

• Ambarawa

Borobudur • • Yogyakarta

B A L I
• Bedulu
Denpasar
Sanur
Semarapura / Klungkung
Ubud

J A V A

Indian Ocean

Brunei ▶

ADDRESS
Jalan Kota Batu
Bandar Seri Begawan BD1510
Brunei

CONTACT INFORMATION
T: +673 2 244 545 / 6
F: +673 2 242 727
E: bmarch@brunet.bn

OPENING HOURS
9am–5pm Mon–Thu, Sat–Sun;
9am–11.30am, 2.30pm–5pm
Fri.

ADMISSION
Free.

FACILITIES
Good museum shop by
the entrance.

HOW TO GET THERE
Bus: 2, 11 or 39 from
the centre of Bandar
Seri Begawan.

Taxi: From the centre of
Bandar Seri Begawan.

AROUND THE MUSEUM
The restaurants of Bandar Seri
Begawan are a few minutes
away by car.

Brunei Museum

The largest and oldest of Brunei's museums, the Brunei Museum, located in the capital, offers a broadly focused overview of the country's culture, natural environment, industry and history.

▪ **THE BUILDING** The Brunei Museum is part of a wider cultural body known as the 'Brunei Museums' which links eight distinct public institutions and cultural sites. Including the Brunei Museum, the Malay Technology Museum, the Royal Regalia, the Art Gallery, Bubongan Dua Belas, Merimbun Heritage Park, the National Archive of Brunei Darussalam (a reference institution open to the public) and the Brunei Arts & Handicrafts Training Centre, these sites offer a wealth of information about the country's archaeology, ethnology, Islamic art, royal regalia, technology, natural history and petroleum industry.

The most comprehensive of the country's museums, the Brunei Museum was established in 1965 and has occupied its present site in Kota Batu, five kilometres from Bandar Seri Begawan, the capital of Brunei Darussalam, since 1970. Officially opened by Queen Elizabeth II in 1972, the building is set on a hilltop and so commands a picturesque view of the Brunei River below. An elongated, low-rise, three-winged structure of international Modernist design typical of the period, the building's façade is decorated with richly engraved patterns based on traditional Malay ornamentation. These were inspired by the tomb of Sultan Bolkiah, the fifth ruler of Brunei, and effectively lend an otherwise innocuous building some indigenous flavour.

Featuring a temporary exhibition gallery in its lobby and six large permanent galleries documenting widely diverse themes, the visitor short of time and interested in an overall introduction to the country had best make this museum his first stop.

▪ **THE COLLECTION** The Brunei Museum's collections are relatively young but span a broad number of subjects. Whatever is lacking in terms of objects is amply made up for with intelligently crafted information.

▪ **THE GALLERIES** The museum's exhibition spaces are all located on the ground floor. Not to be missed is the **Islamic Gallery** which features some 1,500 objects belonging to the Sultan of Brunei. Well presented and labelled,

▲ **Hammered bronze ewer**
North East Iran or Central Asia | 9ᵗʰ–10ᵗʰ century |
H: 36cm

▲ **Glazed ceramic bowl**
Scraffiato decoration, polychrome enamels on
cream slip under a clear glaze | Bamiyan,
Afghanistan | 12ᵗʰ century | D: 17.8 cm, H: 8.5 cm

the collection assembles a wide range of works covering the artistic production of various Islamic regions from the transitional and early Islamic periods through to the late 19ᵗʰ century. Elucidating all aspects of Islamic religious and secular life, the Qur'ans, glassware, calligraphy, metalware, pottery, arms, tools, scientific instruments, carpets, textiles, carved stones, coins and jewels are grouped into main sections including calligraphy, ceramics, metalwork, glass, jewellery and coins.

Distinctive to the Brunei Museum's Islamic Gallery is the documentation of the 19ᵗʰ-century Islamic world's taste for the revival of Mamluk styles of the 14ᵗʰ and 15ᵗʰ

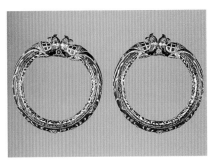

▲ Pair of bracelets
Enamel and diamond-set on gold I India I 19th century I D: 9.5 cm

century. Another interesting curatorial tack taken here is the examination of 17th- to 19th-century East-West trade relations' influence on the respective cultural heritages of the Western and Islamic worlds.

In the ceramics section look out for a series of rare vessels from 12th-century Bamiyan in present-day Afghanistan, in particular a red earthenware bowl decorated with incised cream slip and overlaid with clear, green and manganese glazes. Also see a rare Iranian ewer of the 12th to 13th century with an inscribed border. Finally, a 15th-century architectural element made in China for the local Islamic market confirms Islam's broad cultural and religious radius around wider Asia.

The metalwork section, though not huge, among other good pieces boasts an oblong parcel gilt repoussé silver bowl from the transitional or early Islamic period (6th to early 7th century). As well as being rather rare, this work's iconography is highlighted as having inspired the decorative styles of many later objects of the same genre.

The glass collection features several early wares from the 10th to the 11th century while the jewellery section highlights Mughal-style adornments of the 19th century.

The Brunei Museum's calligraphy section, considered the noblest part of any Islamic art collection due to the written text's unique religious role, includes a number of distinguished pieces. See a North African leaf from the 10th century with gold and silver calligraphy on vellum.

The gallery space devoted to the **Brunei Shipwreck**, not far from the Islamic Gallery, is also highly recommended. Here, a sampling of the over 13,000 objects recovered in the late 1990s from an early 16th-century shipwreck off the Brunei coast are displayed. Split into various categories, including ceramics, beads, metalware, glass and lithics, the collection is predominantly composed of ceramics, these originating from the main ceramic-trading nations of the period—China, Siam and Vietnam. As well as heavy stoneware storage jars, utilitarian in function, the find included several thousand porcelain and celadon wares. The best of these are displayed here and comprise some very good Ming dynasty blue and white vessels. See, for example, a well-conserved 15th- to 16th-century underglaze blue *kendi* as well as an underglaze blue dish decorated with a peacock design of the same period. The latter, and more, are from China's Jingdezhen kiln, the most technically accomplished porcelain manufacturing site of its day. Mass-produced Chinese white ware as well as celadons from Guangdong province are also displayed. Siamese wares constitute nearly half the ceramics retrieved. Of these, the most attractive are the Si Satchanalai pieces. See a 15th-century brown

▲ Miniature ceramic ewer
Lustre-painted and bearing an inscription I Kashan, Iran I Late 12th–early 13th century I H: 13 cm

glazed elephant-shaped pouring vessel representative of period taste in Siam.

Fewer Vietnamese pieces were recovered from the wreck doubtless because trade links between Brunei and Indochina were less developed at the time than those shared by Brunei and its Chinese and Siamese partners. Nonetheless, those not familiar with Vietnamese ceramics will still be able to view several

▲ Qur'an casket
Wood, inlaid with gold and silver, of Mamluk inspiration I Egypt I 19th century I 28.5 x 48.5 x 48.5 cm

▲ Qur'an section
Ink and gilding | Egypt or Syria | Mamluk period, late 14th century | H: 34.5 cm

examples of Annamese blue and white wares, the section offering the viewer a chance to compare the widely different styles of vessels being made in Asia five hundred years ago.

Though the metal, glass, lithic and bead sections are not as extensive, these are still worth a trawl and will give the visitor an idea of the huge variety and scale of period trade.

The **Brunei Malay Culture Gallery**, or **Gallery 4**, presents a cultural panorama depicting the Malay life cycle in Brunei Darussalam from birth through marriage. Different stages of life with their related ceremonial and religious aspects are explored through objects, mini-dioramas and explanatory panels. Malay babies are shown along with items evoking birth-related rituals. Older children are shown learning passages from the holy Qur'an while a recitation is being prepared. Circumcision instruments are shown, relating to the circumcision ceremony that marks a male child's coming of age. Finally, Brunei marriage ritual is documented, the related mix of indigenous and Muslim cultural material displayed underscoring Brunei's cosmopolitan cultural background.

As well as the panorama, a collection of utilitarian and socio-cultural objects are shown. Among the most interesting is a section concerning local traditional games, kite flying and top spinning being the most popular.

A case devoted to betel boxes and another to headgear emphasise the link between purely functional objects and the social status these can confer according to their style, wealth of material and quality of manufacture. Finally, a collection of predominantly early 20th-century brass ware, including several small cannons, provides evidence of the skill and sophistication of Brunei's traditional brass manufacturers.

Those seeking further information about Brunei social customs, indigenous and Muslim, should pay a visit to the Malay Technology Museum (see p. 190).

The **Archaeology and History of Brunei Darussalam Gallery** is of mixed appeal. Boasting sections devoted to Prehistory, Migration, the Discovery of Brunei, Early Trade, the Brunei Sultanate, and the Arrival of the European Powers, the gallery is rich in information though not uniformly in works of art. The Prehistory section displays Neolithic tools but more interesting perhaps are a number of pieces from the Limbang gold hoard. Discovered in Limbang, Sarawak, Malaysia in 1899, the trove comprises 13th- to 16th-century gold objects displaying Hindu iconography. Attributed to the Majapahit Empire of East Java that dominated the region from the 13th to the 16th century, 25 items from the hoard were given to Brunei in 1967 and it is these the visitor will see today at the Brunei Museum.

The Early Trade and Arrival of the European Powers sections of the gallery, though less object-based, are fascinating. Here, Brunei's considerable importance as a Southeast Asian commercial hub, trading raw materials—namely camphor (considered the best in the world at the time), rattan, sandalwood, bees' wax, sago and tortoise shell—against manufactured goods of Chinese origin such as cloth and ceramics from the 10th to the 16th century, is illustrated and explained in depth with photographs, objects, maps and text panels. The arrival of the Portuguese and their swift domination of exchange systems in non-mainland Southeast Asia changed the regional balance of power, and this too is evoked in some detail here. The visitor not familiar with this transitional but crucial period in Southeast Asian history and its influence on political and social developments thereafter will find much to stimulate him here.

The Migration, Brunei Sultanate and Discovery of Brunei exhibits all offer additional information about the country and its development through the centuries.

The Natural History and Oil & Gas Galleries propose a different take on the country, reminding the visitor that Brunei, for all its

Qur'an leaf
Gold kulfic script on blue vellum | North Africa, probably Qayrawan | Early 10th century | H: 29 cm

This leaf is thought to originate from a Qur'an belonging to the Great Mosque of Qayrawan located in modern-day Tunisia. Though the major part of the manuscript is now housed in the Tunisian National Library, Brunei is fortunate to have this leaf in its collection as an example of early North African script.

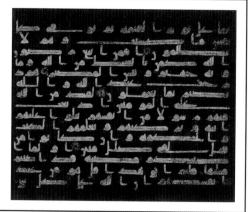

modern, petrol-financed infrastructure is, on the northern coast of Borneo, one of the most exotic destinations in the world.

From a tropical backwater at the beginning of the 20th century, Brunei Darussalam has developed into an important Asian economy a century later. The discovery of the Seria oilfield in 1928 led to the Sultanate becoming an exporter of oil by 1932, and today, the country remains a significant source of petroleum for the expanding economies of Southeast Asia (see a gallery map showing the country's oilfields). In 1963, the Ampa field was explored and offshore oil too became a cornerstone of the economy. Brunei is also an important exporter of liquefied natural gas and boasts one of the largest natural gas plants in the world at Lumut.

The Brunei Museum's **Oil & Gas Gallery** presents the state's major industry, which has so miraculously transformed the small country, in an innovative and intelligent way.

▲ **Pair of Chinese ceramic dishes from the Brunei Shipwreck**
Underglaze blue | 15th–16th century | D: 20 cm

Blown glass bottle
Free blown, cobalt and tuquoise blue glass | Iran | 11th–12th century | H: 23 cm

Applied trailed glass decoration was a Roman innovation improved upon by Muslim craftsmen from the Middle East.

Covering less than 6,000 square kilometres and with a population of around 350,000, Brunei is one of Asia's smallest countries. Yet its economy is large and this gallery shows how a single commodity can transform a nation. Descriptive narratives, photographs, maps and interactive displays explain in depth the origin and formation of oil. Drilling, refining, uses in the market as well as the history of petroleum exploration and industry in Brunei are all covered. Divided into sections, each of the above is explored in depth, the final part of the gallery focusing on oil and petroleum in the wider world context. Not overly technical, the explanations are well made and even visitors with no particular predilection for black gold will be fascinated.

The **Natural History Gallery** too is enlightening, particularly for those with little time to wander beyond the modern confines of

▲ **Inscribed marble panel**
Afghanistan, Ghaznavid | 10th–11th century | H: 48cm

the city. The collection of animal, insect, plant and shell specimens is well developed, if recent, with samples first assembled in the mid-1960s. See in particular the bottlenose dolphin skeleton and the vast collection of butterflies. The gallery is currently being renovated so the visitor may expect a fuller and yet superior documentary approach to the tropical flora and fauna of Brunei when it finally reopens.

Broad in its mission as both an educational and research tool for its home audience as well as providing an excellent introduction to the country's culture, natural environment, industry and history to visiting foreigners, the Brunei Museum should figure prominently on all visitors' itineraries. Its excellent facilities and labelling, and dynamic exhibition strategies also ensure the museum's place as one of Brunei Darussalam's most popular attractions.

Cambodia ▶

ADDRESS
Street 13, Chey Chumneas
Khan Daun Penh, Phnom Penh
Cambodia

CONTACT INFORMATION
T/F: +855 23 211 753
E: museum_cam@
camnet.com.kh

OPENING HOURS
8am–5pm daily.

ADMISSION
US$3.

FACILITIES
Guided tours are available
in Khmer, English, French
and Japanese.

A research library containing
publications about Khmer art
is open from 8.30am–11am
and 2.30–4.30pm daily.

A small shop at the entrance
selling postcards and replicas
of museum pieces made in a
workshop first established on
the premises in 1920; cold
drinks available adjacent to
the ticket booth.

HOW TO GET THERE
By taxi.

AROUND THE MUSEUM
The Royal Palace (see p. 25)
is not far away, as are the
many cafés and restaurants
of Sisowath Quay, the most
famous of which is the
Foreign Correspondents Club
on the corner of the Quay and
Preah Sothearuos Boulevard.

National Museum of Cambodia

The National Museum of Cambodia in Phnom Penh, housed in an elegant Khmer-style, purpose-built colonial building, presents one of the finest collections of Khmer art in the world.

■ **THE BUILDING** Set in a verdant tropical garden north of the Royal Palace, the museum was designed in traditional Khmer style by French archaeologist George Groslier in tandem with the local Ecole des Arts Cambodgiens. As well as the building's architect, Groslier, whose distinguished contribution to the field of Khmer art history is still relevant in academia today, was also the institution's first director. The building's construction was started in 1917 and it was inaugurated three years later, in April 1920, as the Musée Albert Sarraut, in honour of the then French Governor General of Indochina. The structure, like many early 20th-century

▲ *The museum's inner courtyard and sculpture garden.*

public buildings of its kind in Indochina, is a European-local stylistic hybrid.

A solid brick quadrangle with galleries arranged on all four sides, the latter well ventilated and lit by natural light from outside as well as from the museum's large inner courtyard, the building is reminiscent in basic structural design of many late 19th-century European museums. However, the French in early 20th-century Cambodia, presumably quite smitten by the Khmer art and culture of which they had become the colonial custodian when Cambodia became a French protectorate in 1864 (only a few years after Angkor's rediscovery), made a number of concessions to local architectural style. A layered, elongated gabled roof, raised porticos and interior galleries, a temple-like, red, columned façade, wide shaded galleries, and Khmer-style decorative devices such as elegant roof finials and spindly stupa-esque towers, also adorning the roof, are some of the distinctive features of the building. Cambodian artists and sculptors were in charge of the Angkor-style carved reliefs positioned above the museum's doors and windows. Of these reliefs, the two most significant examples, doubtless inspired by 10th-century stone carvings at the Banteay Srei site, are two panels positioned above a pair of main doors on the building's façade.

Whatever its mixed stylistic and architectural origins, the museum is airy and pleasant, not overwhelming in size—though certainly overflowing with art—and with its shaded inner galleries, courtyard and

▲ **Bronze figure of Vishnu-Vasudeva-Narayana**
Kapilapura, Angkor | Angkor Wat style, first half of the 12th century | H: 43.5 cm

numerous resting spots, is one of the most rewarding and contemplative destinations in Phnom Penh whether or not one is interested in Khmer art.

Though shut down and abandoned during the reign of the Khmer Rouge from 1975 to

1979, the institution was thankfully spared destruction and much of the collection, neglected and bat-infested as it was, survived intact, faring much better than its curators, many of whom lost their lives during the four-year regime of terror.

■ **THE COLLECTION** The publicising of the temple complexes at Angkor after French naturalist Henri Mouhot's 1860 visit numbers among the most important archaeological events of the 19th century. It also fuelled over a century of art theft that has not stopped yet. Hence the museum's important role as a study collection of Khmer art from pre-Angkorian times to the 13th century.

Numbering around 1,000 objects when the museum opened in 1920, the collection has grown to include some 14,000 pieces and continues to expand as more works are discovered, donated or returned to the nation. During the civil war in the early 1970s, a number of pieces from provincial collections were transferred to Phnom Penh for safekeeping and have remained in the National Museum ever since.

Run by the French from 1920 until Cambodian independence in the 1950s, the National Museum's directors during the French period include many notable names in Khmer scholarship in the West such as Pierre Dupont, Jean Boisselier (still a very important reference) and Madeleine Giteau. The first Cambodian directors of the museum, Chea Thay Seng and Ly Vou Ong, took their positions in 1966.

The permanent collection features Khmer art from the prehistoric period to the 20th century with a particular focus on stone and bronze sculpture from the 6th to the 13th century.

Later periods are also represented with a variety of material, much of it secular and some a gift to the museum from the Cambodian Royal Household.

■ **THE GALLERIES** The museum houses 15 exhibition galleries as well as an inner courtyard open to the elements where large

Sandstone figure of Harihara

Praset Andet, Kompong Thom | Pre-Angkor period, Praset Andet style, late 7th century | H: 197 cm

The god Harihara, who combines the Hindu gods Vishnu the preserver (Hari) and Shiva the destroyer (Hara), was revered in Cambodia from the 6th to the 10th century. A particularly finely carved example, this life-size figure boasts a realistically modelled *sampot* and belt, the design of the latter based on Indian metalwork styles of the period.

▲ **Sandstone figure of Durga**
Phum Tonlap, Kompong Speu | Prei Khmeng style,
8th century | H: 89 cm

sculptures and architectural ornaments and fragments are attractively displayed.

The visitor first accesses the building through the museum gates and, passing the ticket office into a small, leafy compound which appears not to have changed much since French days, enters the institution's main door. Beyond a small souvenir stand positioned on the left, the visitor will begin his tour proceeding left and then clockwise into the first of the long galleries that make up the museum's sides.

The museum's objects are assembled more or less chronologically and according to medium, and are well labelled in Khmer, French and English. A number of particularly

◄ **Sandstone figure of Shiva and Uma**
Prasat Banteay Srei | Late 10th century | H: 64.8 cm

significant pieces have extended labels explaining their provenance and cultural meaning in greater depth.

The rooms seen on entering the museum are the **bronze galleries** which assemble roughly 500 pieces from the pre-Angkor and Angkor periods (6th to 12th century). A particular highlight here is the 12th-century bronze Angkor Wat-style statue of Vishnu-Vasudeva-Narayana.

Beyond is the **prehistory gallery** where primitive stone tools and early pottery are displayed. If time is short, the visitor can make his way directly to the next several rooms where the masterpieces of Khmer civilisation's high periods are housed.

Two **pre-Angkor galleries** beyond the prehistory section contain works in stone and bronze. While some pieces are displayed in cases, many others are shown in the open, visible on all sides, a pleasure at a time when museums are becoming increasingly clinical in their display. Though the gallery is full of masterpieces, see in particular here an elegant (despite its missing arms) and naturalistic late 7th-century sandstone life-size figure of Harihara in Prasat Andet style from Kompong Thom. Finely modelled, the figure is half Shiva (Hara) and half Vishnu (Hari), as confirmed by the statue's headdress, alternately displaying the stylised curled locks of Shiva the destroyer's hair on the right side, and Vishnu's cylindrical mitre headdress on the left. Shiva is also represented by half a third eye carved in the middle of the figure's forehead. An elegant, elongated, life-size early 7th-century sandstone Vishnu from Tuol Dai Buon is also worth seeking out. Compare this with a monumental Phnom Kulen Vishnu of the first part of the 9th century—far stockier, less naturalistic and more stylised, auguring the high Angkor style to follow—in the same gallery. Also see the remarkably well-preserved sandstone sculpture of an 8th-century figure of Durga in Prei Khmeng style.

Beyond, as one turns right into the back gallery, is a group of four rooms containing

objects in various styles from the **Angkor period**, including Kulen, Banteay Srei, Koh Ker, Baphuon, Angkor Wat and Bayon. Seek out here a Bayon-style, powerfully serene sandstone sculpture of Jayavarman VII, the potent Khmer monarch of the late 12th to early 13th century who was responsible for building the Bayon as well as Angkor Thom and who liberated Angkor from Cham invaders. Imposingly large, the seated figure of the monarch has eyes downcast in a stance reminiscent of Buddha (during Jayavarman VII's reign the kingdom had reverted to Buddhism as its state religion). Realistic in style (indeed experts consider the piece to be a portrait), the work's great

▲ **Sandstone figure of Vishnu**
Tuol Dai Buon | Pre-Angkor period, early
7th century | H: 184 cm

simplicity and ornamental sobriety lend it a startling grace and majesty.

Following the Angkor period rooms are the **post-Angkorian galleries** which feature items such as weaponry, wooden sculpture, a carved river cabin, the funerary urn of His Majesty King Sisowath, lacquer and inlay work, textile technology, textiles, royal palanquins and regalia, ceramics and paintings. Though the works here are of much later vintage—some are of quite recent manufacture—than the high period sculpture that has made the Khmer civilisation famous, these objects will give the visitor a good indication of life in Cambodia in modern times.

On the left, at the far end of this gallery, is an extraordinarily imposing, 11ᵗʰ-century, bronze Angkor-period reclining Vishnu from the West Mebon in Siem Reap. The complete figure in its original pristine condition would have been over six metres in length, thus making it one of the largest bronze sculptures ever cast in Southeast Asia.

Down the stairs from the Vishnu is a room dedicated to the display of Buddhist sculpture from the post-Angkorian period. Like the rest of the museum, the area also has an active function as a religious space. From the **post-Angkorian Buddha gallery**, the visitor can access the other half of the bronze gallery explored upon his first arrival.

A museum visit ends with a leisurely stroll in the **central courtyard garden**. An ideal place to rest, the courtyard is dotted with stone benches as well as four cool lotus ponds surrounding a pavilion housing a seated figure from Angkor's Terrace of the Leper King. The garden offers a bucolic setting for admiring stone lintels and other architectural elements, inscribed steles and the many pieces of sculpture displayed here.

Though not as modern as some institutions, and still recovering from its chequered recent history, as the repository of the most comprehensive public collection of Khmer art in the world, the National Museum of Cambodia is undoubtedly one of the region's top museums.

Jayavarman VII
Carved sandstone | Angkor Thom | Bayon style, late 12ᵗʰ–early 13ᵗʰ century | H: 136 cm

Despite its missing arms this imposingly scaled portrait subtly evokes both the majesty and dignity of its subject while also conveying the monarch's humility, with Jayavarman VII's eyes downcast in a peaceful, meditative stance reminiscent of Buddha. Aesthetically powerful, the sculpture underscores the force of the ruler as well as the nobility of Buddhist devotion.

ADDRESS
Preah Sothearuos Boulevard
Sangkat Cheychumnah
Khan Daun Penh
Phnom Penh
Cambodia

CONTACT INFORMATION
T/F: +855 23 223 724
E: domrei@online.com.kh

OPENING HOURS
7.30am–11am, 2pm–5pm
daily;
closed on public holidays.

ADMISSION
US$3;
US$2 photo fee;
US$5 video fee.

FACILITIES
Wheelchair access.

Guided tours are available in
English, French and Mandarin.

Cold drinks and souvenirs by
the entrance gates.

HOW TO GET THERE
By taxi.

AROUND THE MUSEUM
The National Museum (see pp.
20–24), National Assembly
and Wat Botum are nearby.

A number of cafés and
restaurants are located a
short walk away on Sisowath
Quay, including the Foreign
Correspondents Club on the
corner of the Quay and Preah
Sothearuos Boulevard.

The Royal Palace's Silver Pagoda

On the grounds of the Royal Palace, in Phnom Penh's old town, the Silver Pagoda or Wat Preah Kaeo
Morokat is a richly ornate temple that houses an eclectic collection of Buddhist art.

■ **THE BUILDING** Surrounded by a pleasant green belt close to the banks of the majestic Tonle Sap just as it merges with the Mekong, Wat Preah Kaeo Morokat (Temple of the Emerald Buddha) was built by King Norodom in 1892 to enshrine royal ashes. It was reconstructed 70 years later by King Sihanouk. Designed in traditional Khmer style, the *wat*, located in the southern section of the Royal Palace compound, does not house monks and was originally used by the royal family and members of the court for performing ceremonies throughout the year.

The *wat* itself is modern, and though not architecturally distinguished, is thoroughly opulent. Its terrace and columns are clad in Italian marble and its floor completely covered with silver tiles weighing over one kilogram each, explaining why the temple is often referred to as the Silver Pagoda.

▲ *View of the Silver Pagoda from the temple's
front entrance.*

As appealing as the temple itself are the high, shaded galleries that enclose the compound. These are decorated end-to-end with religious frescoes dating between 1903 and 1904, and covering some 642 metres of wall in length and nearly four metres in height. The frescoes illustrate epic scenes from the Khmer adaptation of the *Ramayana*. The visitor interested in following the narrative in sequence should start at the southern end of the **Eastern Gallery**, reading from left to right. Restoration work in the 1980s halted their decline somewhat. More renovation is slated and may be ongoing when this publication goes to press. Whatever their state of repair, however, the frescoes are worth detailed examination.

Also located on the *wat* grounds are several early 20th-century stupa and other historical monuments such as a bell tower, statue of King Norodom, bath, sanctuary, library, *dhamasala* (assembly hall) and small sacred mountain.

■ **THE TEMPLE OBJECTS** The temple, largely spared during the Khmer Rouge years (1975–1979), houses an impressive collection of over 1,600 artefacts including Buddhist icons made of precious metals or stones, royal jewellery, Buddhist relics and

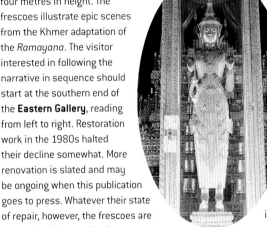

▲ **The Gold Buddha**
1906 | H: 175 cm

assorted gifts presented to the Khmer monarchy by foreign heads of state.

Many of the smaller objects are contained in curio cabinets dotted around the temple and arranged rather eclectically. Porcelain mingles with gold and silver vessels, weapons, jewellery, ceremonial objects, dancing and theatrical regalia, boxes, trays, small Buddhas and many more items.

Though perhaps not great works of art, the Gold and Emerald Buddhas are the most sought-after icons in the temple and are undeniably arresting in their glittery ostentation. The encased gold statue of Buddha Maitreya weighs 90 kilograms and is studded with 2,086 diamonds, the largest of which, decorating the Buddha's crown, weighs 25 carats. The statue, made in 1906, is of religious significance because it was reputedly cast from the gold urn that contained the cremated remains of King Norodom.

The Emerald Buddha, which gives the temple its name, is housed at the centre of the *wat*, behind the Gold Buddha.

A visit to Phnom Penh's Royal Palace and its extensive grounds will give visitors the opportunity to imagine princely life in pre-1970s Cambodia. The Silver Pagoda is doubtless the highlight of such a visit.

Indonesia ▶

ADDRESS
Jalan Raya Tampaksiring
Bedulu, Blahbatuh
Gianyar, Bali
Indonesia

CONTACT DETAILS
T: +62 361 942 347
F: +62 361 942 354
E: bpppbali@dps.centrinnet.id

OPENING HOURS
8am–3pm Mon–Thu;
8am–12.30pm Fri.

ADMISSION
Free.

HOW TO GET THERE
The museum is a 10-minute
taxi ride north of Ubud on the
Bedulu-Mount Batur Road.

AROUND THE MUSEUM
Nearby are the outdoor
archaeological sites of Goa
Gajah and Yeh Pulu.

Pura Kebo Edan, Pura
Pusering Jagat and Pura
Panataran Sasih are three
small but old temples in the
immediate vicinity.

Purbakala Archaeological Museum

Located in a rice paddy between two villages southeast of Ubud, the open-air Purbakala
Archaeological Museum offers the appeal of the Balinese countryside in tandem with interesting
archaeological material.

■ **THE SITE** Between the villages of Bedulu
and Pejeng and not far from Goa Gajah, the
Purbakala site is one of several in a sacred
area of Bali inhabited since the Bronze
Age. Presenting about 40 temples,
the area, known as the regency
of Gianyar, is home to massive
stone carvings, sarcophagi,
Buddhist sanctuaries and
bathing sites. A number of
bronze artefacts have also
been found in the region.
Though a fair bit of material
has been moved to more
important museums in Bali and
beyond, many of the larger pieces have
remained as they were found, on their
original sites—in temples, fields, and
by river banks.

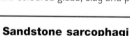
▲ *Pottery vessel
found on site.*

The Purbakala Archaeological Museum,
established in 1974, consists of a collection
of sarcophagi, Neolithic tools, Hindu and
Buddhist relics, iron and bronze jewellery,
clay pots and glass beads, all housed in open-
air pavilions in the middle of a field. The
museum is structured as a Balinese temple,
the space divided into three enclosed outdoor
areas including inner, middle and front
courtyards. The buildings are designed in
traditional Balinese style.

■ **THE COLLECTION** The sarcophagi, housed
in the museum's inner courtyard, are without
a doubt the most impressive part of the
collection. Numbering around a dozen, they

are either full-length, medium or small in size.
While some sport carved, stylised geometric
designs or finials, most are not decorated.

Labelling in English is provided but the
information is sketchy, seldom
going beyond the piece's
geographic origins.

A good number and
variety of Paleolithic
implements and tools are
also on display, these in the
museum's middle courtyard.
Here, the visitor
will find hand axes, flat iron
choppers, high-backed choppers
and bronze spades. Primitive
jewellery, too, is featured in the form
of iron, bronze, glass and wood
bangles of generally plain design, bronze
finger rings, earrings and a series of strung,
multi-coloured glass, clay and perforated

seashell beads. Utilitarian as well as ritual
pottery vessels—several plain, others
decorated, many broken or in poor
condition—are displayed as well, though here
the labelling leaves much to the imagination.

Finally, a series of Hindu and Buddhist
relics are presented. These include assorted
shards of pottery amulets adorned with worn,
seated Buddha images, a bronze bell with
nandi decoration and a much eroded 16th-
century bronze figure of a standing Buddha
disinterred in the local vicinity.

The Purbakala Archaeological Museum,
charmingly ad hoc in feeling and uncrowded
is worth a stop for those pursuing an
archaeological itinerary centred around Ubud.
Combined with a visit to the relief carvings
of Goa Gajah and Yeh Pulu nearby, this
museum set in the rice paddies will give
visitors a good idea of the extent of Bali's
archaeological wealth.

Sandstone sarcophagi
Bronze Age, c. 300 BCE

These sarcophagi are among the most
complete in the museum, their lids and
bodies intact. Varying from one to two
metres in length, they would have enclosed
either adult corpses laid out in a straight
position or adults in foetal position, a pose
associated with reincarnation. As well as
the body, such sarcophagi would also have
contained a selection of bronze funerary
gifts such as jewellery.

ADDRESS
Jalan Hang Tuah
Sanur Beach
Banjar Pekandelan
Sanur Kaja
Denpasar 80227, Bali
Indonesia

CONTACT INFORMATION
T: +62 361 286 201

OPENING HOURS
7.30am–3.30pm Sun–Thu;
7.30am–1pm Fri.

ADMISSION
Adult Rp 750;
child Rp 250.

HOW TO GET THERE
By taxi or *bemo* to
Sanur Beach.

AROUND THE MUSEUM
Pura Desa, west of the
museum, is a village temple
most probably built early in
the last century.

Pura Segara, on Sanur Beach,
is one of the best of several
beach temples built of coral.

There are many cafés and
restaurants located along
Sanur Beach.

Le Mayeur Museum

Bali's Le Mayeur Museum celebrates the oeuvre and life of Belgian painter Adrien-Jean Le Mayeur de Merprès, one of many European artists made famous by his views of Bali and Balinese beauties.

▪ **THE BUILDING** Located in Sanur along Bali's east coast in a garden positioned well away from the road, the museum occupies the house where Adrien-Jean Le Mayeur de Merprès lived with his Balinese wife, dancer Ni Pollok, from 1935 to 1958. Though Sanur has changed immensely since the advent of mass tourism in Bali, the Le Mayeur house, surrounded by lush gardens, retains much of the village's pastoral charm of yore.

Those familiar with the colourful Impressionistic paintings of Le Mayeur also know the artist's house, garden and beach views because he used these recurringly as settings for his portraits of Ni Pollok and the other Balinese women he was so fond of painting.

Designed and built by Le Mayeur, the house is true to local Balinese style in décor and layout though visitors may be surprised to note the artist's predilection for the colour red, perhaps more Chinese than Balinese in taste. With a single ground floor and an expansive tiled and shaded verandah, the house suits the climate and tropical environment it inhabits. Left more or less as it would have been at the time of the artist's death, the various rooms, fitted with furniture and other domestic accessories designed by the artist, now constitute the museum's exhibition galleries.

▪ **THE COLLECTION** Established in 1958 after Le Mayeur's death, the museum was run by Ni Pollok until her death in 1985. After this, as established by Ni Pollok's will, the house,

Adrien-Jean Le Mayeur de Merprès
Balinese Girl Weaving | Oil on canvas | 1957 | 100 x 120 cm

Of Belgian origin, the artist (1880–1958) settled in Bali in 1932 and quickly established himself as one of the island's best-loved expatriate painters. Here, his evocation of Balinese women weaving in the garden of his Sanur home is characteristic of much of his work, juxtaposing human sensuality, local culture, and the lush Balinese landscape.

paintings and other objects it contained were taken over by the Indonesian government to be run as a public museum.

The collection consists of 88 paintings on canvas, hardboard, dashboard, paper or *bagor* (traditional cloth); Le Mayeur's domestic belongings including furniture, ceramics, books and Balinese stone sculpture; and finally, an interesting and eclectic personal collection of old photographs of Ni Pollok, sometimes dancing or conversing with local

and international dignitaries, taken by Le Mayeur and the couple's friends.

The 88 paintings in the museum, selected and donated by the artist and his wife before Le Mayeur's death, are fairly representative of the artist's oeuvre, some still in their original, hand-carved, Balinese wooden frames. Depicting atmospheric beach or garden scenes, light-dappled in the artist's characteristic palette of pretty yellows, pinks, oranges and greens, most of the paintings and drawings included feature young Balinese women at rest, weaving or involved in religious activities.

Set in a charming garden well shielded from the flurry and noise of Sanur's cafés and clubs, the Le Mayeur Museum provides the visitor with a taste of Bali before mass tourism engulfed the island. Enthusiasts of Le Mayeur's work will also get an accurate sense of how the landscapes and seascapes that surrounded him directly shaped his artistic vision and expressive vernacular.

▲ *Ni Pollok.*

▲ *Balinese dancer.*

ADDRESS
Jalan Mayor Wisnu
Denpasar 80232, Bali
Indonesia

CONTACT DETAILS
T: +62 361 235 059 / 222 680
F: +62 361 222 680

OPENING HOURS
8am–3pm Mon–Thu,
Sat–Sun;

8am–12.30pm Fri.

ADMISSION
Adult Rp 750;
child Rp 250.

FACILITIES
Auditorium.

HOW TO GET THERE
By taxi or *bemo* to the centre
of Denpasar.

AROUND THE MUSEUM
Next door to the museum is
Pura Jaganatha.

The museum is located at
the centre of Denpasar
where there are plenty of
restaurants and cafés.

Museum Bali

In the heart of the Balinese capital, Denpasar, the Museum Bali, one of the island's oldest art institutions, combines a good ethnological collection with interesting architecture.

■ **THE BUILDING** On the east side of Puputan Square, the museum was first conceived in 1910 by W.F.J. Kroon, a colonial administrator in South Bali. The initial goal was to preserve an exemplary core collection of Balinese cultural artefacts at a time when important archaeological and ethnological material was flowing out of Bali at an increasingly alarming pace. The combined effort of Curt Grundler (a German architect), I Gusti Ketut Rai, I Gusti Ketut Gde and an Undagi (an expert on

▲ **Geringsing ceremonial cloth**
Natural dyes on cotton | Tenganan Pegeringsingan village | L: 211 cm, W: 50.5 cm

Balinese architecture) using the *Hasta Kosala Kosali* (Book of Balinese Building Principles), resulted in a museum boasting combined *puri* (palace) and *pura* (temple) architectural styles with the practical attributes essential to a functioning museum.

Thus, the hybrid structure includes a *jaba* (outer courtyard), a *jaba tengah* (an area that functions as a combined outer courtyard and inner section) and a *jeroan* (inner section), each separated by walls with *candi bentar* and *candi kurung* (forms of Balinese gates) as entrance ways.

Typical of palace architecture are the *bale bengong*, a four-poster resting pavilion used by royalty for meeting commoners and sharing news of life outside the palace, and a *beji* (royal bath) located in the Tabanan Pavilion. Typical of temple architecture are the *bale kulkul*, a drum tower located on the south side of the *jaba tengah* which would normally serve as an information gathering station, and an *ijuk* (jaka palm tree fibre) rooftop.

The *jeroan* consists of three exhibition buildings, the Gedung Tabanan, Gedung Karangasem and Gedung Buleleng, representing indigenous architectural attributes characteristic of various regencies located in different parts of Bali, in particular the South, East and North of the island.

Officially opened in 1932, the Museum Bali became a government museum after independence in 1945 and its name was altered to Museum Bali Foundation. The museum has changed its name so frequently

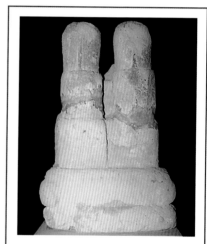

Twin *linga*
Sandstone | Bedugul, Tabanan, Bali | 11th century | H: 62 cm

Twin *linga* on a single foundation are extremely rare and this example is unique in Indonesia. The two phalluses probably symbolise the pairing of the gods Shiva and Parvati.

thereafter that visitors reading dated guidebooks to Bali will be thoroughly confused. In 2000, however, the museum reverted to the Bali Provincial Administration and so changed its name once again, returning to the original Museum Bali. The museum was extensively expanded southward in 1969, the original 2,600-square-metre floor space increased to cover around 6,000 square metres.

■ **THE COLLECTION** Ranging from prehistoric material to recently produced cultural works, the Museum Bali collection aims to be a representative survey of Balinese ethnology, archaeology, history, philology, coins and visual arts. Featuring some 14,000 items, only a small fraction of the museum's holdings are shown at one time, the objects divided into five sections housed in different pavilions.

▲ **Polychrome wooden mask used for performing the *topeng* dance**
20th century | H: 18.8 cm

■ **THE GALLERIES** The visitor penetrates the museum on its west side, facing Puputan Square. Beyond the ticketing office is the **Bale Kulkul** (Drum Tower) that was part of the original building. Further back, on the compound's east side, the **Gedung Buleleng** (Buleleng Pavilion) houses the textile collection as well as weaving equipment of various sorts. Though the labelling here is perfunctory, the visitor will be impressed by the technical and artistic merit of the *ikat, songket, prada* and *geringsing*. See in particular a rare collection of Tenganan cloth adorned with the *pat likur isi* motif.

To the left of the textile gallery, still in the original building, are the Gedung Tabanan and the Gedung Karangasem (Tabanan and Karangasem Pavilions). **Gedung Karangasem** was the original museum's largest gallery and houses Balinese calendar and ritual paraphernalia. **Gedung Tabanan** is home to objects related to dance and performance.

Walking back through the gardens and courtyards past the Bale Bengong and entrance, the visitor enters the museum's later annex. The long and narrow **Ruang Pameran Lukisan** (Painting Exhibition Pavilion) presents paintings ranging in style from traditional Balinese to contemporary international. Though displaying a fair number of works, painting is doubtless not the museum's strongest category and many of Bali's top 20th-century painters are not represented here.

Hugging its east side, the expanded museum's largest gallery is **Gedung Timur** (Eastern Pavilion). Built on two floors, this gallery alone will keep the curious visitor busy for several hours. The ground floor houses the museum's archaeological artefacts while the upper level features traditional technology including farming and fishing tools, household implements, weapons, carpentry paraphernalia, and medical and healing materials. A highlight of the archaeological section is the twin *linga* made of volcanic stone found at Bedugul in Tabanan, Bali. *Linga* are usualy found singly or in pairs close together. Adjoined twin *linga* are extremely rare and Museum Bali's is a fine example of one.

Located in a series of attractive courtyards and well-kept gardens inspired by Balinese temple and palace architecture, Museum Bali offers a cool and quiet respite from dusty, overcrowded Denpasar. The museum's collections, particularly archaeology and ethnology as opposed to fine art, afford the visitor a comprehensive view of the breadth and depth of Balinese culture.

▲ **Pratima Dewa Dewi carved polychrome wooden ceremonial icon in the form of a mythological beast** | *20th century | 55 x 49.7 cm*

ADDRESS
Jalan Pengosekan
Ubud 80571, Bali
Indonesia

CONTACT INFORMATION
T: +62 361 976 659
F: +62 361 975 332
E: info@armamuseum.com
W: www.armamuseum.com

OPENING HOURS
9am–6pm daily.

ADMISSION
Rp 20,000.

FACILITIES
Guided tours in English and
Japanese are available upon
request (US$50 for 2 hours).

HOW TO GET THERE
The museum is a 5-minute
taxi ride from the centre
of Ubud.

AROUND THE MUSEUM
Other Agung Rai facilities
including restaurants and
their commercial art gallery.

Agung Rai Museum of Art

The Agung Rai Museum of Art is one of Bali's privately owned and run museums. Set in a lush garden, it features a good collection of Indonesian paintings and frequent performances.

■ **THE BUILDING** A few kilometres south of Ubud, the Agung Rai Museum of Art, known locally as ARMA, is designed in a modified, traditional Balinese style and composed of two large pavilions (North and West) juxtaposing Balinese, European and Javanese architectural features such as high ceilings, interior columns, a peaked roof, Javanese *ukiran* carvings ornamenting the ceilings, and natural ventilation. Surrounded by a well-developed and shady garden, ARMA is but one branch of the Agung Rai empire which includes the museum, a commercial art gallery, a Thai restaurant, a café and a resort, all within a stone's throw of one another between Jalan Pengosekan and Jalan Peliatan.

While the **North and West Buildings** house the museum's permanent painting collection, the smaller **South Building** holds photographs of older Balinese performers. Visitors can also expect to watch theatrical and dance performances in a special **open pavilion** off the main exhibition hall. Temporary exhibitions are also presented in either of the main pavilions. In addition, cultural workshops and music, dance and painting classes are held in an annex. The compound also includes a café, bookshop, research library and reading room.

■ **THE COLLECTION** Agung Rai, one of Bali's foremost art entrepreneurs, began his professional life as a street pedlar in Kuta

Raden Saleh
Bangsawan Jawa | Oil on canvas | 1837 | 192 x 127 cm

This impressively large double portrait of an Indonesian regent couple came to the museum in poor condition but has now been restored. Raden Saleh (1807–1880) is known as the father of Indonesian painting because he was the first Indonesian exponent of Western-style oil painting in the country, perfectly mastering both the European medium as well as oil painting's formal and compositional aspects. He trained and worked in Europe and indeed found fame there as well.

▲ *View of an exhibition pavilion set in lush grounds.*

selling souvenirs. An excellent eye combined with a deep-rooted passion for Balinese culture quickly led him to sell art and he soon gained importance backing local artists and promoting their work abroad. ARMA, financed with profits from Agung Rai's commercial art activities and administered by the ARMA Foundation, opened in 1996 and has since become one of Bali's more established small art museums. Known for the quality of its Balinese and Indo-European works, it has about 250 paintings on permanent display, with canvases on loan from Agung Rai and his wife's personal collection sometimes supplementing the foundation's holdings.

The collection includes traditional Kamasan-style paintings on tree bark, works by Batuan school artists of the 1930s and 1940s, and paintings by two artists of key importance to the development of Indonesian art history—Walter Spies, credited for regenerating Bali's cultural scene in the 1930s, and Raden Saleh, considered the father of Indonesian painting. Works by both painters are very rare.

■ **THE GALLERIES** The **Bale Dauh (West Gallery)**, more Western in feeling than the North Gallery and located on the compound's left side, houses paintings by local and foreign painters working in non-Balinese style. Naturalistic to abstract, academic to contemporary, the artists exhibited here include 19th-century Javanese painter Raden Saleh, early 20th-century Mexican painter Miguel Covarrubias, Walter Spies, Rudolf Bonnet, Donald Friend, Adrien-Jean Le Mayeur,

Walter Spies
Calonarang | Oil on canvas | c. 1930 | 56 x 46 cm | Mr and Mrs Agung Rai Collection
Walter Spies (1895–1942), probably Bali's most famous expatriate painter and the most sought-after by collectors today, left Europe for Indonesia in 1923 and settled in Bali in 1927. As well as representing the Balinese landscape in his characteristic chiaroscuro mode dubbed 'magic realism', Spies was instrumental in founding the Pita Maha painting society that did much to bring modern Balinese painting into the international forum.

▲ **I Gusti Nyoman Lempad**
Dance Lesson | Ink on paper | 1950 | 19 x 29 cm

Theo Meier, Arie Smit, Willem Hofker, Auke Sonnega, Made Djirna and other seminal Indonesian or Indo-European artists. See in particular *Calonarang*, a magnificent 'magic realist' work by Walter Spies from the artist's early Balinese period, and *Bangsawan Jawa*, an early 19th-century portrait of a young Javanese couple by Raden Saleh, quite remarkable in its pared-down Modernism.

The **Bale Daja (North Gallery)**, smaller than the Bale Dauh, is very Balinese in both style and content. Artists featured here include Sobrat, Lempad and Ida Bagus Made among others.

Showcasing works by many of the great names of 20th-century Balinese art history, the Agung Rai Museum of Art is a must for anyone spending a few days in bucolic Ubud and keen to understand local culture in greater depth.

ADDRESS
Jalan Raya Ubud
Ubud 80571, Bali
Indonesia

CONTACT INFORMATION
T: +62 361 975 136 / 971 159
F: +62 361 975 136
E: museumpl@indo.net.id
W: www.mpl-ubud.com

OPENING HOURS
8am–4pm daily.

ADMISSION
Adult Rp 20,000;
free for children.

FACILITIES
A consultation library
is located in the
administration building.

Children's *barong* dance takes
place on the museum grounds
every Sunday afternoon.

HOW TO GET THERE
By foot from the centre
of Ubud.

AROUND THE MUSEUM
Puri Saren on the corner of
Jalan Kajeng, along Jalan

Raya Ubud, and the market at
the junction with Jalan
Monkey Forest, where crafts
can be purchased, are nearby.

There are a number of good
restaurants and cafés along
Jalan Raya Ubud.

Museum Puri Lukisan

Museum Puri Lukisan, at the centre of Ubud, is one of Bali's most historically fascinating fine art museums. Its grounds adjacent to a small ravine are as seductive as its collection.

■ **THE BUILDING** Built on Ubud's main thoroughfare, Jalan Raya Ubud, on land purchased from a relative of the prince of Ubud, Museum Puri Lukisan (Palace of Painting), though first mooted in the 1930s, was finally opened to the public in 1956 after the turbulent war years followed by the country's struggle for independence.

Separated from the road by a small brook, the museum is accessed by crossing a wooden bridge to the hillside beyond. Entering the compound, a small ticket office and *gamelan* pavilion hosting regular performances are located on the right or east side. Further up, the main museum complex is composed of three exhibition pavilions—North, East and West—that enclose a lush, terraced garden with two charming lotus ponds at its centre.

Designed in traditional Balinese style by expatriate Dutch painter Rudolf Bonnet, with

▲ **Ida Bagus Nyana**
Sleeping Woman | Carved jackfruit | 1956 |
H: 18.4 cm

characteristic peaked roof, brick walls and stone architectural features, the museum's original pavilion (North Building)—located at the rear of the compound as one approaches from the road—is distinguished by two murals by I Gusti Nyoman Lempad. They were painted on the building's outer façade in 1956 and restored by the artist in the early 1970s, just a few years before his death. Not many other changes have been made since the building's inauguration over five decades ago.

As the main building could not hold the entire collection, however, two new wings, East and West, also designed by Bonnet, were added to the museum in 1969. A library and administrative office are in a fourth pavilion, behind the East Building.

■ **THE COLLECTION** A joint initiative of the prince of Ubud, Tjokorda Gde Agung Sukawati, and his close friend, the Ubud-based artist Rudolf Bonnet, the museum was designed as a showcase for the ideas and artistic

achievements of Pita Maha (1936–1942). The latter, translated as 'Great Ancestor', was a short-lived but influential pan-Bali cooperative of indigenous and expatriate artists founded in the 1930s to promote Balinese art internationally and protect its nascent reputation by enforcing strict quality control. In Bali's increasingly tourist-oriented and commercial art forum of the 1930s, the credibility and integrity that the Pita Maha association afforded its members was not to be underestimated.

The enterprise was originally spearheaded by Bonnet, his friend Walter Spies (the German expatriate painter and musician who, once settled in Bali in 1927, had, within a few short years before his death in 1942, revitalised the island's fine arts, music and dance practices), the House of Ubud, and famous local painter I Gusti Nyoman Lempad. The collection, including both painting and sculpture, was assembled in the 1930s as Bonnet drove around the island visiting artists and discussing their work. As well as being culled essentially from Bonnet's private holdings, the collection has been supplemented over the years by gifts from other patrons gravitating around Pita Maha, artists, and a small acquisition fund garnered from proceeds of the annual selling exhibition, Kebyar Seni, that was instituted in 1998.

After World War II and Indonesia's independence from the Netherlands, Bonnet once again pledged the work that he had secured on his motor tours of Bali in the 1930s.

▲ *View of one of the museum's several lotus ponds with an exhibition pavilion in the background.*

Thus, some 150 paintings and 60 woodcarvings by Bali's most innovative and skilled artists of the 1920s and 1930s found their way into Museum Puri Lukisan. In 1953, a non-profit cultural and educational foundation, Yayasan Ratna Wartha, was established to uphold the ideals of Pita Maha and run the museum. Ratna Wartha still oversees the institution.

Since then, the collection has expanded, the foundation securing philanthropic patronage and raising its own funds to purchase works to fill gaps. The museum's holdings now include 200 paintings and 100 works of sculpture, of which most are on permanent display. One of the best collections of Modernist and neo-Classical Balinese painting in Indonesia, it also ranks among the best in the world.

For those interested in Bali's seminal Pita Maha period, an excellent museum catalogue simply titled *Museum Puri Lukisan* and penned by art historian and long-time Bali resident Dr Jean Couteau, as well as documenting the collection in some depth, provides insightful essays chronicling the complex development of 20th-century Balinese art history. The visitor who does not have time for the museum would do well to acquire this intelligent and well-researched catalogue.

■ **THE GALLERIES** The North, East and West exhibition halls positioned contiguously constitute the museum's galleries.

▲ **Ida Bagus Made Kembeng**
The Priest Advises the Animals | Tempera on paper | 1934 | 48.6 x 41.5 cm

▲ **Anak Agung Gede Sobrat**
Dance of the Barong Landung | Tempera on plywood | 1934 | 60.8 x 91.5 cm

The **North Building** or **Building I** is the original exhibition pavilion. Built in 1956, it is identified by two Lempad murals depicting typical indigenous rice-planting scenes flanking its entrance. Split into four galleries, this pavilion houses the collection's core of Transitional Painting, also termed Renewal Painting, dating from the mid-1930s to the mid-1940s. Modernist in their emphasis, examples here include the work of Ida Bagus Gelgel (see the spectacular 1935 work on paper, *The Priest Frees the Monkey, Tiger and Snake from a Well*), Ida Bagus Kembeng and Cokorda Oka Gambir. Amateurs of the luminous and lively inks on paper of I Gusti Nyoman Lempad will delight in the artist's economy of line in a 1940 frieze-like composition titled *Kris Dance*, and a second work that is distinctly Balinese, yet totally modern in feeling for its variation in scale, *The Dream of Dharmawangsa* of 1957.

Though the emphasis of the museum's collection is on later work, the small section devoted to pre-1930s, *wayang*-style painting—the dominant style prior to the modernisation of Balinese art in the 1920s—is worth looking at. The *wayang* works are situated in the **East Building** or **Building III**. See in particular paintings by Nang Ngales and Nang Ramis. As well as art, the East Building features a gift shop and a small café.

The museum's **West Building** or **Building II** contains paintings in the Young Artists style in the pavilion's first room, located to the left of the entrance. See in particular the work of I Ketut Soki and I Ketut Boko. A further three galleries are devoted to neo-Classical works in the Modern Traditional Balinese style represented by descendants and students of Pita Maha members from Ubud, Pengosekan and Batuan. Highlights include the works of I Made Sukada, Dewa Nyoman Leper, I Ketut Gelgel and I Ketut Murtika. The West Building also houses temporary exhibitions that focus on a particular aspect of Pita Maha.

Sculptural works from the corresponding periods crafted from indigenous woods are displayed throughout the museum, with the majority dating to the Transitional Painting period mentioned earlier.

In its shaded, terraced gardens, with the sound of a gurgling brook masking the bustle of Ubud's centre just over the bridge, Museum Puri Lukisan is an idyllic and rewarding place to learn about one of Balinese art history's most exciting periods.

Ida Bagus Gelgel
The Priest Frees the Monkey, Tiger and Snake from a Well | Natural pigments on paper | 1935 | 68.1 x 48.9 cm

One of the early 20th century's most important Balinese artists, Ida Bagus Gelgel's work is characterised by its clear colours, flat perspective and narrative idiom. Here, he depicts an episode from the *Tantri Kamandaka* cycle of animal stories derived from the Indian *Panchatantra*. The story underscores the generosity of animals and the treachery of humans.

ADDRESS
Barat 12
Central Jakarta 10110
Indonesia

CONTACT INFORMATION
T: +62 21 386 8172 / 344 7778
F: +62 21 381 1076
E: munas@budpar.go.id
W: www.budpar.go.id

OPENING HOURS
8.30am–2.30pm Tue–Thu,
Sun;
8.30am–11.30am Fri;
8.30am–1.30pm Sat.

ADMISSION
Adult Rp 750;
child and student Rp 250.

FACILITIES
Guided tours in English, French
and Japanese. Available in
German, Spanish, Dutch and
Finnish upon request.

HOW TO GET THERE
Bus: Take Bus Way running
between Blok M and the
city and alight at the
National Museum.

AROUND THE MUSEUM
The museum is less than 5
minutes away by taxi from
Gambir Railway Station and
a short walk from the
Presidential Palace (built in the
same style as the museum).

National Museum

The National Museum, presenting Indonesian antiquities, Chinese works of art, prehistoric material and ethnological works, is one of the country's oldest and most distinguished museums, housed in an elegant and just-expanded colonial building.

■ **THE BUILDING** A short walk from the Presidential Palace, on the west side of central Jakarta's Medan Merdeka (Freedom Square), the National Museum (Museum Nasional) was established in 1868 by the Dutch-run Batavian Society of Arts and Sciences, itself founded in 1778 and the oldest association of its kind in Asia. Jakarta residents know the museum as the Gedung Gajah (Elephant Building) because of the large bronze statue of an elephant marking the building's entrance. The statue was given to the city by Thai King Chulalongkorn when he paid a state visit to Jakarta in 1871.

Originally a neo-Classical structure set around a courtyard with typical tropical colonial architectural features such as a Doric-columned and porticoed façade, high ceilings, airy rooms and large shuttered windows, the museum has now been extended. The new B Wing, incorporating two additional basement levels and seven floors, is due to open in 2005, the extension and the old space combined providing the museum with some 23,000 square metres of floor space. The local architects in charge of the project have cleverly extended the principal façade up and out to the rear, substantially increasing the exhibition space while retaining the essence of the museum's appearance.

■ **THE COLLECTION** Though the museum proper was set up in the second half of the 19th century, the collection itself predates the building by some 80 years. The museum's founder, the Batavian Society of Arts and Sciences, a humanistic, forward-thinking institution, had accumulated indigenous 'curiosities' (including books, manuscripts, musical instruments, coins and dried plants) which eventually developed into a collection able to further the society's principal objective which was research and the study of the cultural history of Indonesia in all its aspects. This original brief no doubt explains the breadth, depth and excellence of the museum's holdings.

When the British briefly replaced the Dutch in the East Indies in the early 19th century, the society came under the patronage of Sir Stamford Raffles, the new Lieutenant Governor of Java. Raffles, as he did in Singapore a few years later, took a keen interest in indigenous arts and culture, collecting cultural objects from many regions of the archipelago and raising the institution's public profile as well. At this time the collections were considerably expanded and a new, larger building was sought to house them.

The society's holdings continued to increase (though both the zoological and geological sections were discontinued around this time) and in 1862 the Dutch government, now returned to power in their former colony,

▲ **Chinese charger found in Sumatra**
Porcelain | Decorated in underglaze blue | Ming dynasty, 15th century | D: 44 cm

▲ *Statue of a bronze elephant, a gift from King Chulalongkorn of Thailand, with the National Museum in the background.*

decided to build a new museum, the now familiar premises at Jalan Merdeka.

The collection saw ups and downs in the 20th century: it was considerably enriched when the Dutch collector E.W. van Orsoy de Flines donated more than 6,000 ceramics to the museum, but impoverished in 1931 when part of it was destroyed in a fire in Europe, the museum having sent star pieces for exhibition at the Indonesian pavilion during the Paris World Fair. The insurance money was used to extend the museum building in Jakarta. At this time, the book and manuscripts department, in effect the society's library, also grew in stature and ranked as one of the largest libraries, if not the largest, in Southeast Asia.

After Indonesia's independence from the Netherlands, the society was renamed the Institute of Indonesian Culture. By the 1960s, the Institute, now administered by the Indonesian government's Department of Education and Culture, had become a public institution named the Central Museum, which in 1987 finally became the National Museum. At this time as well, the painting collection was moved to its own building and museum across Medan Merdeka, the National Gallery.

The collection, luckily spared damage during World War II and the struggle for independence, numbers close to 200,000 objects and constitutes the world's most comprehensive grouping of artworks and ethnological pieces documenting the Indonesian archipelago's cultural history. Covering prehistory, the Classical period from the 4th to 15th century, the rising influence of Islam in the 16th century, and the period of European influence beginning in the 17th century, the collection continues to expand today through acquisition, donation and excavation. Extremely broad in scope, it covers the country's entire geography and virtually all its history. It has traditionally been divided thematically into nine sections including Prehistoric, Archaeological (Hindu and Buddhist period relics are here), Numismatic, Historical (Verenigde Oostindische Compagnie (VOC) or Dutch East India Company period), Geographical, Ethnographical, Textiles and Ceramics. The ninth section, Fine Arts, as stated, has since moved to its own museum, the National

▲ **Stone stele depicting Shiva and Parvati**
Klaten, Central Java | 8th–9th century | H: 198 cm

Gallery. All remaining sections are strong, with many works unique in artistic quality, spiritual associations, state of conservation and rarity.

The trove of foreign ceramics found in the archipelago, mainly Chinese and Southeast Asian but also Japanese and European, most donated by de Flines—also the museum's first curator until his departure in 1957—is remarkable, dating back as far as the Han dynasty (205 BCE—220 CE) and including a number of fine Ming dynasty (1368–1644) pieces. The collection is of particular significance because, as well as numbering many artistically resplendent pieces, rare and valuable in their own right, it documents the historical importance of Indonesian trade links over the centuries with the two great and powerful centres of ancient international commerce, China and India. The origin of foreign ceramics in Indonesia is closely related to trade and, indeed, ceramics were frequently a medium of trade themselves.

Exchanged by the Chinese against Indonesian spices, ceramics of Chinese origin were often of export quality, but some were fine or specifically commissioned and thus kept in the family as heirlooms. One such example from the de Flines donation is a large and rare early Ming charger decorated in underglaze blue, found in Jambi, Sumatra. The Chinese did not much favour large plates but the indigenous culture's taste for communal eating explains the vessel's size and discovery in Sumatra, presumably ordered by a local family. A second large plate found in Sumatra—17th-century Ming Swatow ware painted in overglaze *wu t'sai* enamels—was clearly also commissioned as it is decorated throughout with Arabic script. A green-glazed water vessel, dating to the middle of the Tang dynasty (circa 8th century) is thought to have been brought to the archipelago by Chinese Buddhist priests and novices visiting the kingdom of Srivijaya between the 7th and the 10th century.

The museum's collection of metalware —bronze, silver and particularly gold—is also outstanding. The archipelago is rich both in copper and tin—the alloys used to make bronze; and indigenous cultures as well as the Dong Son culture, which spread from Annam to Indonesia around 300 BCE and continued to influence local taste for several centuries, are well represented here. Dong Son-style bronze kettledrums, produced in Java and Bali well after Dong Son had waned, are a highlight of the collection and enthusiasts of bronze ceremonial weapons will find much to please them. Best of all, perhaps, are the bronze Hindu-Buddhist relics of the 7th to the 15th century, many of fine quality and well conserved. See in particular a central Javanese icon of Kuvera from the 8th to 9th century, the figure's throne still intact.

As Indonesia is a producer of gold and silver, wonderful precious metal objects thus come from every corner of the archipelago, with death masks, jewellery, beads, ceremonial wares and religious icons figuring prominently in the national collection. A silver central Javanese figure of Shiva from the 8th to 9th century is a highlight, as are two gold Hindu icons worked in repoussé, a 9th-century Shiva from Central Java of exquisitely stylised design, and a figure of Harihara, larger and of the same origin and period. Weaponry and tribal jewellery of more recent manufacture, many pieces unique in the world, are also worth the detour.

Perhaps the museum's most dazzling collections, however, are stone, ethnology and textiles. The ethnological section, numbering some 30,000 pieces, many of which were collected before other world collections were

▲ **Silver figure of Shiva**
Central Dieng, Central Java | 8th–9th century | H: 11.6 cm

◄ **Detail of a stone figure of Prajnaparamita**
Malang, East Java | 13th century | H: 126 cm

even founded, is representative of every corner of the archipelago. Prow ornaments from Central Malaku, hair combs from East Sumba, rice harvesting implements from South Kalimantan, shields from Irian Jaya, spirit effigies from Central Sulawesi, ceremonial hats from Sumatra, stone heads from Timor, architectural ornaments from Bali, wall decorations from West Java and two full *gamelan* orchestras give visitors an idea of the breadth and scope of the trove. Fine examples of utilitarian objects such as basketry, woodcarving and weapons also abound. Vast and unrivalled, this part of the museum's collection is worthy of several visits in itself and even those visiting the storerooms cannot hope to absorb the entire collection, though it is thought the building's renovation will allow much more material to be displayed at one time.

Concepts of ancestor worship established in prehistoric Indonesian society are reflected in the still surviving stone works. Indeed, this culture continues to be closely tied with stone statuary in various parts of the archipelago such as Nias, Toraja, Flores and Sumba. Indian Hindu influence, present from before the 5th century, also marked statuary form, and grafted onto indigenous culture, furthered the development of a local Hindu vernacular. As well as Indian-type statuary, Singasari-Majapahit sculpture from Indonesia's Classical period is a significant part of the collection. Worth seeking out in particular are a life-size 8th- to 9th-century relief of Shiva and Parvati and a naturalistically carved kneeling figure of Dwarapala from 10th-century Central Java. Again, the museum's expansion should make much more of this spectacular and unrivalled collection visible to the public.

The grandeur of Indonesia's textile tradition arises from the great variety of its

ethnic groups whose distinctive cultures are most vividly revealed in their textiles. The role of textiles in Indonesian society remains important even today, present in life rituals and embodying supernatural powers. The National Museum's collection includes a number of rare examples, among others a Balinese double *ikat* in perfect condition dating from the beginning of the 20th century or earlier, an outstanding Sumatran ship cloth, a 19th-century West Kalimantan *songket*, and a 19th-century sarong from North Sulawesi.

■ **THE GALLERIES** The museum has traditionally been laid out thematically and according to medium. Galleries devoted to

▲ **Gold relief of Shiva**
Gemuruh, Banyukembar, Leksono, Wonosobo, Central Java | 9th century | H: 20.5

▲ **Ship cloth** | *Cotton* | *Lampung, Sumatra* | *Second half of the 19th century* | *61 x 282 cm*

ethnography, for example, were grouped together, sub-sections presenting works according to their geographic origin. Textiles, bronzes, ceramics and coins were all displayed in their own space while some stone pieces were viewed in the museum's inner courtyard. Two treasure rooms displaying precious metal and jewelled objects from the ethnography and archaeology holdings were located on the second floor. The expanded gallery design, not available at the time of printing, is expected to increase dramatically the number of objects on display as well as clarify the viewing experience. However, the groupings are likely to remain the same.

The National Museum collection, more than housing an extraordinary cache of priceless works of art, documents the rich and complex history of Indonesia and the links of Southeast Asia to the world beyond.

One of the most distinguished museums in Southeast Asia, in terms of its collection and history, the National Museum also provides an

interesting post-colonial framework for socio-political discussion. Indeed, it has been argued by Indonesian scholars that the national collection, assembled largely by the Dutch, present in the archipelago for over 300 years, reflects a somewhat Eurocentric understanding of art and cultural history. While for Europeans a work of art or cultural object is defined by its intrinsic aesthetic quality and age, Indonesians, for their part, tend to recognise an object's spiritual power or historical associations as essential criteria in determining its cultural value and legitimacy as an heirloom. This concept of the *pusaka*—an object handed down from generation to

▶ **Earthenware** *kendi***, China**
Glazed earthenware | *Found in Palembang, Sumatra* | *Tang dynasty, 8th century* | *H: 25.5 cm*

generation, accorded special veneration and in some cases seen as having spiritual and healing powers—does not necessarily coincide with the European understanding of heritage and art. Thus, to some Indonesians, the National Museum, though called 'national', is the product of 'an alien cultural sensibility' and thus not really a flagship national institution after all (it should be noted that a reasonable number of Indonesians, albeit Westernised, were members of the Batavian Society of Arts and Sciences from the mid-19th century onwards). Whatever the nature of the nationalist theoretical debate, and however 'alien' its sensibility, the National Museum should on no account be missed by anyone interested in art, history or Indonesia.

ADDRESS
Jalan Prabu Geusan Ulun 40B
Sumedang 45311
West Java
Indonesia

CONTACT INFORMATION
T/F: +62 261 201 714
E: mayasujat@hotmail.com

OPENING HOURS
8am–2pm Sat–Thu.

ADMISSION
Adult (foreigner) US$1;
student Rp 2,500.

FACILITIES
Guided tours are available in
Bahasa Indonesia, Dutch,
English and Sundanese.

A small shop selling snacks
and souvenirs.

HOW TO GET THERE
Taxi: From Bandung,
Sumedang is 45 km east.
Picturesque local roads run
through plantation areas and
the scenic Cadas Pangeran
(Prince Rock Hill).

AROUND THE MUSEUM
The West Java countryside.

Museum Prabu Geusan Ulun

In Sumedang, some 45 kilometres from Bandung, Museum Prabu Geusan Ulun, housed in a charming series of old buildings, is the most comprehensive museum of Sundanese culture in West Java.

■ **THE BUILDING** The museum comprises five main buildings, all erected at different times over the course of the last two centuries. The earliest building was constructed in 1706 by Dalem Adipati Tanumaja and was originally the regent of Sumedang's residence. A plain, square edifice with deep overhanging eaves, interior support columns and large, rounded windows on all sides, the Srimanganti Building is now used as an auditorium.

The Bumi Kaler Building, erected in 1850 by Pangeran (Prince) Sugih, follows traditional Sundanese architecture (Julang Ngapak) characterised by the use of high-quality teak.

A third edifice, the Pusaka Building, was also built by Pangeran Sugih but was remodelled in the 1950s so that few of its mid-19th-century architectural traits remain.

Two further buildings house *gamelans* and motor vehicles respectively.

■ **THE COLLECTION** The museum was named after a charismatic proponent of Islam. Its collection includes Sundanese works of art and cultural objects from the 15th to the 19th century.

■ **THE GALLERIES** The **Srimanganti Building** is the first encountered by visitors and houses a large antique clock, paintings, antique china, royal costumes from the house of Sumedang, carved antique furniture from Jepara and Pangeran Kornel's bed. Pangeran Kornel, famous in this part of Java, was the Sundanese prince governing Sumedang at the beginning of the 19th century. He is remembered for his bravery

▲ *Binokasih coronation regalia including a man and a woman's crown and various other ornaments.*

in opposing the Dutch colonial government who wished to build a new road using local labour.

The **Bumi Kaler Building** houses Sundanese and Arabic manuscripts dating back to the 18th century, as well as other books, coins, and a collection of 17th-, 18th- and 19th-century ceremonial umbrellas.

The **Pusaka Building** is the museum's most important in terms of exhibits. *Pusaka*, or sacred traditional weapons such as *keris*,

badik, *kujang* and swords are kept here. At the centre of the room, in a pyramid-shaped, bulletproof case, are the Binokasih coronation regalia, including a crown and male and female accessories such as belts, bracelets, necklaces, hair pins and other assorted ornaments.

The **Gamelan Building** presents a number of complete orchestras including a 19th-century *gamelan* known as Sari Oneng Parakan Salak that was exhibited in Holland in 1883, Paris in 1889 during the ceremony marking the opening of the Eiffel Tower, and finally, Chicago in 1893. The Sari Oneng was so well regarded that it toured abroad for another hundred years and was only returned to Java in 1990.

The **Kereta Building** holds a collection of vehicles including the official Naga Barong and common public transport vehicles such as the *delman* or *keretek*.

Set in a typical West Javanese backwater, Museum Prabu Geusan Ulun's small collection provides many clues to provincial Sundanese life in pre-colonial and colonial times.

Sari Oneng Gamelan Orchestra

A complete 19th-century orchestra, the Sari Oneng Gamelan was one of the first Indonesian *gamelan* orchestras to travel to the West when European interest in Southeast Asian culture first dawned in the late 19th century. Initially exhibited in Amsterdam, it caught the fancy of many and thus travelled to Paris and then Chicago.

ADDRESS
Jalan Laksda Adisucipto
Yogyakarta 55281, Java
Indonesia

CONTACT DETAILS
T/F: +62 274 562 593
E: musaff@yogya.
wasantara.net.id
W: www.affandi.org

OPENING HOURS
9am–4pm Tue–Sun;
9am–1pm Mon.

ADMISSION
US$2 (includes a soft drink).

FACILITIES
Guided tours in English,
French, Mandarin or other
languages are available
upon request.

Café; museum shop.

HOW TO GET THERE
Taxi: The museum is a 20-
minute taxi ride from the
centre of town.

AROUND THE MUSEUM
Gajahwong River and some
local *warungs*.

Museum Seni Lukis Affandi

A very personal and charming museum on the edge of Yogyakarta, the Museum Seni Lukis Affandi offers Affandi's pioneer Modernist work as well as his personal collection, in buildings designed by the artist.

■ **THE BUILDING** Until his death in 1990, the museum complex and garden were developed progressively by Affandi over several decades on 3,500 square metres of terraced land on the west bank of Yogyakarta's Gajahwong River. The complex was established in 1975 when Affandi designed and built a house for himself on this land and later kept part of his collection there. The house, which garnered him the 1981 Aga Khan Award for design (he refused the honour, explaining he did not deserve it because he was a painter, not an architect), combines a low, overhanging, banana leaf-shaped roof made of palm leaves, and organically shaped, concrete supporting columns. He chose the banana leaf for its perceived protective and indigenous connotations.

The house is now occupied by a café on the ground level, while Affandi's private quarters, a floor above, can be viewed as part of the museum visit.

Three more pavilions, constructed later but along the same lines as Affandi's house, contain the collection as well as temporary exhibitions featuring other Indonesian artists.

A *gerobag* (a traditional cart that resembles an old fashioned horse-drawn caravan) that Affandi built for his wife, which now functions as a prayer hall for family and visitors, also has a home in the compound.

▲ **Affandi**
*The Painter and His
Daughter | Oil on canvas |
1950 | 176 x 98 cm*

■ **THE COLLECTION** The Affandi Foundation, the body that runs the Affandi Museum, owns some 300 paintings by the master. A portion of these are exhibited at the museum at all times, the works rotated every six months or so.

Along with paintings by Affandi, the collection features a number of canvases by fellow pioneer Modernists, including Sudjojono, Hendra Gunawan, Muchtar Apin, Popo Iskandar and numerous others.

■ **THE GALLERIES** Three permanent exhibition galleries are housed in the compound. The first, around 300 square metres in size, was opened in the 1970s and is used as a survey space, displaying artworks in all media and from every period of Affandi's life. Several sculptural self-portraits are here, as is the artist's Mitsubishi Gallant, transformed into a fish, and his bicycle. Some of Affandi's favourite paintings include an early portrait of his wife, a portrait of the artist with his daughter Kartika as she leaves her father for married life, a self-portrait with his father and mother, and a self-portrait with a grandchild.

A second 350-square-metre, government-sponsored gallery was opened in 1987. This space is used for exhibiting the museum's works by other modern Indonesian artists.

▲ **Affandi**
Self Portrait | Oil on canvas | 1964 | 128 x 99 cm

The third gallery, opened in 2000, was built by the Affandi Foundation to house and exhibit various works and provide a space dedicated to teaching art to children. Though built well after the artist's death in 1990, this structure's architecture resembles that of the other buildings in the complex. Its first floor is used as a temporary exhibition space and studio for children, while the second floor is devoted to restoration, and the basement for storage.

Affandi's engaging personality and huge talent is nowhere more present than in this museum set in a verdant garden. Visitors unfamiliar with the artist as well as admirers of his characteristic impasto and expressive language will delight in the Affandi Museum.

ADDRESS
Jalan Boyong Kaliurang
Sleman, Yogyakarta, Java
Indonesia

CONTACT INFORMATION
T: +62 274 880 158 / 895 161
F: +62 274 881 743

OPENING HOURS
9am–3.30pm Tue–Sun.

ADMISSION
US$4.

FACILITIES
Guided tours in English and
Bahasa Indonesia are
available, and others as
requested by appointment.

Welcome drink; souvenir
shop; elegant restaurant.

HOW TO GET THERE
Taxi: Head 25 km north from
downtown Yogyakarta, about
half an hour by road.

AROUND THE MUSEUM
Rural Java.

Ullen Sentalu Museum

Yogyakarta's Ullen Sentalu ('Light of Life') Museum celebrates local Javanese court culture through the display of an eclectic collection in an attractive garden setting.

■ **THE BUILDING** The Ullen Sentalu Museum is located in the countryside north of Yogyakarta which, with its cool air and leafy vistas, attracts Yogya weekenders. The recently built museum, designed by KP Dr Samuel J. Haryono Wedyadiningrat, features hybrid architectural elements that marry local stone with a mock Tudor style of Dutch colonial inspiration. The compound is lovely, punctuated with different gardens set among the pavilions, some of which display sculpture. A cinnamon and pine forest borders the grounds on the west side.

■ **THE COLLECTION** The Ullen Sentalu Museum was established in 1997 by the Haryono clan in the family compound. Though of mixed Chinese descent, the family, long involved in the home batik industry, successfully absorbed classical Javanese tradition in their art in terms of both aesthetics and iconography. Innovators as well, a later generation of the family was part of the 'batik renaissance' that took hold in Java in the first half of the 20th century and thus adapted

the style of their designs to appeal to a broader, more international audience. So distinguished was their batik that the Haryonos became the sole supplier to several royal families in Solo and Yogyakarta and thus grew close to court life as well as members of the royal families.

The collection includes an eclectic assortment of royal effects given to the Haryonos by their royal patrons, including family memorabilia, paintings of the Mataram Kingdom royal family, ancient batiks from the *kraton*, silverware, Javanese ceremonial crafts, sculpture, miniatures of royal carriages and much more.

■ **THE ROOMS AND OUTDOOR SPACES** The visitor first encounters **Guwo Selo Giri**, an underground stone cavern in Tudor style, where portraits of the Mataram Kingdom family members are displayed.

Next is **Kampung Kambang**, the museum's richest interior space, housing **Tineke's Room** (memorabilia belonging to Princess Tineke from Kraton Surakarta) and **The Adoring Princess' Room**, dedicated to Princess Nurul Kusumawardhani from Mangkunegaran, Surakarta. Two further rooms, perhaps of greater interest to an international public, house the museum's collection of batiks, respectively from South Central and North Central Java. Differences in colouring and iconography are well elucidated here by the guides whose anecdotes about royal family history and personal affairs bring the collection to life. Finally, the **Pengantin Paes**

▲ **Detail of modern copy of an 1897 portrait of Sunan Paku Buwono X** | *Oil on canvas* | *200 x 200 cm*

Ageng houses Javanese women's wedding costumes from Kraton Yogyakarta.

The third and last public building is the underground **Djagad Academic Gallery**, presenting temporary exhibitions staged by young artists, local and foreign.

Not yet open as this book goes to press, the **Kaputren** on the compound's far east side is a house featuring personal effects and recreations of women's ceremonies.

Ullen Sentalu is a small, eclectic museum that, in marrying one family's history with a glimpse of royal life, provides a snapshot of Javanese high society's relative hierarchical fluidity.

▲ **Detail of a batik**
Cotton | Urang Wetang | 1930s

Laos ▶

ADDRESS
Souphanouvong Road
Pakham Village
Luang Prabang
Laos

CONTACT INFORMATION
T: +856 71 212 122
F: +856 71 212 044
E: nangpheng@hotmail.com

OPENING HOURS
8am–11am, 1.30pm–4pm daily.

ADMISSION
20,000 kip.

FACILITIES
Guided tours are available in English.

HOW TO GET THERE
On foot or by bicycle.

AROUND THE MUSUEM
Luang Prabang is small and easy to get around on foot.

Cafés, handicraft shops and temples surround the museum.

Mount Phousi is across the street.

Luang Prabang National Museum

The Luang Prabang National Museum, or the Royal Palace Museum, located along the Mekong River and opposite Mount Phousi, houses an eclectic collection of Lao Buddhist art.

■ **THE BUILDING** Situated at the centre of Luang Prabang and set in a pretty, shaded garden, the Golden Palace (or Ho Kham as the building is known locally) is relatively modern, having been constructed at the beginning of the 20th century for King Sisavangvong's coronation. The French, in an attempt to strengthen their protectorate, were keen to tie the Lao monarchy more closely to the colonial administration. Thus, they had an earlier, more modest wooden palace on the same site demolished, and in 1904 began construction of a new building. Completed in 1909 (the lateral wings were extended a few years later), the palace combines elements of Lao vernacular architecture with French turn-of-the-19th-century Beaux-Arts style.

Approaching the palace from Luang Prabang's main street, Phothisarath, the visitor is met by a rather French-looking, palm-lined avenue leading to the museum's main door. The palms were planted in the 1920s, and during the same period, the roof's original pinnacle was altered by the king, who preferred Lao design to French.

The palace's raised, horizontal façade is lined from one end to the other with a covered verandah that protects the building from the blazing midday sun (mornings and nights in Luang Pabang are dry and cool) but the balustrade and supporting pillars are reminiscent of late 19th-/early 20th-century European Atlantic boardwalk architecture rather than Asian in appearance. The monumental columned entrance is not particularly indigenous in style either (fleurs-de-lys adorn the columns), though it is surmounted by a gilded relief of a three-headed Lao elephant symbolising the unification of the three former Lao Kingdoms under the Luang Prabang monarchy.

■ **THE COLLECTION** The palace housed the royal family until their overthrow by the Lao communists in 1975. Crown Prince Sisavang Vatthana (who was to be crowned king the same year) and his family never returned to the palace which was converted into a national museum and opened to the public in 1976. It remains more or less as it was left by the exiled royals in 1975.

The collection presents more than 20,000 objects ranging from textiles to musical instruments, royal accessories, decorative arts, ceramics, documents, Buddhist art and furniture, among other things.

▲ *The Ambassadors' Room, featuring murals by Alex de Foutereau.*

It includes some fine works of art (or their copies) worth seeking out, including the most famous of the trove, the Prabang—an ancient, gold Buddha reputedly made in Sri Lanka sometime before the 9th century and brought to the Khmer kingdom in the 11th century. Legend has it that due to a royal alliance between the Lao and the Khmer, the Prabang was given to the Lao kingdom by the Khmer at the end of the 14th century. A chief source of spiritual inspiration for Laotians since then, and marking the official arrival of Theravada Buddhism in the kingdom, the Prabang gave the city its name. A copy of the original is housed in a small, private chapel on the north side of the complex. The real Prabang is now locked away for protection.

Other items of significance are a series of fairly well-conserved Dong Son drums, Buddhist sculpture from different periods dating back as early as the 12th century

▲ *View of the Royal Palace's façade from the front garden.*

collected from various temples around the city, ornamented domestic articles, precious metal Buddhist alms bowls, ornate royal furniture from different periods, and an eclectic assortment of gifts presented to the royal household by foreign dignitaries and governments. One such present, rather incongruous here, are fragments of moon rocks from the Apollo 17 mission presented to the kingdom of Laos in 1973 by Richard Nixon on behalf of the American people (Laos was an important American ally during the Vietnam War).

▲ **Standing Buddha**
Gold | 14th century | H: 83 cm

embedded Japanese glass mosaic figures depicting scenes from Lao festivals and history. The throne and gilded furniture are also majestic, but perhaps more interesting is a collection of precious Buddhist items including several gold Buddhas from That Mak Mo, a local *wat* that collapsed in 1910. Swords and other items belonging to the royal regalia are also housed here in cases.

Left of the entrance is the **Secretariat**, where guests were registered prior to their audience with the king, and beyond this is the **Queen's Reception Room**. These rooms contain

furniture and a large selection of state gifts, including the abovementioned moon rocks and portraits of the royal family.

The private apartments of the royal family, rather dim and airless due to their corridor location, are tucked behind the public reception rooms. They are decorated simply with dark furniture. The most interesting of these rooms is the former **Nursery** where traditional Lao performance material is shown, including instruments, masks and costumes used for interpreting the *Ramayana*.

The Luang Prabang National Museum is as interesting for its river setting as for the trove it houses. In addition to presenting a unique, if mixed collection, the museum provides the visitor with an insightful look into the life of the two last generations of Lao monarchs.

■ **THE ROOMS** The palace is of cruciform shape with 11 rooms open to visitors. Its grand public reception rooms are positioned at the front and sides of the building while the royal family's private chambers, far more modest, are located at the rear.

The visitor first enters the **Main Entrance Hall**. Originally only a point of entry, the hall gradually took on additional functions and over time, was to host religious and other traditional ceremonies. A number of sculptural Buddha icons from around Luang Prabang are displayed in cabinets here, as they were in the former king's day.

To the right of the hall is the king's **Audience Room** or the **Ambassadors' Room**. The walls here feature a mural painted in 1930 by French artist Alex de Foutereau depicting daily life in Luang Prabang according to the time of day. Cleverly, the panels are positioned such that morning light falls on the morning activities scene, while afternoon sunshine illuminates the afternoon activities scene. In addition to the mural, a pair of lacquered and gilded panels evoking scenes from the *Ramayana* by Laotian master Thit Tanh can also be viewed.

The **Throne Room**, behind the entrance, is quite impressive with its red lacquer walls and

Throne Room
Red lacquered walls embedded with Japanese glass

The Throne or Coronation Room was redecorated between 1960 and 1970 in anticipation of Prince Sisavang Vatthana's coronation which was postponed because of the war in Indochina. Embedded into a brilliant red lacquer background further enhanced with gilded woodwork that together recall Luang Prabang's vivid traditional temple decoration, the Japanese glass is positioned so as to describe charming scenes from a variety of Lao festivals. Though undeniably exotic and luxurious, this decorative scheme, in borrowing its iconography from parochial life, is simultaneously regal and close to all Laotians.

ADDRESS
Route 13
Pakse
Laos

CONTACT INFORMATION
T: +856 31 212 501

OPENING HOURS
8.30am–11.30am,
1.30pm–4.30pm, daily;
closed on public holidays.

ADMISSION
5,000 kip.

FACILITIES
Guided tours are available
in Lao.

HOW TO GET THERE
On foot or by *tuk tuk*.

AROUND THE MUSEUM
The bustling morning market

just east of the museum is
excellent for purchasing
Laotian and tribal textiles.

With its market-town
ambience, the Mekong and
dusty, untouched colonial
architecture, Pakse, not overly
built-up, offers some
enjoyable walks.

The ruins at Wat Phou can be
accessed by road or, perhaps
more pleasantly, by river.

Champasak Provincial Museum

Located in Pakse, close to the Thai border at the confluence of the Xe Don and Mekong rivers, the Champasak Provincial Museum houses some fine pre-Angkorian stone works as well as tribal material.

■ **THE BUILDING AND TOWN** Pakse is southern Laos's largest town and was established by the French at the beginning of the 20th century as a commercial hub for the south. A number of old French colonial buildings, though decrepit, remain, lending Pakse a certain faded charm. The town is not as quiet as it once was, however, due to the opening in 2000 of the Lao-Japan Bridge (known as the Friendship Bridge and funded by the Japanese) that spans the Mekong at Pakse, linking Laos with Thailand.

Those travelling to Pakse to visit the 7th-century, pre-Angkorian Khmer ruins at Wat Phou (considered among the finest of the genre outside Cambodia) may wish to stay in Pakse rather than Champasak so as to visit the museum.

Located on the eastern side of town, close to the new market, 500 metres north of the banks of the Mekong and next to the site leading to the point of access for the new bridge, the museum is housed in a recent, two-storey concrete building

▲ **Cotton-reeling device**
Carved wood | Early 20th century

Stone fragments of architectural elements
Two fragments of lintels or other architectural remains | Khmer (pre-Angkor), 7th century

Remains of architectural elements such as these were once part of the ancient Khmer temples in the vicinity of Pakse. Though not in marvellous condition, these lintel fragments attest to the artistic vigour and technical accomplishment of Khmer temple art beyond Angkor.

of undistinguished but vaguely traditional style. The building is nonetheless airy and reasonably well appointed, enjoying a good view of the surrounding landscape from its second floor.

Founded in 1995 to disseminate information about Champasak Province's cultural past and present, the museum's two floors present approximately 600 square metres of exhibition space.

■ **THE COLLECTION** The collection, only recently formed, was first assembled in the mid-1970s and continues to expand as new material is found in the province. It includes ancient bronzes (see a number of drums), ancient stone sculpture and architectural elements from Wat Phou, iron ware, indigenous ethnic textiles, costumes and a few examples of tribal jewellery and basketry, as well as an extensive series of modern propagandist photographs documenting socio-economic development in the province (consisting mainly of Lao government officials

presiding over school and factory openings). Labelling is succinct and in Lao but the stone material coming from either the Champasak site or around the province does not need much explanation to be appreciated.

■ **THE GALLERIES** The museum's ground floor houses the province's historical cultural material and the floor above features photographs documenting the contemporary history of the province. Visitors with little time should concentrate on the ground floor.

The archaeological, Khmer and tribal material is shown in a rather ad hoc fashion in three spaces at the centre of the gallery with the pre-Angkorian sandstone architectural elements located towards the rear. In this section, see a pair of well-conserved, elaborately carved 7th-century lintels.

Though neither large nor exhaustive in scope, the Champasak Provincial Museum presents a good collection of archaeological material in an airy and pleasant setting.

ADDRESS
Samsaenthai Road
Vientiane
Laos

CONTACT INFORMATION
T: +856 21 212 462
F: +856 21 212 408
E: laonationalmuseum@
hotmail.com

OPENING HOURS
8am–12pm, 1pm–4pm daily;
closed on public holidays.

ADMISSION
5,000 kip.

FACILITIES
Shop selling souvenirs and
cold drinks.

HOW TO GET THERE
On foot as the location is very
central.

AROUND THE MUSEUM
Located in the heart of
Vientiane, the museum is a
short distance from hotels as
well as Wat Sisaket and
Ho Phra Keo.

Lao National Museum

Housed in a pleasant French colonial building, the Lao National Museum documents the country's archaeological and cultural history, its many ethnic cultures and the revolutionary war and its effects.

■ **THE BUILDING** The museum is located in the former residence of the French colonial governor (the French claimed control of Laos at the end of the 19th century) and is one of many examples of French colonial architecture remaining in Vientiane. Built in 1925, the rather plain two-storey, flat-fronted house with a small columned entrance portico was enlarged in the 1950s, thus providing the museum, established there in 1980, with adequate floor space for its collection. The institution, positioned in the centre of Vientiane and a short walk from the Mekong and two major temples, is set in a garden where two large burial urns from the Plain of Jars are displayed.

■ **THE COLLECTION** The national collection has been housed in a number of different places and under different names since its founding in 1917. Initially assembling Buddhist works of art, the collection and focus of the museum have been modified as history has

▲ **Pipe bowl**
Clay | Sisattanak District, Vientiane | 17th century | 4.5 x 6.5 x 3.8 cm

unfolded in Laos in the course of the 20th century. At one point being the Lao Revolutionary Museum, the institution became once again a National Museum in 2000.

The museum covers Lao history chronologically, with works of art as well as more prosaic cultural material, photographs and text information providing evidence of key historical developments and ruptures. As well as Buddhist art of different periods worked in various media, the collection now includes prehistoric works of art and artefacts, including some examples of the megalithic urns from the 2,500-year-old Plain of Jars culture, ceramics of different periods and origins, Hindu religious art, traditional musical instruments and theatrical paraphernalia and some tribal material (the Hmong, Mien and Akha are some of the country's hill tribes) among others. The text panels and labels are generally in Lao, English and sometimes French.

■ **THE GALLERIES** Spread over the old house's ground and upper floors, the objects tend to be grouped by periods such as **Prehistory and Early Culture**, the **Formation of States**, the **Lan Xang Period** and **The**

▲ **Figure of Ganesha**
Sandstone clay | Dong Kong, Champasak Province | 7th century | H: 48 cm

Twentieth Century, thematic areas of investigation associated with these periods determining the objects' arrangement. While the first floor presents the archaeology of the Mekong Valley, the second works its way forward from the mid-14th century and the founding of Lan Xang—the first independent Lao kingdom, in 1353—to the 20th century with French colonialism, independence, the American war in Indochina and after 1975, the country's Marxist revolution.

The museum also features various exhibitions about Lao ethnic culture, religious practices and ecosystems. A well-presented display documenting a Swedish-Lao archaeological team's discovery near Vientiane of material dating back as far as the 11th to 12th century, as well as other fragments many hundreds of years older, was inaugurated in 2004.

Conveniently located in central Vientiane along Samsaenthai Road, the Lao National Museum provides a good survey not only of the country's religious and archaeological cultural history but the important socio-political events that marked the 20th century and are currently shaping its future. It offers interested visitors with limited time to spare a concentrated, one-stop introduction to Laos.

Malaysia ▶

ADDRESS
Jalan Lembah Perdana
50480 Kuala Lumpur
Malaysia

CONTACT INFORMATION
T: +60 3 2274 2020
F: +60 3 2274 0529
E: info@iamm.org.my
W: www.iamm.org.my

OPENING HOURS
10am–6pm Tue–Sun.

ADMISSION
Adult RM 8;
student RM 4;
free for children under 6.

FACILITIES
Wheelchairs and baby
strollers provided.

Conservation Centre.

HOW TO GET THERE
Train: Alight at Kuala Lumpur
Station, a 10-minute walk
from the museum.

By taxi.

AROUND THE MUSEUM
The museum is sandwiched
between landmark attractions

such as the National Mosque,
Lake Gardens, Merdeka
Square and the Kuala Lumpur
Train Station.

Islamic Arts Museum Malaysia

In the heart of Kuala Lumpur's cultural district, set amid lush greenery, the Islamic Arts Museum is one of Malaysia's best-designed cultural institutions, elucidating Islam while providing a rich aesthetic experience.

▪ **THE BUILDING** Neighbouring the National Mosque, and a stone's throw from the Planetarium, the Bird Park, the National Museum and the Central Market, the Islamic Arts Museum is one of Kuala Lumpur's newest landmark public institutions. Completed in 1998, the vast 23,000-square-metre museum is designed to evoke infinite space, and with its domes, free-standing columns and sophisticated ceramic tile decorative devices, to allude to the best of Islamic architecture, both religious and secular.

As well as the objects it houses, the museum building itself plays an important role in promoting the art, culture and architecture of Islam. The building's design was conceptualised by Italian architect Roberto Monsani in tandem with Malaysian architectural firm Kumpulan Senireka Sdn Bhd. The result is an imposing, geometric structure, lightened by its use of glass panelling and lofty dimensions. The building's gridded panels of white marble and glittering domes bring to mind the opulent monuments of Mughal India, while its grand portico and impressive scale suggest the great mosques and caravanserais of medieval Iran.

The museum's otherwise plain, white walls are embellished by panels made up of repeated grids forming the name of the museum in the complex, geometric, Arabic *kufi banaie* script. Also known as the *mo-aqali* script, *kufi banaie* is an ancient and angular form of the traditional *kufic*, frequently used for architectural inscriptions and particularly suited to masonry.

To reach the museum lobby, visitors must pass through the great front portal, the *iwan*. An architectural form originating in pre-Islamic Sasanian times, the *iwan* serves as a monumental entrance to normally sacred places. During Islam's medieval period, the construction of colossal entrances, porticos and gateways was seen as testimony to a ruler's power and strength. The *iwan* of the Islamic Arts Museum, however, was recreated as an abstract form, lacking the standard vaulted hall and pointed archway, and leaving only the rectangular framework. Not only does this form continue the repetition of rectangular frames carried throughout the entire building, it creates a quietly restrained

façade, thus reinforcing the museum's position as a temple of art rather than an institution of religious dogma.

The *iwan* is dressed in striking mosaic tilework, painstakingly produced by Iranian ceramicists. The museum is ornamented with yellow, light and dark green, cobalt blue, turquoise, brownish red, pink and white tiles, contemporary versions of the traditional colours that characterise the tilework of the most magnificent monuments in modern-day Uzbekistan, Iran and Afghanistan. According to the celebrated 12th-century Persian poet Nezami, the Haft Rang or Seven Colours traditionally used in building decoration— black, yellow/gold, green, red, blue, brown and

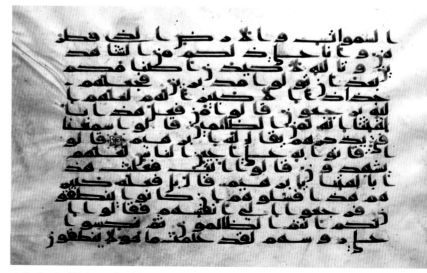

▲ **Qur'an leaf** | *Ink on vellum* | *North Africa or the Levant* | *8th century* | *20.2 x 30.3 cm*

Leaf from a Chinese Qur'an

Ink and gold leaf on paper | Qing dynasty, 17th century | Qur'an size: 27 x 19.5 X 3 cm

Beautifully and richly illuminated, and in a good state of conservation considering its age, this Qing dynasty Qur'an attests to the prosperity of China's minority Muslim community under the Qing.

white—corresponded with the Seven Heavenly Bodies of traditional Islamic culture.

The columns of the *iwan* are embellished with delicate, coiling floral tendrils and cartouches emanating from the Tree of Life motif prevalent in Central Asian tilework. The Tree of Life has carried a symbolic meaning since the pre-Islamic era, representing the divinity of the creator.

Museum-goers can also enter the museum via a second access located at the side of the building, leading directly to the museum's second level. The sloping land on which the museum is located necessitated a multi-level structure with landscaped areas on each plane. Winding paths take visitors to the various gardens scattered around the vicinity of the museum and the second entrance, thus providing easy access to the building without the visitor having to descend to the front entrance. Situated towards the rear of the museum is the Museum Auditorium and Rehal Terrace, the latter offering respite from the Malaysian heat. The terrace is only accessible from the outside of the building and its cool, blue-tiled floors, granite ornaments and benches create a refreshing point for pause.

■ **THE COLLECTION** Including some 8,000 works of art and objects, the Islamic Arts Museum's collection continues to expand.

■ **THE GALLERIES** The museum's first (ground) and second levels house two temporary exhibition halls—**Special Gallery 1** (ground floor) and **Special Gallery 2** (level two)—as well as the entrance hall, ticket hall, locker room, education and art workshop, student room, museum shop, children's library, Fountain Garden, Inverted Dome Pavilion and restaurant. Both a lift and a grand staircase connect level one to level two.

Approaching the top of this grand winding staircase, the visitor is greeted by a vast open space that is the **Inverted Dome Pavilion**. A giant, bronze *ghandil* lamp from Iran, suspended above the staircase, is reflected in the mirrored cartouches embedded in the inverted dome from which the area derives its name.

On the museum's third and fourth levels are 13 permanent galleries with widely differing themes. Though exploring a variety of issues, these galleries have in common their excellent display facilities including

lighting, labelling and a general airiness that encourage a slow, methodical exploration rather than a quick tour.

On the third floor, bordering the Rehal Terrace, is the **Qur'an & Manuscripts Gallery**. The museum's best-endowed and most spectacular gallery, it features a broad variety of religious and secular texts, miniature paintings, scientific treatises and literary works from a range of periods and areas such as Iran, China, India, Egypt, North Africa, Spain, Turkey, Syria, Uzbekistan and the Malay world. This gallery includes some of the museum's most historically important works. Note, among other pieces, a 15th-century illuminated Qur'an leaf from Jerusalem, an 8th-century Qur'an leaf on vellum from the Levant or North Africa, and a 15th-century illuminated leaf of Mamluk origin.

The gallery also highlights different styles of calligraphic script as well as examples of elaborate Qur'anic illuminations.

Beyond the Qur'an & Manuscripts Gallery, also bordering the Rehal Terrace and extending to the front of the museum, is the large **Architecture Gallery** where scale models

▲ *Interior view of the Blue Dome over the Qur'an & Manuscripts Gallery.*

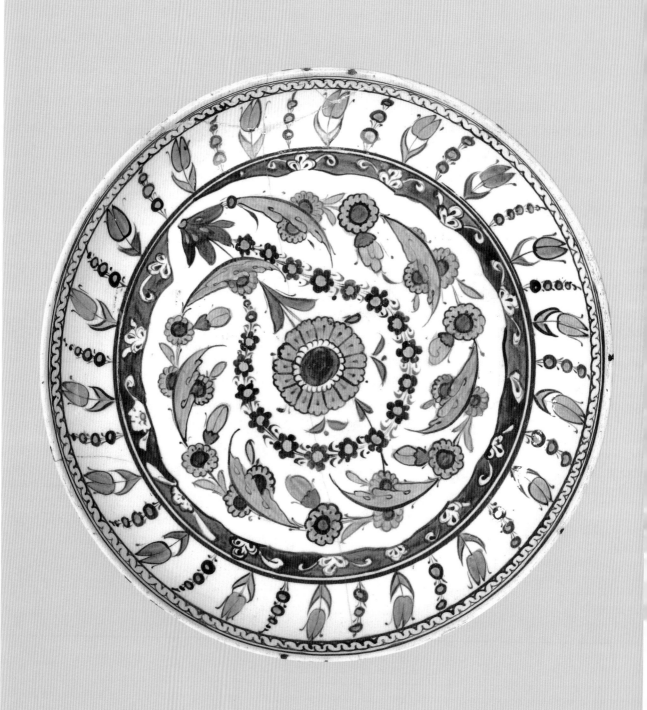

of some of the most important and splendid monuments, structures and holy sites from around the Islamic world are displayed. Look in particular for a magnificent model of Masjidil Haram in Mecca. For those interested in architectural details, decorative tiles and friezes from the Islamic world are also on show here. An alcove within this gallery is dedicated to the Art of the Mosque, with various architectural elements relating to prayer such as a *mihrab* (a prayer niche indicating the *kiblah* or the direction of Mecca) and a *minbar* (a pulpit used by imams during Friday prayer) being featured.

Beyond is the **Standard Chartered Ottoman Room**, a lavishly reconstructed interior of an Ottoman Syrian house of the early 19th century, dated to 1821. Sponsored by the Standard Chartered Bank Malaysia, this splendid room has original floor tiles in hues of warm russet, brick and ochre, as well as carved, lacquered wooden panels and chandeliers of the period. Ottoman Syria was a centre of culture and mixed cosmopolitan influences, and this room carries on the tradition with its juxtaposition of artistic styles that range from Chinese genre foliate bands to Rococo painting, calligraphic *thuluth* panels and a marble mosaic floor in indigenous Syrian taste. Furnished with a carved marble niche, used either as a cupboard or to hide faucets, the room has an opulent and exotic feel to it that successfully transports the visitor to another time and place.

Opposite the Architecture Gallery, areas relevant to Malaysia's three main ethnic groups—the Malays, Chinese and Indians—are given approximately equivalent floor space. Sensitivity to ethnic representation is typical in a country where ethnic harmony is considered key to political stability and economic progress.

The **India Gallery** features decorative works of art from Mughal India. One of the Islamic world's greatest empires, the Mughal Empire was an exemplar both for its military

▲ **Miniature painting**
Mughal portrait of Emperor Shah Jahan | Gouache and gold leaf on paper | India | 17th century | 19.6 x 13.5 cm

might within the subcontinent and for its far-reaching cultural influence. Splendid examples of Mughal jewellery, arms and armour, Qur'ans, manuscripts and folios of miniature paintings are exhibited here. See in particular a 17th-century miniature of the Mughal emperor Shah Jahan.

Dedicated to promoting a better understanding of Chinese Muslim culture, the **China Gallery** presents a wide range of works of art produced by the Muslim ethnic minorities of China dating from the 15th to the 20th century. Including calligraphic scrolls,

manuscripts, porcelain and bronzes, the collection showcases the parallels, differences and influences of Chinese Islamic art in relation to art from other parts of the Islamic world.

To the left of the China Gallery, looking from the museum's front to its back, is the **Malay World Gallery** where over 150 objects from the Malay Peninsula, Indonesia and Southern Thailand are exhibited. Illustrating the cultural diversity and refinement of both Malaysia and the Muslim world, this section features examples of costumes, textiles, Qur'ans and jewellery. Of particular importance is the 18th- to 19th-century Qur'an belonging to Sultan Zainul Abidin II of the Malaysian state of Terengganu. Known as the 'Gold Edition', this Qur'an was specially copied and bound in red, tooled Moroccan leather and written in *naskh* script, with gold borders on every page and gold roundel verse markers.

A number of smaller permanent galleries are housed on the fourth floor. Beyond the Main Dome and View Terrace, bordering the façade, are the Coins, Textile, Jewellery, Arms & Armour, Metalwork, Ceramics & Glassware, and Woodwork Galleries.

The **Coins Gallery**, just behind the View Terrace—from which the Kuala Lumpur skyline can be admired—features an extensive range of contemporary and older currency from around the Islamic world.

To the left of the Coin Gallery, the **Textile Gallery** extends in a long corridor-style display.

◀ **Underglaze blue fritware dish**
Iznik, Turkey | c. 1530–1535 | D: 34 cm

▲ **Jade hilted dagger** | *Gemset | India and Turkey | 19th century | L: 44.5 cm*

▲ Standard Chartered Ottoman Room
View of the marble floor and lacquered wood panelling of this reconstructed Syrian room, dated 1820–1821.

Costumes, shawls, hangings and other ornamental items from Central Asia, India, the Middle East and the Ottoman Empire are lined up as if in a frieze, with some examples refined, elegant and subtle in their decoration while others are splendidly colourful. The visitor pressed for time to spend in the museum will not be disappointed here.

Next to the Textile Gallery is the **Jewellery Gallery**. Exhibited is a dazzling array of gemset, lacquered, filigree-worked and gilt jewellery as well as personal accessories from India, Iran, Syria, Egypt, Turkmenistan and the Malay archipelago. Along with classical styles from the Islamic empire, the museum also holds some fine examples of Islamic tribal group jewellery.

Beyond the Jewellery Gallery is the **Arms & Armour Gallery**. Here, daggers, swords, shields, axes, maces, firearms and other weapons are displayed, many lavishly decorated with precious metals and gems, suggesting their ceremonial purpose. Arms buffs should look for a jade-hilted, gemset dagger from 19th-century India or Turkey, its scabbard finely worked in silver and its blade decorated on both sides in gold *koftgari* with calligraphy and formal scroll work.

Behind the Coins Gallery and beside Arms & Armour lies the **Metalwork Gallery**. This room provides an overview of the wide range of metalwork embellishment techniques used in the Islamic world while also highlighting the innovation and technical accomplishment of Islamic metalworkers as well as the richness and variety of materials used.

Moving on from the Metalwork Gallery is the **Ceramics & Glassware Gallery**. Dispensing information about the numerous styles and techniques used to produce ceramics and glassware around the Islamic world, this small gallery holds a number of noteworthy pieces.

Finally, the recently created **Woodwork Gallery** houses a small but expanding collection of Islamic parquetry, papier mâché objects and carved ivory.

Beyond these galleries, at the rear of the building, are the **Patrons Lounge** and a well-stocked library that in due course will be known as the **Scholars' Library**, expected to house 15,000 volumes including books, periodicals and auction catalogues.

Lucidly presented, varied, and aesthetically rewarding, the collection of the Islamic Arts Museum will shed new light on Islamic culture for those familiar with the subject and those who are not. The museum's cool gardens and courtyards, terraces, domes, fountains and Islamic symbols which have been integrated with the decorative scheme, make it a place of beauty, learning and serenity. Well-researched special exhibitions, some organised in collaboration with other prestigious institutions, cover specialist topics: verse inscriptions on Islamic works of art, Persian calligraphy from the 16th to the 19th century, Arabic script through the ages (organised in collaboration with the British Museum), residential architecture in the Islamic world, and Islamic art in China, have been some of the themes explored in the museum's varied and highly engaging temporary exhibition calendar.

MUZIUM NUMISMATIK MAYBANK

ADDRESS
Menara Maybank
1ˢᵗ floor, 100 Jalan Tun Perak
50050 Kuala Lumpur
Malaysia

CONTACT INFORMATION
T: +60 3 230 8833 ext. 2420
F: +60 3 2072 2504
E: publicaffairs@
maybank.com.my

W: www.maybank2u.com.my

OPENING HOURS
10am–6pm daily;
closed on public holidays.

ADMISSION
Free.

FACILITIES
Guided tours are available
by appointment.

Cafeteria; ample free parking.

Talks and lectures.

HOW TO GET THERE
Located within walking
distance of Plaza Rakyat and
Masjid Jamek LRT Station.

AROUND THE MUSEUM
There are plenty of shops and
cafés around the museum.

Maybank Numismatic Museum

Located in Menara Maybank, a stone's throw from the heart of Kuala Lumpur, is the small, specialist Maybank Numismatic Museum where visitors can trace Malaysia's history through coins.

■ **THE BUILDING** The only numismatic museum affiliated with a commercial bank in Malaysia, the Maybank Numismatic Museum is housed in an air-conditioned room on the bank's first floor. The bank itself is located in an imposing and sculptural modern high-rise building fronted by cool, marble-clad fountains.

■ **HISTORY** As far back as the 3ʳᵈ century, the Malay peninsula was a central emporium of trade for Chinese merchants from the East and Indian and Arab traders from the West. The earliest method of conducting the commercial exchange of goods and services was through barter, where one item was traded for another of roughly the same value. This rather approximate method was eventually replaced by a primitive currency system using precious commodities with established but not always intrinsic value such as gold dust, silver bars, coloured beads, cowrie shells, brass, bone, ivory and tin for the payment of goods. This system was eventually supplanted by the modern paper and non-precious metal currency system we know today.

■ **THE COLLECTION & GALLERY** By assembling a collection of rare coins and currencies dating back to the Melaka Sultanate of the 15ᵗʰ century, the museum has succeeded in tracing the country's history over the last 500 years through coins. The museum has also gathered numismatic material from the various states of Malaysia and other Southeast Asian countries.

The material is displayed more or less chronologically within the gallery and labelled in both English and Malay.

The early barter currencies are most interesting and yield surprises in the form, for example, of a brass kettle used as a medium of exchange in Borneo. Glass and stone beads, also found in Borneo, were probably brought to the island over many centuries by Chinese, Arab and African traders. In some parts of East Malaysia, beads of this style continue to be used today to display social status and wealth. Miniature brass cannons were also a form of currency in Borneo; however, with the introduction of paper money they fell into disuse and many were consequently melted down. Hence the examples shown here are relatively rare and unusual.

The first real coins to gain currency in Melaka have been ascribed to the reign of Sultan Muzaffar Shah in the second half of the 15ᵗʰ century (see several tin coins of this period). During the Portuguese occupation of Melaka in the 16ᵗʰ century, local coins were ordered to be minted. The museum displays several Portuguese soldo and dinheiro coins made of an alloy of tin and lead. Later, as the Dutch took control from the Portuguese in the mid-17ᵗʰ century, Dutch guilders replaced the soldo and dinheiro. Other interesting currencies include animal money in the form of a fighting cock from 16ᵗʰ-century Kedah as well as tin ingots in the shape of elephants used in Selangor and Perak.

▲ *Tin ingot in the shape of an elephant.*

The collection works its way through Johor, Perak, Selangor, Pahang, Penang, Terengganu, Kelantan, the British Straits Settlements, Malaya, British Borneo and 19ᵗʰ-century Singapore. It covers Brunei, Indonesia, Thailand, the Philippines and modern Singapore, and features notes from India, China and Australia as well.

Though a specialist collection, the Maybank Numismatic Museum will appeal to those interested in Southeast Asia's commercial history as much as it will to the coin enthusiast.

▲ *Coinage of various periods including the Dutch East India Company (VOC) and Portuguese-Melaka periods.*

ADDRESS
2 Jalan Temerloh, off
Jalan Tun Razak
53200 Kuala Lumpur
Malaysia

CONTACT INFORMATION
T: +60 3 4025 4990
F: +60 3 4025 4987
E: info@artgallery.org.my
W: www.artgallery.org.my

OPENING HOURS
10am–6pm daily;
9am–5pm during Ramadan.

ADMISSION
Free; children under 12 must
be accompanied by an adult.

FACILITIES
Wheelchair access.

Guided tours are available.

Art classes for children.

HOW TO GET THERE
Bus: 14D from Central Market
to General Hospital Kuala
Lumpur; 169, 165 or 195.

Putra LRT: Ampang Park
Station or KLCC Station.

Star LRT: Sentul Timur Station
or Titiwangsa Station.

Taxi: Five minutes from Kuala
Lumpur City Centre (KLCC)

AROUND THE MUSEUM
Sculptures in the gardens
including five public pieces by
local artists.

The National Theatre and the
National Library are in the
museum's vicinity.

National Art Gallery

A new Kuala Lumpur architectural landmark though an old institution, the National Art Gallery fulfils an important educational and developmental role with its unique collection of Malaysian modern and contemporary art.

■ **THE BUILDING** The National Art Gallery, changing addresses several times in four decades, has finally come to rest in its own purpose-built, state-of-the-art building, a striking and ambitious work of art in itself.

Established in 1958, the museum was initially billeted in borrowed space in Dewan Tunku Abdul Rahman, Malaysia's first House of Parliament. Though housed in the Jalan Ampang building for 25 years, and despite limited space and facilities there, the collection grew in size and profile.

In 1984, the museum moved to Kuala Lumpur's former Hotel Majestic, a rambling, colonial-era building of Dutch design built in 1932. Though seemingly not well suited to accommodate a growing collection of national contemporary art as well as the many public programmes and exhibitions that were now the museum's hallmark, the old hotel was transformed and well equipped for its new vocation. Indeed, the newly listed heritage building, by providing a new home for the National Art Gallery, had spared itself the wrecker's ball at a time when there was considerably less public interest in architectural conservation.

In 1998, however, the museum moved again, its collection having once more outgrown its quarters. At 40, the National Art Gallery was finally given its own building, custom-designed to house a still-expanding flagship collection and a full calendar of public events. Officially inaugurated in 2000, the new National Art Gallery building is a

▲ *The museum's light-filled atrium entrance area.*

vast, Modernist structure with a high, asymmetrical sloping roof that has ensured the museum's place as a Kuala Lumpur architectural landmark.

Located just north of the city centre and next to the Istana Budaya and the National Library, the building was designed by local architect Dato' Mir Shariman Mir Sharuddin on a five-hectare site. Covering some 13,500 square metres of floor space, the high-tech structure is equipped with the latest in lighting, atmospheric controls and public facility features and provides ample space for the display of the permanent collection, loan

exhibitions and the gallery's various educational programmes. Built with aesthetics and functionality in mind, the exterior projects a dramatic interplay of solid and translucent elements, and particularly with its dramatic, steeply sloping roof, merges traditional Malay architectural lines and visual style with contemporary volumes and planes.

The museum houses six galleries on three floors, arranged around an attractive, light-filled atrium space topped by a steep cathedral ceiling. The galleries are accessed by a lift or, more interestingly, by a broad corkscrew ramp that connects the ground floor to the top as it twists around the atrium void. As with the celebrated Guggenheim Museum in New York, both art and museum building can thus be enjoyed from different levels and angles as the visitor looks either up or down from his vantage point on the ramp.

The largest gallery, boasting 1,650 square metres, is devoted to exhibitions from the gallery's permanent collection. The other five host art by local and foreign artists. Though these spaces are smaller than Gallery 1, ranging from 1,300 square metres to 200 square metres, they are all versatile and well-equipped areas designed to accommodate large, site-specific installation work as well as smaller, conventional pieces.

■ **THE COLLECTION** The collection has mushroomed exponentially. A beneficiary of both purchase and philanthropy, it has grown from four pieces in 1958 to 2,500 today and is still expanding. Works by Malaysian and Chinese modern and contemporary artists predominate. Included are names such as Wong Hoy Chong, Ahmad Fuad Osman, Raja Azidin, Abdul Latiff Mohidin, Abdullah Ariff, Cheong Soo Pieng, Yong Mun Seng, Georgette Chen and Redza Piyadasa, to name a few. An eclectic assortment of foreigners is also represented including Robert Rauschenberg, Anupam Sud, Ansel Adams and Sir Frank Swettenham (a 'local foreigner') among others. Aboriginal art, folk art, design, architecture and, recently, electronic, video and multimedia art are other aspects of the collection.

■ **THE GALLERIES** Actively involved in educational, research, publication and exhibition activities, the National Art Gallery has been known to stage as many as six simultaneous art shows in its six galleries. By holding its exhibitions for relatively brief periods of two to six weeks and thus constantly offering a display of new artwork, the gallery aims to conduct a continuous,

▲ *The permanent collection on show on the second floor of the National Art Gallery.*

varied and highly dynamic artistic dialogue with its many museum visitors.

Entering the spacious and naturally lit lobby area, visitors access the **Auditorium** and **Resource Centre** to the left. The latter is an increasingly well-stocked archive of biographical and art information open to the general public. **Gallery 1**, on the ground floor, is devoted to exhibitions from the gallery's extensive permanent collection.

The museum's second floor houses the lower mezzanine—**Gallery 2B** to its left and **Gallery 2A** to its right. The top floor is occupied by the upper mezzanine—**Gallery 3B** to the left and **Gallery 3A** to the right. The latter two spaces are more intimate in scale than the second floor rooms, and Gallery 3B, the smallest gallery, may at times be used for the display of multimedia art, including video performances.

With their parquet floors, excellent lighting and extensive labelling in English and Malay, the galleries, seldom crowded except for parties of school children, provide an ideal setting for the appreciation of innovative and cutting-edge art from Malaysia and beyond.

Some past exhibitions include *New Route of Cuban Art* featuring the latest in contemporary art from Cuba, and *Revival: Evoking the Batik Tradition*, presenting the work of three batik masters.

Reflecting Malaysia's rich and diverse cultural heritage, the National Art Gallery, with its dynamic and varied educational programmes, frequently changing exhibition calendar and elegant architecture, offers an exciting taste of contemporary Malaysian culture at its best.

Abdul Latiff Mohidin
Pago-pago | Oil on canvas | 1964 | 98 x 98 cm

Abdul Latiff Mohidin (b. 1941) is Malaysia's most celebrated living artist. Also a poet, the painter, who received his art education in Germany, was one of the first artists in Malaysia to define and present a truly indigenous pictorial style derived from his personal interpretation of local iconographies and surrounding forms taken from nature or tribal culture.

ADDRESS
29 Jalan Raja
50050 Kuala Lumpur
Malaysia

CONTACT DETAILS
T: +60 3 2694 4590 / 1 / 2
F: +60 3 2694 4640
W: www.nationalhistory
museum.gov.my or
www.jma.gov.my

OPENING HOURS
9am–6pm daily;
closed on the first day
of Hari Raya Aidilfitri and
Hari Raya Aidiladha.

ADMISSION
Free.

FACILITIES
Wheelchair access.

Guided tours in Bahasa
Malaysia and English are
available upon request.

Shop; parking at Plaza Putra.

HOW TO GET THERE
Putra LRT: Central Market
Station (10-minute walk).

Star LRT: Masjid Jamek Station
(15-minute walk).

AROUND THE MUSEUM
Restaurants and cafés in
Plaza Putra and Dayabumi.

The High Courts, Sultan Abdul
Samad Building, the Royal
Selangor Club, Merdeka
Square, Masjid Jamek and the
National Mosque are in the
museum's vicinity.

National History Museum

Housed in an imposing colonial building in central Kuala Lumpur, the National History Museum explores Malaysia's history from prehistoric times, through Islamisation, colonisation, and the two World Wars, to mid-20th-century nation-building.

■ **THE BUILDING** For colonial history buffs, the National History Museum building is perhaps as interesting as the collection it contains. The museum site, first developed at the end of the 19th century to house Kuala Lumpur's first bank—the earlier Chartered Bank of India, Australia and China (forerunner of Standard Chartered)—brings to mind the country's colonial past. The Chartered Bank building, demolished at the turn of the last century, was rebuilt in 1910 and is now one of Kuala Lumpur's better known architectural landmarks.

Designed by British former State Architect A.C. Norman, who was also responsible for the design of the capital's Sultan Abdul Samad Building, the structure combines late Victorian and Moorish-style architectural features. A fairly pedestrian, pillar-fronted, white stucco and brick façade that might have graced London's Bayswater has been strategically 'Islamised' with four rooftop domes, pointed arches over the ground-floor windows and central entrance porch, and a series of miniature minaret-type appendages jutting out from the roof along the façade. Though not among the most elegant colonial buildings of Southeast Asia, and seemingly making few concessions to the tropical climate, the building is nonetheless full of character and will give visitors a good idea of what Malayan towns looked like under the British.

Covering over 2,000 square metres on three floors, the building was converted into a museum in the early 1990s and officially opened as the National History Museum in 1996.

■ **THE COLLECTION** Covering prehistoric to contemporary times, the objects in the collection are displayed more or less chronologically, labelled in Malay and English, and exhibited in well-lit galleries. Although the galleries show evidence of a clear political point of view, the museum gives the visitor with limited viewing time a comprehensive and coherent understanding of Malaysia's history in all its complexity.

Comprising approximately 1,000 pieces, the collection has been built up essentially through excavation, donation, loan and bequest. It features an eclectic assortment of objects of national historic interest including the first independence flag of the Federation of Malaya, unfurled in 1957, the 19th-century Pangkor Treaty Table, prehistoric tools, early Buddhist relics, official colonial statuary, and examples of works of art from the Dong Son culture.

■ **THE GALLERIES** The galleries are separated by partitions erected between the

▲ **Cast bronze bell with green patina**
Dong Son culture, found in Muar, Johor, Malaysia | c. 2nd century | H: 56 cm, Weight: 10.7 kg

building's original support columns and are spread over the museum's ground, second and third floors. Entering through the ground floor's shaded porch—one of the building's concessions to the city's tropical heat—the visitor will encounter the wood-clad **Introduction Gallery**. Here, old European trade route maps of the region and a cast bronze anonymous Malay warrior in full 15th-century Melakan battle-dress tell the country's story in highlight form. Beyond are three rooms devoted to prehistory—the **PreHistoric, Proto-Historic** and **Megalithic Culture Galleries**—where a large assortment of Neolithic tools, stone fragments, pottery and human skulls are displayed, all well-documented with informative labels and photographic interpretation panels.

To the right of the entrance, behind the bookstore but partitioned off from the prehistory section, are several rooms designed to be visited at the end of the museum tour. The **Historical Heritage Gallery** features photographic documentation of Malaysia's colonial architectural landmarks, while the **National Features Gallery** offers images relating the country's varied geography and geology. The next few rooms, further to the right, contain references to modern historical themes and feature small displays detailing the **Communist Insurgence**, **Japanese Occupation**, and the **British and Dutch Periods**, all of which are left for the end of the museum visit as a chronological tour is intended.

There are two staircases servicing the second and third floors, the first on the façade's left side for ascending and the second on the façade's right side, for descending.

The six second-floor galleries examine several centuries of history starting with the **Spread of Islam in Melaka** and **The Melaka Sultanate Galleries** where objects representing the period of the Melaka Kingdom are displayed. Among the items visitors will find here are a wooden seal dated 1423, information concerning the tomb of Sultan Mansor Shah (1459–1477), and tin coins from the reign of Sultan Muzaffar Shah. Other rooms on this floor delve into the **Johor-Riau Empire** which was established after the fall of the Melaka Kingdom by the latter's last descendant. Artefacts shown include Bugis armour, shields, kris and other weapons. The **Foreign Interventions Gallery** is divided into three sections portraying the chronological intervention of European powers in the peninsula. The first section exhibits Portuguese weapons and helmets, the second features the Dutch period in Melaka and the third concentrates on the British in Malaya, illustrated by British coins and medals. **The Malay States 1824–1900 Gallery** focuses on the Malay States after the Anglo-Dutch Treaty of 1824 and the Pangkor Treaty of 1874. This period was vital since it marked the introduction of the British Residential System in the Malay States. Displayed here are the Pangkor Treaty Table and animal tin coins which were used as currency then. Finally, the **Foreign Interventions in Sabah and Sarawak Gallery** looks at the British administration in Borneo as embodied by the British North Borneo (Chartered) Company in North Borneo (Sabah), and the Brooke dynasty in Sarawak. Artefacts exhibited here include the currency

Bronze figure of Buddha
Found at Jalong, Sungai Siput, Perak, Malaysia | 9th century | H: 52.5 cm

This large statue is known as the 'Jalong Buddha' because it was found at Jalong by a Chinese worker in 1962. Though not in excellent condition, the icon is historically significant because it presents material evidence of a Hindu-Buddhist cultural presence in the Malay Peninsula in pre-Islamic, pre-colonial times.

produced by the company and indigenous traditional weapons.

The third and top floor, where foreign visitors may wish to spend more time, cover events in the 20th century through six

galleries. In the **Nationalism** section, the movement's proponents are portrayed, and key nationalist magazines produced during the Japanese occupation are displayed. The **Japanese Occupation 1941–1945 Gallery** exhibits period propaganda and currency produced by the Japanese as well as Samurai swords and a Japanese two-wheeler, representing the fleets of bicycles used to invade the peninsula. Over in **Malay State Administration**, the British post-war administration in Malaya is highlighted. This includes a section on the Malayan Union and the resistance it met which proved a catalyst for the growth and development of Malay nationalism. The communist threat, which led to the Emergency of 1948–1960 is also documented here. Artefacts on display include weapons used during the Emergency such as secret society machetes. Malayan Independence, established on 31st August 1957, is illustrated with the First Flag of the Malaya Federation and the Merdeka Signing Table. The process leading up to the signing is also covered comprehensively. The **Yang Dipertuan Agong Malaysia** (Head of State and a symbol of Malaysian sovereignty) section explains the selection process for the head of state and exhibits the throne of the first Yang Dipertuan Agong of Malaysia. In **Formation of Malaysia**, the 16th September 1963 linking of Malaya, Sabah, Sarawak and Singapore (Singapore withdrew from Malaysia in 1965 to become an independent republic) as one entity is documented. **Prime Ministers of Malaysia**, where all the country's prime ministers since independence are featured, brings visitors to the end of the tour.

Though injected with a predictable dose of nationalism, the top-floor displays deserve the visitor's closest attention, the 20th century having been the most politically and socially tumultuous in Malaysia's history.

With its well-designed, extensively labelled exhibits and varied cross-section of displays, the National History Museum will appeal to those interested in making sense of Malaysia's and the wider region's complex history.

ADDRESS
Jalan Damansara
50566 Kuala Lumpur
Malaysia

CONTACT INFORMATION
T: +60 3 2282 6255
F: +60 3 2282 6434
E: info@jma.gov.my
W: www.jma.gov.my

OPENING HOURS
9am–6pm daily;
closed on the first day of Hari
Raya Aidiladha.

ADMISSION
Adult RM 2;
child and senior RM 1.

FACILITIES
Guided tours are available
upon request.

Research library; café;
parking lot.

HOW TO GET THERE
Bus: Take 33 or 35 and alight
at Jalan Travers. The museum
is a 5-minute walk from there.

LRT: KL Sentral Station.

By taxi.

AROUND THE MUSEUM
The museum is close to the
Bird Park, the Planetarium,
the Railway Station and the
National Mosque.

National Museum

Located not far from Kuala Lumpur's centre, in an imposing, purpose-built complex, the National Museum offers material documenting Malaysia's history, cultures and natural environment.

▲ **Cheong Lai Tong, Malaysia** | *One of a pair of Italian mosaic murals adorning the museum's façade.*

■ **THE BUILDING** The present museum was built on the site of the old Selangor Museum, a small British-run collection that was established in 1906. Destroyed by a stray bomb during World War II due to the museum's proximity to the railway station, the collection was built up once more in the 1950s and a new museum building was mooted in 1959, two years after independence. The National Museum or Muzium Negara opened in 1963 and at the time was the most modern and ambitious public art institution in Malaysia.

Conceived by local architect How Kok Hoe, the building's design was inspired by traditional Minangkabau-Malay palace architecture and embellished with Malay motifs. The two-tiered central roof, curved gable faces, sloping gabled screens and forked gable tops provide a direct reference to indigenous architectural features. A symmetrically placed pair of imposing murals, each roughly 6.5 metres high and 35 metres long, adorn the façade, thus distinguishing the building from other large public venues in the capital. Designed by Cheong Lai Tong of Kuala Lumpur and made of Italian mosaic, the murals depict Malaysia's history and many cultures.

Three storeys high, the museum houses its exhibition galleries on the second and third floors, reserving the first floor for administrative offices and the museum shop. Though the main façade faces the road, visitors arriving by car will in fact access the building from the back. Here, beyond the parking lot, a broad alley leading to the museum's rear entrance is flanked by covered galleries where models of various vehicles are displayed, with an industrial fishing boat and locomotive probably the most interesting items.

Beyond the main museum building in the compound, an annex known as **Gallery Three** houses a number of temporary exhibitions. The history of bound feet in China, Malay gold, and an introduction to ghosts of the world are three examples of recent month-long temporary exhibitions.

■ **THE COLLECTION** The museum's collection numbers approximately 300,000 artefacts, including ethnographic, archaeological and natural history material.

■ **THE GALLERIES** The museum presents its collection thematically, dividing its space into

▲ *Embroidered silk women's slippers from China, specially designed to fit feet that have been 'let-out' after binding.*

▲ *Diorama depicting Malay kite making in anticipation of a religious festival.*

four sections harbouring five galleries that explore culture, Malaysian identity, weaponry, traditional music, ceramics and natural history.

Upon entering the museum on the second floor, the visitor initially encounters an airy central reception hall that usually hosts temporary exhibitions on a variety of themes. **Gallery A**, located on the left as one faces the back of the museum, houses the **Cultural Gallery**. Here, the many strands of Malaysia's multi-ethnic society are examined through the display of national costumes and dioramas illustrating various ethnic rituals and traditions. Those with memories of Malaysia's communal riots of the 1960s and aware of the country's affirmative action laws applied along ethnic lines, will be interested to know that national pluralism is discussed here in a deliberately positive way.

Opposite the Cultural Gallery, to the right of the entrance hall, **Gallery B** houses the **Faces of Malaysia Gallery**. Here, Malaysia's cultural and ethnic melting pot is explored in detail through the investigation of individual communities and their customs. Photographs, information technology, dioramas and traditional explicative text boards highlight the various peoples, viewed from the perspective of their ceremonies and festivals. The Malays, Indians, Chinese, Orang Asli aborigines, and the Sabah and Sarawak contingents, as well as smaller communities such as the Portuguese (a few enclaves established in the 16th and 17th centuries remain), Thais and Gurkhas are touched upon as well, the museum clearly burnishing the country's image as a haven of multi-racial and multi-ethnic harmony and tolerance. This pluralistic approach to ethnic representation, considered against the background of contemporary Malaysian society, is refreshingly positive.

▲ **Prada cloth** | *Gold-stamped sarong, Bugis design* | *Selangor, Malaysia* | *c. 1800* | *L: 211 cm, W: 139 cm*

Dioramas representing Indians enjoying festivals such as Deepavali and Thaipusam, Orang Asli dancing ceremonies, a Chinese scholar at his desk and Malays confecting traditional kites celebrating Hari Raya Aidilfitri are among the highlights of this gallery.

The museum's top floor houses three galleries. **Gallery C**, the **Natural History Gallery**, is among the museum's most interesting. The Malaysian rainforest, one of the world's oldest forests, and its varied fauna and flora are highlighted here. Dioramas replicating Malaysia's jungle environment and display cases featuring a large variety of reptiles, birds and insects provide visitors with a glimpse of the rainforest.

Opposite this gallery, on the other side of the third floor lobby, is **Gallery D**, harbouring the museum's **Weaponry & Musical Instruments Gallery** as well as the Ceramic Gallery. The former, on the left, displays an array of weapons

▲ **Jawa Demam Keris**
Gold and ivory | *Kelantan, Malaysia* | *Late 18th century* | *L: 40.5 cm*

such as kris, knives and indigenously styled axes—the weapons' overall form common to several related Southeast Asian cultures. Beyond the weapons section, at the rear of the gallery, the traditional musical instruments of some of Malaysia's main cultures are featured. A Malay-style *erhu* and drums are some examples to look out for.

The **Ceramic Gallery** houses a small collection of essentially local pottery. Some Southeast Asian vessels are also showcased along with ceramics found in shipwrecks dotting the Malaysian coast.

Popular with local residents, the National Museum provides an overview of Malaysia's ethnic and cultural make-up as well as a taste of its unique and spectacular natural environment.

▲ **Gold coins**
Johor, Malaysia | *From the reign of Sultan Muzaffar Shah (1564–1570)*

ADDRESS
KM 24 Jalan Pahang Gombak
53100 Kuala Lumpur
Malaysia

CONTACT INFORMATION
T: +60 3 6189 2113 ext. 216
E: info@jheoa.gov.my

OPENING HOURS
9am–5pm Sat–Thur;
open on public holidays.

ADMISSION
Free.

FACILITIES
Parking available.

HOW TO GET THERE
Taxi: The museum is roughly
15 minutes from the centre
of Kuala Lumpur.

Orang Asli Museum

Recently opened, the Museum of the Jabatan Hal Ehwal Orang Asli (Museum of the Department of Aboriginal Affairs) provides insight into the history, traditions and material culture of the indigenous tribal populations of Malaysia.

■ **THE BUILDING** The museum was opened by Malaysia's Department of Aboriginal Affairs in 1987. Originally housed in the former residence of the Director General of the Department, the museum moved to its current premises in 2000.

The building was constructed in 1995, its style inspired by traditional local architecture. Part of the building is raised off the ground on sturdy pillars, allowing for air circulation, while the typical multi-tiered, steeply pitched roof with deep overhanging eaves affords both the efficient drainage of monsoon rains as well as protection of the interior from the sun.

■ **THE COLLECTION** Peninsular Malaysia has more than 116,000 aborigines of differing tribal origins. The three main tribes, the Senoi, Negrito and Proto Malay, are each further divided into

▲ *Examples of natural fibre jewellery and basketry in the Orang Asli Museum.*

six smaller sub-tribes for a total of 18, all speaking different dialects, including Malay. As a result of this large number of sub-tribes, the collection is a varied one, with the objects displayed according to cultural function.

■ **THE GALLERIES** The **Hunting Equipment** exhibition is one of the museum's most interesting. Here, the hunting tools presented tend to be made of materials found in the tropical rainforest. These include blowpipes, bows and arrows, booby traps and spears made of bamboo, poisonous roots and other indigenous organic material. Though some of these tools are not recent, most tribes continue to use similar equipment today.

The section devoted to the **Wedding Ceremony** in the Orang Asli community documents both the ceremony's decorative trappings as well as the tradition itself. Sharing some similarities with Malay matrimonial customs, the aboriginal version is nonetheless unique in its rituals for warding off bad luck, teeth filing, henna painting and bridal bathing.

The **Clothes and Costumes** and **Jewellery** displays feature numerous types of apparel and personal ornaments. The unusual wood-pulp clothing is worth looking at in particular, as are the bead and raffia necklaces and the decorative hair combs made of horn and bone.

The museum's **Musical Instruments** section is fairly large, reflecting the importance of music in the daily life and rituals of the Orang Asli. Used for healing as well as entertainment, the instruments shown here are generally made from organic materials originating in the rainforest such as wood, bamboo or animal skin, but brass and other metals can also be present in certain types of drums and gongs. Examples of tribal instruments unique to the Orang Asli are the *ngengong* and the *pensol*, a sort of bamboo flute.

The museum's **Sculpture** section illustrates Orang Asli tribal aesthetics and documents the aboriginal belief system.

Kuala Lumpur's Orang Asli Museum, though not huge, provides a good introduction to the tribal culture of peninsular Malaysia.

▲ *Carving ritual masks.*

ADDRESS
Lot 341–343
3rd level, Suria Kuala Lumpur
City Centre (KLCC)
50088 Kuala Lumpur
Malaysia

CONTACT INFORMATION
T: +60 3 2051 7770 / 3 / 8
F: +60 3 2051 7170
W: www.galeripetronas.com

OPENING HOURS
10am–8pm Tue–Sun;
open on public holidays
except the first day of
Hari Raya Puasa and Hari
Raya Aidiladha;
the gallery closes at 5pm
during Ramadan.

ADMISSION
Free.

FACILITIES
Free guided tours.

Art Resource Centre; gallery
shop; Artist-in-Residence
programme; art classes;
annual conference.

HOW TO GET THERE
Bus: 23, 24A, 24C, 28, 34A,
34D, 176, 178, 182, 183, 185,
259 or 270.

LRT: KLCC Station.

Taxi: To KLCC. Alight at
the Ampang and
Ramlee entrance.

AROUND THE MUSEUM
Located at the heart of KLCC,
the gallery is surrounded by
shops and cafés.

Petronas Gallery (Galeri Petronas)

Housed in Kuala Lumpur's most famous modern architectural landmark, Petronas Twin Towers, Petronas Gallery or Galeri Petronas offers a varied menu of local and international art and design in a well-appointed space.

■ **THE BUILDING** Petronas Twin Towers, when its construction was completed in 1998, was the world's tallest building. Though recently surpassed by a skyscraper in Taiwan, the two 88-storey towers remain an extraordinary and impressive symbol of Malaysia's status as one of Southeast Asia's most powerful 'tigers' during the pre-Southeast Asian economic crisis years of the mid-1990s. Conceived by American firm Cesar Pelli and Associates Architects, the towers are of a tapering design on a geometrically polygonal plan, the latter a clear reference to one of Islamic art's most cherished and oldest geometric designs. Though the towers' Art Deco-like architectural style has proved controversial, the structure magisterially dominates central Kuala Lumpur's skyline.

Galeri Petronas is located on the third level of the Suria Kuala Lumpur City Centre or KLCC shopping complex in Petronas Twin Towers Two.

▲ **Simryn Gill**
Dalam | Colour photograph, one of a series | 2001 | 23.5 x 23.5 cm

■ **THE GALLERY** Galeri Petronas was founded in 1993 by the national petroleum corporation Petronas (Petroliam Nasional Berhad) to further the understanding and appreciation of visual art among Malaysians. The gallery moved to its current Twin Towers premises in 1998. Boasting versatile, international standard, state-of-the-art electronic and technological facilities, the 2,000-square-metre gallery was designed to accommodate a broad range of displays for the benefit of the widest possible audience.

The gallery features a circular exhibition space surrounding a central rectangular core that functions as a service area. The space has an innovative lighting system that uses a series of radial ceiling louvres that emanate rays of virtual sunlight from the core area. A combination of textures and materials, such as stone, concrete, granite, cast aluminium, steel, clear resin and floating glass elements, provide a contemplative and spare background in which the dynamism and creative energy of the art on display can fully shine. The space features the **Main Gallery** and the **Bustle Gallery** which operate separately or can be integrated into a single space capable of holding voluminous installation displays. The **Main Entrance Area** and two **Multimedia Spaces** are also available for exhibition.

Though over the years the gallery has built a varied 1,000-work permanent collection that includes prints, painting, sculpture, drawings, photographs, textiles, ceramics and other crafts of Malaysian origin, as a space, it has opted to make its name as an initiator of excellent,

▲ **Abdul Latiff Mohidin**
Daun Agave and Pago-Pago | Oil on canvas | 1964 | 101 x 102 cm

curated thematic temporary exhibitions that promote a fascinating and varied cross-section of visual practice, local or foreign, cutting-edge or more traditional. The gallery also hosts loan exhibitions curated by external organisations. In addition it offers art workshops, demonstrations, classes, lectures and video screenings, all open to the public. Coupled with its Art Resource Centre (a library and Malaysian artists database), these educational programmes have made the gallery one of the most highly regarded art learning and appreciation spaces in Malaysia.

Housed in Kuala Lumpur's most high-profile architectural landmark, Galeri Petronas offers a visually and intellectually stimulating cultural experience to audiences interested in local as well as foreign art practice.

ADDRESS
5 Jalan Perdana
50480 Kuala Lumpur
Malaysia

CONTACT INFORMATION
T: +60 3 2272 5689
F: +60 3 2273 6598 / 5690

OPENING HOURS
10am–6pm Tue–Sun.

ADMISSION
Free.

FACILITIES
Guided tours are available
upon request.

Library; photo library;
auditorium; talks.

HOW TO GET THERE
Bus: Take 15, 16, 331 or 33D
from Chow Kit to Central
Market and walk past
the National Mosque to
the museum.

Train: Kuala Lumpur Station
is a 15-minute walk from
the museum.

By taxi.

AROUND THE MUSEUM
A 10-min walk from the
Islamic Arts Museum (see pp.
60–64) and near the National
Mosque, Lake Gardens,
Merdeka Square and the Kuala
Lumpur Train Station.

Royal Malaysian Police Museum

A short walk from Kuala Lumpur's Islamic Arts Museum, the Royal Malaysian Police Museum offers a view of Malaysia's social and political history seen through the prism of law enforcement over the centuries.

■ **THE BUILDING** The museum is housed in a single-storey complex composed of three linked buildings that were once the Police Senior Officers' Mess. At the top of a steep hill, the museum is set in a well-kept garden which serves as a striking display for assorted police equipment. Visitors are permitted to approach and touch these exterior exhibits which include an armoured vehicle and a single-engine Cessna airplane. The principal museum structure is designed in traditional indigenous-colonial hybrid style, and features airy, high-ceilinged rooms, wide, overhanging eaves along the building's length to provide shaded walkways, and a broad porch at the entrance.

■ **THE COLLECTION** The museum was established in 1952 and officially opened in 1961 by the third king of Malaysia, Tuanku Syed Putra Al-Haj. The collection, which continues to grow, holds around 3,000 documentary photographs as well as 4,000 objects, some of which date back to the Melaka Sultanate of the early 16th century. Within the museum, approximately 2,500 items are on permanent

▲ *Chinese insurgent's typewriter.*

display. These depict various aspects of crime prevention and include objects relating to illicit activities such as gambling, counterfeiting, secret societies, drug trafficking, and on the political side, communist insurgency. Weapons, uniforms, medals, motor vehicles and police paraphernalia also feature prominently.

■ **THE GALLERIES** The museum sets a theatrical stage for the display of its material, the lighting in the galleries kept to a minimum except for the display cases and dioramas.

Three principal galleries, corresponding to the complex's three buildings, are connected by covered walkways also used for exhibition purposes. The museum's artefacts are displayed thematically in historical order.

The first gallery approached from the museum's entrance is **Gallery A**. Here, the visitor will find exhibits devoted to the Sultanate, Portuguese, Dutch and British periods spanning the 16th to the 19th century. Uniforms, arms, medals, and well-made dioramas and explanatory panels give an account of the world of law enforcement through different periods of foreign control.

Radar and other surveillance equipment is presented along the walkway leading to **Gallery B**. Here, objects from the 19th century to the present provide in-depth coverage of Malayan and Malaysian law enforcement history. Along with cases of weapons, and a complete brass band of the early 20th century, a large collection of miniature automobiles and a police motorcycle are displayed.

Gallery C is probably the museum's most appealing. Here, the visitor will get a strong sense of 20th-century history with direct references to the important political and social events that have shaped contemporary Malaysia. The Emergency (1948–1960), which occurred when initially the British, and after 1957, Malaysia's first independent government, fought communist insurgents in the Malaysian jungle, figures prominently here. A particularly graphic diorama depicting a life-size, just-shot, communist insurgent in a jungle setting is one of the gallery's more dramatic displays. Other exhibits such as a period communist flag, a Chinese typewriter, and showcases featuring insurgents' paraphernalia, especially the female communist's gear which includes a bright fuchsia brassiere, all give some indication of the period's explosive atmosphere and rather dramatic flavour.

The display case documenting illicit drug manufacturing is also riveting, with weighing scales and a wide assortment of instruments featured. Of less historical interest, but surely appealing to memorabilia buffs, are the medals and trophy sections.

Varied, well presented and with excellent Malay and English labelling, the Royal Malaysian Police Museum collection is rewarding on many levels. Those interested in the machinery of law enforcement will find much to please them here, as will those keen to understand better Malaysia's social and political history through the centuries.

ADDRESS
Labuan International Sea
Sports Complex
Jalan Tanjung Purun
87008 Wilayah Persekutuan
Labuan
Malaysia

CONTACT INFORMATION
T: +60 8 7425 927
F: +60 8 7414 462

E: shawali@jma.gov.my

OPENING HOURS
9am–5pm daily,
closed on the first day of
Hari Raya Aidilfitri and Hari
Raya Aidiladha.

ADMISSION
Free.

FACILITIES
Guided tours in English are
available by appointment.

Recreational park; conference
room; souvenir shop;
restaurant; free parking.

HOW TO GET THERE
On foot: A 20-minute walk
from the town centre.

Mini-Bus: 1, via Jalan Tanjung
Purun. Alight at the Luban
Clock Tower.

By taxi.

AROUND THE MUSEUM
Other attractions of the
Labuan International Sea
Sports Complex.

Labuan Maritime Museum

On Pulau Labuan, the Labuan Maritime Museum provides a fine introduction to the varied and fascinating marine life of the South China Sea.

■ **THE BUILDING** Labuan, a small island off the Sabah coast on the state's southwest side and just north of Brunei, was better known a century ago for its coal and fine anchorage than for its beaches. The island also played a significant role in World War II, the Japanese first landing in Labuan in early 1942 and from there invading British North Borneo, which they occupied until 1945. Lately, however, the Malaysian government has sought to capitalise on the island's beaches and diving opportunities, and the new Maritime Museum is thus the centrepiece of the island's recently developed series of tourist attractions.

The museum is located within the Labuan International Sea Sports Complex in the centre of Labuan Town (formerly Victoria), on the island's southeast side. The complex was completed in 1999 and the museum was established in 2002. Designed to resemble a stylised open clam, the museum is a luminous two-storey building with international standard displays and state-of-the-art technology.

■ **THE EXHIBITS** The museum aims to both impart specific information about the aquatic life of Labuan and Borneo and develop visitors' interest in environmental heritage and conservation. The exhibits are split into two sections. The **Lower Gallery** focuses on the display of live marine specimens, featuring in particular eight large aquariums and a touch pool filled with fish found in Labuan's waters, including those living around the island's various shipwrecks (several World War II and post-war shipwrecks lie off the island's south

▲ *Coral and fish in their simulated natural habitat.*

coast). The display is further divided into five sub-sections including Marine Life, Coral Reefs, Shipwrecks, Mangrove Swamps and Scenes of Labuan Based on Habitat.

The **Upper Gallery** presents graphic explanatory panels, models and replicas of marine life, and three aquariums containing live coral. It is divided into eleven sections including Labuan Marine Life, Coral Reefs, Shark and Ray Habitat, Marine Reptiles, Commercial Fishes, Marine Mammals, Marlins, Oceanography and Marine Biology, Fishing Activities, Diving, and Molluscs.

In addition to documenting local marine life, this gallery offers some fairly detailed exhibits on fishing equipment, diving paraphernalia and shipwrecks.

Though small, with its thoughtful and comprehensive displays, airy galleries and welcome emphasis on environmental conservation, visitors to Labuan will find the Labuan Maritime Museum worth exploring.

▲ *Sharks and rays in the Upper Gallery.*

ADDRESS
Jalan Tun Abang Haji Openg
93566 Kuching
Sarawak

CONTACT INFORMATION
T: +60 82 244 232 / 482 / 202
F: +60 82 246 680
E: museum@po.jaring.my
W: www.museum.sarawak.
gov.my

OPENING HOURS
9am–5.30pm Mon–Sun.

ADMISSION
Free.

FACILITIES
Ample parking;
research institute.

HOW TO GET THERE
Walk or take a taxi from the
centre of town.

From the airport, buses
stop along Jalan Tun Abang
Haji Openg

AROUND THE MUSEUM
The many cafés and shops of
Kuching's historic centre.

Sarawak State Museum

Located in Kuching, the state capital of Sarawak on the island of Borneo, the Sarawak State Museum boasts one of Malaysia's oldest and most distinguished collections, displayed in a 19th-century colonial building.

■ **THE BUILDING** The museum and its collection of largely ethnological material reflect Victorian architectural and collecting tastes. Proposed in 1878 by Sarawak's second 'White Rajah', the Englishman Sir Charles Brooke, the Sarawak Museum was initially set up in 1886 in a temporary space overlooking the market place in Kuching. Two years later, Sir Charles decided that the holdings warranted a purpose-built home and an attractive garden site was selected in the centre of Kuching. The present museum building, a long, three-storey construction with a flat façade, thought by its 19th-century designers to resemble a Normandy town hall, was opened in 1891. Extended in 1911(its front double stairway also removed) and again in 1940, the museum's stylistically hybrid façade was altered, its upper verandahs enclosed, and a central protective porch added to shelter the main entrance from Sarawak's tropical heat and rain. Numerous windows, affording the interior galleries abundant natural light and a cooling draught, are

▲ **Woodcarving of the *Kenyalang* or hornbill icon** | *Iban, made for the hornbill festival* | *20th century* | *L: 218.3 cm*

partially shaded from the sun by deep, overhanging eaves on the second floor and a wide lateral ridge on the first.

Over the years, the museum complex has been developed so that the compound now consists of seven buildings of different vintages and architectural genres including the original exhibition hall, a museum extension, a large and excellent reference library and archive (the former British Council building), a Spirit Hall, an Administrative Block/Reference Collection, a workshop, and a block of barracks.

■ **THE COLLECTION** The first foundations of the Sarawak Museum collection were laid in 1878 when Sir Charles Brooke began assembling objects for his proposed public institution. In 1886, however, H. Brooke Low's holdings of ethnological specimens from the Rajang river area were added and it is these that are generally considered the nucleus of the collection. In the course of the 20th century, the holdings grew in fits and starts as Sarawak's tumultuous political events allowed, all new material entering the museum meticulously researched by specialists

▲ *View of the museum in 1891.*

▲ **Wooden masks**
Dayak | 20th century

according to Brooke's original brief—to this day the museum incorporates a research institute. Now containing some 22,500 artefacts, the museum covers ethnology, natural history, botany and art. Floor space is devoted to Sarawak's fascinating history, including a century of rule by the Brooke dynasty. The material collection is further supplemented by a fairly extensive collection of multimedia documentation.

■ **THE GALLERIES** The present museum complex includes two main exhibition spaces comprising the original turn-of-the-19th-century building, its galleries housed on its ground and second floors; and the late 1960s/1970s museum extension known as Dewan Tun Abdul Razak (named after the second Malaysian prime minister), also presenting two floors of display area. Together,

the two buildings provide 3,700 square metres of display space.

A visit to the museum will probably start in the original building, the first structure encountered and the most inviting with its period architecture.

Entering on the ground floor through the porch shading the main door, the visitor will find the museum's central staircase and information counter.

Those particularly interested in Sarawak's flagship collection of ethnological works (this celebrated aspect of the collection could easily stand alone) may wish to ascend directly to the floor above. However, the ground floor's non-art displays, including several seashell and animal galleries, are well presented and worth seeing. The **Mammal Gallery**, **Technology Section** and **Petroleum Gallery** are positioned to the right of the entrance while the **Reptile**, **Bird**, **Invertebrate** and **Mollusc Galleries** flank the entrance on the left. Behind the stairwell are the **National Parks and Geological Sections**. Amongst the most engaging on this floor are the Mammal and Bird Galleries, which document the varied and very exotic fauna of the Borneo rainforest. Worth seeing are the numerous species of monkeys and the rare hornbill, a beautiful bird that is also one of Sarawak's most potent cultural icons. The gallery's text panels emphasise environmental conservation, a positive initiative in a part of Malaysia subjected to extensive logging in recent years.

On the second floor are many of the galleries the museum is best known for. Assembled here are, in a clockwise

▲ **Orang Ulu baby carrier**
Beaded wood and rattan frame | 20th century | H: 42 cm

configuration of display cases from the front to the rear, on the stairwell's right-hand side: Weapons, Beadwork, Boat Models, Masks and Wood Carving, with Basketry and Fish Traps displayed at the centre. Particularly interesting are four cases housing a spectacular array of masks, many over 80 years old and some depicting white men, reflecting Sarawak's unusual 19th century political structure. The basket section is equally appealing with many older examples.

On the other side of the rectangular gallery are the Musical Instrument and Games sections and an extensive display devoted to Traditional Houses. On the far left-hand side is a life-size model of an Iban longhouse.

The museum extension is a square building across Jalan Tun Haji Openg, a short walk from the other buildings in the compound. It houses a number of temporary exhibition galleries and administrative offices.

Though somewhat off the beaten track in Kuching, the Sarawak State Museum holds one of the country's best ethnological collections. Those visiting East Malaysia, even if only briefly, should not miss it.

▲ **Assorted basketry**
Orang Ulu | 20th century

▲ **Assorted traditional musical instruments**
Orang Ulu | 20th century

ADDRESS
50 Jalan Tun Tan Cheng Lock
75200 Melaka
Malaysia

CONTACT INFORMATION
T/F: +60 6 283 1273

OPENING HOURS
10am–12.30pm;
2pm–4.30pm daily.

ADMISSION
Adult RM 8;
child between 5 and 12 RM 4.

FACILITIES
Guided tours are available
upon request.

HOW TO GET THERE
Bus: 17 from town.
On foot.

AROUND THE MUSEUM
Located on one of the Chinese
quarter's most attractive
streets, the museum is
surrounded by curio shops,
restaurants and cafés.

Baba Nyonya Heritage Museum

Located in two renovated Peranakan houses in Melaka, the private Baba Nyonya Heritage Museum affords a taste of Straits Chinese hybrid culture and life at the end of the 19th century.

■ **THE BUILDING** Situated in adjacent shophouses west of the Melaka River, the museum was once home to three generations of a single Peranakan family. Built by a wealthy Straits Chinese tycoon in 1896, the Chinatown house (the old Dutch quarter is on the east side of the river), with its narrow, plain and columned façade, stucco decoration and covered porch, does not give much away from the outside, its adapted Chinese architecture typical of turn-of-the-19th-century Singapore, Melaka and Penang construction. But inside, the house is grand and ostentatious indeed, extending at least 50 metres to the back and naturally lit by interior courtyards and light wells. The Chan family mansion, as the house was known, is described as 'Chinese Baroque' or 'Chinese Palladian' in style.

■ **THE COLLECTION** Assembling mainly furniture and porcelain, the museum is set up

▲ The Heritage Museum's ground floor with its unique, richly carved staircase in the foreground.

on two floors more or less as the house would have been a century ago, with much of the dwelling's original interior architectural features still intact. Neo-Classical European columns decorated with swags and cornucopia of a type popular in Victorian England, Art Nouveau floor tiles adorned with stylised foliate motifs, and elaborately carved and gilded doorways of Qing dynasty inspiration all coexist happily here. An ornate carved and gilded hardwood staircase, thought to be the only one of its kind in Malaysia, links the ground floor to the second.

The furniture, too, is an eclectic mix of styles, with ostentation always preferred to discretion. The richly decorated and monumental bridal bed, with its silks, veils and tassels is typically Peranakan in its exuberant excess and can be contrasted with a pair of far more sober hardwood Chinese chairs flanking a huge sideboard. The latter, a massive locally made wooden piece which, though of Dutch-inspired design rather than Straits Chinese, is just as heavy-looking and ornate as the Peranakan furniture. As well as elaborate carvings, gilt wood and intricate floral designs, Peranakan patrons were very fond of mother-of-pearl inlay in dark wood

▲ **Peranakan plates**
Porcelain dinnerware made in China for export to the Straits Settlements, c. 1900.

designs, and a number of pieces shown here attest to this particular predilection.

At the rear of the museum, on the ground floor, an ancestral altar, typical of those common in Chinese homes to this day, commemorates the Chan family ancestors and is equipped with all the appropriate paraphernalia such as incense burners and images of the deceased.

Displayed in glass cases are pieces of Peranakan porcelain. Made in China specifically for export to the Straits Settlements, these ceramics, often heavily potted, are richly decorated and brightly enamelled with gold, turquoise, yellow and pink. Though Chinese in iconographical inspiration, Peranakan ceramics are nonetheless thoroughly tropical in palette and flamboyant in taste.

Another display, highlighting Baba and Nyonya clothing, encapsulates the hybrid aspect of Peranakan culture with its mixed strands of Chinese, Malay and Western iconographies and styles.

A small but fascinating museum, the Baba Nyonya Heritage Museum documents one of Southeast Asia's lesser known but intriguing hybrid peoples. The institution also acts as a reminder of Southeast Asia's history of cultural fluidity and cosmopolitanism.

ADDRESS
Melaka Museums Corporation
Kompleks Warisan Melaka
Jalan Kota
75000 Melaka
Malaysia

CONTACT INFORMATION
T: +60 6 282 6526
F: +60 6 282 6745

OPENING HOURS
9am–6pm Sat–Thu;
9am–12.15pm,
2.45pm–6pm Fri;
closed on Hari Raya Aidilfitri
and Hari Raya Aidiladha.

ADMISSION
Adult RM 2;
student RM 0.50.

FACILITIES
Museum shop.

HOW TO GET THERE
Bus: 17/SK

AROUND THE MUSEUM
The museum is located in
Melaka's busy tourist area
where there are plenty of
shops and restaurants.

Melaka Sultanate Palace Museum

The Sultanate of Melaka is the institutional core of the traditional Malay system of government. The Melaka Sultanate Palace Museum provides an introduction to both early Malaysian political history and traditional royal architecture.

■ **THE BUILDING** While the majority of the original imperial Melakan buildings of the 15ᵗʰ century were destroyed in the wake of the Portuguese occupation of 1511, the Melaka Sultanate Palace was in fact razed in a fire in the late 15ᵗʰ-century, some years before the Portuguese arrived.

At the foot of St Paul's Hill, next to the Dutch Graveyard and the Porta De Santiago in the heart of Old Melaka, the new Sultanate Palace is a recently built recreation of the 15ᵗʰ-century royal Melaka court.

Closely replicating the original both inside and out, the new Sultanate Palace's design is based on detailed written descriptions found in the 17ᵗʰ-century *Sejarah Melayu* (Malay Annals), as well as other literary sources of the period that provide a record of Malay history and document the Empire's expansion under Sultan Mansor Shah (reigned 1456–1477).

The palace, constructed in 1984, was built with hardwood in traditional *bumbung*

▲ *International representatives in the Main Hall.*

panjang (long roof) style, a vernacular still evident in some Malaysian kampong houses today. It is characterised by a raised ground floor, deep overhanging eaves to protect the interior from the heat, and steeply pitched sloping roofs designed to drain the heavy monsoon rains efficiently and quickly. The rebuilt palace also displays traditional architectural features such as a structural system totally free of nails that, instead, relies on a combination of interlocking cuts, slots and grooves supplemented by wedges and dowels to provide basic support. Some nails are nonetheless integrated into the building's secondary, non-structural elements.

■ **THE COLLECTION** The museum presents more than 700 cultural and other objects including clothing, weapons and ornaments.

■ **THE ROOMS** The museum was added to the palace in 1986. Once inside the palace, the visitor will tour the **Throne Room** or the **Main Hall**. Along with its interesting inner construction, all hardwood support beams and panelling reminiscent in general style of much indigenous Southeast Asian architecture, the palace's spare opulence is quite striking. Models of courtiers and officials are placed in the Main Hall, realistically conveying the room's atmosphere as the political and decisional heart of the palace and government. In addition to the local Melakan entourage, several messengers are represented, thus evoking the importance

of 15ᵗʰ-century Melaka as a commercial trading centre. Present there might have been Gujerat messengers discussing the trade of their merchants' cotton, camphor and opium. Arab messengers might have been there as well, presenting their glassware, oil, beads, corn, silk, weapons and copper for barter. As Muslims, the Arab traders were particularly favoured and protected by the Melakan court of Sultan Muzaffar Shah (reigned 1446–1456) and as a result, some of the merchants decided to stay in Melaka, thus increasing the city's importance as a centre for the dissemination of Islam in the peninsula. Trade between China and Melaka had already developed in the 15ᵗʰ century, so Chinese messengers were a common sight at court as well. While the Chinese delivered silk, gold, tea, porcelain, pearls, mother-of-pearl and gunpowder to Melaka, they returned to China with Middle Eastern and Southeast Asian products. Finally, the Javanese traded rice, spices, sugar and wood.

Other exhibits include the intimately scaled **Royal Bedchamber**, **Islamic Chamber**, **Malay Traditional Dress Gallery** and the diorama of the **duel between Hang Tuah and Hang Jebat**, two brave warrior brothers from the reign of Sultan Mansor Shah, as well as displays of traditional Malay games and musical instruments.

The Melaka Sultanate Palace Museum documents the early history of Melaka, highlighting the city's importance as a trading hub and centre for the dissemination of Islam.

ADDRESS
Lebuh Farquhar
10200 Penang
Malaysia

CONTACT INFORMATION
T: +60 4 261 3144
F: +60 4 261 3144
E: muzium@po.jaring.my

OPENING HOURS
9am–5pm Sat–Thu.

ADMISSION
Adult RM 1;
child RM 0.50.

FACILITIES
Guided tours are available
upon request.

Library; theatrette; museum
shop; car park.

HOW TO GET THERE
Free city shuttle bus.

AROUND THE MUSEUM
The large anchor of the French
ship *Mosquet*, and an original
funicular carriage from
Penang Hill's Funicular
Railway are positioned in
front and on the left side of
the museum building.

Museum & Art Gallery, Penang

Documenting the history of Penang's diverse population, as well as aspects of the island's political and commercial history, the museum, part of Penang's Museum & Art Gallery, is housed in an attractive colonial building.

■ **THE BUILDING** The museum's current home dates back to the early 19th century when the East India Company's socially enlightened chaplain, Reverend Robert Sparke, established a school open to local children irrespective of ethnicity, religion or class. The Penang Free School was initially housed in rented quarters, but moved into Mortimer's Hall, a building adjacent to Penang's St George's Church (constructed in 1817 under the direction of Englishman Captain Robert Smith of the Royal Engineers) along Farquhar Street, in 1821. A second structure was added in 1897 just in front of the school (the current museum building).

It remained there until 1928, when the Hutchings School took over the premises. Though the structure lost its East Wing to bombing during World War II, it continued to house the Hutchings School until 1961.

Exhibiting late Victorian references to Classical architecture, including columns, a small cupola and large arches, combined with tropical architectural features such as a broad, shaded porch and high-ceilinged rooms, the building is as eclectic in appearance as the collection it contains.

■ **THE COLLECTION** The original private collection, built in the 1930s and housed in St Xavier's Institution in 1941, was destroyed during the Japanese occupation. Subsequently, the collection was built up once more, only to be scattered a second time. Finally, in 1962 a permanent museum building was mooted and the Museum & Art Gallery, Penang, was declared open in 1965.

Containing over 1,000 objects from the late 18th century to the present day, the collection preserves the state's historical and cultural artefacts and documents the history of the island's cosmopolitan population of Malay, Chinese, Indian and Peranakan origin.

■ **THE GALLERIES** On the museum's ground floor, beyond the entrance, visitors are introduced to the various ethnic populations present in Penang. Through a mixture of utilitarian wares, cultural objects, religious items, photographs and text panels, the museum presents insights into the lives of the island's three dominant ethnic communities— the Malays, Chinese and Indians.

In the **Malay Room (Room 2)**, to the right of the main entrance, beyond the **People Room (Room 1)**, visitors learn of the Malay tradition of inhabiting rural parts of the island and their engagement in activities such as

▲ **William Daniell**
View of the Cascade, Prince of Wales Island | Aquatint from the oil on canvas by Captain Robert Smith | 1821 | 45.5 x 35.4 cm

fishing and agriculture. Their culture is documented through jewellery, costumes, the kris and images of the oldest extant mosque in Penang, the Lebuh Acheh Mosque.

Past the Malay Room is the **Indian Room (Room 3)**. Here, Indian religious diversity and trading practices are explored, and Indian Muslim intermarriage with the indigenous Malays documented. Though many Indian workers returned to the subcontinent after their sojourn in Malaya, many other migrants stayed on, their children regarding the new country as home. Conversely, Penang's Sikh

▲ *Photographic image of the Penang waterfront and Swettenham Pier in the early 20th century.*

community, often traders and civil servants, kept their native traditions and rarely intermarried. Their customs and religious practices are examined here as well.

Next to the Indian Room is the **Chinese Room (Room 4)**, illustrating the Chinese migrants' important role in the cultural and economic history of Penang. The gallery features ornate and opulent Chinese furniture of the 19th century set up to resemble the interior of a wealthy Chinese entrepreneur's home a century or more ago. Quite evocative of the lifestyle of the first generation of well-to-do Chinese traders—originally migrants from Southwest China who established themselves at the end of the 18th century during the period of early British rule—the gallery shows that the Chinese valued education and enjoyed a British-influenced lifestyle that included European-style accommodation.

Visitors intrigued by the history of the Peranakans, or Straits-born Chinese—the offspring of Chinese traders who, as early as the 15th century are known to have intermarried with the locals—will find much documentation in these two rooms. Illustrating their traditions and unique mixed culture, the **Nyonya Costumes Room (Room 7)** and the **Wedding Chamber Room (Room 5)** present a wide selection of objects. Their costumes, combining local Malay styles and Chinese patterns, porcelain, often imported from China but more elaborate and bolder in colouring than contemporary Chinese Qing dynasty wares, and jewellery, incorporating Chinese iconography and local goldsmithing techniques, are all displayed in these galleries. Richly ornate wedding paraphernalia, including a majestic canopied wedding bed, are a highlight of this part of the museum.

The different peoples of Penang, having been examined in individual contexts on the ground floor of the museum, are all brought together in the **Streets of Penang Room (Room 6)** where the island's hawker culture is explored with a recreation of local street life and a display case enclosing Penang's most evocative street names.

Finally, the museum's top floor is dedicated to Penang's history.

The **History Gallery** is a vast section divided thematically to underscore places and events that chart the early history of the island. With the use of panoramic displays, the rise of Penang as a strategic port on the East India Company's India-China trade route is explored. Text panels, audio-visual displays, images and period memorabilia explain Penang's development over the centuries. Penang's formal takeover by the British in 1786 is discussed, along with its status as a free port and one of the region's busiest trading settlements.

A highlight on this floor consists of eight early 19th-century landscapes of the island by Captain Robert Smith (1787–1873). These provide invaluable topographical references to Penang in the days before photography.

Holding its own among the island's most distinctive architectural landmarks, the Museum & Art Gallery, Penang, presents a well-labelled and displayed collection elucidating the history of one of Southeast Asia's most cosmopolitan enclaves.

Peranakan wedding bed
Lacquered, carved and gilded wood hung with silk draperies | 19th century | H: 252 cm

The central showpiece of the museum's Peranakan display, the elaborately decorated, richly ostentatious wedding bed has become emblematic of the Baba Nyonya culture of Penang, Melaka and Singapore. More than a piece of furniture, the wedding bed was a material reflection of an elaborate wedding ceremony that would often last several days and was one of the central social pivots of the culture.

ADDRESS
Jalan Tamingsari
34000 Taiping, Perak
Malaysia

CONTACT INFORMATION
T: +60 5 807 2057
F: +60 5 806 3643
E: zainal@jma.gov.my or
sahabudin@jma.gov.my

OPENING HOURS
9am–5pm daily;
closed on the first day
of Hari Raya Aidilfitri and
Hari Raya Aidiladha.

ADMISSION
Free.

FACILITIES
Guided tours are available by
appointment.

Library stocking a fair number
of 19th-century publications.

HOW TO GET THERE
On foot from the centre
of town.

By taxi.

AROUND THE MUSEUM
In Taiping itself there are
many shops and restaurants.

Maxwell Hill, the colonial hill
station, is a short drive to the
east for those who have a day
to spare.

Perak State Museum

The oldest museum in the country, the Perak State Museum, formerly the Taiping Museum, harbours a mixed zoological, anthropological and historical collection in an attractive, old, colonial building.

■ **THE BUILDING** Located in the old mining town of Taiping, less than an hour's drive from Ipoh, Perak's state capital, the Perak State Museum is housed in a purpose-designed museum building constructed by the British colonial authorities in 1886.

At a time when Kuala Lumpur was barely on the map, Taiping was a town of prosperity and 'firsts', its surrounding tin mines driving the British colony's growing wealth. As well as being the site of Malaya's first museum, it also claimed the first railway, the first English language school, and Malaya's maiden English language newspaper.

As Taiping was at the helm of British colonial implantation in Malaya, it was only natural that the town should be home to the peninsula's first museum, established not long after the colonists' administrative buildings were erected.

Opposite Taiping Prison (another late 19th-century English institution) on the northwest side of town, the museum is a short walk from the town centre. Renovated and expanded in the 1990s, the museum remains functional despite its age. Though the galleries lack the latest technology, this is compensated for by the airy, old world charm of the institution.

Of white stucco construction with a red tiled roof, the building, with its mock turrets and fussy façade, is in typical Victorian style. The two wide verandahs at the front and rear of the museum are the only real concessions to Taiping's tropical climate.

Though the main part of the building was finished in 1886, a shortage of funds prevented the construction of verandahs and the West Wing until 1893. The museum, however, was quickly filled with artefacts and in 1903 a second two-storey building was added to the complex.

■ **THE COLLECTION** Upon the initiative of the then British Resident in Perak, Sir Hugh Low, the collection was first assembled in 1883 by fellow Englishman and botanist/geologist Leonard Wray Junior, who was instructed to collect historical, cultural and natural history material for 'the enlightenment of posterity'. Initially displayed in two rooms in a government building, the collection focused at first on the region's flora and fauna (typical of this late 19th-century collecting style are the various slightly musty animal trophies of the period still proudly displayed around the galleries), but subsequently evolved to include Orang Asli artefacts (one of the more interesting aspects of the collection today), local costumes, ceramics, other cultural and historical material, as well as vehicles, boats and cannons, the latter part of the more recent outdoor exhibit. There are currently some

▲ *View of an outdoor exhibit featuring three aboriginal dugout canoes from the early 18th century.*

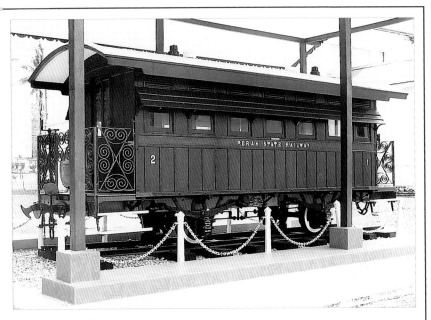

Railway coach
19ᵗʰ century

This coach was among the first railway carriages to operate on the all-important Taiping Railway Line in the last decade of the 19ᵗʰ century. Taiping was a large economic centre of colonial Malaya, its tin mines generating significant income, and thus the new railway's contribution to transporting the commodity to market was crucial to the town's increasing development and prosperity.

5,250 objects in the collection, 3,000 of which are at least 120 years old, having for the most part been assembled in the 1880s. Objects are labelled in English and Malay.

■ **THE GALLERIES** The museum is laid out in an 'L'-shaped formation, its main building housing two permanent galleries and the two-storey annex at the rear of the building on the left enclosing two more. Several covered **outdoor display spaces** on the grounds of the museum provide shelter for large exhibits such as a mid-19ᵗʰ-century cannon, a 19ᵗʰ-century railway carriage among the first to operate on the Taiping line and in use between 1885 and 1895, a 20ᵗʰ-century bus, rickshaws, an 18ᵗʰ-century horse gharry, romantically decked with flowers and interior draperies, a hand-pumping fire extinguisher of the same period,

and three Orang Asli dugout canoes dating back to the early 18ᵗʰ-century.

Penetrating the museum, beyond the entrance and ticket desk, and next to a small temporary gallery and the distinguished museum library on the right, are the largest of the museum's rooms, the **Natural History Gallery** and the Ethnological Gallery. In the former, glass cases lining the walls and running down the middle of the space enclose a variety of regional animals including snakes, rodents and larger mammals. Some specimens are as old as the museum itself and though presented in a rather arcane manner, are of particular interest to those keen to spot species no longer common or altogether extinct in modern Malaysia. Some animal skeletons

in the same room are impressive in scale and will likely appeal to children.

Leading off the Natural History Gallery toward the rear of the museum is the **Ethnological Gallery**. Here, a wide range of cultural material is shown including Malay textiles of different types and periods, weapons—see a large collection of kris, some quite old, finely worked 18ᵗʰ-century nielloware, old machinery and hunting paraphernalia. Also displayed are personal ornaments and costumes—see in particular the development of the costumes of Perak dignitaries over the years, musical instruments and an ornate early 20ᵗʰ-century throne belonging to the Perak Sultanate. Slated to be upgraded soon, this gallery, probably the museum's most interesting, may be yet more so in the near future.

The later-built, two-storey annex at the rear of the compound houses the **Indigenous People Gallery** and the Ceramic Gallery. The former contains a small collection of tribal masks and sculpture as well as some clothing, household items, basketry and jewellery. See in particular a series of early 18ᵗʰ-century bark cloths woven by the Orang Asli as well as some of the tools and implements used to manufacture these textiles.

The **Ceramic Gallery** contains a fairly large group of similar Malay utilitarian ceramics from the 18ᵗʰ century.

The Perak State Museum, though not large, provides the visitor with an accurate idea of 19ᵗʰ-century British collecting style in a traditional museum setting.

▲ *Outdoor exhibit of the Long Jaafar Cannon.*

Myanmar ▶

ADDRESS
66/74 Pyay Road
Yangon
Myanmar

CONTACT INFORMATION
T: +95 1 282 563 / 608 or
279 652

OPENING HOURS
10am–4pm daily.

ADMISSION
US$5.

FACILITIES
There are two bookshops and
a souvenir shop on the
museum's ground floor.

HOW TO GET THERE
On foot or by taxi.

AROUND THE MUSEUM
The National Museum is
located in the embassy
district, close to People's Park
and the Planetarium.

The Shwe Dagon Pagoda is a
few minutes away by car and
20 minutes to the northeast
on foot.

National Museum of Myanmar

Housed in an expansive five-storey modern building, the National Museum of Myanmar harbours an impressive collection of Burmese cultural material embracing periods from the prehistoric to the contemporary.

■ **THE BUILDING** The National Museum was first established in the 1950s at Jubilee Hall on Shwe Dagon Pagoda Road. It moved to larger premises in 1970, before being relocated once again to its current purpose-built museum building in 1996.

The museum is sited in the embassy district on the southwest side of Yangon, along the broad north-south artery, Pyay Road, that runs from the docks in the south to beyond Inya Lake in the city's northern reaches. A 20-minute walk southwest of the famous Shwe Dagon Pagoda, the museum is also near People's Park and the Planetarium, making it easily accessible to visitors with limited time in the capital.

Though built in the 1990s, the museum's cream-coloured symmetrical façade with recessed, oblong, heat-deflecting windows evokes a generic international Modernism more characteristic of the 1960s than today.

■ **THE COLLECTION** Assembling thousands of objects, the collection covers a wide variety of subjects from royal regalia (some royal artefacts are replicas of the originals not yet returned by the British who removed them from the country further to the various 19th-century Anglo-Burmese Wars), to musical instruments, reproductions of ancient cave paintings and Buddhist icons, the latter, as well as the dazzling jewelled gold ornaments belonging to King Thibaw (the last Burmese monarch, reigned 1878–1885), among the museum's most memorable.

▲ **Carved wooden figures of Buddha**
With pigment | Depicted in bhumisparca mudra (calling Mother Earth posture) | Nyaung Yang period, 17th–18th century | H: 40.5 cm and H: 66 cm

▲ **Carved wooden figure of Buddha**
Gilt and lacquered | Depicted in bhumisparca mudra | Innwa period, 15th century | H: 49.53 cm

■ **THE GALLERIES** The collection is displayed on five floors in 14 galleries, the museum housing roughly 5,000 square metres of exhibition space. The three galleries on the ground floor, encountered by the visitor upon entering through the large covered portico, are representative of the museum as a whole in their variety of focus.

The high-ceilinged, elaborately decorated **Lion Throne Showroom** is lodged in the area behind the central entrance and is probably the museum's most glittery and visually overwhelming gallery. Dating to the mid-19th century when it was built for King Mindon, the eight-metre-high gilded and carved clog-wood Lion Throne was named for the 108 lions that adorn its base. Later belonging to King Thibaw, it is the only Burmese royal throne of importance remaining intact in the country. Indeed, further to the occupation of Mandalay by the British in 1885, and to fires during the bombings of World War II, all

others were destroyed. The easily dismantled Lion Throne, which had been appropriated by the British and shipped to the Indian Museum in Calcutta at the beginning of the 20th century, after the takeover of Mandalay, was returned to the country by Lord Mountbatten in 1948 after the declaration of Burmese independence.

To the right of the entrance and the previous gallery is the **Myanmar Epigraphy and Calligraphy Showroom**. Here, in a space similar in size to the Lion Throne Showroom, the museum exhibits a collection of manuscripts and other objects that document the history and evolution of Burmese script through the ages. An inscribed pair of 16th-century teak columns from Kanbawzathadi Palace in Bago is one impressive example. Others are very ancient.

See in particular the gold leaf Pali manuscript found in the relic chamber of Khin Ba's Mound, Hmawza, Pyay district, dated to around the 4th to 5th century. An inscribed Pyu stone funerary urn dated 1st to 5th century is also worth examining. In addition to objects themselves, a series of photographs depicting inscribed monuments and rubbings, taken from steles left *in situ* around the country or kept in storage for conservation, are displayed in this gallery.

Still on the ground floor, to the left is the large **Yadanabon Period Showroom** which features models, photographs and paintings of the Mandalay Myanansankyaw Palace as well as royal furniture and ceremonial costumes, many dating to the 19th century. See in particular a spectacular carved ivory chair belonging to King Thibaw.

Shwe Pay Chat gold leaf manuscript
Pyu period, 4th–5th century | Leaves approximately L: 17.7 cm, W: 3.8 cm

Pyu gold Buddhist scriptures are not only important works of art, giving clues to the period's aesthetic leanings, but of acute historical significance. Indeed, being inscribed on gold, the over 1,600-year-old texts have survived where scriptures on paper, bamboo or palm leaf, even of much later manufacture, have not.

▲ **Ayoe Ore clay burial urn**
Beikthano | Pyu period | 1ˢᵗ–5ᵗʰ century | H: 28 cm

On the second floor the museum presents four galleries including the **Royal Regalia Showroom**, the Historic Period Showroom, the Natural History Gallery and the Myanmar Prehistoric Period and Protohistoric Period Showroom. The first highlights a wide assortment of precious objects—betel boxes, jewelled baskets, silver and gold spittoons and many more—used for royal ceremonies, and whether they are of the period or reproductions, are quite dazzling in their workmanship and ostentation. Opposite, towards the rear of the museum, the **Historic Period Showroom** presents bronze, stone and terracotta Buddhist icons and votive tablets as well as some household items. Authentic pieces mix with reproductions here. See in this section a 5ᵗʰ-century Pyu period silver reliquary in the form of a Bodhi Tree that gives some idea of the sophistication of Pyu period artistic and technical skills. A collection of

◄ **Stone Buddhist stele**
With traces of pigment | 5ᵗʰ–9ᵗʰ century | H: 30.5 cm

authentic Pagan pieces ranging in date from the 11ᵗʰ to the 13ᵗʰ century is also noteworthy. The **Natural History Gallery** on the left at the rear of the museum features a number of fossils including a 40-million-year-old primate as well as land and sea vertebrates and invertebrates, and fossilised flora of various kinds. The **Myanmar Prehistoric Period and Protohistoric Period Showroom** assembles prehistoric stone tools, beads, selected reproductions of ancient cave paintings, and Bronze Age tools and arrowheads.

The floor above comprises two galleries, the **Myanmar Traditional Folk Art Showroom** and the Myanmar Performing Arts Showroom. The first, on the left and the largest, displays a broad grouping of religious and domestic artefacts that highlight the talent of indigenous craftspeople. The arts of lacquer—at which the Burmese are particularly accomplished, gold, copper and silver smithing, painting, pottery, wood and ivory carving, weaving, stucco work and masonry craft are all illustrated with some fairly recent objects as well as older ones. The **Myanmar Performing Arts Showroom** contains puppets, instruments and costumes relating mainly to classical Burmese performance. A full traditional Burmese orchestra decorated with glass mosaic is displayed here as well.

The next floor up is devoted principally to painting (copies of Pagan temple murals as well as some works dating to the introduction of Western painting to Burma) in two rooms, **Myanmar Art Gallery (1)** and **Myanmar Art Gallery (2)**. It also houses an interesting if small collection of ancient jewellery and ornaments in the adjacent **Myanmar Ancient Ornaments Showroom**. See in particular good examples of Pyu gold in this gallery.

▲ **Bronze bell**
Thayekhittaya | Pyu period, 5ᵗʰ century | H: 29.2 cm

▲ **Carved wooden figure of Buddha**
Gilt and lacquered | 15ᵗʰ century | H: 56 cm

The museum's last floor explores indigenous ethnic cultures and Buddhist iconography. The large **Showroom for the Culture of the National Races** displays mannequins representing the different tribal peoples of Myanmar wearing their respective traditional dress. A collection of musical instruments and cultural objects relating to the ethnic identities are also shown. Finally, the museum's last room, the **Buddha Images Showroom**, on the right side at the front of the museum, is of particular interest to visitors keen on Burmese religious art and architecture as a representative collection of Buddhist sculpture gathered from and originating in the country's ancient monasteries and temples is housed here.

Though the National Museum of Myanmar's building lacks the architectural charm and period character of some of Southeast Asia's other national museums, its large, airy rooms and displays provide a good backdrop against which visitors can view a comprehensive collection. English labelling is on the succinct side, but much of the art speaks for itself, the museum assuring an excellent introduction to Burmese culture through the ages.

The Philippines ▶

ADDRESS
University of San Carlos
P. del Rosario Street
Cebu City
The Philippines

CONTACT INFORMATION
T/F: +63 32 253 1000
E: museum@usc.edu.ph

OPENING HOURS
8.30am–12pm,
1.30pm–5.30pm Mon–Fri;
8.30am–12pm Sat.

ADMISSION
30 pesos;
student 10 pesos;
free for USC students.

FACILITIES
Wheelchair access.

Guided tours are available
in English.

Bookshop.

HOW TO GET THERE
On foot, or by taxi or jeepney.

AROUND THE MUSEUM
P. del Rosario Street is close to
Cebu's downtown core of
Colon Street.

Sto. Rosario Parish Church is
not far from the university, as
are cafés and small shops.

University of San Carlos Museum

With its eclectic collection of cultural and natural science material, the University of San Carlos Museum in Cebu City provides an introduction to pre-colonial funerary archaeology and indigenous tribal culture.

■ **THE BUILDING** The museum is located on the ground floor of the university's Main Building, to the right of the entrance on P. del Rosario Street.

■ **THE COLLECTION** The University of San Carlos Museum was founded in 1967 by the German Father Rudolph Rahmann SVD, an anthropologist and the university's former president. The collections were assembled somewhat earlier. Starting with a modest grouping of ethnological and archaeological material, the holdings were expanded as Dr Marcelino Maceda and Father Rahmann contributed material from the Buhid Mangyans of Mindoro, the Negritos of Antique, Panay

▲ *Religious icons in the museum's Spanish Colonial Gallery.*

Island and the Mamanuas of Surigao. Some of the archaeological finds were the result of Dr Maceda's studies on Kulaman Plateau burial urns. Added through either acquisition or university fieldwork in the vicinity, the Spanish colonial and natural science objects further enlarged the museum's collection.

■ **THE GALLERIES** Composed of four galleries, the museum features rooms devoted to Spanish Colonial, Ethnological, Archaeological and Natural Science material. Modern in concept, the museum seeks to present its objects in such a way that they 'speak' to the visitor, relating stories about the country's Christian heritage, tribal life, ceremonial practices, and ecological issues.

The **Spanish Colonial Gallery** contains altarpieces, religious icons, woodcarvings, reliefs, coins and baptismal records documenting Catholic heritage in the Philippines.

The **Ethnographic Gallery** displays the material culture of many indigenous tribal communities as well as a well-made ethnolinguistic map showing the distribution of different communities throughout the country. Weapons, tools, costumes, ornaments, jewellery and betel nut chewing paraphernalia are exhibited here. See in particular painted wooden statues used as protective house idols from the Mansaka tribe of Davao. Tribal practices such as teeth mutilation are also explained.

The **Archaeological Gallery** houses pre-Hispanic burial artefacts such as boat coffins from Bohol, limestone burial jars from

▲ *A wealth of stone and pottery material in the museum's Archaeological Gallery.*

Cotabato, earthenware coffins and jars from Negros Oriental, and containers for the ashes of cremated bones from Laguna, all exhibited on a plinth in the middle of the gallery. The display explains the different burial practices associated with these objects and attests to pre-Christian Filipinos' belief in life after death as well as to the aesthetic taste of pre-colonial Filipino culture. Surrounding the burial material is a small collection of early trade ceramics excavated at Lipa, Cebu and Batangas as well as tools from Cebu housed in glass cases.

The **Natural Science Gallery** exhibits examples of Filipino flora and fauna including rare and endangered species. The display aims to sensitise visitors to the ecological problems currently being faced by the Philippines, the country's natural environment and ecosystem often threatened by burgeoning industrialisation and urbanisation.

A small museum, the University of San Carlos Museum is worth a visit if one is spending a few days in Cebu.

ADDRESS
Makati Avenue,
corner De la Rosa Street
Greenbelt Park, Ayala Center
Makati City, Metro Manila
The Philippines

CONTACT DETAILS
T: +63 2 757 7117
F: +63 2 757 2787
E: inquiry@ayalamuseum.com

W: www.ayalamuseum.org

OPENING HOURS
9am–6pm Tue–Sun.

ADMISSION
Adult 350 pesos;
child, student and senior
250 pesos.

FACILITIES
Wheelchair access.

Guided tours are available at
an extra charge; audio guides
available.

HOW TO GET THERE
LRT: Ayala Station at Ayala
Center. The museum is a 10-
minute walk towards
Greenbelt Park.

AROUND THE MUSEUM
The hotels, restaurants and
shops of the Ayala Center.

Ayala Museum

In a stunning Modernist building, the Ayala Museum is one of the Philippines' best private ethnological and fine art museums, tracing the country's history from pre-colonial times to the 20th century.

■ **THE BUILDING** Having moved three times since its inception in the mid-1960s, the Ayala Museum has finally come to rest in a state-of-the-art Modernist glass, steel and stone building designed by Leandro Y. Locsin Jr and his team (Locsin's father Leandro V. Locsin designed the Ayala Museum's previous premises). The new institution covers over 6,000 square metres of space and consists of two structures connected by a bridgeway on the second and third levels. A Zen-inspired landscaped plaza on the ground level seamlessly connects the museum to the rest of Greenbelt Park while an elevated walkway links the building with the Greenbelt complex and the Makati Business District.

■ **THE COLLECTION** The Ayala Museum was founded in 1967 by the Filipinas Foundation Inc. which later became the Ayala Foundation. The museum was the brainchild of Fernando Zóbel de Ayala y Montojo (1924–1984), not only a scion of the powerful and philanthropic Ayala family, but a distinguished abstract artist in his own right who worked in the United States and later in Spain.

The collection's roots lie in the rational analysis of Filipino history and the determination of its critical turning points. Once these were established, objects related to them—ethnological, archaeological or fine art—were assembled and displayed in conjunction with 60 handcrafted dioramas illustrating particular historical episodes in the rich tapestry of Philippine history.

Thus, the museum's ethnological, archaeological and fine art collections are intelligently interwoven to illustrate distinct historical epochs covering prehistory to the present. Rare 19th-century paintings by Juan Luna and Damian Domingo are complemented by gold jewellery and religious icons from the Spanish colonial period. The boat gallery illustrates the Filipinos' affinity with the sea and their particular competence as boat-builders and navigators. And in addition to the historically oriented holdings, two further 20th-century fine art collections have been assembled, the first representing the oeuvre of Fernando Zóbel, the museum's principal founder, the second an important body of work by Fernando Amorsolo (1892–1972). The Amorsolo collection is one of the most significant in the Philippines.

■ **THE GALLERIES** In its new premises, the museum's focus has changed from that of an institution dominated by its permanent collection to an institution whose core collections are regularly enriched by outside

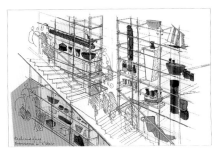

▲ *Architectural drawing of the new building.*

▲ *Brass and silver betel nut boxes.*

loans so as to present a constantly changing and open face to the public.

In the permanent galleries, the Philippines' historical narrative is recorded moving backwards through time, from the second to the fourth floor. Here, the multimedia **People Power Hall** is a highlight, recounting Filipino history from the birth of the country as a modern democracy in 1946 to the present.

The **second floor** presents the museum's most didactic galleries. Housing a collection of handcrafted model boats including Spanish galleons, Chinese junks and native outriggers, the visitor is reminded of the country's past as a trading hub in pre-modern Southeast Asia. Fine art (19th and 20th centuries) and object-based works are on the **third floor** while the **fourth** traces the country's development from early pre-colonial times to the 18th and 19th centuries through a wealth of cultural and fine art material.

With its dazzling new building coupled with a dynamic approach to public involvement in history and the arts, the Ayala Museum is one of the Philippines' most exciting private museums.

ADDRESS
Kaisa-Angelo King
Heritage Center
Anda Street,
corner Cabildo Street
Intramuros, Manila
The Philippines

CONTACT INFORMATION
T: +63 2 527 6083 / 526 6798
F: +63 2 527 6085

E: kaisa@philonline.com
W: www.philonline.com.ph/
ffkaisa/khc_btsinoy.html

OPENING HOURS
1pm–5pm Tue–Sun.

ADMISSION
Adult 100 pesos;
child 60 pesos.

FACILITIES
As well as a museum, the
Center houses a library
and provides community
activities, lectures and
film screenings.

HOW TO GET THERE
By taxi or jeepney.

AROUND THE MUSEUM
The walls of Intramuros ring
the area.

Manila Cathedral and Fort
Santiago are not far, as are
many restaurants and cafés.

Bahay Tsinoy: Museum of Chinese in Philippine Life

The Bahay Tsinoy, housed in Manila's Kaisa Heritage Center, is a permanent showcase of the history of the Chinese in the Philippines from prehistory to the present.

■ **THE BUILDING** A relatively new institution, the Bahay Tsinoy (or the Chinese-Filipino House) was conceived in the mid-1980s by a University of the Philippines anthropologist of Chinese descent, Professor Chinben See. Though Professor See died in 1986, his dream was taken up by members of the Chinese business community and the museum was launched in 1999 within the framework of the Kaisa-Angelo King Heritage Center, the latter inaugurated simultaneously.

The 1,300-square-metre Kaisa Heritage Center building is located in the heart of Manila's historic Intramuros district, close to Manila Cathedral. The three-storey, stone, colonial-style structure, designed by celebrated contemporary local architect Rogelio Villarosa, houses a library, an auditorium, the centre's offices, as well as the Bahay Tsinoy.

■ **THE COLLECTION** Though the collection contains important examples of Chinese cultural material including ancient books, maps, paintings, prints, rare archival material, sculptures and ceramics, it is the museum's explicative documentation, dioramas, photographs and a new interactive centre on the third floor that constitute its main wealth.

■ **THE GALLERIES** Relations between the Filipinos and Chinese predate Magellan's arrival in the Philippines by many centuries. According to early records, commercial relations between the two were already well developed by the 10th century.

▲ *Diorama of Chinese food pedlars.*

The collection and related dioramas, text panels and mixed-media displays document the shared history of the Chinese and Filipinos through the role and cultural contribution of the migrant Chinese to the Philippines. And as an extension of Kaisa, the museum promotes Tsinoy culture, values and history.

The collection, initially divided into five sub-sections, is now split into 14 major information clusters.

Early Contacts evokes the Ice Age period when land bridges connected what is now the Philippines with mainland Asia. Some historians point to a Chinese presence in the Philippines in prehistory as evidenced by a local knowledge of terraced rice paddy farming. By the late 10th century, trade was well established between China and the Philippines, with exchange systems involving the archipelago from north to south. China bartered silk, pottery, tame buffalo, hardware and farm equipment against tortoiseshell, cotton, betel nuts, shark's fin, mother-of-pearl, wax and pearls from the Philippine islands. The display documenting this early history includes ancient Chinese maps and annals that mention this trading system. The gallery also showcases a Chinese sampan containing trade wares such as porcelain, gold, glass, beads and cloth.

The **Parian** section describes the first integrated involvement of the Chinese in the Philippine economy through several dioramas.

Three porcelain vessels
China | Northern Song dynasty, 960–1127 | H (largest ewer): 21.3 cm

All manufactured in South China's Guangdong province at the Xicun kiln, these 1,000-year-old ceramic ewers and bowl are three of many Sung wares in the collection. Found in the Philippines, they attest to the ancient, extensive and well-developed trade relations between China and the archipelago a millennium ago.

Postcard of a Binondo street
*Calle Santo Christo, Binondo, Manila |
Early 20th century*

By the 16th century, trade links between Spain, Mexico and the Philippines were well established and as the Spanish settled the Philippines, Chinese immigration (notably from Fujian and Canton) increased, the foreigners providing the backbone of the Spanish colonial economy. Though the Chinese were necessary as labourers, merchants and artisans, they were also distrusted by the Spanish and persecuted as a result. In 1582, in a bid to segregate the Christian colonists from the Chinese, the Spanish established the Parian, a Manila ghetto where non-Christian Chinese were confined outside the walls—'*extramuros*' as opposed to '*intramuros*'—of the Spanish city. However, Christian Chinese were allowed to live among the Spanish. In 1790, when the last Parian was destroyed, the Chinese were permitted to join the baptised Chinese in Binondo (Chinatown) and Santa Cruz.

The **Colonial Culture: Shared Hands** section features examples of early Filipino books printed by Chinese artisans. One of the Chinese immigrants' most significant contributions to Filipino culture was printing. The first three books printed in the colony, all of them catechisms, were printed by Keng Yong of Binondo in 1593, Chinese printing hugely facilitating the dissemination of Christianity in the colony. Chinese influence is also apparent in early Catholic icons, church decoration and vestments, many of the stone churches of this period having been built by Chinese artisans.

The next two sections involve politics and are among the museum's most interesting.
Emergence of the Chinese Community

illustrates the first stirrings of political cohesion within the Chinese community at the end of the 19th century. Despite many generations of Chinese participation in Philippine life, they continued to be persecuted, and as a result resisted by forming institutions for self-protection. Schools, hospitals, a cemetery and a Chinese Chamber of Commerce were founded, as were the first distinctly Chinese businesses (China Bank, for example). Again, dioramas document this transitional time in Chinese-Filipino history. **In Defense of Freedom** documents the leadership of the educated Chinese-Filipinos in their quest for reform and liberation from the colonial yoke at the end of the 19th century. The history of Jose Ignacio Paua, a fighter of purely Chinese origin who emerged as a key figure of the revolution, is also covered in some detail here.

Sari-Sari Store and **Tool Shed** shifts back to Chinese commercial practices in the mid-19th century by showing a diorama of a Chinese run *sari-sari*, the retail agent of the large *cabecilla* (wholesaler) of imported goods.

▲ **Epitonium Scalare**
Rare Philippine Shell Collection

The next two sections concern domestic material culture. The **Mestizo House – Sala** gallery documents the Chinese-Filipino house with its large public reception room visible from the street (a tradition that was adopted by the Filipinos), while the **Mestizo House – Bedroom and Kitchen** gallery shows through dioramas a Chinese interior with furniture made by famous Binondo Chinese cabinet maker Eduardo Ah Tay.

National Leaders of Chinese Descent highlights the contribution of Filipinos of Chinese origin to public life, thus suggesting that today's Chinese can be fully integrated within mainstream Filipino society. The **Gallery of Rare Prints and Photographs** mainly comprises images of Binondo, the centre of commerce at the end of the Spanish era up until the American period. **Martyrs Hall** documents Chinese participation in the

resistance to the Japanese during the occupation of World War II. **Porcelain Collection** features a group of Chinese ceramics dating from the 10th to the 17th century recovered exclusively from the Philippine archipelago.

Tsinoys in Nation Building is one of the museum's most recent galleries, a hologram display tracing the transformation of the early barefoot and illiterate peasant immigrant into today's Tsinoy, a special kind of Filipino of Chinese descent who combines the best of both cultures. The role of the Tsinoy in a variety of community projects and affairs is explored here.

The last gallery, unrelated to the museum's core theme but interesting too, is the **Rare Philippine Shell Collection**, with a wide array of indigenous seashells, including a number of extinct species of crustaceans.

Though a small museum, with its intelligently designed displays and ample explicative information, the Bahay Tsinoy provides the visitor with an insightful view of Philippine history from the Chinese perspective, with particular emphasis on the unique blending of two cultures over time. The Chinese diaspora in other parts of Southeast Asia has yet to be so well documented.

▲ **Coloured newspaper illustration**
Soirée Musicale at Manila from 'Sketches from Manilla and Hong Kong', The Illustrated London News | *19th century | approx. 15 x 10 cm*

ADDRESS
Bangko Sentral ng
Pilipinas Complex
Roxas Boulevard
Manila
The Philippines

CONTACT DETAILS
T: +63 2 523 7855 / 521 1517
F: +63 2 523 7855
E: art4all@info.com.ph

OPENING HOURS
10am–6pm Mon–Sat.

ADMISSION
Adult 50 pesos;
senior 40 pesos;
student 30 pesos.

FACILITIES
Art and architecture tours are
available upon request.

Pinoy Lab museum shop;
trendy museum restaurant;
parking available.

HOW TO GET THERE
The museum is near Pablo
Ocampo Street, diagonally
across from the Cultural
Center of the Philippines
(see pp. 106–107).

LRT: Quirino Station or Vito
Cruz Station.

Bus/Jeepney: On Taft Avenue
get off at Pablo Ocampo and
take the CCP orange shuttle
to the service road of Roxas
Boulevard. Take a walk down
the Boulevard towards
Luneta Park.

Metropolitan Museum of Manila

Recently focusing on Filipino contemporary art, the privately run Metropolitan Museum of Manila also presents 19th-century Filipino painting, pre-colonial and applied art, and international painting.

■ **THE BUILDING** Located in central Manila and housed on three floors of a purpose-built, brutalist structure with a streamlined façade completed in 1977 by architect Greg Zamora, the museum has an expansive state-of-the-art exhibition space for its very diverse permanent collections.

■ **THE COLLECTION** The Bangko Sentral ng Pilipinas (BSP) collection is one of the most wide-ranging collections of Philippine art in the world. Largely ascribed to the vision of

Dr Jaime C. Laya, governor of the Central Bank from 1981 to 1984, it is significant in the breadth of its holdings which include 19th- and 20th-century Filipino painting, furniture, pre-colonial gold and pottery, as well as foreign art.

The Filipino collection is particularly noteworthy for the presence of works by painters from provinces beyond Manila. Many lovers of Filipino art are familiar with the canvases of early Filipino pioneer artists such as Juan Luna and Felix Resurreccion Hidalgo. However, their provincial contemporaries, who often lacked formal art training and, unlike Luna and Hidalgo, did not travel abroad, are less well known. The BSP collection endeavours to correct this imbalance and presents paintings by Vincente Villasenor of Lucban and Tayabas, Pedro Ardena of Capiz, Juan Senson of Angono, and Pedro Salazar of Batangas, thus considerably expanding the geographical horizons of early Filipino paintings.

The collection is also unusual because of its interest in the work of 19th-century female artists such as Paz Paterno, whose still-lifes or *bodegones* are presented here.

The pre-colonial gold and pottery collections of the Bangko Sentral ng Pilipinas are also noteworthy. First begun in 1981 and initially comprising barter rings used as a means of exchange, the collection gradually expanded with significant discoveries from Samar, Batuan and Suriago—made during the construction of infrastructure in these areas. The trove, dated between the 10th

▲ **Gold belt**
Pre-colonial, 6th–11th century

▲ **Pottery burial jars**
c. 10th century

and the 13th century, remains shrouded in mystery and was possibly part of a king's treasure, hidden to keep it out of the Spanish conquerors' hands, or buried during a volcanic eruption.

One of the finest Suriago discoveries are the massive and intricately woven and decorated gold belts that attest to a high level of pre-colonial technical sophistication, belying standard notions that Filipino civilisation began with the Spanish conquest. The display also confirms the importance of gold in early Filipino societies where it was plentiful and hence widely owned. Despite its abundance, however, it was then, as it still is today, considered a status symbol of major significance. Finally, the role gold played in early Filipino burial practices is also explored here.

The pottery collection, dating even further back in time and also of importance, includes objects and vessels designated for both ritual and household use.

While the museum presents key pre-colonial material as well as significant oil paintings by the luminaries of the Philippines' 19th-century academic school, the highlight of the institution's core permanent collection are its extensive holdings of paintings and sculpture by mainly contemporary Filipino practitioners. Collected relatively recently, most of these works were acquired during the 1990s at a time of increased awareness of social issues. Internationally exposed Filipino artists such as Ben Cabrera (born 1942), Pablo Beanse Santos, Charlie Co, Pacita Abad, Julie Lluch and Ana Fer are but a few of the artists featured in this section. See in particular here a poignant 1995 portrait of Flor

Felix Resurreccion Hidalgo
Las Virgenes Cristianas Expuestas Al Populacho | Oil on canvas | 1884 | 115 x 157 cm

This allegorical work depicting innocent virgins being leered at by the crowd was painted by Hidalgo (1853-1913) at the height of his career. Hidalgo, who worked extensively in Europe and was in his day one of the Philippines' most successful and internationally-known artists, favoured romantic themes and an academic style even as Impressionism was taking hold in Europe.

Lippo Memmi
Altarpiece of Five Saints | Siena, Italy |
Gold and egg tempera on panel | 14th century |
220 x 200 cm

Contemplacion, the Filipina maid who made headlines around Southeast Asia in 1995 when she was hanged, convicted of the murder of another Filipina maid in Singapore. This picture by Cabrera, like so many by the current generation of Filipino artists, uses paint and canvas to underscore pressing socio-political issues (in this case the problems faced by unemployed Filipinos obliged to leave their country in search of work as domestic helpers in countries where they are unrepresented by the local legal system), relevant both at home and abroad.

The museum continues to expand as works are acquired and donated, its holdings including some foreign examples as well. These collections are rotated periodically according to exhibition themes.

■ **THE GALLERIES** Upon entering the museum from the street, the visitor ascends a broad staircase to the first-level entrance and lobby. To the right of the entrance is the well-stocked and trendy Pinoy Lab museum shop—one of Manila's better museum shops—and beyond the shop, the stylish museum café, decorated with contemporary art.

A library and auditorium are also housed on this floor, with the central part of the space presenting the expansive **Tall Galleries**, and opposite these, the **Galeriya Bangko Sentral ng Pilipinas**. The latter space features special thematic exhibitions organised around various aspects of the permanent collections.

The basement level, accessed via lift or staircase from the first floor, houses the museum's permanent collections in two large, rectangular galleries—the **Pre-Colonial Gold Gallery** at the rear, and the **Pre-Colonial Pottery Gallery** at the front. In these pleasantly hushed rooms visitors should look in particular for gold death masks from the 6th to 11th century that were used to cover the faces of the dead upon burial; boldly designed jewellery of the same period; and an intricately worked gold handle of a kris, also from this period.

The museum's upper level, connected to the first floor by an elegant, circular staircase, offers a large central space flanked at the rear by the **Galeriya Calma**, the **Galeriya Magsaysay-Ho** and the **Galeriya Luz**, and opposite, bordering the museum's façade, the long and narrow **Catwalk Galleries** where temporary exhibitions are staged. Varied in medium and subject, and international in flavour, past themes of loan exhibitions held in different museum spaces here include contemporary handmade art from Colombia, *The Turns of the Terno*, a show featuring the indigenous *terno* (the Philippines' full-skirted

▲ **Ana Fer** | *India and Ilustrada* | *Oil on canvas* | *1991* | *228.3 x 289.3 cm*

Pacita Abad
House of Incest | *Plastic beads, coral, cowry, buttons, broken glass, yarn and oil on canvas, stiched and padded* | *1991* | *134.78 x 177.8 cm*

Pacita Abad (b. 1946) has spent much of her career wandering the globe. Her flamboyant and abstract-leaning paintings and sewn fabric collages (known as 'Trapunto' and referring to women's craft art) are inspired by her keen interest in the peoples, societies and cultures she has encountered on her travels.

and puff-sleeved women's national dress) and its makers, 30 years of printmaking in France, and water in Khmer arts and life.

Less formally identified display areas include the intimate **Library Gallery**, the **Stairwell Gallery** for very large works, and the **Auditorium Hallway**.

With 'Art for All' as its tagline, the Metropolitan Museum of Manila is indeed engaging and dynamic in its educational approach. Intrepid about documenting the most divergent of art forms, periods, nationalities and aesthetics—where else might a museum-goer find showing at one time exhibitions about architecture, cars, sports, ancient gold and non-Filipino visual art?—the institution strives to encourage both curiosity and appreciation in its viewers. Showing strong and varied permanent collections along with a broad, international programme of temporary loan exhibitions, the museum's excellent presentation, labelling and state-of-the-art galleries will appeal to Filipinos

and foreigners alike while attesting to the astonishing wealth of Filipino cultural material through the ages.

▲ **Ben Cabrera**
Portrait: Flor Contemplacion | *Oil on canvas* | *1995* | *153.5 x 123 cm*

ADDRESS
Roxas Boulevard,
corner South Drive
Manila
The Philippines

CONTACT INFORMATION
T: +63 2 523 1797 / 8
F: +63 2 522 1246
E: mpfi@museopambata.org
W: www.museopambata.org

OPENING HOURS
9am–12pm, 1pm–5pm
Tue–Sat Apr–Jul;
8am–12.30pm, 1.30pm–5pm
Tue–Sat Aug–Mar;
1pm–5pm Sun;
closed on public holidays.

ADMISSION
Adult and child 60 pesos;
free for infants, street

children and Manila
residents (Tue).

FACILITIES
Wheelchair access.

Parking.

HOW TO GET THERE
By jeepney.

LRT: On the A. Mabini route,
alight at United Nations

Avenue and walk to
Roxas Boulevard.

AROUND THE MUSEUM
The museum faces Manila Bay
where people stroll and dine.
Just a few blocks away are
several museums.

Museo Pambata

Sandwiched between the US Embassy and the Quirino Grandstand, the Philippines' premier children's museum, Museo Pambata, offers both young and old a stimulating and educational experience through interactive, hands-on exhibits.

■ **THE BUILDING** Museo Pambata has been located in the Elks Club Building since its inception. This building, a historic Manila landmark dating to 1911, was built by American architect William Parsons on reclaimed land near Luneta, looking out over Manila Bay. Designed in typical American colonial style, the building was central to American expatriate community life in Manila until World War II. During the war, however, the building suffered extensive damage and had to be rebuilt in the late 1940s. Since then, it has remained similar in appearance with its elongated façade, large windows and shallow, overhanging eaves.

■ **THE HISTORY OF THE MUSEUM** Museo Pambata, a non-profit institution run by the private Museo Pambata Foundation, was the brainchild of Nina Lim-Yuson, an early childhood educator and mother of four. When visiting the Boston Children's Museum with her offspring, Lim-Yuson witnessed them learning and having fun. Sensitive to the great need of many

underpriviledged children in her own country, she decided to work towards providing them with a similar place and experience.

Faced with a country where many youngsters are deprived of a formal education and have no access to stimulating learning centres, the idea struck a chord with senior government officials. Endorsed by the former mayor of Manila, Alfredo Lim, and backed by prominent figures in business and the arts, the museum opened at the end of 1994.

■ **THE ROOMS** The museum has eight themed rooms that expose visitors to local and international topics through touch-and-play.

The **Kalikasan Room** explores the environment. Here, visitors can enjoy nature treks in a simulated rainforest and seabed and be inspired to protect the environment.

The **Maynila Noon Room** provides a glimpse of old Manila at the turn of the 19th century. Children are invited to put on clothing worn by their grandparents' generation, board a Spanish galleon, or step into a miniature cathedral and *bahay na bato* (stone house).

The **Bata sa Mundo Room** is dedicated to children in the global village. Here, visitors can view dolls in national costume and play with toys, indoor games and musical instruments from all over the world.

The **Tuklas Room** promotes science through discovery. Scientific principles behind daily occurences are illustrated and demonstrated here. A particular attraction in this gallery is a moon rock from the Apollo 11 expedition.

▲ *Heroes' Circle in the Old Manila Room.*

Other spaces include the **Paglaki Ko Room** which explores career options including broadcasting, theatre and sports; the **Craft Room**, where children can make art with recycled material and view works made and displayed by other visitors; the **Pamilihang Bayan Room**, a simulated market place where visitors can trade and bargain; and finally, the **Katawan Ko Room** which provides the opportunity to see and experience the workings of the human body. This last room is one of the most exciting, allowing visitors to find answers to their most common questions about the body through play. The hands-on exhibit, Miss Digestion, traces the digestive process by peeking through the throat and intestines.

A children's library, resource centre, multi-purpose hall, changing exhibition space, outdoor theatre and playground complete the list of facilities gracing the museum, while a bevy of ongoing outreach activities involving theatre, visual art and music ensure the museum is accessible to children of different social strata.

▲ *Under the Sea in the Kalikasan Room.*

ADDRESS
Ground Floor, National
Historical Institute Building
T.M. Kalaw Street
Ermita, Manila
The Philippines

CONTACT INFORMATION
T: +63 2 524 9952
F: +63 2 524 3181
E: info@nhi.gov.ph

W: www.nhi.gov.ph

OPENING HOURS
8.30am–12pm, 1pm–4.30pm
Tue–Sat;
closed on national holidays.

ADMISSION
Free. Donations are welcome.

HOW TO GET THERE
By jeepney or taxi.

LRT: On the A. Mabini route,
alight at United Nations
Avenue, walk to Roxas
Boulevard and cross over
into the Park.

AROUND THE MUSEUM
Nearby, in Rizal Park, is the
National Library.

Towards the east side of the
park is the National Museum

(see pp. 102–103), while the
Museo Pambata (see p. 99)
can be reached by crossing
Roxas Boulevard.

Manila City Hall is 10 minutes
away as is the contemporary
art space Kanlungan ng
Sining (see p. 192).

Museum of Philippine Political History

Housed on the ground floor of the Philippines' National Historical Institute in Manila, the Museum of Philippine Political History provides an excellent introduction to the country's quest for independence and nation-state-building.

■ **THE BUILDING** With its façade of columns and capitals, the four-storey building housing the Philippine Cultural Heritage Institute and the Museum of Philippine Political History appears to be of Spanish colonial origin at first glance. However, the institute, a government agency for promoting and preserving Philippine cultural heritage that oversees a number of the country's landmarks and historical museums, is in fact situated in a Classical Revival-style building of modern construction erected in 1993 by the architects of the state's Historic Preservation Division, led by architect Reynaldo Inovero. There are eight niches in the lower part of the building, each featuring a mural by a different local artist who has depicted a historically significant battle of the Spanish period.

With an area of 3,744 square metres spread over four floors, the building is well equipped to accommodate both the Museum of Philippine Political History on the ground floor and administrative space on the three levels above. The Museum of Philippine Political History occupies roughly 600 square metres of floor space.

■ **THE COLLECTION** Though small, the museum offers a telling panorama of the Philippines' complex political history. The institution's collection currently numbers 145 pieces—both original and reproduction—of which 30 key exhibits include original memorabilia of past presidents, pre-Hispanic swords and cannons, and documents.

▲ **Japanese instrument of surrender**
Signed by General Tomoyuki Yamashita, Baguio City, 3 September 1945

Garnered from the various monuments and historical landmarks administered by the institute, they and other supporting material have been chosen for their ability to relate, record and bring to life the country's political history, in a thematic manner. Some pieces such as the cannons and swords are on long-term loan from the National Museum (see pp. 102–103). Still seeking to expand and diversify its collection as it tracks Philippine political history in the making, the

museum accepts donations from various private and public sources.

■ **THE GALLERIES** The museum presents a single gallery documenting five distinct chapters particularly significant in Philippine political history, covering 5,000 years from pre-colonial times to the present.

The first chapter, **Bayan**, covers the pre-colonial *barangays* (municipal districts) up to the time of the reformists. Key pieces here include native swords such as the *barung* and *kris* as well as *lantakas* (small cannons). Facsimiles of *Noli Me Tangere* and *El Filibusterismo* (influential novels by Jose P. Rizal) are located here too. A sound and light presentation simulating a *pueblo* (village) completes this section.

The **La Liga Filipina, Katipunan, and First Philippine Republic** chapter covers the founding of La Liga Filipina, an association formed in the late 19th century to put forward ideas on political reform, the Kataas taasang Katipinan ng mga anak ng Bayan or Katipunan

General Luciano San Miguel's War Standard
With three blue four-pointed stars and inscribed 'Viva la Republica Filipina Viva!!!' | Early 20th century | 119 x 177 cm

This flag belonged to General Luciano San Miguel who was assigned to lead Filipino forces north of the Pasig River during the Filipino-American war of 1899 to 1913.

▲ **Ceremonial chest made to hold the 1935 constitution** | *Wood, metal and gold leaf* | *c. 1935* | *H:78 cm*

The fifth chapter, **People Power in Nation Building**, covers the administrations after Martial Law including those of President Corazon Aquino, Fidel V. Ramos, Joseph Ejercito Estrada and Gloria Macapagal-Arroyo. Through video, the two People Power revolutions of 1986 and 2001 are documented.

The museum regularly updates its displays as events unfold in the country. The latest event to be covered is the second EDSA Revolution in January 2001 which brought about the downfall of President Estrada and gave then Vice President Gloria Macapagal-Arroyo the presidency. The museum will extend its feature on President Arroyo once her term has ended in 2010.

Though the museum material can be perceived as complex, the gallery's presentation is designed to pull in and engage a broadly composed audience. Interactive computer programmes, a hologram of the freedom fighter Andres Bonifacio exhorting Filipinos to cherish liberty, touch-screen computers, light and sound shows, dioramas, and more conventional displays aid in the lively and compellingly didactic approach to historical interpretation and narration.

The only one of its kind in the country, the museum focuses on Filipino history from an indigenous point of view as it traces the evolution of the Filipino nation-state and the democratic traditions which have emerged from the nation's struggle for independence.

(1872), a nationalist organisation that aimed to boot out the Spanish, The Malolos Republic, and American Colonisation. Key exhibits here are facsimiles of Katipunan documents signed by the members with their own blood, pictures of the framers of the Malolos Constitution, the original flag of General Luciano San Miguel inscribed with *Viva La Republica Filipina Viva!!!*, and General Emilio Aguinaldo's *rayadillo* (war uniform) as well as his shoulder epaulettes. The display also features a life-size talking hologram of Andres Bonifacio in the Pamitinan Cave.

The third chapter, **The Nation Within a Colony**, covers the Commonwealth government led by President Manuel L. Quezon (1935–1944), the Japanese occupation with Jose P. Laurel as president, and Sergio Osmeña

(1944–1946). Visitors will see the massive Commonwealth seal made by Tiffany's N.Y., the ceremonial chest where the 1935 Constitution was kept, and the Japanese Instrument of Surrender signed by General Tomoyuki Yamashita in Baguio before his execution.

The fourth chapter, **The Nationhood of a Free People**, covers the period spanning 1946 to 1972. It features, among others, Presidents Manuel A. Roxas, Ramon F. Magsaysay, Diosdado P. Macapagal and Ferdinand E. Marcos. Displayed here are copies of campaign paraphernalia and video presentations of the achievements of the presidents, as well as the tumultuous days of Martial Law. Also found here are documents detailing the forming of the 1973 Constitution and a niche for the martyrs of Martial Law.

▲ **Bronze lantaka or native cannons**
c. mid-19ᵗʰ century | *L (longest lantaka): 91.5 cm*

ADDRESS
National Museum of the
Philippines (Main Building)
P. Burgos Street
Manila

The Museum of the
Filipino People
Agrifina Circle, Rizal Park
Manila
The Philippines

CONTACT INFORMATION
T/F: +63 2 527 0278 /
528 4912

OPENING HOURS
10am–4.30pm Tue–Sun.

ADMISSION
100 pesos;
free on Sun.

FACILITIES
Guided tours in English and
Tagalog are available.

HOW TO GET THERE
By taxi.

AROUND THE MUSEUMS
Rizal Park, the Planetarium
and the National Library are
all nearby.

National Museum of the Philippines

In two imposing colonial buildings, the National Museum of the Philippines and its sister institution, the National Museum of the Filipino People, offer a broadly focused collection of cultural and natural history material.

■ **THE BUILDING** Established in 1901 as an ethnography and natural history museum, the institution is housed in two buildings. The Old Congress Building, designed in 1918 by American architect Daniel Burnham, is now the museum's main building where the Arts, Natural Sciences and other support divisions are housed, while the former Finance Building in the Agrifina Circle of Rizal Park, across P. Burgos Street, now called the National Museum of the Filipino People, houses the national Anthropology and Archaeology Divisions.

The museum's administrative history is chequered. First called the Insular Museum of Ethnology, Natural History and Commerce, it then became the Philippine Museum in 1904, and in 1916 its Ethnology and Fine Arts Divisions merged with the National Library to create the Philippine Library and Museum, the Natural History Division remaining under the

Bureau of Science. After several changes to its name and administrative structure, the museum finally became independent in 1998 as the National Museum of the Philippines.

With its grandiose four-storey white-stone façade, elegant staircases, Doric columns and imposing scale, Daniel Burnham's state building makes no concessions either to the climate or the indigenous locale. Designed in a conventional neo-Classical style, it appears better suited to represent the lofty ideals of an executive office building rather than a public art museum. While the structure would not be out of place in Washington DC or London, the formal façade fronts a museum harbouring a collection within that does much to redeem the exterior rigidity of its premises.

■ **THE COLLECTION** Covering geology, zoology, botany, art, archaeology and anthropology, with sections devoted to education, conservation and the laboratory, the museum offers as complete a picture of the Philippines as a museum could. The foundations of the ethnological collection date back to the 1904 St Louis World's Fair when, as an American colony, the Philippines was keen to show the world visiting St Louis the best of her indigenous culture.

The museum's Anthropology Division is one of its most important and holds over 10,000 items in its material collection. The section documents and studies the Philippines' various ethno-linguistic groups and using its reference collection of

▲ **Detail of a Tausug headcloth**
Silk | Jolo, Sulu | Probably 19ᵗʰ century | L: 90 cm, W: 88 cm

Maitum anthropomorphic burial jar
Earthenware | c. 1ˢᵗ century | H: 70 cm, D: 36 cm

The anthropomorphic secondary burial jars from Pinol, Maitum, Saranggani Province in Mindanao date back to the Metal Age and with their naturalistic human facial features are exceptional. Other objects excavated with the jars include metal implements, glass beads and bracelets, shell ornaments and a spoon. Non-anthropomorphic burial jars in the collection display incised designs and cut-out foot-rings.

ethnological material, explores different aspects of indigenous ethnic culture. As well as boasting a particularly strong material collection, the division is an active protector of ethnic culture, conducting research and initiating activities geared towards the preservation of extant aspects of traditional culture such as vernacular architecture and boat building. Groups such as the Maranao, the Palawan, the Sama d'laut, the Subanen and the Ifugao are looked at specifically in terms of their traditions, and examples of their material culture illustrating these traditions are displayed.

The **Archaeology Division** examines the past through objects, ecofacts and ancient structures with a focus on the prehistory of the Philippines in relation to that of Southeast Asia as a whole. Both terrestrial and underwater archaeology are touched upon.

The **Botany Division** has made a systematic inventory of Philippine flora and vegetation and maintains the national herbarium which is the reference collection for plants found in this country. Currently the collection harbours about 170,000 specimens.

Permanent exhibition galleries feature, for example, pottery and other household articles from Southwest Philippine culture whereas the **Hiyas at Palamuti Gallery** shows personal ornaments (clothing and jewellery) from the prehistoric period to the present time.

The new National Museum of the Filipino People showcases, among others, two permanent archaeological exhibits, The Prehistory of the Philippines (Pinagmulan), and Archaeological Treasures (Kaban ng Lahi). The San Diego galleon is a long-term temporary exhibit.

The **Prehistory of the Philippines** gallery features prehistoric material focusing first on the geological formation of the archipelago, moving through subsequent periods and into the modern age, examining specifically the Age of Trade Goods, Luxury Goods (carnelian, jade and glass), Pottery, Asian Trade, the Butuan Boat, International Trade, conservation of underwater materials, a featured site—the

Terracotta Manunggul jar
Incised and polychromed | Palawan | 890–710 BCE | H: 66.5 cm

Found in Chamber A of Manunggul Cave in Palawan, this elaborately designed burial jar displays anthropomorphic figures on the cover that represent souls sailing to the afterworld in a death boat. The figure at the rear is holding a paddle with both hands while the front figure's hands are folded across his chest in a manner evoking corpse-arranging practice prevalent in the Philippines and Southeast Asia. The prow is carved to resemble a head with eyes, nose, and mouth. This motif is still found on traditional sea vessels of the Sulu Archipelago, North Borneo, Malaysia. The execution of the ears, eyes and nose bear similarities with the contemporary woodcarvings of Taiwan, the Philippines, and many areas of Southeast Asia. The Manunggul jar is a National Treasure and is depicted on the Philippine 1,000 peso bill.

Batanes Archaeological Project—and ending with general archaeology.

The **Archaeological Treasures** display includes some of the museum's most important cultural objects and works of art. See in particular the Maitum anthropomorphic potteries, the Manunggul jar, Leta-leta potteries from Palawan, limestone urns from Kulaman Plateau, Cotabato, and a number of early gold artefacts. The latter include gold ornaments from the Central Bank of the Philippines collection such as the Bolinao, Pangasinan gold teeth peggings, a nose disc and gold eye

mask retrieved from an open burial site in Barangay San Antonio, Central Philippines dating from the late 14th or early 15th century as well as gold artefacts from underwater archaeological sites. These facial orifice coverings are delicately worked sheets of gold used to cover the eyes, nose, and mouth of the dead. The Southern Chinese and a limited group of Filipinos practised this burial custom which persisted through the early Spanish era.

Vast and filled with treasures, the National Museum of the Philippines, in its period buildings, should not be missed.

ADDRESS
Grand Hall, Mezzanine,
UST Main Building
Espana, Manila
The Philippines

CONTACT INFORMATION
T: +63 2 781 1815
F: +63 2 740 9718
E: museum@ust.edu.ph
W: www.ustmuseum.org

OPENING HOURS
9am–4.30pm Tue–Fri;
Saturday viewing by prior
arrangement, and visits must
be booked three days ahead.

ADMISSION
Adult 30 pesos;
student 20 pesos;
free for UST students.

FACILITIES
Souvenir shop; library;
conservation laboratory;
ample parking.

HOW TO GET THERE
By jeepney.

Bus: Look for buses that
display 'UST' or 'DAPITAN'.

LRT: Alight at Legarda Station
and hop onto a jeepney.

AROUND THE MUSEUM
There are plenty of shops
and restaurants in the
neighbourhood around the
university campus.

University of Santo Tomas Museum of Arts and Science

Housed in the Philippines' oldest university, the Museum of Arts and Sciences' collection of natural history, ethnographic and religious material is nearly as ancient as the University of Santo Tomas itself

■ **THE BUILDING AND THE UNIVERSITY** Both the institution and the building where it is housed are rich in history.

The University of Santo Tomas (UST) was founded in 1611 by two Fathers and the third Archbishop of Manila, Msgr Miguel de Benavides, OP. The oldest existing university in Asia, it is also the largest Catholic university in the world located on one campus. Originally named Colegio de Nuestra Señora del Santisimo Rosario, it was renamed Colegio de Santo Tomas in memory of St Thomas Aquinas and in 1645 was elevated to the rank of university by Pope Innocent X. Since its foundation, the university's academic life has been interrupted only twice, from 1898 to 1899 during the Philippine revolution, and from 1942 to 1945 during the Japanese occupation of Manila when the institution was used by the Japanese as an internment camp for American and foreign civilians.

Originally located in Intramuros, the university's campus moved beyond Manila's walls in the first quarter of the 20th century.

The UST Museum of Arts and Sciences, the oldest museum in the country, is located within the university at the centre of the leafy campus. The Main Building was the first structure of the new campus to be designed in the then prevailing Art Deco style by Fr Roque Ruano, OP, an engineer and the university's Dean of the Faculty of Engineering from 1923 to 1927. Of hybrid style, the stone Main Building blends Art Deco features such as geometric angularity and a flat linear façade with Classical-genre mouldings, swags and column-like elements. Ornamentation in the form of 15 realistically carved statues of figures of religious and historical importance by Italian sculptor Francesco Monti (1888–1958) surmount the façade. The Main Building is further dominated by a nine-storey tower topped by a concrete cross which has long been a dominant feature of the Manila skyline.

▲ **Chinese porcelain dish**
*Underglaze blue | Ming dynasty,
16th century | D: 20.5 cm*

■ **THE COLLECTION** The collection dates back to 1682 when it was contained in what was referred to then as the 'Gabinete Fisica', the room where the university's medical students pursued their biological, zoological and other scientific studies.

The museum as an institution was born in 1871 when natural history professor Fr Ramon Martinez Vigil, OP began systematically cataloguing the collections. Originally on the Intramuros site within the confines of the university, the UST museum was later transferred to its present site in Sampaloc.

The permanent collection includes natural history, ethnological and Philippine religious

▲ *Seashells from the Natural History and Archaeological section.*

▲ **Bas relief of St Thomas Aquinas, the university's patron**
Recovered from the library at Intramuros | Carved polychrome wood | 17th–18th century | 105 x 77 cm

material as well as coins, medals and memorabilia, Oriental objects (ceramics in particular), and painting from the 16th to the 20th century.

■ **THE GALLERIES** On two levels, the airy mezzanine-style UST museum exhibition space is of long, rectangular plan with its galleries repeating the oblong configuration on opposite sides.

Passing the registration desk and beyond the small souvenir shop on the left is the **Hall of Philippine Religious Images**. One of the most significant collections of religious work in the country, it assembles mainly three-dimensional icons of different periods from around the country as well as some brought to the Philippines by the Spanish in the 16th century. Displayed soberly in niches on the sides of the long gallery, the sculptures document the Philippines' various phases of religious history as well as stylistic and

aesthetic developments from province to province over the centuries.

At the centre and rear of the gallery are the museum's **Natural History and Archaeological** holdings, the oldest part of the collection and probably its most impressive. Two displays on the left show indigenous birds while opposite, on the right-hand side, are cases devoted to seashells. Two very long and narrow displays, running the length of the gallery on opposite sides, focus on Philippine animals. Specimens, fossils, minerals and corals are also shown, while at the back of the gallery a well-made diorama of selected Philippine fauna is featured. Because many of the animals represented are either endangered or extinct, the collection is of significant value to scientists and students.

On the far right of the room is a long hall housing the **Gallery of Painting** where religious canvases by early Spanish and Filipino artists are shown as well as works by more familiar 20th-century painters such as Fernando Amorsolo, Carlos Francisco, Vicente Manansala and Galo Ocampo.

The museum's upper level is somewhat more compact than its ground floor. Here, **Oriental Arts** are represented on the gallery's left side, the collection including pre-colonial ceramics from China and Southeast Asia. While the majority of the vessels are Chinese, wares from Japan, Thailand and Vietnam are also featured. Though not a dauntingly large collection, it aptly records the well-developed trade links between the Philippines and the rest of Asia before the arrival of the Spanish.

Coins, Medals and Memorabilia is a small, mixed display at the back of the gallery. Of particular interest in this gallery are the antique coins from as far away as Rome and Greece.

Ethnography is located on the right side and includes a good selection of indigenous cultural material such as ceramics, burial jars,

▲ **Glazed earthenware jar**
Probably Vietnamese | 17th century | H: 38.4 cm

household wares, tribal musical instruments (at the front, right of the gallery), weapons and metalware. Finally, a wooden replica of the oldest locally made printing press in the country is presented opposite the musical instruments on the left.

As well as the permanent galleries, temporary thematic exhibitions are organised by the museum throughout the year.

Above the exhibition space on the third floor are the museum's conservation laboratory and a small research library.

One of the Philippines' most distinguished small private museums, the UST Museum of Arts and Sciences offers an eclectic but attractive mix of cultural and natural material in a pleasant setting.

Pablo Amorsolo
Fruit Vendor | Oil on board | Late 1930s | 45 x 32 cm

Pablo Amorsolo (1898–1972) was the brother of the more famous Fernando Amorsolo and the nephew and pupil of Fabian de la Rosa, the well-known, early 20th-century academic master. Though he was an exponent of Modernism, steering clear of Romantic idealisation, Pablo Amorsolo's style remained classical, one of his themes being local people at work.

ADDRESS
CCP Complex
Roxas Boulevard
Pasay City, Metro Manila
The Philippines

CONTACT DETAILS
T: +63 2 832 5094 / 3702
F: +63 2 832 3702 / 3674
E: museo@culturalcenter.
gov.ph

W: www.culturalcenter.gov.ph

OPENING HOURS
10am–6pm Tue–Sun;
10am–10pm on performance
evenings.

ADMISSION
Galleries: Free.

Museum guided tours:
professional 40 pesos;

student with ID 30 pesos.

Museum walk-in visits:
professional 30 pesos;
student with ID 20 pesos.

FACILITIES
Wheelchair access.

Guided tours are available in
English and Tagalog.

Library; gift shop.

HOW TO GET THERE
MRT: From EDSA Metrorail
Station, get off at Taft Avenue.

LRT: Alight at Vito Cruz Station.
Orange shuttle jeepneys will
take you to the CCP Complex.

AROUND THE MUSEUM
The Metropolitan Museum
of Manila (see pp. 96–98)
is nearby.

Cultural Center of the Philippines

One of the Philippines' most dynamic and progressive public art institutions, the Cultural Center of the Philippines (CCP) offers a comprehensive view of modern and contemporary Filipino culture through both the visual and performing arts.

■ **THE BUILDING** The CCP's purpose-built exhibitions and performance building was designed in the mid-1960s by national architect Leandro V. Locsin, responsible for a number of distinguished cultural buildings in the Philippines. Inaugurated in 1969, the stunningly spare brutalist CCP main building is set on reclaimed land in a sprawling 21-hectare park and with the site's other structures, collectively known as 'The CCP Complex', enjoys a unique view of Manila Bay to the west. Comprising a main building with three theatre facilities, the Main, Little and Experimental Theaters (known for the excellence of their acoustics), the CCP also houses the Main and Small Galleries as well as

a number of hallways and niches used as temporary exhibition spaces.

The Museo ng Kalinangang Pilipino (Museum of Philippine Humanities) is yet another art venue, established in 1988 as part of developments after the EDSA Revolution that toppled the Marcos regime. The new museum aims 'to highlight and provide a deeper understanding of Filipino creativity and aesthetic expression within the perspective of a national culture evolving with and for the nation'.

The complex also includes the Coconut Palace (see p. 192), the Philippine International Convention Center, the Product Design and Development Center, the Folk Arts

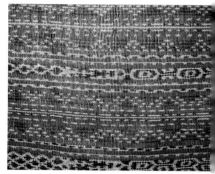

▲ **Detail of a *tabi* (tubular garment)**
B'laan group of Davao Del Sur, South Central Mindanao | Abaca and natural dyes | First half of 20th century | Whole piece L: 250.5 cm, W: 164.5 cm

Theater, the Manila Film Center and the Philippine Center for Trade and Exhibitions.

■ **THE COLLECTION** Though housing a substantial permanent collection, the CCP—more than a static museum focusing only on historical works—as a non-commercial venue for the temporary exhibition of experimental and multidisciplinary pieces, is a dynamic institution constantly investigating the new. Thus, as a non-commercial bell-wether for new forms and ideas, the CCP has become a launching pad enabling Filipino artists to enter the international forum at the highest level. The CCP also plays an important role as an implementing agency for cultural programmes and agreements between the Philippines and other countries, thus ensuring the exposure of young Filipino artists abroad, while bringing foreign talent to local audiences.

Victorio Edades
The Builders | Oil on plywood | 1928 | 119.5 x 320 cm

Victorio Edades' (1895-1985) long life straddled his country's firmly rooted academic tradition and its post-war Modernist surge. His seminal work, *The Builders*, painted after a nine-year stint in America, is a pioneer Modernist work. Exhibiting the dark palette of Philippine academism, it also presents a dynamic Modernist composition and form that shocked the Filipino public of the day.

The CCP Visual Arts Unit is responsible for the care and management of the CCP Visual Arts Collection. Its strength lies in its holdings of visual expression from the 1970s and 1980s. The works were obtained through bequests made by artists and patrons and by acquisitions made by the CCP and the former Museum of Philippine Art (MOPA, 1977–1985). The sum of the CCP and MOPA holdings adds up to almost 1,000 pieces comprising painting, sculpture, prints and photographs.

Among the significant pieces in the collection are works by Filipino masters and National Artists who represented the avant garde of Filipino Modernism. Painters such as Arturo Luz, Vicente Manansala, Jose Joya and Victorio Edades are included here, among many others.

The CCP Museo Unit showcases the CCP Ethnological Collection consisting of tribal textiles, weapons, ritual paraphernalia, personal ornaments, household items and musical instruments of Asia (mostly gifts presented to former First Lady Imelda Marcos from the early 1970s to the 1980s by the governments of India, Indonesia, China, Thailand and Japan). Philippine and Korean examples of instruments are of more recent acquisition. This collection, housed in the Museo ng Kalinangang Pilipino, holds approximately 1,000 artefacts.

▲ **Vincente Manansala** | *Mother and Child* | *Oil on canvas* | *1966* | *65 x 83.8 cm*

■ **THE GALLERIES** Six CCP spaces of varying size and configuration are devoted to temporary exhibitions of contemporary practice, with the **Bulwagang Juan Luna**, the CCP's third floor **Main Gallery**, being the largest with 440 square metres. An average of 20 contemporary art exhibitions in differing media are held over a regular 12-month period. Past exhibitions include *Traditions of Personal Ornamentation* and *Circles in My Mind*, featuring Pacita Abad's work on paper from 2004.

With its permanent collection featuring works by the Philippines' most important and influential exponents of Modernism and a constantly changing menu of exhibitions in its galleries and hallways, Manila's Cultural Center of the Philippines is one of the capital's most compelling contemporary art venues.

▲ **Jose Joya** | *Dimension of Fear* | *Oil on canvas* | *1965* | *101 x 298 cm*

ADDRESS
Ground Floor,
Benpres Building
Exchange Road,
corner Meralco Avenue
Pasig City, Metro Manila
The Philippines

CONTACT DETAILS
T/F: +63 2 631 2417
E: pezseum@skyinet.net

W: www.lopezmuseum.org.ph

OPENING HOURS
8am–5pm Mon–Sat.

ADMISSION
Adult 70 pesos;
student 60 pesos;
child 50 pesos.

FACILITIES
Guided tours are available.

Library containing material on
Philippine history and culture;
museum shop.

Changing exhibitions; lectures
and workshops.

HOW TO GET THERE
MRT: Alight at Shaw Station,
and walk towards EDSA
Central. Take a jeepney or FX
going to Antipolo, Angono or

Binangonan and alight at
Benpres Building.

Bus: Alight at Crossing. Take a
jeepney or FX going to Antipolo,
Angono or Binangonan and
alight at Benpres Building.

AROUND THE MUSEUM
There are several shopping
malls in the vicinity of
the museum.

Lopez Memorial Museum

The crowning philanthropic achievement of the industrialist Lopez family of Manila, the Lopez Memorial Museum is one of the most important private collections of indigenous 19ᵗʰ-century paintings in the Philippines.

■ **THE BUILDING** The Lopez Memorial Museum was founded in 1960 by Eugenio Lopez Sr in honour of his parents Benito Lopez and Presentacion Hofilena. Formerly located in Pasay City in a four-storey building (now demolished) designed by architect Angel Nakpil, the Lopez Memorial Museum moved to the Benpres Building (formerly the Chronicle Building) in Pasig in the 1980s. The museum is on the ground floor of this six-storey building which is near the Philippine Stock Exchange in Pasig City. Of note as one enters the museum is the broad wooden door sculpted by Modernist artist Napoleon Abueva.

■ **THE COLLECTION** The museum's collection of fine art, maps, archaeological artefacts, manuscripts and Filipiniana books was assembled from the personal holdings of Eugenio Lopez Sr and is considered one of the finest of its type in the country. With over 16,000 Filipiniana titles by 12,000 authors as well as rare books, manuscripts and literary works in various languages acquired from the best antiquarian booksellers in Europe and America, the collection is so distinguished that of the only 215 Philippine imprints published from 1597 to 1800 in Manila and other Filipino towns, the Lopez Museum has impressively managed to acquire as many as 21 titles.

Better known internationally, however, is the outstanding fine art section of the collection which was built up progressively as different series of works were added to the original nucleus amassed by Eugenio Lopez. This core section includes works by the celebrated 19ᵗʰ-century Philippine masters Juan Luna (1857–1899) and Felix Resurreccion Hidalgo (1853–1913) as well paintings by the later 20ᵗʰ-century master of light, National Artist Fernando Amorsolo (1892–1972). The museum now holds an unrivalled number of paintings by Luna, Hidalgo and Amorsolo, the latter constituting the anchor of its collection. Among the 38 works by Luna, see in

▲ **Felix Resurreccion Hidalgo**
En El Jardin | *Oil on board* | *1885* | *25.4 x 20.32 cm*

particular the historically important allegorical *Espana y Filipinas* of 1886 and the atmospheric *Ensuenos de Amor* of 1887, a portrait of the artist's wife Paz as she lies sleeping. A third painting by Luna, *Street Flower Vendors,* is also of interest as it commemorates the Paris funeral of the French 19ᵗʰ-century novelist Victor Hugo, the writer's funeral cortege faintly visible in the canvas' background. Of the formidable 182 works by Hidalgo in the collection, see in particular two oil studies for *La Barca de Aqueronte*, considered to be one of the artist's key masterpieces, as well as the lyrical *En El Jardin*, painted in 1885. The prolific Amorsolo, well known for his bucolic rural scenes featuring buxom maidens

▲ **Juan Luna**
Street Flower Vendors | *Oil on canvas* | *1885* | *78 x 43.3 cm*

bearing mangoes, is also represented here with the historically significant 1942 oil *Burning of the Intendencia*.

A second layer was added to the holdings when Eugenio Lopez's son Robbie Lopez, who had also been a keen collector but unlike his father, had focused instead on Modernist work, left his own collection of 45 paintings to the museum upon his death in 1992.

Since 1995, as decided by the late Eugenio Lopez, the museum has embarked upon an acquisition programme designed to 'strengthen and round out the collection'. The museum's aim is to eventually assemble a collection that covers the full length and breadth of Filipino pictorial art history with Luna and Hidalgo's works figuring as a historical starting point.

Thus, the 20th-century art acquired during the last decade to fill the collection's gaps includes paintings by Ray Albano, represented by *Uva* of 1982 and *Where Will You Be Today* of 1979, H.R. Ocampo, Cesar Legaspi with his early work of 1949 entitled *Idol*, Arturo Luz, represented by the work *Trumpeters*, and J. Elizalde Navarro, whose 1975 hanging wood found-object sculpture is featured. The collection also boasts a number of paintings by pioneer Modernists Fernando Zóbel and Ang Kiukok. See Zóbel's 1961 *La Vision* as well as his sophisticated 1967 oil *Dialogue with a Sketch by P.P. Rubens*. Finally the Chinese-

Anita Magsaysay-Ho
In the Marketplace | Egg tempera on board | 1955 | 58 x 76 cm

Anita Magsaysay-Ho, born in 1914, is one of the Philippines' pioneer Modernists, among a handful of exponents who developed a new fully Filipino artistic language in the mid-20th century. Magsaysay-Ho's work, though changing formally over the years, is generally characterised by her depiction of animated Filipina women in market place or rural settings.

▲ **Fernando Zóbel de Ayala**
La Vision | Oil on canvas | 1961 | 165 x 203 cm

Filipino artist Ang Kiukok is represented by his stunning *Seated Figure* of 1977.

Works by Carlos Francisco, Vicente Manansala, Nena Saguil, Juvenal Sanso, Romeo Tabuena, Anita Magsaysay-Ho and Jose Joya, among many others, are also shown.

A small collection of archaeological artefacts including blue and white ceramic ware, earthenware vessels and jewellery recovered from various burial sites in Calatagan, Batangas, in the Southern Tagalog region is also on view.

The museum boasts a strong programme of internally researched, thematic temporary exhibitions, holding two to three different shows every year. An example of a well-received specialist exhibition is the 2002 presentation of works by Juan Luna and Felix Resurreccion Hidalgo executed during their stay in 19th-century Paris around the time

when both were gaining exposure in Europe, having won acclaim at the 1884 *Exposicion General de Bellas Artes in Madrid*. Part of a tri-museum collaboration entitled *Zero In*, the following year's show had the Lopez Museum focusing on works done by other expatriate Filipino artists. Further exhibitions have featured a wide collection of maps, a show about collectors and their collections, and projects relating to and by contemporary Filipino artists. The Lopez Memorial Museum is also one of the first museums in the Philippines to have invited local artists working with video media to show their work in a museum setting.

Neither bibliophiles nor followers of Southeast Asian art history should miss Metro Manila's Lopez Memorial Museum which is considered one of the finest of the Philippines' small and privately established collections.

ADDRESS
Ground Floor, Rizal Library
Ateneo de Manila University
Loyola Heights
Quezon City, Metro Manila,
The Philippines

CONTACT DETAILS
T: +63 2 426 6001 ext 4160
F: +63 2 426 6488
W: http://decode.ateneo.edu

OPENING HOURS
8am—12pm, 1pm—5pm
Mon—Fri;
8am—12pm Sat.

ADMISSION
Free.

FACILITIES
Guided tours are available by
booked request.

Exhibition catalogues for sale.

HOW TO GET THERE
MRT: From Makati Business
District, take MRT 3 to Cubao
Station. Transfer to MRT 2 and
alight at Katipunan Station.
Walk or take a jeepney to the
University of the Philippines.
Along Katipunan Avenue,
alight at Gate 3 of Ateneo
University. The gallery is in
the first building on your left.

LRT: From Quiapo, take LRT 1
and alight at EDSA Station.
Transfer to MRT 3, alight at
Cubao and follow the same
route as above.

AROUND THE MUSEUM
Restaurants abound along
Katipunan Avenue.

Ateneo Art Gallery

The Ateneo Art Gallery, situated on the ground floor of the Rizal Library on the campus of Manila's private Ateneo de Manila University, is the country's first museum of modern Philippine art.

▪ **THE BUILDING** First housed in Bellarmine Hall in 1961, the museum moved to its present location in 1967 and has remained there ever since. As part of the well-established Ateneo de Manila University, itself founded in 1859, the gallery benefits from the university's pleasant and leafy 33-hectare campus. The Rizal Library, built by local architect Jesus Bondoc in typical 1960s International Style, is a three-storey structure, with the gallery on its ground floor.

▪ **THE COLLECTION** The Ateneo Art Gallery holds close to 600 works including paintings, prints, drawings, sculpture, photographs and posters. Though not huge, the collection is recognised as one of the country's most important, documenting pioneer Filipino Modernism of the post-World War II period.

The Ateneo's principal patron was Fernando Zóbel de Ayala (1924–1984), an art scholar, teacher and collector, as well as one of the Philippines' most recognised Modernist painters. Over the course of several years Zóbel donated some 200 works on paper and canvas to the university gallery to form a study collection for the university's students, thus institutionalising Modern art in the Philippines. Most of these works form the core of the Ateneo's Modern Philippine Art Collection.

Including some paintings by an earlier generation of academic painters such as Fabian de la Rosa and Fernando Amorsolo, the Zóbel bequest principally concentrated on key post-war Modernists who, moving away from Classical Eurocentric artistic language, were

▲ **David Cortez Medalla**
My Sister at the Sewing Machine | Mixed media | 1956 | 92 x 61 cm | Gift of Fernando Zóbel

the first generation of artists to truly institute an indigenous Filipino vernacular, both in their style and concerns.

Most of these pioneer artists had been involved in the legendary Philippine Art Gallery, known locally as PAG. The PAG, a crucial player in post-war Filipino art history, was founded in 1951. The first real art gallery in the country, the PAG was, during the 1950s, the only exhibition venue for Modern visual expression and was instrumental in the acceptance of Modern art in a country dominated until then by a strong Classical art tradition. Both Abstraction and Cubism were first shown at the PAG, and Zóbel,

a member of the PAG group, acquired much of his Philippine art there.

Today, the collection holds some of the finest works by these pioneer artists, including Vicente Manansala, Hernando R. Ocampo, Arturo Luz, Cesar Legaspi, Jose Joya, David Cortez Medalla, Anita Magsaysay-Ho, Lee Aguinaldo and Ang Kiukok, as well as 37 of Fernando Zóbel's own works—nine oil paintings, 21 prints and three drawings.

The original Zóbel bequest, initially a modest study collection, has expanded over the years to become a national cultural resource of importance, accessible to the general public and incorporating much art beyond the pioneer years.

The Ateneo also boasts a small but broad **Prints and Drawings Collection**, the core of which came from Fernando Zóbel's bequest and the rest from artists' and collectors' donations. Works from this part of the collection consist of over 200 etchings, engravings, woodcuts, lithographs and other graphic arts media by local and international masters from the Renaissance to the 21st century. Considered one of the finest collections in Southeast Asia, it includes prints and drawings by Rembrandt van Rijn, Francisco Goya, Eugène Delacroix, Henri Toulouse-Lautrec, Pablo Picasso, Edouard Manet, Oscar Kokoschka and Käthe Kollwitz. A number of American artists are also represented, among others Ben Shahn, Chaime Koppelman, Varujan Boghosian and Leonard Baskin. Asian practitioners figure here as well, including Juvenal Sanso, Virgillio Aviado, Filemon de la Cruz, Cheung Yee (China), Masaji Yoshida (Japan), Sugai (Japan) and the Philippines' father of modern print-making, Manuel Rodriguez Sr.

The third part of the collection focuses on **Contemporary Philippine Art**, works produced from the 1960s to the present day. All modern movements, from neo-Realism and Abstract Expressionism of the 1950s and 1960s, to Social Realism of the 1970s and 1980s, to today's post-Modern hybrid mix, are surveyed here.

Finally, the gallery also holds important sculpture, with many leading Filipino sculptors represented. Among key works are National Artist Arturo Luz's first sculpture, *Kristo*, of 1952, and National Artist Napoleon Abueva's *Judas Kiss* of 1955, both carved from adobe, a local limestone. Of the more recent works, Julie Lluch's large, exuberant and feminist consciousness-raising terracotta *A House on Fire* of 1991 stands out. Other sculptors represented are Abdulmari Imao, Lamberto Hechanova, Eduardo Castrillo, Ros Arcilla, Ramon

▲ **Fernando Zóbel de Ayala**
Carroza | Polymer on plywood | 1953 | 119 x 59.5 cm | Gift of the artist

Vicente Manansala
Jeepneys | Enamel on panel | 1951 | 51 x 59 cm | Gift of Fernando Zóbel

Jeepneys is one of Modernist painter Vicente Manansala's (1910–1981) best-known works. Depicting the Philippines' ubiquitous open-air public utility vehicles jammed together in Manila traffic, all dust, heat and sweat, this small work is considered a seminal Modernist Filipino painting for its unromanticised evocation of the bustle and grime of street life in the metropolis. Formally, too, the work moves away from the conventional and idealised aesthetics of academism, and with its frieze-like composition and acidic palette contributed to the early stages of the development of a new Filipino artistic language.

Orlina, Impy Pilapil, Egai Fernandez, Jose Tence Ruiz, Junyee and USA-based Ben Gonzales.

Protest icons from the last two decades, familiar to those close to the Filipino democracy movement, can also be seen at the Ateneo Gallery. Among others, Pablo Baens Santos' *Krista* of 1984, closely associated with the Martial Law and post-Martial Law periods, Imelda Cajipe-Endaya's *Bintana ni Momoy* of 1983, Lazaro Soriano's *Jack en Poy* of 1987, a satirical statement on the First People Power Revolution, and Anna Fer's lyrical watercolour *Green Orchid* of 1996 are noteworthy.

■ **THE GALLERIES** With roughly 500 square metres of exhibition space spanning three galleries, the museum is not overwhelming, rotating its collection regularly according to exhibition themes. The **Main Gallery**, divided into three sections, houses a changing display of works as well as large sculptures. The **Inner Gallery**, devoted to prints and drawings, is half the size of the Big Gallery, while the **New Gallery** is just a little smaller than the previous one. The museum's three galleries are either combined for a single exhibition, or sometimes used individually for three smaller shows running in tandem. As well as its excellent core collection, the Ateneo often borrows seminal works from other Filipino institutions, together initiating scholarly surveys.

With its broadly reaching and ambitious exhibition calendar, and one of the Philippines' most stimulating core collections of modern art, Metro Manila's Ateneo Art Gallery is one space not be missed.

ADDRESS
Roxas Avenue
University of the Philippines
Diliman, Quezon City
Metro Manila
The Philippines

CONTACT INFORMATION
T: +63 2 928 1927
F: +63 2 928 1925
E: vargas.museum@up.edu.ph

W: www.vargasmuseum.org

OPENING HOURS
8.30am–4.30pm Tue, Thu–Sun;
8.30am–7.30pm Wed;
closed on Mon.

ADMISSION
20 pesos;
free on Wed.

FACILITIES
Guided tours are available
(call to make a booking).

HOW TO GET THERE
By UP campus jeep or taxi.

Jeepney: From
Commonwealth Avenue, get
off at Philcoa and then take a
UP campus jeep.

AROUND THE MUSEUM
Visitors taking a walk around
the campus will enjoy
sculpture, a bonsai garden
and lagoon.

Almost all buildings on
campus have a restaurant or
café open during office hours.

Jorge B. Vargas Museum & Filipiniana Research Cente

Among the memorabilia, stamps and coins at the Vargas Museum is a unique collection of paintings, sculpture and drawings that tracks Philippine artistic achievement from the 1880s to the 1960s.

▪ **THE BUILDING AND SITE** The rationally Modernist three-storey building was designed by government architects from the Department of Public Works and Highways. It offers 3,600 square metres of space devoted to galleries, activity areas, public facilities and offices. The University of the Philippines itself was established in 1908 while the Diliman Campus, where the Vargas Museum is located, was founded in 1948. The University of the Philippines has a long and historic association with the fine arts. One of the Philippines' most distinguished painters, Fabian de la Rosa, was named the first Filipino dean of the former University of the Philippines School of Fine Arts in 1926.

The 400-hectare Diliman Campus is an art destination in itself, with its public sculpture, buildings and parks. Note sculptures by Ildefonso Marcelo, Guillermo Tolentino and Napoleon Abueva lining the walkways of University Avenue and around the University Oval. Tolentino's larger-than-life sculpture, *Oblation*, figures as the University's emblem. On the north side of the campus is the 1955 Roman Catholic chapel designed by National Artist for Architecture Leandro V. Locsin. Other National Artists are also associated with the chapel: Napoleon Abueva created the wooden cross at the centre altar, Vicente Manansala painted the mural-sized *Stations of the Cross*, and Arturo Luz designed the floor of the aisles. Many more sculptures and paintings can be found dotted around the university grounds.

Another campus landmark is the almost 40-metre-high University Carillon. Designed by Felipe de Jesus Nakpil, it is the tallest structure on campus. The Carillon plays twice daily, in the morning and afternoon, breaking the silence of the otherwise peaceful university compound. The Sunken Garden, Amphitheatre and Lagoon, all lined with trees and landscaped lawns, provide open spaces ideal for rest and contemplation.

▪ **THE COLLECTION** Jorge B. Vargas (1890–1980) was the Philippines' first Executive Secretary during the Commonwealth period (1935–1941) and also served as the Mayor of Manila in 1942. He donated his personal papers, memorabilia of public office, and collections of stamps, coins, books and art to his alma mater, the University of the Philippines, in 1978. A museum housing Vargas's extensive collection was opened in 1987.

The Vargas Museum's Library and Archives enclose a rich collection of Filipiniana archival material, manuscripts, papers, rare books, journals, photographs, scrapbooks and magazines relating to 19th- and 20th-century history for general and specialist reference. Having served in various government posts, Vargas's personal papers and archival material constitute a unique and primary source of historical information for the American colonial period, the Commonwealth era, and the Japanese occupation. Moreover, Vargas's personal archives shed the appropriate contextual light on the museum's art collection and Vargas as a collector. Much of the memorabilia are currently exhibited in the

▲ **Fernando Cueto Amorsolo** | *Harvest Scene* | *Oil on plywood* | *1942* | *90.2 x 182.9 cm*

museum's basement. One of the most notable pieces here is the unpublished manuscript of Vargas's *Sugamo Prison Diary*, recounting the author's internment at a detention camp outside Tokyo at the end of World War II. His diary sheds light on life as a prisoner-of-war and events occurring between December 1945 and July 1946.

More interesting to the foreign visitor without a specialist interest, however, is the collection of fine art documenting one of the Philippines' most important and seminal periods of development in art history. Vargas's art collection began with the painting *Village Woman with a Bundle of Hay* by 19th-century Filipino artist Felix Resurreccion Hidalgo. Presented as a birthday present to him by a group of his friends, the gift inspired him to collect Philippine art. Though only a third of the holdings are on display at one time, frequent temporary exhibitions are organised to rotate the collection. A third-floor open-storage system is currently being designed to provide researchers with more access to the assembled works.

▲ **Juan Luna y Novicio** | *Picnic in Normandy* | *Oil on canvas* | *1885* | *88.9 x 128.9 cm*

Strong on academic painters, the collection is particularly noted for its 56 paintings and drawings by Fernando Cueto Amorsolo. Documenting five decades from 1919 to 1969, these canvases span most of the artist's career and are amongst the country's richest holdings of his work. Amorsolo, one of the Philippines' best internationally known early to mid-20th-century artists, defined national identity in a new way with his scenes of rural life, women vendors and cockfights, which were still, however, academic in style. The collection also includes works by seminal Modernists who broke away from European-style academism to forge a new, indigenous artistic language. Arbitrarily listed by the former leader of avant garde painting, Victorio Edades, 13 Modernist painters known as the '13 Moderns' were regarded as challengers of the conservative and academic tradition. Ten of them are represented in the Vargas Museum collection: Edades, Arsenio Capili, Bonifacio Cristobal, Cesar Legaspi, Diosdado Lorenzo, Arturo Luz, Vicente Manansala, Hernando R. Ocampo, Ricarte Purugganan and Jose Pardo. The three members not represented here are Galo Ocampo, Carlos 'Botong' Francisco and Anita Magsaysay-Ho.

■ **THE GALLERIES** The **Main Gallery**, where much of the permanent collection is displayed,

is located on the museum's second floor and presents 132 paintings. See in particular Juan Luna y Novicio's luminous and painterly *Picnic in Normandy*, circa 1885—the artist's interest in light and surface have prompted some to define the work as Filipino Impressionist—and the more classically academic *The Penitent* by Felix Resurreccion Hidalgo, from the same period. Examples of work by Simon Flores and the prolific Fernando Cueto Amorsolo are also presented. Sculpture is presented in the **Main Lobby**. The **Vargas Memorabilia Gallery** in the basement includes 21 paintings of Vargas and his family members along with sculpture and items such as certificates, diaries, documents and trophies. The **Library** and **Archives** of Jorge B. Vargas are situated on the third floor.

The **Lobby**, **Third Floor Landing**, **Third Floor Lobby** and **Edge Gallery** are spaces dedicated to temporary exhibitions. Other areas such as the basement, porch and gardens are open to workshops and special events.

The University of the Philippines' lush and centrally located Diliman compound offers a pleasant respite from the bustle of Metro Manila. Located within the academic oval, at the heart of the campus, the Jorge B. Vargas Museum houses a collection of Filipino art that while neither fully representative nor exhaustive, gives an excellent idea of the vast scope and depth of Filipino painting of the late 19th to the mid-20th century.

Fernando Cueto Amorsolo
Ambassador Jorge B. Vargas with Decoration | *Oil on canvas* | *1944* | *90.2 x 64.7 cm*

Singapore ▶

ADDRESS
39 Armenian Street
Singapore 179941

CONTACT INFORMATION
T: +65 6332 3015
F: +65 6883 0732
E: nhb_acm_pa@nhb.gov.sg
W: www.nhb.gov.sg/
acm/acm.shtml

OPENING HOURS
1pm–7pm Mon;
9am–7pm Tue–Thu, Sat–Sun;
9am–9pm Fri.

ADMISSION
Adult S$3;
child, senior and
student S$1.50;
free for children under 6;
free 7pm–9pm Fri.

FACILITIES
Wheelchair access.

Guided tours are available in
English and Japanese.

Museum shop.

HOW TO GET THERE
Bus: No. 190.

MRT / NEL: City Hall Station /
Clarke Quay Station.

AROUND THE MUSEUM
The Substation (see p. 193)
and the Singapore Philatelic
Museum (see pp. 134–135)
are in the museum's vicinity.

Fort Canning Park is just a
short walk away.

Asian Civilisations Museum (Armenian Street)

The Asian Civilisations Museum's first home in Armenian Street is currently being turned over to the specific documentation of Peranakan culture and history.

■ **THE BUILDING** The Armenian Street Asian Civilisations Museum (ACM) building was erected in 1910 to house the expanding student population of the Tao Nan School, a Chinese institution established by the Hokkien community of Singapore. In 1982, the school closed its Armenian Street building and moved to another site on the island. Mooted as a home for the new Asian Civilisations Museum, renovation work on the building began in 1994 and was completed in 1996, the museum moving in the following year.

Of hybrid design, a style described locally as 'Eclectic Classical', the building presents a mixture of classical European architectural features and tropical attributes. While the white stucco columned façade is generically Western in character, the elegant, deep verandahs adorning the three-storey building are well adapted to Singapore's climatic conditions, shielding the interior from both intense heat and monsoon rains. A broad interior air-well spanning the building's full height also provides constant air circulation within the rooms.

Though the bulk of the ACM collection moved to the museum's much larger Empress Place location in 2003 (see pp. 118–122), most of the material relating to the Peranakan Chinese is now housed in Armenian Street. Those with no time to visit the latter will nonetheless get a taste of Peranakan culture through a small display of artefacts documenting Chinese influence in Southeast Asian culture, located in The Mary and Philbert Chin Gallery at the ACM Empress Place.

The ACM Armenian Street has not yet been officially re-named the Peranakan Museum, but this change of name, as well as extensive modification of the building's interior space to accommodate the museum's shift in focus, is anticipated some time in 2006.

■ **THE COLLECTION** The Peranakans, Straits Chinese, or Nyonyas and Babas as they are

▲ **Wedding portrait of a Peranakan couple in front of their ancestral home**
Singapore | Early 20th century | Collection of Lee Hin Ming

variously known, were members of the immigrant Chinese communities of tradesmen who, for economic reasons, travelled to Nanyang (the South) in the 18th and 19th centuries, or perhaps earlier. Opting to settle along the Melaka Straits, mainly in Singapore and Penang, they most commonly intermarried with local Malay women or, if not, integrated with various aspects of Malay culture. Though Chinese tradesmen were operating in numbers in Southeast Asia and absorbing local culture as early as the 18th century, a true Peranakan identity and culture only began to emerge in the mid-19th century as a response to a renewed influx of Chinese migrant workers from the North.

The museum's Peranakan material includes thousands of different pieces exhibiting widely differing media and creative techniques. As many as 600 exhibits are featured in the galleries at this time, but more may be displayed when the galleries are redesigned further to the museum becoming an official 'Peranakan Museum'. The collection is divided into various categories, including jewellery, furniture, textiles and garments, beadwork and embroidery, and old photographs, ceramics and silver, and is probably the largest of its type in the world. It provides an excellent introduction to Straits Chinese life, especially around the turn of the last century. Much of the material originates from Singapore, Melaka or Penang, three of the largest and best known centres of Peranakan culture in Southeast Asia.

■ **THE GALLERIES** Currently the museum has six functioning exhibition galleries covering roughly 1,400 square metres of floor space. Located on the second and third floors, the rooms are accessible by lift or elegant, reconstructed period staircase. The ground floor is slated to be redesigned in 2005.

A particular highlight of the museum is its permanent exhibition called the **Peranakan Legacy**, housed in **Galleries 3, 4, 5 and 6** on the second level. Here, the Peranakan wedding in Gallery 4 (the museum's southeast corner) and the ancestral altar in Gallery 6 (northeast corner), two important features of Peranakan culture and daily life, are showcased. The

▲ **Beaded cigarette case**
*Padang, Indonesia |
Early 20th century*

Peranakan wedding, known for the elaborateness of its ceremony and the wealth of its material display, is documented complete with all appropriate contextual accoutrements: a sumptuous carved, lacquered and gilded wedding bed from 19th-century Penang hung with the richest of silks, surrounding furniture such as a dressing table, washstand and wardrobe, and most impressive, a case featuring the bride and groom's intricately worked wedding costumes. In the second part of the Peranakan Legacy is a fully equipped ancestral altar, the **Tan Kim Seng Altar Table** (Tan Kim Seng was a wealthy Singapore entrepreneur and philanthropist of Peranakan descent), shown

▲ **Studio photograph of a Peranakan Chinese family**
Singapore | Early 20th century | Collection of Lee Hin Ming

with incense holders, offering dishes, candle holders and a large pair of vases all presented in traditional fashion. The gallery also contains an extensive selection of Peranakan furniture, porcelain, silver and betel boxes, all displaying the juxtapositions in varying proportions of Chinese, Malay and Western form, aesthetics and technique that constitute Peranakan art.

On the museum's third floor, in **Galleries 9 and 10**, are two recently conceived temporary exhibitions. The first, **Tok Panjang** ('the long table'), presents a typical Peranakan feasting table set for all the close and extended family who would have participated in traditional festive day meals. The second, **The Gilded Age**, features a large and broadly chosen selection of black and white photographs documenting Peranakan life in Singapore and Penang (principally domestic views) in the early 20th century, a period of particular Peranakan prosperity and social establishment.

The ACM Armenian Street already provides a thoughtfully conceived introduction to Peranakan life in Southeast Asia. Documenting the culture's special fusion of Chinese, Western and Southeast Asian traditions and tastes, the museum's unique approach invites every object displayed to tell a story. Once the Asian Civilisations Museum Armenian Street has assumed its new identity as the Peranakan Museum, visitors can expect a yet more complete and rewarding interpretation of Straits Chinese art and culture.

Detail of a Nyonyaware *kamcheng* with floral and insect motifs
Porcelain | Jingdezhen, China | Commissioned by members of the Straits Settlements Chinese Community | Late 19th–early 20th century | On loan from the Mariette Collection

Peranakan-commissioned polychrome enamel porcelain of the mid to late 19th century is distinctive for its vividly coloured palette and rich ornamentation, juxtaposing a tropics-inspired range of hot pinks, strong yellows, sky blues and rich violets with more typical late Qing iconography.

ADDRESS
1 Empress Place
Singapore 179555

CONTACT INFORMATION
T: +65 6332 7798
F: +65 6883 0732
E: nhb_acm_pa@nhb.gov.sg
W: www.nhb.gov.sg/
acm/acm.shtml

OPENING HOURS
12pm–6pm Mon;
9am–7pm Tue–Sun;
9am–9pm Fri.

ADMISSION
Adult S$8;
child, senior and student S$4;
free for children under 6;
free 7pm–9pm Fri.

FACILITIES
Free guided tours in English,
Chinese and Japanese.

HOW TO GET THERE
MRT: Raffles Place Station.

AROUND THE MUSEUM
The Fullerton Hotel, a restored
colonial era building, and One
Fullerton, an entertainment
complex just across from the

hotel, are in the museum's
vicinity, as is Esplanade's
Jendela Gallery(see p. 193).

The museum is located in
the historic civic district,
and there are many
restaurants, cafés and
pubs nearby.

Asian Civilisations Museum (Empress Place)

Singapore's relatively new Asian Civilisations Museum houses the city's oldest and most distinguished collection. This, along with its architecture and effective use of technology, makes it one of the region's most attractive museums.

▲ *Detail of the Asian Civilisations Museum's façade seen from the Singapore River.*

■ **THE BUILDING** The Asian Civilisations Museum, referred to locally as ACM, was opened in 1997 on Armenian Street (see pp. 116–117) in the converted colonial Tao Nan School. In 2003, lack of space for the museum's rapidly growing collections prompted a move to the much larger and newly renovated Empress Place site. This landmark building designated to accommodate the expanding Asian Civilisations Museum was constructed in 1867 along a breezy bend of the Singapore River to house the colonial government's administrative offices. Overlooking Boat Quay, Empress Place and its gardens are of undoubted historical importance as they mark Sir Stamford Raffles's Singapore landing site in 1819. Furthermore, the building, designed by colonial engineer J.F.A. McNair and built by convict labour, is particularly distinctive with its combination of neo-Palladian Classical elements typical of

mid-19th century European taste and tropical architectural features such a wide, columned, shaded porch, high ceilings and many shuttered windows characterising the façade. Though renovating and expanding this historical landmark to 21st-century technological standards was to prove more complex than building a new museum from scratch, Empress Place's unique location on the river—the city's lifeline, locus of original settlement and centre of trade in its early years and indeed until quite recently—as well as its distinctive architectural features, are particularly suited to an institution devoted to history and culture.

The result of the six-year-long renovation and extension project is a museum that offers an exciting combination of advanced display technology, historically evocative 19th-century neo-Palladian Classical architecture, and unique city and river views.

■ **THE COLLECTION** Though founded in the 1990s, the ACM traces its roots back to the 1887 British-established Raffles Library and Museum, and its collections to the late 19th century. In the late 1960s, the museum became the National Museum, which in 1991 was split into three distinct institutions—the Asian Civilisations Museum, the Singapore Art Museum (see pp. 126–129), and the Singapore History Museum (see pp. 130–133). The ACM is currently the only museum in Southeast Asia to present art comprehensively from the dominant civilisations and cultures of

Asia, including China, India, the broader Muslim world and Southeast Asia.

■ **THE GALLERIES** With its move to Empress Place, the museum has acquired ten new permanent galleries and a special exhibition gallery providing over 3,000 square metres of space. This is more than double the area of its old premises. In order to fulfil the museum's mission as an institution established to tell the story of Singaporeans' ancestral cultures, important and varied bodies of material have been acquired through purchase, loan and donation in the last decade, vastly enlarging the old ethnological collection. For clarity of exposition, the current display of about 1,300 artefacts has been organised into four regional sections—Southeast Asia (including most of the 19th-century Raffles Museum artefacts), China, South Asia and West Asia/Islamic World. The museum's four

▲ **Dayak Mask**
Carved wood | Sarawak, Malaysia | c.1900 | H: 33 c▮

clusters of geographically defined galleries are arranged thematically over three floors.

The **South Asia Galleries**, positioned just beyond the gift shop which adjoins the main entrance foyer, have been housed on the ground floor due to their wealth of heavy stone sculpture that could not have been supported on the floors above without extensive reinforcement. Such important structural alterations as would have been required for this reinforcing process would have violated the building's strictly enforced conservation requirements. **Galleries 7 and 8** are home to the subcontinent's statuary, architectural elements, utensils, jewellery and costumes, all of which successfully evoke Indian culture as a whole.

Sculptural works from South Asia—many never yet properly exhibited—form a recently established part of the ACM collection. Though including a number of North Indian pieces as references, the ACM has historically concentrated on South Indian material because Singapore's Indian population hails principally from that part of the subcontinent. The gallery layout and storyline for South Asia is thematic, though chronology provides connecting links between works. Themes explored include religions, festivals, performing arts and architecture, while music and literature are investigated with the aid of multimedia software. Aspects of Hinduism, Islam and Buddhism, which travelled to Southeast Asia through trade, migration and missionaries, thus linking Singapore and India over the course of history, are also presented.

Most aesthetically powerful in these galleries are the carved stone works. Look in particular for the rare 97 CE Kushana seated Buddha, an early Buddhist icon whose vigorous facial expression and muscular posture (he is represented seated in *abhaya hasta*) admirably reflect the young religion's dynamism; the lively 10th-century buff sandstone dancing Ganesha from Madhya Pradesh; and the impressive carved, pink sandstone gateway from late 17th-century

Dancing Ganesha
Buff sandstone | Central or East Madhya Pradesh, India | First half of the 10th century | H: 46.4 cm

This relief of Ganesha comes from the exterior wall of a temple in *nagara* style where niches faced the cardinal directions. In the museum's South Asia gallery, the sculpture is displayed on a pilastered wall simulating its placement in its niche of origin and thus giving the viewer a good idea of how it might have appeared in its original context. Vigorously carved, despite its broken arms and trunk, the figure sensually conveys its dynamism and Ganesha's passion for dance.

West Uttar Pradesh, painstakingly reassembled after much study in **Gallery 7**.

The historical core of the museum's collections under the Raffles Library and Museum includes ethnological material culled

from the region, essentially examples of the tools, crafts, weapons, utensils and costumes of the Malay and other indigenous cultures of Southeast Asia. These early acquisitions are now housed in the **Southeast Asia Galleries**.

Within the new Empress Place configuration, these galleries are located on the building's second and third levels (**Galleries 3, 4 and 4A**). Occupying the most floor-space, these rooms explore the complex cultural mix of Southeast Asia's communities over the centuries by organising their permanent display of regional art around four central themes—Hindu Buddhist Kingdoms, the Malay World, the Sinicised Southeast Asian, and Tribal Southeast Asia.

This last part of the ACM collection is one of the museum's particular strengths and includes many tribal artefacts from the original Raffles Museum holdings.

The tribal groupings in Gallery 3 and 4 are probably the museum's most comprehensive in a single category, covering populations in island Southeast Asia such as the Dayaks, Nias and Bataks, and those from interior hill regions such as the Yao, Hmong and Karen tribes. Jewellery and textiles of tribal and non-tribal origin figure prominently in Gallery 4 where they are organised aesthetically rather than ethnographically. Though institutions in

▲ **Tribal 'soul lock' amulet**
Silver | Hmong and Yao people, North Thailand | Early 20th century | H: approximately 5 cm

Europe may hold excellent island textiles and ornament collections, the two are seldom paired as thoughtfully as at ACM. Here, curators have drawn a link between the two art forms in a joint thematic display that underscores the connection between their iconographies, symbolic associations and ritual functions. With this in mind, compare gold *mamuli* ornaments from early 20th-century East Sumba in Gallery 4 with the adjacent Hinggi warp *ikat* of the same period

and origin displaying shared bird motifs. Also compare the *mamuli* with a T'boli warp *ikat* from South Central Mindanao in the Philippines featuring stylised geometric motifs recalling those on the gold ornaments. Other tribal artefacts of note in Gallery 3 include Northern Thai silver jewellery and a delicately worked Dayak mask from early 20th-century Sarawak.

The most balanced and distinguished group among those presented in the Southeast Asian galleries, and certainly one of the museum's strongest, is the **Edmond Chin Collection of Southeast Asian Gold**, located in Gallery 4. Built over the last 20 years by local collector and connoisseur Edmond Chin, and including a selection from his donation of over 300 pieces, the collection showcases a remarkably full range of works that not only cover well-researched, Classical-age Javanese examples, but also those from ethnic groups outside the court cultures of Bali and Java. In their careful and comprehensive representation of Austronesian, Indo-Javanese, Islamised and Chinese traditions and cultures of the region, the Chin objects are unique in their genre and

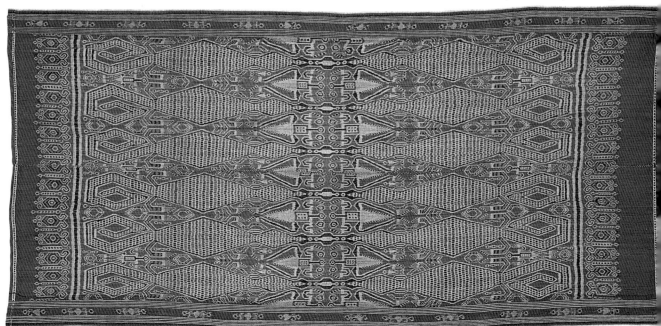

▲ **Sacred cloth (*pua kumbu*)** | *Cotton | Sarawak, Malaysia | c. 1900 | L: 255 cm, W: 120 cm*

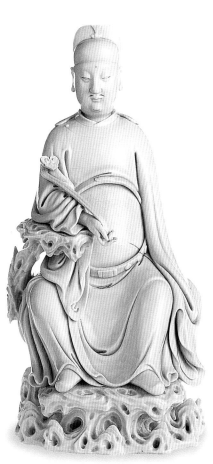

▲ Blanc de Chine figure of Wenchang
Porcelain | Dehua, China | Early 17ᵗʰ century |
H: 34 cm

arguably constitute one of the most significant collections of its type. In Gallery 4, look for an intricate, three-dimensional gold headdress from West Sumatra. Other noteworthy examples include silver and gold *padung-padung* Karo Batak head ornaments from late 19ᵗʰ-century Sumatra; a gold, double *lamba* head ornament from 19ᵗʰ-century East Sumba with a bold and beautifully balanced incised design; and another 19ᵗʰ-century gold ceremonial headdress from West Sumatra.

The museum's Chinese holdings are housed in **Gallery 6**, the **China Gallery**, on the building's second floor. The collection, built up largely in the last decade through meaningful grouping and ancillary audio-visual prompts does an admirable job of telling the complex story of China's political and social systems with an emphasis on their relationship to the development of Buddhism, the literati elite,

Confucianist-based patriarchy, funerary traditions and economic dynamics through the changing dynasties. The China Gallery holds some fine Buddhist stone works. Look for a large Eastern Wei (6ᵗʰ century) triad stele, distinguished by its quality of carving and fine state of conservation; and a rare limestone Guanyin from the Tang Dynasty (7ᵗʰ–8ᵗʰ century) with traces of original pigment. Compare the latter, a purely votive piece, to the cast gilt bronze 14ᵗʰ-century Guanyin, intricate and decorative in its aesthetic, more *objet d'art* than devotional in vocation. The ACM also features a fine and comprehensive series of *blanc de Chine* from Southern Fujian province donated by local collectors Frank and Pamela Hickley. The **Hickley Collection**, ranging from *blanc de Chine*'s earliest production in the 12ᵗʰ century, includes some 170 pieces, at least 70 of which remain on permanent display. Highlights include religious pieces from the 17ᵗʰ century such as the seated Wenchang with potter's mark, and a meditating Shakyamuni, highly expressive and realistic in rendition.

Much of the material in the museum's **West Asia/Islamic Galleries** has been acquired fairly recently. Housed in **Galleries 5 and 5A**, on the second and third floors respectively, the pieces have been selected for their formal significance as well as their ability to tell the story of one of Singapore's ancestral cultures. Rather than attempting a comprehensive representation of Islamic culture's many strands—far too broad a mission for an institution with so many other world cultures to champion—ACM's choice of world Islamic material focuses rather on explaining the religion's culture and history.

In order to better illustrate the links between world Islam and developments in Southeast Asia, ACM curators have split the material thematically. Because a minority of Singaporeans are Muslims—around 15 per cent—curators have endeavoured to arrange the objects so that not only are the basics of the religion explained, but Islam is portrayed as a way of life. A number of Qur'ans are used

to illustrate this, including a well-preserved and large 8ᵗʰ-century North African version, and a fine 16ᵗʰ-century Iranian one.

A second theme explored in the two galleries is calligraphy and Arabic script's close association with Islam. A number of Qur'an folios and leaves are displayed along with writing paraphernalia such as pen boxes and ink wells. A highlight is the inlaid pen-case from 17ᵗʰ-century Turkey of particularly bold design. Contrast a 14ᵗʰ-century Anatolian Qur'an leaf with elegantly stylised later illuminations, with an early 17ᵗʰ-century leaf from Mughal India, florid and refined in both

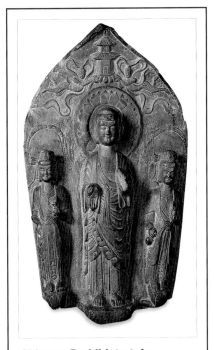

Chinese Buddhist stele
Limestone | China | Eastern Wei dynasty,
534–550 | H: 84.5 cm

This finely carved stele probably came from a niche in a cave temple of the type seen at Longmen. The sweetly smiling, gentle expressions of the central Buddha and two flanking *bodhisattvas* are characteristic of Buddhist art of this period, reflecting the religion's still relatively recent introduction to China.

▲ **Qur'an leaf, West Asia**
Ink, colour and gold on paper | *Probably Anatolia with later illuminations* | *14th century* | *28 x 18.5 cm*

to the viewer. The exhibits and documentation presented in text panels, touch-screen panels and videos are aimed at setting the displays and themes in the context of current Asian traditions and practices. Asian Civilisations Education Zones—informal activity stations set up throughout the galleries that are particularly popular with children—instill a sense of play and encourage self-exploration through hands-on interactive discovery. Also in place is a dedicated discovery centre—Asian Civilisations Education Space—located in the museum's basement and catering to younger visitors.

The ACM's fresh and cogent approach to the complex story of Singapore within Asia, the museum's technical virtuosity where display and conservation are concerned, and the breadth and quality of its collections, make the institution one of the most compelling in Southeast Asia, playing a unique role in explaining Singapore to the world.

script and illumination. Also note a colourful series of delicately worked wooden calligraphic panels from 18th- to 19th-century North Africa. Underscoring the museum's interest in tying history with living culture, examples of contemporary calligraphy are also displayed.

The last theme explored in these galleries is knowledge. Mystical knowledge, religious sciences and knowledge of the world are considered through works of art that include astronomical instruments (see a finely worked brass astrolabe from 18th-century Iran), musical instruments, manuscripts, scientific books (a well-preserved, illustrated, 17th-century Iranian anatomical manual), and books of poetry.

■ **TECHNOLOGY** Through vision and intelligence, ACM curators have made much of their institution's still-burgeoning collections. Creatively designed interactive technology brings the artefacts to life, explaining their function and social role on video screens dotted around the galleries. Virtual hosts, interactive maps and computer programmes provide user-friendly and engaging information

▲ ***Karalama*** or calligraphic exercise
Ink on paper | *Turkey* | *16th–17th century* | *35.3 x 31.6 cm*

ADDRESS
1,000 Upper Changi Road North
Singapore 507707

CONTACT INFORMATION
T: +65 6214 2451
F: +65 6214 1179
E: changi museum
@pacific.net.sg
W: www.changimuseum.com

OPENING HOURS
9.30am–5pm daily.

ADMISSION
Free.

FACILITIES
Wheelchair access.

Guided tours are available in English (adult S$8 and child S$4 for about 45 minutes).

Café on the museum's grounds; small shop in the museum; car park.

HOW TO GET THERE
Bus: No. 2 (from Tanah Merah MRT Station) or No. 29 (from Tampines MRT Station).

MRT: Alight at Tanah Merah Station or Tampines Station and take a bus or taxi from there.

AROUND THE MUSEUM
There are local eateries within 10 minutes of the museum and a large food court in Changi Village (about 15 to 20 minutes by bus).

The Changi Museum

Somewhat off the beaten track, The Changi Museum collection provides a poignant record of the lives of prisoners-of-war and civilian internees incarcerated in Singapore during the Japanese occupation years of 1942 to 1945.

■ **THE BUILDING** Opened at its current site in 2001, the building covers 570 square metres, its windowless structure a simple, almost square shape with the chapel (a symbolic replica) located at the centre of its courtyard.

The museum is located in the Changi area because this was the site of the main prisoner-of-war camp during the Japanese occupation. Some 50,000 POWs from the allied ranks were incarcerated there. Around 3,400 mainly British and Australian civilian internees, including women and children, were also imprisoned in Changi Gaol.

■ **THE COLLECTION** The museum's primary role is to show visitors how the lives of POWs, civilian internees and the local population in general were affected during the Japanese occupation. Educating the public as well as honouring the commitment of those who sacrificed their lives to the defence of Singapore, the museum, despite its nationalistic bent, avoids the overt propaganda often associated with homeland institutions.

Though small, its collection provides an insightful snapshot, through a Singapore lens, of conditions in war-torn Southeast Asia during the years leading to the Japanese defeat.

Through an assortment of items including military equipment, uniforms, textiles, diaries, photos, sketches and other personal items, the museum weaves a vivid and compelling story of the lives of the prisoners during their three and a half years of captivity.

The focus of the museum, particularly for visitors with connections to ex-prisoners and their families, is undoubtedly Changi Chapel. Though not the original chapel built by the prisoners, this structure is a fairly faithful replica of the type that would have been erected at the time. As basic in design and construction as the original would have been, Changi Chapel continues to operate as a functioning site of worship with Sunday services open to all. A cross made from period shell casing is housed in the replica chapel.

Other exhibits include reproductions of the Changi Quilts. The original quilts, now returned

▲ *Changi Chapel.*

to Australia and Britain, were handmade by the interned women and children, and given to the POWs at the women's request. The Japanese allowed these quilts to be given to their male prisoners, not realising that they bore personal news and morale-building messages of hope from the women. Many POWs have credited the quilts with giving them the courage to live through a hopeless situation.

The Changi Murals, painted by British POW Stanley Warren, offer more testimony to the prisoners' spirit of resistance. Consisting of five religious narratives, the murals are housed in what is now a high-security military area. Although the originals are not kept at the museum, faithful copies by Romanian artist Valeriu Sepi are on display.

Though the number of ex-prisoners visiting the establishment is dwindling, the museum and its archive continue to grow. For those interested in the history of Singapore during the Japanese occupation, The Changi Museum offers a poignant glimpse of the era from foreign POW and civilian points of view.

▲ *Letters, photographs and personal items belonging to internees are displayed in the main gallery.*

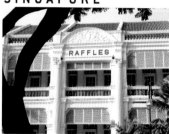

ADDRESS
#03-07, Raffles Hotel Arcade
328 North Bridge Road
Singapore 189673

CONTACT INFORMATION
T: +65 6412 1310
F: +65 6339 7650
E: raffles@raffles.com
W: www.raffleshotel.com

OPENING HOURS
10am–7pm daily.

ADMISSION
Free.

FACILITIES
Wheelchair access.

HOW TO GET THERE
Bus: Bus to City Hall, Beach
Road or Bras Basah Road.

MRT: City Hall Station.

AROUND THE MUSEUM
The hotel arcade includes a
number of antiques shops
and art galleries.

Raffles Hotel boasts several
top restaurants, the most
famous being Raffles Grill.

CHIJMES, a block away, is a
refurbished convent and
includes many restaurants.

Raffles Hotel Museum

Raffles Hotel Museum's small but well-displayed collection of hotel memorabilia offers a glimpse of colonial Singapore in the elegant setting of one of Southeast Asia's oldest and most graceful hotels.

▲ The earliest known photograph of the façade of Raffles Hotel taken from Beach Road, circa 1890.

■ **THE BUILDING** Housed on Raffles Hotel's third and top floor, the Raffles Hotel Museum opened in 1991 after the hotel's renovation. The hotel's reputation as a colonial haven of peace and gracious European living amid the bustle and wilting heat of tropical Southeast Asia dates to the establishment's 1885 acquisition and expansion by the Sarkies brothers—Armenian hoteliers who also built and owned Rangoon's famous Strand Hotel and Penang's Eastern and Oriental Hotel.

Designated a listed monument of Singapore's cultural heritage, Raffles Hotel started life in the second half of the 19th century as a modest bungalow and small restaurant nestled on Beach Road, which at the time commanded a view of both the beach and ocean. Singapore's ambitious land reclamation schemes have long since pushed the sea view several blocks eastward, but the hotel to this day remains on the original Beach Road. If the hotel's vistas are long gone, its 1880s shaded verandahs, covered walkways, cool inner-courtyard fountains and gardens, and broad marble galleries and staircases have survived. And despite a large shopping arcade—albeit exclusive—on the ground and second floors, and piped music infiltrating every corner of the hotel, Raffles' atmosphere of high Victorian refinement and elegance remains intact. Sensitively restored in 1989, original architectural elements such as teak floors, wrought iron balustrades, light fixtures, ceiling cornices, column pediments and most particularly original room proportions have been maintained or accurately replaced.

■ **THE COLLECTION** Serving as a repository for documentation pertaining both to the hotel and to its many notable guests, as well as more generally to Singapore's unique status from the late 19th century to the mid-20th as the 'crossroads of the East', the museum will appeal to history buffs and romantics alike, making for a pleasant change of pace from what is now one of the region's most dynamic metropolises.

Most of the museum's material—and indeed the most interesting—focuses on a period that extends from the fourth quarter of the 19th century to World War II, a period that corresponds with what is considered the golden age of travel in colonial Southeast Asia, a time when travelling in style was still beyond the means of most and a far cry from today's mass-market tourism.

Assembled during the hotel's renovation period, the Raffles memorabilia have been sourced from the far corners of the world and include postcards, photographs, luggage labels, menus, guidebooks, stamps and brochures as well as vintage tableware from the hotel's archival collection.

■ **THE GALLERIES** The museum is housed in three small but airy rooms in the Raffles Hotel Arcade, adjacent to the hotel's theatre, function rooms and the legendary Long Bar (birthplace of the lethal Singapore Gin Sling, the recipe for which is exhibited in the museum).

Most interesting is the museum's first and largest **Gallery-cum-entrance**. Lined with display cases, one of the room's most fascinating displays, on the left wall beside the entrance, is a large and detailed plan of Singapore town, dated 1893. Important swathes of Singapore's west flank were still uninhabited at this time and the island's eastern littoral is quite different from what we know today, after decades of land reclamation. Worth noting as well at the rear of the same gallery is a topographical etching of Singapore, circa 1850, showing the island's harbourfront to be nearly as busy and populated as it is today.

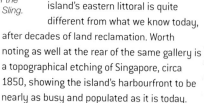

▲ Ngiam Tong Boon, creator of the Singapore Sling.

The Sarkies brothers

Of Armenian descent, the Sarkies brothers were undoubtedly Southeast Asia's most famous hoteliers and with their grand 'palace style' hotels in Singapore and Penang, were in part responsible for revolutionising hotel standards in the region at the turn of the 19th century. Penang's E&O Hotel and Raffles Hotel in Singapore are a testament to their vision of style and elegance in hoteliering.

ndeed, in his late 19th-century travel account *From Sea to Sea* (housed in a central display cabinet), English author Rudyard Kipling famously recommends Raffles Hotel as the place to dine but not to sleep. More telling is his description of 'the view of miles of shipping' from the hotel's wide verandah, confirming Singapore's early status as one of the region's busiest and most prosperous ports.

For those interested in hotel trivia, cabinets on the gallery's far wall enclose advertisements from the beginning of the 20th century illustrating Raffles' ballroom with the caption 'coolest ballroom in the East', a reminder of sticky conditions in tropical Singapore before air conditioning. Fifty years later, a brochure advertises Raffles' 'newly air-conditioned rooms', non-fan cooling still a luxury in Asia at that time. A large and varied collection of travel labels, referring to a number of famous Southeast Asian hotels as well as Raffles, displays the genius of Art Deco graphic art.

Photographs of early 20th-century affairs—May balls, New Year dances, coronation balls, fancy-dress balls (all in a cabinet on the south wall)—remind one that grand and elegant hotels of the East, as well as lodging travellers, served as outposts of 'home' and offered comfort to their colonial patrons, far away from 'civilised life' in mother Europe or America.

For those interested in the anecdotal life of the hotel rather than its more glamorous side, reproductions of newspaper clippings documenting events at the hotel also make fascinating reading. See in the first gallery's left wall the report concerning the shooting of a tiger under the billiard table in 1902. Further dramatic events include the sighting of a boar in the hotel gardens and the disposal of a very large snake found wandering the grounds, also at the beginning of the 20th century.

The heyday of Southeast Asia's great 19th-century hotels ended with the ebbing of colonial power. And though the collection does not explicitly say so, Raffles Hotel went into gentle decline in the 1970s, a few years after Singapore's independence. A selection of 1950s and 1960s photographs of film stars and celebrities at Raffles (north wall of the first gallery)—Ava Gardner, Elizabeth Taylor, Han Suyin—attest to a last hurrah, but other than a 1992 letter to the hotel's manager from former American President George Bush, the post-renovation material is scant.

An exception in the second and smaller **South Gallery** is a series of photographs taken of the hotel during its renovation. Architecture enthusiasts will be fascinated by the peeling away of different layers of the hotel—partitions, false ceilings, decorative devices—to rediscover the original Victorian shell.

The third and smallest room, the **West Gallery**, is something of an afterthought and less interesting than the larger entrance and South galleries, containing a few bits of vintage but pedestrian hotel furniture, and books by writers who have stayed at the hotel.

Resurrected from decline by renovation, though no longer playing a central role in local social life, Raffles Hotel is still considered the best in the city. Though perhaps more nostalgic than historic in flavour, the Raffles Hotel Museum provides the traveller with a little time to spare a concise but accurate snapshot of early colonial life in Singapore at a time when the city was still considered the 'crossroads of the East'.

▲ *A view of hotel memorabilia and travel-related objects in the museum.*

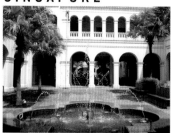

ADDRESS
71 Bras Basah Road
Singapore 189555

CONTACT INFORMATION
T: +65 6332 3222
F: +65 6334 7919
E: nhb_sam_programs@
nhb.gov.sg
W: www.singart.com

OPENING HOURS
10am–7pm Mon–Thu,
Sat–Sun;
10am–9pm Fri.

ADMISSION
Adult S$3;
child, senior and student
S$1.50;
free for children under 6;
family ticket (max. 5) S$8;

free 6pm–9pm Fri.

FACILITIES
Wheelchair access.

Guided tours are available
in English, Japanese
and Mandarin.

Museum shop.

HOW TO GET THERE
Bus: Nos. 7, 14, 16, 36, 77, 97,
131, 162, 167, 171, 602, 603,

605, 607 or 700.

MRT: Dhoby Ghaut Station,
City Hall Station.

AROUND THE MUSEUM
CHIJMES, which includes
many of the city's trendiest
restaurants and pubs, is
two blocks east along Bras
Basah Road.

Singapore Art Museum

The Singapore Art Museum, founded in 1996, offers an enriching introduction to the modern and contemporary art of Singapore and Southeast Asia in a delightful architectural setting.

▲ *Façade of the museum with its covered arcades seen from Bras Basah Road.*

■ **THE BUILDING** The third offshoot of the old National Museum, the Singapore Art Museum, or SAM as the museum is referred to locally, is housed in one of the city-state's most elegant and architecturally distinguished colonial edifices in the heart of the museum district on Bras Basah Road. The mid-19th-century St Joseph's Institution, partly designed by French priest Charles Benedict Nain, was once home to one of the island's leading Catholic

schools for boys run by the order of La Salle. Converted into a state-of-the-art museum in the early 1990s by local firm C.P.G. Architects, many of St Joseph's original features—grand, shuttered windows and an airy, inner quadrangle space—as well as early 20th-century additions—a central dome and sweeping, curved, lower and upper floor arcade verandahs—have been preserved. Indeed, wherever possible, period features have been integrated into the renovated design, with parts of the original stone façade of 1867, which were uncovered during restructuring work, and small expanses of old tile flooring and inner arches adorned with Latin script, left exposed. Original stone plaques by the museum's main entrance list a number of benefactors, including—it may surprise and amuse some to know—an 'Opium & Spirit Farm', in 1903.

A successful marriage of period and contemporary architecture, the building boasts a dramatic glass hall decorated with contemporary glass sculpture by American master glass artist Dale Chihuly. Neatly fitted into the middle of the old school's inner quadrangle where the old gymnasium used to be, it is now flanked by two stone-paved courtyards where sculpture is displayed. Though the building's second-floor verandahs have been glassed-in to maximise exhibition space, the ground floor's characteristic high-ceilinged, columned arcades still afford the passer-by respite from the scorching, tropical heat and seasonal monsoon rains.

■ **THE COLLECTION** The museum was originally established to house the national collection of Singapore art and assemble works by 20th-century Southeast Asian masters. Though the original nucleus of the museum's holdings dates back to National Museum days (the old National Museum was devolved in 1991 into SAM, the Asian Civilisations Museum, see pp. 116–122, and the Singapore History Museum, see pp. 130–133), much of the art now on rotation in the museum's galleries has been acquired since 1996. With broadening state endorsement of the arts, increasing art trade between Southeast Asian countries (auctioneers Sotheby's and Christie's have been active in Singapore since the early 1990s) and a growing pool of Singaporean and wider Asian contemporary practice to choose

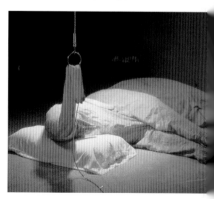

▲ **Sutee Kunavichayanont, Thailand**
Elephant (Breath Collecting) | Rubber and mixed media installation | 1998 | Dimensions vary according to degree of inflation

▲ **Tang Da Wu, Singapore**
Tiger's Whip | Mixed media installation | 1991 | Dimensions variable

from, it should come as no surprise that acquisitions in the last decade have far exceeded any in the past. With some 6,500 works at last count, the museum now boasts the largest public collection of 20ᵗʰ-century Southeast Asian art in the world, the growth spurt showing no sign of stopping as SAM competes actively with two rival institutions with similar briefs, the Fukuoka Asian Art Museum in Japan and The Queensland Art Gallery in Australia.

Widening its scope beyond showcasing modern and contemporary Singaporean and Southeast Asian art, since 2001 the museum has targeted Asia as a whole in its collecting sights, with curators seeking Chinese, and more recently, Indian works to further the collection's appeal. As can be expected with any broadly focused brief, SAM's collection, though impressive and extensive, is not comprehensive. Singapore being home to a majority of Chinese, China is naturally the best represented of East Asia, the museum striving to acquire Chinese modern and contemporary art in both traditional and international idioms (Western-style oil on canvas, mixed media, video art or installation practices being defined as international rather than traditional). Contemporary artists from China whose practices fall into the international category include Hai Bo, Fang Lijun, Liu Xiaodong, Zhong Biao and Su Xinping for example.

Modern Chinese artists working with ink and paper in more traditional mode are also

well represented, the museum's stores including paintings by Qi Baishi, Xu Beihong, Qi Gong, Huang Zhou, Hong Zhu An, and Yu Youren to name a few.

The museum also presents an ambitiously international mixed-media exhibition programme so that the visitor is as likely to see the work of a mid-20ᵗʰ-century Indonesian Modernist as that of Pablo Picasso or a Swedish glass blower. This broad approach to art presentation makes the museum a perfect destination for visitors in search of a quick taste of world culture as well as those looking for a pan-continental brush with Asian art.

■ **THE GALLERIES** SAM's 14 climate-controlled galleries, library, auditorium, multi-purpose hall, museum shop, outdoor courtyards and café occupy some 10,000 square metres of floor space on two storeys.

The museum's lobby-cum-ticketing area, the modest scale of which will remind museum-goers of the institution's former life as a school, is accessible through the main entrance. Beyond the ticket area, on its right and left, are two symmetrically disposed curved **Galleries, 1 and 2** on the east side, and **3 and 4** on the west side. Due to the impressive size of SAM's collection, these four galleries present semi-permanent

▲ **Hong Zhu An, China**
Crystal Moon, Water & Sky | Chinese ink and pigment on rice paper | 1996 | 82 x 78 cm

displays of works from the museum's permanent holdings which, assembled thematically, are rotated more or less on an annual basis. Past titles of theme exhibitions featured in these galleries have ranged from the generically dubbed *Highlights from the Singapore Art Museum Permanent Collection* to *The Landscape in Southeast Asian Art: Works from the Singapore Art Museum Permanent Collection*, to *Curatorial Readings from the Permanent Collections*. Containing as many as 30 or 40 works, these four galleries give the visitor an accurate though brief overview of SAM's extensive holdings. Keen to publicise its ever-expanding permanent collection, SAM is currently elaborating a change of exhibition policy and aspires to show a greater number of its works (60 to 80) by 2005 in a score of

galleries for three-year periods. Thus, with paintings rotating less frequently, the museum hopes to cultivate familiarity with a permanent collection that is largely unknown to the Singapore public as well as to those visiting from overseas.

Beyond Galleries 1 to 4—note the 100-year-old ceramic floor tiles in the small area to the left of the circular staircase—lies the Chihuly-decorated **Glass Hall** which is much sought-after for external and internal functions. Located at the centre of the old school courtyard, the hall features floor-to-ceiling glass walls on three sides in a show of restraint and elegance that admirably complements the old building's period grace.

From the museum's central foyer, adjacent to the entrance, a majestic circular staircase (built during the museum's renovation) leads

▲ **Georgette Chen, China**
East Coast Vendor | *Oil on canvas* | *1965* | *92 x 73 cm*

to second-floor **Galleries 5 to 8**, located above Galleries 1 to 4. These spacious rooms accommodate various international and local loan exhibitions that span about three months. Past exhibition titles include *swedenmade design 4 stories* and *Pierre & Gilles*, a show featuring stylised kitsch portraits by French artists Pierre Commoy and Gilles Blanchard.

To the west of Galleries 7 and 8, **Galleries 15 and 16** showcase an annually changing display of cyber art. Reflecting the museum's commitment to new technology in art, much of the work in the cyber galleries is interactive, with visitor participation necessary to call up images on computer screens.

Galleries 9 and 10 are the **Art Education Galleries**. Housed on the second floor of the museum in the glassed-in, west-side, curved verandah, these galleries are devoted to art education for children. An 'Art Lab Corner' at one end of the space invites young museum-goers to create and produce artworks of their own.

SAM's largest gallery space, known as the **Upper and Lower Galleries**, occupies the museum's east side, with a grandiose, tiered staircase connecting the first- and second-storey rooms. Reserved for major travelling

Hendra Gunawan, Indonesia
War & Peace | *Oil on canvas* | *94 x 140 cm*

Because Hendra Gunawan (1918–1983) is best known for his portraits of languid young women collecting seashells and nursing children on the beaches of Bali, this painting depicting Indonesian independence fighters lying in wait in the Javanese countryside is particularly important in his oeuvre. Referring to Indonesia's independence war with Holland of the late 1940s, Hendra here juxtaposes a key historical theme with his signature painterly style that is recognised as playing an important role in defining the beginnings of a home-grown Indonesian Modernism.

Bui Xuan Phai, Vietnam

Halong Bay – Cat Ba Island | Oil on canvas | 1953 | 45 x 60 cm

Bui Xuan Phai (1920–1988) is considered one of the most important painters of 20th-century Vietnam. Principally known for his depictions of Hanoi street life, he was part of a small group of Vietnamese painters (along with Nguyen Tu Nghiem and Nyuyen Sang, among others) who championed Modernism in the mid-20th century and, marrying Vietnamese iconography and aesthetics with Western-style technique and media (oil, watercolour, canvas or whatever other material might be available in a country often deprived of essentials), developed an indigenous artistic language. Usually favouring intimately scaled street-scapes and portraits of local Cheo actors, the artist's view of Halong Bay, though thematically exceptional within his oeuvre, remains characteristic of Phai in its frieze-like composition, use of impasto, and concern with local working folk.

ban exhibitions or locally organised shows ighlighting established artists of particular istoric significance, these galleries often oast a high-profile artist whose work is isplayed to appeal to an international udience. Past loan exhibitions sited here nclude *German Art: 1960s–1990s*, *The*

Origins of Modern Art in France, and *Leonardo Da Vinci: Scientist, Inventor, Artist*.

For those confused about the elliptical gallery nomenclature, be advised that Galleries 11 to 14 do not exist at present.

Even visitors who are not intimately acquainted with modern Asian art will

appreciate the quiet, cool confines of the Singapore Art Museum. The inner courtyards, with their sculpture and fountains, are a pleasant place to while away a few hours, and the galleries, with their innovatively conserved 19th-century architectural elements, are a pleasure to discover.

ADDRESS
Riverside Point
30 Merchant Road
#03-09/17
Singapore 058282

2006:
93 Stamford Road
Singapore 178897

CONTACT DETAILS
T: +65 6332 3659 / 5642

F: +65 6332 3587
E: nhb_shm@nhb.gov.sg
W: www.nhb.gov.sg/shm

OPENING HOURS
12pm–6pm Mon;
9am–6pm Tue–Thu, Sat–Sun;
9am–9pm Fri.

ADMISSION
Adult S$2;
senior and student S$1;

free for children below 6;
free after 7pm Fri.

FACILITIES
Wheelchair access.

Guided tours are available in
Japanese from Tue to Fri at
10.30am; in English from Tue
to Fri at 12pm; schedules are
subject to change, call ahead.

HOW TO GET THERE
NEL: Clarke Quay Station.

Taxi: To Merchant Road,
opposite Clarke Quay.

AROUND THE MUSEUM
Many restaurants and pubs
lie just across the river at
Clarke Quay.

Singapore History Museum

The Singapore History Museum, soon to be rehoused in the superbly renovated National Museum Building, should not be missed for its elegant architecture and inspiring approach to national and regional history.

■ **THE BUILDING** During the National Museum building's four-year renovation, the Singapore History Museum is being housed on two floors of Riverside Point, a shopping mall conveniently positioned on the banks of the Singapore River, opposite Clark Quay. Though the gallery area at Riverside Point is much smaller than the museum's permanent home, the complex offers a breezy riverside setting in tandem with attractive river views.

In 2006, the museum will return to its original Stamford Road premises in the National Museum Building, one of Singapore's grandest and most distinctive colonial architectural landmarks and long the site of the island-state's only national museum. Nestled at the foot of Fort Canning Hill,

another of the city's landmark locations, and at the heart of Singapore's designated museum precinct, the National Museum Building is the country's original purpose-built museum complex. Designed by colonial engineer Henry McCallum and built in 1887, the museum, then called the Raffles Museum and Library, combines late Victorian neo-Palladian style with idiosyncratic tropical attributes such as a deep, covered porch and well-recessed, high shuttered windows. Its outside appearance has remained largely unchanged since its inception and is characterised by an elegant, columned façade surmounted by an airy, stately entrance rotunda.

The renovation work has involved the construction of an extension behind the

▲ *Images of the National Museum galleries as they appeared in the early and mid-20th century.*

original building, digging a large basement underneath and updating the two floors above to 21st-century state-of-the-art standards of conservation, lighting and general infrastructure. The total gallery space upon completion will be over 6,000 square metres, an area that should easily accommodate the expansion of future collections and their permutations. At the time of going to press, a core gallery devoted to telling the Singapore story had been apportioned around 1,400 square metres while the well-made and engaging Children's Discovery Gallery, so popular at Riverside Point, is slated to get 235 square metres once the collection moves back to Stamford Road on the refurbishment's completion. Furthermore, looking to the future, the new museum building will boast an imposing column-free, climate-controlled, high-ceilinged gallery covering 1,300 square metres designed to accommodate temporary exhibitions and travelling shows of all kinds. Thus, as well as presenting and documenting Singapore's history, with this versatile and

▲ *View of the façade and elegant cupola of the National Museum Building, Stamford Road.*

large-scale new exhibition space, the Singapore History Museum aims to be an active and engaging participant in the region's blossoming cultural forum.

■ **THE COLLECTION** The Singapore History Museum has its roots in the city-state's first public art institution which, as the Raffles Library and Museum, was opened in 1887 by Governor Frederick Weld. Initially a natural history museum, its early collections, like those of the Asian Civilisations Museum, date as far back as the early 19th century. A four-metre-long whale skeleton, now in Kuala Lumpur, was one of the early stars of its natural history displays. The museum's Singapore collection, first started in 1918, grew extensively over the decades that followed. The general collection, growing rapidly in the course of the late 19th and 20th centuries, expanded so that it increasingly reflected the social and cultural history of Singapore and the wider region. By the 1970s, the museum had abandoned its earlier emphasis on natural history. At this time, much of the natural history material was transferred to various institutions including the National Museum of Malaysia in Kuala Lumpur (see pp. 70–71) and the National University of Singapore.

The Singapore History Museum as we know it today was established in 1991 when the National Museum was split into three institutions—the Singapore Art Museum (see pp. 126–129), the Asian Civilisations Museum (see pp. 116–122), and the Singapore History Museum.

Today the museum's collection continues to grow through purchase and donation. It is hugely diverse, an emporium of items reflecting all manner of historical, cultural and societal developments in Singapore. Among other pieces, the visitor will see archaeological relics, facsimiles of historic documents such as treaties signed by Sir Stamford Raffles, old advertisement boards, street signs, cameras and movie projectors, video footage, photographs and postcards, Chinese opera costumes, historical prints and paintings,

▲ **Black Handed Gibbon – Mangosteen** | *From the museum's collection of William Farquhar Botanical and Zoological drawings* | *Artist unknown* | *Watercolour on paper* | *Early 19th century* | *49.5 x 35 cm*

headgear worn by *samsui* women (labourers), merchandise found at the local department store John Little during the colonial era, modern sculpture and much more.

A highlight of the collection, however, is the Haw Par Jade assembled by Tiger Balm entrepreneur Aw Boon Haw and donated to the museum in 1980. As well as jade, the 385-

▲ *Fragment of the Singapore Stone.*

piece collection of mainly Qing dynasty carved semi-precious minerals also features stones such as crystal and lapis lazuli.

Perhaps more internationally recognised than the jade collection are the museum's William Farquhar Botanical and Zoological Drawings. Important for their documentary value as well as for their artistic merit, the drawings were commissioned by Major-General Farquhar during his administrative stint in Melaka from 1795 to 1818 (posted in Singapore from 1819 to 1823, he was later dismissed by Sir Stamford Raffles). Executed by anonymous local Chinese artists, the drawings, faithfully reflecting the characteristic vibrancy and colour of their tropical Southeast Asian subjects, are unique

in combining traditional Chinese painting techniques and characteristics (a flat, frieze-like composition without shadow or depth) and the accuracy and detail displayed in Western scientific drawings of the period. Farquhar, returning to London after his dismissal by Raffles, donated the drawings to the Royal Asiatic Society. In 1995, the latter sold them back to Singapore patron Goh Geok Khim who then donated them to the Singapore History Museum. The 477 drawings, displayed in small, rotating batches, depict birds, plants—including flora seen in the vicinity of modern Malaysia's Mount Ophir, and medicinal flora, fish, insects, mammals and reptiles.

The replica and fragment of the Singapore Stone, though not particularly significant to foreign visitors, constitute an important local draw. Rather than wonderful works of art, they are historical artefacts documenting old Temasek well before colonial times. The Singapore Stone was a large boulder that once stood at the mouth of the Singapore River and bore an inscription in an unknown language which might, speculatively, have shed light on early Temasek history. Blown up by the British

in 1843 to make way for military construction, the text on the stone was never deciphered. Because neither the language nor the nature of the stone's inscription are known, both the stone's replica and its fragment are shrouded in mystery, making them, with their rather self-conscious, anti-colonial, political connotations, a must-see exhibit for those interested in Singapore's history and post-1965 political discourse.

Another national treasure is the Majapahit gold jewellery discovered accidentally by workers in 1926 during excavations for the construction of a reservoir on Fort Canning—the ridge bordering Stamford Road, behind the museum and to the south. What survives of the hoard today consists of several 24-carat gold rings or perhaps earrings, each with a socket joint and a wire hinge, as well as a large, flexible gold armlet with fine strands of chain ending in a tongue. The tongue slips into a plaque of repoussé work depicting a Javanese *kala* head. The representation of a demon-like lion is closely related to examples decorating the entrances to Javanese temples.

■ **THE GALLERIES** At Riverside Point, the Singapore History Museum occupies part of the third and fourth floors of the commercial complex, harbouring at least 650 square metres of gallery space.

The museum is fairly unique in its broad and expansive approach to local and regional history. Thus, rather than simply being presented with a musty collection of old artefacts, however interesting, the visitor is likely to be shown unusually composed photographs of modern Singapore taken by a talented local photographer, well-put-together dioramas documenting Singapore's pivotal role as a port and trading centre in the 19th and 20th centuries, or interactive settings documenting the city-state's industrial development and the complex history of its many waves of immigrant influxes. The presentation, whether through interactive technology, dioramas or multi-sensory activities is user-friendly and thought-provoking, bringing life and an

▲ **Boorong Java – Pelican** | *From the museum's collection of William Farquhar Botanical and Zoological drawings* | *Artist unknown* | *Watercolour on paper* | *Early 19th century* | *38.5 x 54.5cm*

element of discovery to Singapore's heritage. Appealing to visitors of all ages and levels of historical knowledge, the museum is as much a repository of the rich collective heritages of the people of Singapore as it is a dynamic and inspiring educational institution open to all interested in local history.

One of Riverside Point's most popular exhibits, **Rivertales** is an intelligently assembled work that relates the history of Singapore through stories revolving around the Singapore River. It traces events over seven centuries using artefacts, text and interactive media displays. The visitor can enter the exhibition at any point since it is organised thematically rather than chronologically. Themes covered include Long Ago, A Trading Town, Politics, Celebrations, Conflicts, Everyday Life, The River at War, and The River of Life Reborn. An innovative and engaging highlight here is the short video, *The Old Man and the River*, commissioned by the museum from award-winning local film-maker Royston Tan. Tan filmed 77-year-old Singaporean coolie and road-sweeper Chia Tiong Guan who, in narrating his life in his native Hokkien dialect, takes the audience on a poignant, informative, yet non-sentimental 12-minute journey down the Singapore River.

Another highlight, to be reconstructed at the Stamford Road premises in a specifically conceived area, is the interactive **Children's Discovery Gallery**. Specially designed for children aged 7 to 12, the gallery provides youngsters with the opportunity to see an archaeological pit and examine and measure shards. A second section of the gallery is devoted to the exploration of ethnic roots, where children are encouraged to examine their ancestors' motives for immigration. In a third part of the gallery, visitors can 'experience' the hardships of immigrant life by trying their hands at pulling a rickshaw, balancing a heavy load on a pole across their shoulders, and rowing a sampan. These well-designed, interactive exhibits are engaging, fun and educational, leaving a vivid impression on all young visitors.

Ornaments discovered at Fort Canning Hill
Earrings or rings and an armlet | 24-carat gold | Javanese | Majapahit period, c. mid-14th century

These items are part of a small hoard found on Singapore's Fort Canning Hill in 1926. Their dating is somewhat uncertain, however, archaeologists have surmised that the jewellery must have been manufactured before the 15th century as by that time Islamic iconoclasm (the armlet displays animal-like iconography) was already an important influence in Javanese decorative art. The presence of Javanese works of art in pre-colonial Temasek sheds light on an elusive period of Singapore's history.

For adults interested in Singapore's pivotal role during World War II, audio interviews with survivors of the Japanese offensive and occupation are available.

Those spending a few weeks in Singapore will appreciate the well-designed programme of public lectures, hands-on archaeology field trips and tours which supplement the exhibits.

One of Singapore's most thoughtfully designed museums, the Singapore History Museum meets the challenge of fulfilling its role as a living repository of history, heritage and culture, engaging visitors both local and foreign on both fundamental and more sophisticated levels. Truly a museum for the people, it addresses all sectors and all levels of the population. In its newly refurbished and enlarged Stamford Road premises, the museum's intelligent approach will shine all the brighter.

ADDRESS
23B Coleman Street
Singapore 179807

CONTACT INFORMATION
T: +65 6337 3888
F: +65 6337 8958
W: www.spm.org.sg

OPENING HOURS
1pm–7pm Mon;
9am–7pm Tue–Sun.

ADMISSION
Adult S$3;
child (4–12 years) S$2;
free for children under 4;
free on public holidays.

FACILITIES
Wheelchair access.

Guided tours in English,
Mandarin and dialects can be
arranged in advance by

calling the museum's
main number.

HOW TO GET THERE
Bus: Nos. 2, 12, 32, 33, 51, 61,
62, 63, 80 or 197.

MRT / NEL: City Hall Station /
Clarke Quay Station.

AROUND THE MUSEUM
The Substation (see p. 193)
and the Asian Civilisations

Museum in Armenian Street
(see pp. 116–117) are in the
museum's vicinity.

Fort Canning Park is just a
short walk away.

Singapore Philatelic Museum

The Singapore Philatelic Museum, founded in 1995 and located in the heart of Singapore's designated museum precinct, spotlights 150 years of Singapore's social and political history through stamps.

■ **THE BUILDING** Located at the foot of historic Fort Canning Rise, and a few paces away from The Substation (see p. 193) and the Asian Civilisations Museum on Armenian Street (see pp. 116–117), the Singapore Philatelic Museum is housed in an early 20th-century building, formerly part of Anglo Chinese School. Designed by Tomlinson and Lermit Architects, a well-established local firm responsible for a number of early colonial edifices, this 1907 structure marries tropical climatic imperatives with the generic classicism of late Victorian architecture. Its façade features symmetrically aligned shaded verandahs, louvred windows and column-enclosed arches. A fire-engine-red Victorian pillar box, still operating as a standard postbox, signals the museum's entrance.

■ **THE COLLECTION** The nucleus of the collection was first established in the 1960s when the Singapore Post Office first began accumulating stamps, first day covers and original stamp artwork. Earlier Straits Settlements stamps were principally acquired through purchase and the odd donation. The museum's holdings continue to grow as new Singapore issues are introduced and international issues acquired. In recent years, some eight to ten new Singapore issues have been produced annually.

■ **THE GALLERIES** Occupying two floors, the Singapore Philatelic Museum has seven airy galleries devoted either to a specific theme or

▲ *Selection of colonial period stamps featuring the British monarchs.*

featuring temporary displays. Though a specialist vocation, philately is explored intelligently so as to capture the interest of a broad spectrum of museum-goers.

As the visitor enters the museum, he is met first by a functioning post office and well-stocked museum shop selling first day covers and an assortment of local and international stamps.

The **Orientation Gallery**, first on the left after the shop, presents an array of vintage Singapore postal equipment such as weighing scales and post boxes, as well as a short, well-made introductory video documenting postal history in Singapore from its Straits Settlements days to the present.

Beyond, in the **Discovery Gallery**, visitors learn about Singapore's high-tech mail delivery system as well as stamp designing and production. These technical subjects, including design and printing errors, printing methods

---

Bisect stamp cover

The 1859 bisect four *annas* stamp cover from Singapore to Calcutta per Australiano line is one of the Singapore Philatelic Museum's rarest and most unusual pieces. Due to an acute stamp shortage at the end of the 1860s, many denominations were not available. As a result, the Singapore Postmaster decided to double the supply by cutting stamps in half along the diagonal. These were the first and last stamps to be bisected in Singapore's history. Very few covers have survived, hence this one's historic significance.

and different printing materials, are approached from a Singaporean perspective, but much of what is explained reflects the general context, making this gallery a must for anyone interested in philately, irrespective of his or her understanding of Singapore's history. Interactive exhibits such as a display that asks the visitor to test his eye for detail by trying to spot printing errors, successfully pull the viewer into this technical field.

At the rear of the museum, the **Stamp Club Room** on occasion welcomes collector stamp exchanges and fairs, and features a broad display of stamps from around the world, with some 180 countries represented.

The final ground-floor gallery, **The Atrium**, acts as a function or temporary exhibit hall, often featuring theme or country-based loan collections such as the recent *Coffee or Tea*.

On the second floor, a third permanent space, the **History Through Stamps Gallery**, greets the viewer. Probably the most universally appealing of the museum's galleries, this compact room explores, through an array of stamps both original and reproduction, explanation panels, historic postcards, first day covers and photographs, how the early postal system functioned in the Straits Settlements, and its subsequent

▲ *A Singapore miniature sheet commemorating the opening of the Esplanade arts complex.*

development. The viewer will learn that under the East India Company, Singapore acquired its postal system in 1854, some 14 years after Britain first introduced it to the world in 1840; and that the Straits Settlements' first stamps were Indian, overlaid with a special chop identifying the Settlements; and the visitor will see a rare 1859 cover of a four *annas* stamp, bisected by the post office because of the difficulty of obtaining stamps in the Settlements at that time. The first airmail service to Singapore, which occurred in 1933, is also documented.

Equally interesting, the gallery explores how stamps have been used through the years to express national identity, and also serve as subtle tools of state propaganda. Indeed, from the 1960s, stamps in Singapore shifted increasingly away from the standard evocation of the British sovereign (eliminated once Malaya gained its independence from Britain in 1957) and grew in importance as ways of displaying Singapore's social, commercial and political achievements. While some stamps illustrate local flora and fauna or traditional shophouses, others, more politically charged, celebrate the government's public housing scheme or Singapore's renowned Changi Airport. The traditional arts of the nation's main ethnic communities (Chinese, Malay, Indian and Eurasian) are also featured, the viewer getting a sense of local social history as the state promotes its different cultures with a deliberately even hand. Finally, global postal developments such as methods of calculating international postal rates, are touched upon.

More can be gleaned about Singapore's unique social history by viewing a

storyboard that narrates the 1876 riots which began when the colonial government disbanded the Chinese community's private postal system as it competed with the government's system for some years after the latter's inception. Twentieth-century Asian history is addressed as well with a display of some stamps defaced by the Japanese when they occupied Singapore during World War II.

Three further galleries complete the display, **Theme Galleries I and II** and the **Exhibition Gallery**. These three rooms, to the right and left of the History Through Stamps Gallery, host a variety of temporary and semi-permanent theme exhibitions produced locally from museum and collector material, or on loan from other countries. Currently dotted throughout the museum, non-permanent small 'explanation stations' take on historical questions such as how stamps changed with the onset of war, while a display case enclosing a colourful range of miniature postboxes from around the world is sure to delight visiting children.

Though the visitor may encounter school groups, part of the museum's appeal resides in its calm atmosphere and intelligently designed setting where erudite philatelist and history buff alike will be captivated by the museum's balanced approach to both philately's technical imperatives and Singapore's history through stamps.

▲ *Selection of post-independence stamps.*

▲ *Display featuring postboxes from around the world.*

Thailand ▶

ADDRESS
6 Soi Kaseman 2
Rama I Road
Bangkok 10330
Thailand

CONTACT INFORMATION
T: +66 2 216 7368
F: +66 2 612 3744
E: info@
jimthompsonhouse.com

W: www.
jimthompsonhouse.com

OPENING HOURS
9am–5pm daily.

ADMISSION
Adult 100 baht;
student 50 baht;
free for children under 10.

FACILITIES
Mandatory tours in Thai,
English, French and Japanese
start every 15 minutes.

HOW TO GET THERE
Bus: Along Rama I Road.

Sky train: National Stadium
Station.

AROUND THE MUSEUM
On the museum grounds is a
pleasant open-air café, a large
Jim Thompson shop and an
exhibition space referred to as
The Arts Centre featuring
temporary displays relating to
both traditional and
contemporary art (p. 194).

Jim Thompson House

Jim Thompson House, with its small but excellent collection of Southeast Asian works of art, extraordinary subversion of traditional Thai architecture, and garden-on-the-canal setting, is a jewel of a museum that should not be missed.

■ **THE BUILDING** Jim Thompson's mysterious disappearance while on vacation in Malaysia in 1967 is largely responsible for the legendary aura associated with the Thompson name. Yet the American architect-turned-spy-turned-entrepreneur deserves far more credit than any strange death can confer, and a visit to this delightful museum that was once Jim Thompson's home confirms the man's unique vision and place in modern Thai history.

Though his role in the shadowy world of espionage may have been responsible for his death, Jim Thompson should be remembered as the foreign architect in Thailand who, in the 1940s and 1950s, beamed an outsider's

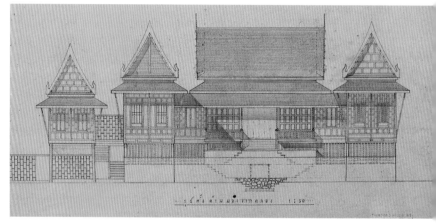

▲ *Architectural drawing of the Thompson House, prepared by Thompson and his Thai architect.*

▲ *Entrance hall and stairway.*

appreciative and knowledgeable eye on traditional Thai craft and architecture at a time when there was little local interest in indigenous art forms. Revitalising the Thai silk industry virtually single-handedly in the early 1950s, Thompson settled in Bangkok and bought a plot of land bordering the Thai capital's longest canal, Klong Saen Saep. The land was strategically located, with the Bangkrua district, home to Bangkok's Muslim community of Cham descent, which at the time was one of only a few groups in the country with any experience and recollection of ancient regional weaving skills, lying on the other side of the *klong*. Indeed, weaving in the country had been in slow decline since the introduction of imported, machine-made textiles which are much favoured by the progress-oriented Thais.

Rather than building a house from scratch, Thompson, an art connoisseur with a love of local materials and building methods, opted to purchase six traditional Thai houses and reassemble them on his site with the help of a local architect friend. Built in a matter of months between 1958 and 1959, the result of these six strung-together teak pavilions is a magical, whimsical whole, leaving visitors entranced by both the grandeur and intimacy of a perfectly balanced juxtaposition. While a couple of the houses were acquired in the capital (the largest of which became the drawing room) and date from 1800, the others, as well as connecting buildings, were brought down on barges from Ayutthaya, the historic, former royal capital north of Bangkok. Situated in lush and slightly wild grounds, the amalgamated house proved

▲ Scene from the *Vessantara Jataka*
Pigment on cloth | 19ᵗʰ century | 53 x 42.5 cm

to be admirably functional despite its numerous eccentric departures from Thai convention.

The visitor familiar with typically prefabricated and easily moved Thai housing (the structures were generally manufactured in parts and brought to the site by barge or cart, with buildings moving as whole villages relocated in search of more fertile land) will delight in the preservation of a number of traditional elements: sloping, extended eaves that provide shade as well as protection from the violence of monsoon rains; vents above doors and along the upper reaches of walls to ensure air circulation and ventilation; a total absence of nails, the structure secured with the traditional system of dowels and pins; a slight sloping of the walls on the outside, top to bottom, to encourage the rise and expulsion of hot air; stilts elevating the house and thus decreasing its vulnerability to flooding and wild animals; high sills between rooms keeping evil spirits and snakes at bay while preventing crawling babies from falling to the ground several metres below; and finally, graceful gable ends shaped like *naga* that lend the six pitched roofs their characteristic grace.

Less conventional and resolutely innovative is Thompson's reversal of walls (in the case of the drawing room), their polished outdoor surfaces, patinated by years of exposure to the elements, turned inward to

be enjoyed by those inside the house. Windows too have been subverted: once looking out but now looking nowhere due to the houses abutting one another, they have been turned into niches used to display ancient sculpture from the region. Western materials such as marble flooring (on both floors of the main house entrance hall) and Occidental room sequences do not so much jar as remind the visitor of the house's thoughtfully hybrid nature.

Surrounded and screened by a tamed jungle garden that includes a large variety of tropical plants, Jim Thompson's house would be charming and worth a visit even without the rich collection of works of art it harbours.

Stone head of Ardhanari
Sandstone | Lopburi, Thailand | 10ᵗʰ century | H: 36.5 cm

This head, of Lopburi School origin and similar in aspect to the Khmer style of Koh Ker, attests to the artistic and technical accomplishment of Khmer or Khmer-inspired art beyond the main Khmer centres. In relatively good condition, this head of the Brahmin deity Ardhanari (representing Shiva in half male and half female form) boasts sensitively carved facial features and an intricately decorated diadem and conical *mukuta*.

▲ **Buddha preaching** | *Painting on panel* | *Bangkok School, 19th century* | *38 x 52 cm*

small, traditional house from the vicinity of Ayutthaya, the entrance hall is distinct from the rest of the house with its boldly tiled black and white carrara marble floor imported to Thailand for use in a 19th-century Bangkok palace. Though unusual against the lustrous tones of the old teak walls, the worn marble is aesthetically pleasing. To the left as one enters, in niches converted from windows, stand carved wooden figures—a gong holder and an 18th century Ayutthaya period standing Buddha—from Burma and Thailand. Ascending the stairs to the hall's upper level and house proper, opposite the landing, the visitor will come across several large Thai paintings on cotton depicting Buddhist scenes dating from the 17th to the 19th century.

The hall's **upper level** houses outstanding early stone sculpture: in the left niche a figure of a Khmer, Angkor Wat-period limestone Vishnu, and to the right, a limestone Shiva of the same period. In a doorway centred between the niche, a sandstone Bayon-style 13th-century Buddha of Thai origin sits on an imposing *naga*.

Beyond the upper hall is the **dining room**. Jutting out at right angles from the drawing room axis, the dining room has windows on three walls, thus improving air circulation and reducing the heat. Two intricately carved Qing dynasty *mahjong* tables form a dining table. The room is lit by a 19th-century crystal chandelier acquired by Thompson in Bangkok. Note the impressive collection of Chinese blue and white porcelain on the tables and adorning the sideboard. Most of the pieces, 16th- and 17th-century exports, came from Ayutthaya (an important Asian trading hub 500 years ago), where they had been buried at the bottom of a river following a shipwreck.

■ **THE COLLECTION** As an architect, it is no surprise that Thompson possessed both a good eye for art and the technical knowledge and feel for materials necessary to confidently buy important pieces. As a wealthy entrepreneur, operating at a time when few moneyed collectors were based in Thailand, Thompson not only could afford to indulge in the best works of art, but also faced very little competition from either foreign or local Thai buyers on the open market. As a result, the Thompson collection includes some resplendent and rare pieces that in themselves warrant a trip to the museum.

As Thompson bought constantly from the time he founded the Thai Silk Company in 1951 to the time of his disappearance in 1967, his collection was initially dominated by fine classical stone and bronze works of art of Thai origin. Asked by the Thai government to give some of his best pieces up, however, he ceased collecting early sculpture (a number of fine pieces remain though) and moved instead toward later Chinese and Thai ceramics and furniture, and local painting and

drawing. The odd European work of art or decorative *objet d'art* also found its way into his collection. Today, the objects are organised more or less as they would have been during the owner's lifetime, their tastefully unpretentious display around the house serving to underscore their exemplar quality.

■ **THE ROOMS** Due to theft some years ago, the museum cannot be freely visited and thus the visitor enters the house in the company of a mandatory guide.

Once the visitor has removed his shoes, he or she is brought to the **entrance hall**, its door flanked by a pair of 19th-century Chinese stone lions from the Qing dynasty (1644–1911). Designed with two levels and originally a

▲ **Painting fragment, Phrai Malai visiting hell**
Pigment on paper | *Bangkok School, 19th century* | *28 x 16 cm*

A large collection of Bencharong enamel ware, prized by Thompson, has been assembled in the **Bencharong room**, an area off the entrance hall that was once the house's kitchen. Bencharong porcelain, made in China for the Thai market from the 17th century, incorporates typical Thai iconography with a heavily worked decorative background.

Thompson's collection, one of the biggest in Thailand, includes examples of most periods and shapes.

The house's **drawing room** is undoubtedly its most elegant. Thompson's ability to recast different objects for use as furniture is most apparent here: a traditional early 19th-century carved teak bed has been transformed into a coffee table; lacquered chests serve as lamp-tables; and lamp-bases have been made from Burmese drums. The large chandelier is a 19th-century Belgian crystal fixture, similar to the one found in the dining room and another antique shop find. As in other parts of the house, window frames in this room have been turned into niches, here accommodating wooden Burmese religious statuary of the early 19th century, given to Thompson by the Burmese in exchange for his advice relating to the modernisation of the Burmese silk industry. Also here, the visitor will find a large and finely carved sandstone 13th-century head of Buddha from the Ayutthaya School.

The drawing room is bordered on the *klong* side by a wide terrace that Thompson used for entertaining. Its floor is paved in 17th-century Ayutthaya brick and its balustrade made of green-glazed Chinese ceramic panels that were used as ballast by ships plying the 18th-century North-South Asian trade routes.

▲ *View of the drawing room.*

Stone torso of Buddha
Brown limestone | Lopburi region | Dvaravati School, 8th century | H: 104 cm

Rare due to its size and good condition, this limestone torso of Buddha is considered one of the most important sculptures in the collection. The simple, pared down style of the icon, the pureness of its pose and the elegance of the Buddha's humbly downcast expression is characteristic of the Dvaravati School (Mon Kingdom) which spanned the period from the 7th to 11th century and was influenced by Indian sculpture of the post-Gupta era.

Off the drawing room are Thompson's study and bedroom. The **study** contains one of the museum's most important pieces as well as one of Thompson's favourites—an 8th-century limestone Dvaravati Buddha from Lopburi Province. Some 15th-century Sukhothai ceramics lie on the desk and on bookshelves while a series of charming French prints depicting Siamese emissaries at the court of Louis XIV hang to the right of the doorway.

Thompson's **bedroom**, rather spartanly furnished, looks over the terrace and *klong* and also boasts some fine treasures. A magnificent carved teak bed, originally belonging to a member of the Thai royal family, dominates the room spatially, competing for attention with some top-quality stone sculpture positioned on a cabinet and low table on the room's left side. Particularly striking are a fine, pre-Angkor, 8th- to 9th-century grey sandstone head of Suriya from the Srivijaya School; an 11th-century sandstone standing figure of Uma in Khmer style found in Thailand; and the head of a Dhammapala in Khmer style, also found in Thailand, probably dating to the 12th century.

As well as having an excellent eye for art, Thompson apparently also enjoyed novelty objects: on the right wall in a glass case sits an early 19th-century miniature wooden maze-house for mice, a Chinese-built object designed to entertain children who would let loose their pet mice inside the house and delight in watching them scramble about trying to find morsels of food.

A small **guest room** behind the master bedroom contains a low, 19th-century, carved wooden dresser built for a Thai princess as well as a Chinese porcelain chamber pot in the shape of a sitting cat.

The **space under the house** that was used for big parties in Thompson's day now holds a number of important works of art. As well as Chinese ceramics, look for two large, grey, Dvaravati School limestone torsos, the first from the 8th century and the second, extremely rare, from the 7th century, considered by scholars to be one of the earliest and best remaining sculptures of the Dvaravati School in Thailand.

In addition to the main house, three separate **garden pavilions** that used to be servants' quarters house a collection of Thai paintings and assorted works of art (essentially gold objects, ceramics and bronzes).

Jim Thompson House, hidden at the end of a *soi* off Bangkok's busy Rama I Road, offers world-class art in a magical setting.

ADDRESS
4 Chao Fa Road
Phranakorn
Bangkok 10200
Thailand

CONTACT INFORMATION
T: +66 2 282 0637
F: +66 2 282 2639 / 2240

OPENING HOURS
9am–4pm daily;
closed on New Year's Day and
Song Kran.

ADMISSION
30 baht;
free for children.

FACILITIES
Guided tours are available
in English.

Auditorium; bookshop;
Museum Café; parking lot.

HOW TO GET THERE
Taxi or river taxi: Alight at Phra
Pinklao Bridge and walk east
or take a *tuk-tuk* along Phra
Pinklao Road from there.

AROUND THE MUSEUM
The National Museum (see pp.
144–147) and the National

Theatre are a few minutes
away, walking south. The
Grand Palace and Wat Pho
are further along in the
same direction.

National Art Gallery

Located on the northern side of Bangkok's Old City, close to the river, the National Art Gallery presents a broad variety of Thai fine art in its permanent galleries and temporary exhibitions space.

■ **THE BUILDING** Opened in 1977, the gallery is housed in an attractive, old, Western-style building of vaguely Italianate appearance. Erected in 1902, a few years after King Chulalongkorn's maiden visit to Europe, when classical European architecture was all the rage in Bangkok, the building was originally designed to house Thailand's first royal mint. Reminiscent of a Birmingham (UK) factory admired by the king, the brick building has a gabled roof, arched windows and decorative columns adorning the façade.

Within, the two-storey, 2,500-square-metre museum is airy and high-ceilinged with two side wings and a rear annex enclosing a central, square, open-air courtyard.

■ **THE COLLECTION AND GALLERIES** The permanent collection is shown in the main part of the building in two large galleries fronting the street to the left and right of the entrance. Focusing on various periods of Thai

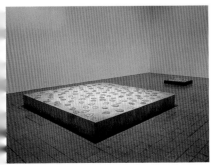

▲ **Pinaree Sanpitak**
*Breast Leaves I and II | Gilded bronze | 2000–2001
| Dimensions variable*

painting history (Western-style painting, predominant here, was introduced to Thailand in the mid-19th century and was firmly established by the early 20th), the art of King Rama VI (King Vajiravudh, reigned 1910–1925) and the present King Bhumiphol, or Rama IX, are presented first in the **Celebration Room**. The work of pioneer Modernists of note is shown in the **Senior Artists Room**, including paintings by Professor Silpa Bhirasri (an Italian by birth, the founder of Silpakorn University, Bangkok, and considered the father of modern art in Thailand), Kien Yimsiri, Fua Haribitak, Sawadi Tantisook and Misiem Yipintsoi (look for her work in Misiem's Sculpture Garden, p.194). Art spanning the late 1960s to the present is also represented in this gallery.

A recently created special section called the **Silpa Bhirasri Memorial Gallery** aims to convey the atmosphere of the distinguished professor's working office.

The second floor galleries are devoted to **Traditional Thai Art**, with religious banners, copies of old temple murals, and early Bangkok period painting displayed.

The left wing and rear of the museum offer totally different artistic fare, for many the true focal point of the museum. Here are housed frequently changing temporary exhibitions of Thai and sometimes foreign **contemporary art** of the more cutting-edge variety that may also be of particular interest to the foreign visitor. Many of Thailand's most dynamic and provocative avant garde practitioners, some

of whom are better known in New York or Berlin than in Thailand, their art at the other end of the spectrum from the mainstream conventional painting seen in the commercial galleries of Sukhumvit, have shown their work here in the last decade.

Indeed, while Bangkok awaits its long promised contemporary art museum (a change of municipal government put the project on hold a few years ago), the National Art Gallery figures as the only government space in Bangkok documenting and promoting Thai contemporary practice. Though the gallery's temporary exhibitions vary somewhat in theme and level of sophistication, more often than not the visitor will be given the opportunity to view new, exciting and thought-provoking contemporary art from Thailand and beyond. Past exhibitions include Bundith Phunsombatlert's *Landscape: Transmitting Thoughts* (2004), Araya Rasdjarmrearnsook's *Why is it Poetry Rather Than Awareness* (2002), Pinaree Sanpitak's *Vessels and Mounds* (2001), Jakraphun Thanateeranon's *Future in Mind* (1999), Sutee Kunavichayanont's *3rd Exhibition by the Cobalt Blue Group* (1996), Montien Boonma and Kamol Phaosavasdi's *Content/Sense* (1995), Vasan Sitthiket's *I Love Thai Culture* (1994), and Kamin Lertchaiprasert's *Muangnging Sae Lao* (1993).

Offering a mixed selection of Thai art, both contemporary and conventional, secular and religious, the National Art Gallery charts the development of visual art in Thailand right up to the moment.

ADDRESS
Na Phrathat Road
Phra Borommaharachawang
Sub-district
Phra Nakhorn District
Bangkok 10200
Thailand

CONTACT INFORMATION
T: +66 2 224 1333 / 1404
F: +66 2 224 1404

OPENING HOURS
9am–4pm Wed–Sun;
closed on New Year's Day and
Song Kran.

ADMISSION
40 baht.

FACILITIES
Guided two-hour tours in Thai,
English (9.30am Wed–Thu),
French (9.30am Wed–Thu),
Japanese (9.30am Wed)
and German (9.30am Thu)
are available.

Auditorium; library; museum
shop; cafeteria.

HOW TO GET THERE
By taxi or river taxi to Tha Phra
Chan pier.

AROUND THE MUSEUM
The museum is close to the
Grand Palace, Wat Phra Kaeo
and Wat Pho to the south
and the National Art Gallery
(see p. 143) across Phra
Pinklao Road.

Some cafés are located along
Na Phralan Road bordering
Wat Phra Kaeo to the south.

National Museum Bangkok

Thailand's foremost and oldest public art museum, Bangkok's National Museum offers an unrivalled introduction to all aspects of Thai art from prehistory to the 20th century in a historic architectural setting.

▪ **THE BUILDING** A stone's throw from Wat Pho and the Grand Palace to the south, the museum has occupied its present site since 1887. Housed in a royal palace that dates back to the reign of King Rama I (reigned 1782–1809) when it was built for the king's brother, the Prince Successor (the king's deputy, a title since abolished), it was known as Wang Na or 'Palace of the Front', a building conceived as a buffer zone for protecting the king. The museum's principal building thus dates to the first year of the Bangkok period which began when the Siamese capital was moved from Thonburi to Bangkok in 1782 and the first Chakri king assumed the throne.

A number of other distinguished historic buildings make up the museum compound. The **Tamnak Daeng** (Red Palace, see the smaller contemporary reproduction of this house in the Prasart Museum, pp. 148–149) built in Ayutthaya style and originally located in the palace grounds at Thonburi, dismantled and relocated to the museum precinct, is one of the loveliest. Another interesting building is the hybrid European-Thai **Issares Rajanusorn**, the residence of King Pinklao, one of King Rama IV's brothers, and containing 19th-century European furniture adapted to Thai taste. Other smaller pavilions dating to the early Bangkok period or later are dotted around the grounds and open to the public.

In addition to the domestic pavilions, the museum boasts sumptuous religious architecture in the form of the 18th-century **Wat Buddhaisawan**, located opposite the Tamnak Daeng and in the axis leading to the main museum building. The *wat* displays richly carved lacquer and gilt-ornamented gables and lacquered doorways which contrast with the otherwise sober column and platform design, a juxtaposition seen in other examples of early Bangkok period architecture. Featuring some of the finest and oldest murals in Bangkok (many are restored, others sadly very faded), the chapel was built to house, and still houses, the much-revered and mythic gilt bronze seated **Buddha Phra Buddhasihing** dating to the mid-15th century, whose place of manufacture remains to this day shrouded in mystery.

When the museum was moved from the Grand Palace to Wang Na in 1887, the collection was displayed in three of its ceremonial buildings, towards the front of the compound. However, in the 1920s the holdings, ever larger, were allowed to spill over into the palace's outer annexes and in 1967, two further two-storey elongated wings were constructed on the peripheral rear edges (north and south) of the principal building to house the museum's vast collection of sculpture. A further two galleries, those of Prehistory and Thai History have since been established on the left side of the compound, at the entrance in one of the palace's original buildings.

▪ **THE COLLECTION** The museum and the core of its collection date back to 1874 when King Chulalongkorn (Rama V, reigned 1868–1910) established the country's first art institution when he opened King Mongkut's (Rama IV, reigned 1851–1868) treasures to the Thai public. Initially displayed in the Grand Palace's Concordia Pavilion, the pieces were

▲ *Scene of the Buddha descending from Tavatimsa Heaven, from one of the better conserved murals in Wat Buddhaisawan, 18th century.*

▲ **Bronze ornaments**
*Ban Chiang culture |
c. 300 BCE–200 CE*

▲ Stone relief of Buddha
Sarnath, India | Early 6th century | H: 119 cm | Gift of the Government of India

subsequently moved to their present location. In 1926 the museum became the Bangkok Museum and after Thailand's constitutional reforms of 1932, the institution was administered by the Department of Fine Arts and changed names once more, becoming the National Museum Bangkok in 1934.

The collection includes every sort of Thai cultural material and is the largest of its kind in the world. It is also unique in presenting, along with the national holdings, broadly and well-selected examples of works of art from around Southeast and South Asia (Khmer, Cham, Javanese and Indian stone sculpture

among others) that intelligently position Thailand and its complex art history in a wider Asian context. Neolithic wares, Ban Chiang culture wares, jewellery, Buddhist and Hindu art in all media from Thailand and beyond, royal regalia, furniture, ceramics, textiles, musical instruments, stamps, coins and even vehicles for transporting royal family members can all be found here.

■ **THE GALLERIES** The collection is split into three major exhibition sites, one of which, in two parts, is on two levels. A number of subsidiary pavilions such as the above-mentioned Wat Buddhaisawan, Tamnak Daeng and Issares Rajanusorn must also be visited for their architecture as much as for their contents. As the museum is rich in objects and rather expansive, a thorough tour requires a full day. The visitor pressed for time should therefore concentrate on a selection of favourite galleries.

The **Thai History and Prehistory Galleries** are located in Siwamokhaphiman Hall on the left of the entrance and behind the museum shop and ticket counter. Here, both prehistory and indigenous history (from the Sukhothai period in the 13th century onwards) are examined through objects—the visitor will see a fair bit of Bangkok period royal memorabilia —and documentary displays such as text panels (in Thai and English) and dioramas elucidating key events. A work of particular local significance is the late 13th-century four-sided stone stele supposedly inscribed by the third king of Sukhothai Ram Kamhaeng and considered Thailand's first work of indigenous literature, describing as it does the Kingdom of Sukhothai in the Thai alphabet. The Prehistory Gallery, at the rear of the building, documents several of Thailand's recently discovered and important prehistoric excavation sites and their finds. Objects from the Dong Son culture, usually associated with Vietnam but also present in Thailand, are shown here.

The site at Ban Chiang, where excavations began in 1967, is featured prominently too. Ban Chiang bronze ornaments and implements

as well as a good assortment of pottery from the 4th millennium BCE to roughly 200 CE are shown here as well as in the **Ban Chiang Gallery** on the top floor of the south wing, where a model of the excavation site has been faithfully constructed.

The largest of the museum's exhibition spaces, the Wang Na's central palace buildings in the middle of the compound house the **Decorative Arts and Ethnological Collection**. Accessed through the **Throne Hall** where temporary exhibitions are held, the large space is divided into rooms where objects are assembled according to function or medium. Moving through the pavilion clockwise, the visitor first encounters the **Gold Treasures Room** displaying a good collection of gold ornaments and jewellery found at U-Thong (these particular pieces are 5th to 7th century) as well as 15th-century gold from Ayutthaya. The larger **Transportation Gallery** boasts several 18th-century royal palanquins and an intricately carved early 20th-century ivory *howdah* (elephant seat) given to King Chulalongkorn by the Prince of Chiang Mai. Other galleries exhibit respectively **Theatre Arts and Games**, **Ivory**, **Ceramics** (Lopburi,

▲ Terracotta head of Buddha
From Wat Phrangam, Nakhon Pathom Province | Dvaravati period, 9th century | H: 17 cm

Lanna, Sukhothai, Bencharong and Lai Nam Thong wares from Thailand as well as Chinese, Japanese and Annamese ceramics and porcelain), **Mother-of-Pearl Inlay**, **Wood Carving** and **Old Weapons** (a large collection with a life-size model of an elephant in full battle array as a centrepiece). **Stone Inscriptions**, historically rather than aesthetically speaking one of the most significant galleries, includes steles in Southern Indian, Sanskrit, Pali, Khmer and Thai languages ranging from the 7th to the 18th century. **Buddhist Religious Articles, Costumes and Textiles** include mainly 19th-century textiles manufactured in Cambodia, China and particularly India, to royal Thai specification (see also some interesting Northern Thai textiles for commoner use). **Royal Regalia & Gold Treasures** are at the centre, and finally,

▲ **Bronze Buddhist triad**
Found in Uthai Thani Province | Lopburi style, 13th century | H: 35 cm, L: 28 cm

Musical Instruments (Thai and a Javanese *gamelan* orchestra) figure at the entrance.

The museum's third section is the **Archaeology and Art History Collection** lodged in the two-storey wings south and north of the Wang Na complex. Here are certainly some of the greatest masterpieces of the national collection and visitors with tight schedules will be well rewarded if concentrating only on this part of the museum. As labelling here can sometimes be succinct and the interweaving fabric of regional and Thai art history complex, a museum guidebook or better still a museum-provided docent tour is recommended for a fuller appreciation of works of art in this part of the museum.

Assembling mainly Brahman and Buddhist art in stone and bronze, the two wings group their respective material chronologically, the south wing displaying general Asian Art, Lopburi Art and Ancient Hindu Sculpture on the ground floor and Srivijaya Art, Javanese Sculpture, Dvaravati Art and Ban Chiang Art on the second. Though the north wing concentrates properly on Thai art, the south wing is highly interesting for its elucidation of cross-cultural artistic and religious fertilisation around Southeast and South Asia in the 1st millennium CE. Highlights here abound and include, from Indian art (in the **Asian Art Gallery**) a large, early 6th-century sandstone Sarnath Buddha in semi-relief. This piece was a gift of the Indian government, but

▲ **Stone figure of meditating Buddha** | *Found at Wat Phra Sri Rattana Mahathat, Lopburi Province | Early Lopburi style, 14th century | H: 100 cm*

a much smaller stone relief of the same period and style displayed here was found in Thailand in Surat Thani Province, underscoring the well-established religious, trade and cultural links between Thailand and India at this time. The **Dvaravati Gallery** is one of the most impressive in this wing of the museum. See here a life-size full stone sculpture of Buddha of the 7th century; and at the end of the gallery, an 8th-century stone wheel of law over two metres in diameter, representing Buddha's first sermon and found in Nakhon Pathom Province (the wheel of law is a characteristic form of Dvaravati art not found in later Thai art). An elegant and large bronze Buddha in preaching *mudra* of the 9th century is also worth seeking out. The **Lopburi Gallery** features Khmer-influenced Thai sculpture in bronze and stone as well as a small selection of ceramics. Though sometimes referred to as 'provincial Khmer art', Lopburi works, powerful and artistically accomplished, are well worth a look in their own right. The adjacent **Srivijaya** and **Javanese Galleries** (second floor, west corner of the gallery), though not as large as the former, include works of art that shed much light on the aesthetic and formal ties linking the region's distinct visual expressions.

Those in search of fully developed Thai art will concentrate on the north wing. Here, the top floor houses large galleries devoted to the art of **Sukhothai** (13th–15th centuries) and **Ayutthaya** (14th–18th centuries), considered the high periods of Thai art and typified by their integration of the serene and aesthetic ideal into the whole work of art. The characteristic religious icon of Sukhothai is the walking Buddha in the full round, a good example here being a gilt bronze 15th-century figure of Buddha in *abhaya mudra* (gesture

▲ **Celadon elephant**
Sawankhalok | Sukhothai period, 14th–15th century | H: 20 cm

for dispelling fear, giving protection or subduing Mara) on a lotus pedestal. Visually, the religious sculpture of this period is lighter and gentler than the contemporary Khmer expression from which Sukhothai broke away among others. Though mostly Buddhist art in bronze and stone, a good number of domestic ceramics (Sawankhalok celadons and stoneware) and a few architectural elements of the Sukhothai period are also shown here. See in particular an imposing, nearly three-metre-high, mid-14th-century bronze figure of Vishnu from Sukhothai and a large bronze Buddha head in Kamphaeng Phet style dated to the 15th century. The **Ayutthaya Gallery**, focusing predominantly on Buddhist art, also features several exquisitely gilded and lacquered cabinets, generally depicting scenes from Buddha's lives. Cabinets of this sort, often the only pieces of furniture to be seen in a temple, were usually made of teak and used to store monasteries' precious and fragile palm-leaf manuscripts of religious scriptures. See in particular here a rare carved and painted teak cabinet dating from around 1750 that, as well as being an astonishing work of art because it is carved and painted, is an important historical document because it represents in some detail the architecture of the royal capital Ayutthaya before its 1767 sacking by the Burmese.

Rattanakosin art evolved at the end of the 18th century when Siam's capital was moved to Bangkok first from Ayutthaya and then from Thonburi, across from Bangkok. As with much 19th-century art in the West, and indeed in China, the art of this period tends to look back to the styles of previous periods. The **Rattanakosin Gallery** and the related adjacent **Decorative Arts Gallery** are located

on the north wing's ground floor, east side, and highlights here are in the *objets d'art* category rather than in the religious.

Further sections in this wing are the **Lanna Gallery** (works of art from Northern Thailand), the **Buddha Images Gallery** and the **Coins, Banknotes and Stamps Gallery**.

A vast museum, as rewarding in its architectural delights as in its extensive and comprehensive collection, the National Museum Bangkok should be the central feature of any visitor's cultural stay in Bangkok. If time is limited, the excellent museum tours given by knowledgeable docents are well recommended.

▲ **Bronze figure of Harihara**
Gilt | Sukhothai period, 15th century | H: 119 cm

ADDRESS
9 Soi Krungtepkreetha 4A
Krungtepkreetha Road
Huamark, Bangkapi
Bangkok 10240
Thailand

CONTACT INFORMATION
T: +66 2 379 3607/ 1 or
253 9772
F: +66 2 253 9772

OPENING HOURS
10am–3pm Fri–Sun;
by appointment only.

ADMISSION
300 baht; snack and drink
included.

FACILITIES
Shop; refreshments served.

HOW TO GET THERE
By taxi.

Sky train: Take the east line to
Onnut Station, then a taxi.

AROUND THE MUSEUM
The museum is in a mixed
residential-commercial area,
with small shops nearby.

Prasart Museum

In a seductive garden, an oasis of greenery and calm in the centre of bustling Bangkok, the Prasart Museum is a private museum boasting a varied collection of predominantly Thai art in a unique architectural setting.

■ **THE BUILDING** Founded in 1981, the Prasart Museum is the culmination of the vision and collecting impetus of Thai entrepreneur and connoisseur Khun Prasart Vongsakul. Wishing to assemble in one locale the best of Thai art and archaeology from their beginnings in prehistory to the Rattanakosin era of the 19th century, Khun Prasart has put the cream of his decades of collecting on display for the Thai and international public at large to enjoy.

Located in the eastern part of the Thai capital, the museum complex and the spectacular ponds and gardens surrounding it are both hybrid juxtapositions of the old and new, traditional and contemporary, and foreign and indigenous.

Assembling various structures, the complex includes a small Buddhist temple reminiscent of Wat Yai Suwannaram in Thonburi's Bangkok Noi Canal, a classic Thai house modelled after a scaled-down version of the Tamnak Daeng (Red Palace) in the compound of Bangkok's National Museum (see pp. 143–147), a teak library on stilts surrounded by water, and a European-style building of vaguely Italianate taste, the sort popular in Thailand at the turn of the 19th century when King Chulalongkorn, the first Thai monarch to visit Europe, had just returned from an admiring stint in the West. Other more recently constructed buildings in the compound are a Chinese shrine to Guanyin, a sandstone temple in Lopburi style, and a Lanna-style house in Northern Thai taste. The museum complex's entrance gate evokes early 18th-century Rattanakosin taste.

The garden, with its old gnarled trees and clipped shrubbery, combines both traditional Thai palace and temple landscape design with more contemporary elements such as paths winding through heliconias and bamboo thickets. Forming a lush and sophisticated backdrop for Khun Prasart's pluralistic mixture of indigenous, foreign, secular and Buddhist architecture, the museum grounds, featuring a number of rare plant species, antique Thai ceramics, Khmer stone, Burmese woodcarvings and Chinese Qing dynasty statuary, are well worth exploring in their own right.

■ **THE COLLECTION** A collector from childhood, Khun Prasart sought from the start to form a

▲ *Buddhist Chapel in Rattanakosin style overlooking the main pond.*

group of objects that would preserve Thailand's cultural legacy for posterity. Convinced of the richness of Thai art history from ancient times, he focused as much on Buddhist art as on early vernacular expression, assembling prehistoric pottery, pre-Thai Khmer wares and Lanna artefacts as well as the more typically collected Thai ceramics, Buddhist sculpture and Bencharong enamel ware of later periods. Chinese ceramics, European decorative arts of many types, Khmer art, furniture, paintings, photographs and much more figure in the museum as well.

■ **THE BUILDINGS AND GARDENS** The museum is set on an oblong piece of land, the visitor entering the complex through the main gate positioned on the side. Directly to the right as one enters is a well-stocked shop and beyond, at the end of a winding path, the **Chinese temple**. The largest building in the complex is the two-storey European-style villa, set more or less in the middle of the grounds. Most of the remaining buildings are located beyond, to the left, clustered around an 'L'-shaped pond at the extremity of the property.

The land on which the museum sits was acquired in two stages. The area where most of its buildings are concentrated, around the pond, is the original, and though the second, later-acquired plot is still being developed, the garden meshes the compound's two halves together seamlessly.

The first building erected by Khun Prasart was the **Buddhist temple**, used both as a functioning meditation space and a gallery to house **Buddhist art**. Located on the far left of the complex, overlooking the pond, it is built on a white marble platform supported in traditional early Bangkok fashion on sunken wooden piling. Not a reproduction of an existing construction, it is an original creation inspired by various artistically important Buddhist sites around Thailand. The building's structure and form is in early Bangkok style such as that seen at Wat Suthat, whereas its elaborate display of carved and gilded gables adorned with Hindu iconography derives from Ayutthaya-type religious architecture as seen at Wat Yai Suwannaram. A building at Bangkok's Wat Po, the Thai capital's oldest temple, served as a model for the decorative devices that surround the windows while the eave brackets were inspired by those supporting the roofs of the 18th-century Wat Buddhaisawan in the compound of the National Museum. The interior is decorated with a series of gold and black lacquer paintings and the floor is tiled in black and white marble. Currently, the temple houses a single 15th-century **Kamphaengphet** seated bronze Buddha positioned on an impressive pedestal that rises in tiers from the floor.

A second unique pavilion in the compound is a *hor trai* (library) made entirely of teak and erected in the middle of the pond opposite the temple. Libraries housing precious religious scriptures in Buddhist complexes were often surrounded by water to safeguard the manuscripts against attack by land parasites such as termites or white ants. Here, the library design is again a hybrid, juxtaposing Ayutthaya and Sukhothai architectural and decorative elements. It contains historical manuscripts, books and old photographs as well as Ban Chiang ceramics and some later Sukhothai wares in cases.

Though most of the buildings that make up the museum were designed and built by Khun Prasart, the **bell tower** overlooking the pond, to the right of the library and the temple, is original, salvaged from an old Nonthaburi temple near Bangkok.

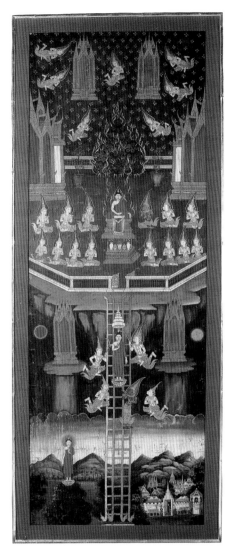

▲ **Buddhist temple painting on cloth**
Third quarter of the 19th century | 242 x 85 cm

Secular traditional Thai architecture is also well represented by the museum. The smaller-scale reproduction of the National Museum's **Tamnak Daeng**, admired by Khun Prasart since his youth, is one of the compound's most impressive architectural efforts. Fairly faithfully reproducing the early 19th-century pavilion which was originally built as a residence for Queen Sri Suriyentara, consort of King Rama II (reigned 1809–1824), and displaying a mixed Ayutthaya-Rattanakosin style, the copy's construction methods have also remained faithful to tradition in every detail, with pegs and dowels used instead of nails. Made of rare and

beautifully rich golden teak collected by Khun Prasart over many years, his recreation is supported by 48 pillars, a number of which date to the 18th century. Divided into five rooms and boasting a long, heat-shielding verandah, the house provides the perfect setting for Khun Prasart's collection of **Ayutthaya** and **early Rattanakosin** works of art. Set up more or less as if lived in, the Tamnak Daeng presents elegant and richly ornate gilded and lacquered Rattanakosin period (mid-19th century) furniture with Buddhist sculpture of the Ayutthaya period (14th–18th centuries).

Eclectic in appearance to the Western eye is the museum's fourth major building and its largest and broadest in exhibition terms, the Italianate-style **villa** to the left of the entrance. Though Khun Prasart originally built the house to live in himself, the size of his collection and its need for air-conditioning have obliged him to give it over to display (Khun Prasart now lives in a smaller pavilion in the complex). Here, the museum's owner has housed his European porcelain, crystal, jewellery, marble statuary, photographs and King Chulalongkorn memorabilia, the latter in particular affording a glimpse of turn-of-the-last-century collecting tastes in Thailand. Also here are the collection's Khmer bronzes, early Sukhothai Buddhist sculpture (in the meditation room), some earlier indigenous Buddhist art (see a Mon terracotta Buddha in particular and a U-Thong-style Buddha of the 13th to 14th century) and Sukhothai ceramics, among others.

As much a constantly evolving architectural exhibition site as an art museum—indeed Khun Prasart is still building new pavilions, with a **Puppet House** destined to hold traditional 18th-century Thai puppets being the latest—the Prasart Museum deserves to be savoured at a leisurely pace. Bearing the very personal imprint of its patron and thus truly a living museum, continuing to grow and respond to Thai art history in the making, the Prasart Museum and its magnificent gardens should not be missed by anyone interested in Southeast Asian art or architecture.

ADDRESS
131 Sukhumvit 21
(Asoke Road)
Bangkok 10110
Thailand

CONTACT INFORMATION
T: +66 2 661 6470 / 7
F: +66 2 258 3491
E: info@siam-society.org
W: www.siam-society.org

OPENING HOURS
9am–5pm Tue–Sat;
closed on public holidays.

ADMISSION
100 baht.

FACILITIES
Guided tours by appointment.

Auditorium; good gift shop;
courses and educational
events; weekly lectures.

HOW TO GET THERE
By taxi.

Sky train: Asok Station
(5 minutes away).

Subway: Siam Society exit.

AROUND THE MUSEUM
The museum is located in a
mixed commercial district.

The Siam Society and Kamthieng House Museum

Bangkok's Siam Society and its Lanna ethnological museum Kamthieng House, set in attractive, peaceful grounds, present a small but engaging collection of Thai art as well as a specialist library open to Society members.

■ **THE SIAM SOCIETY** Outward reaching and forward thinking, the venerable Siam Society, celebrating its centenary in 2004, was established by a group of local and expatriate residents of Bangkok keen to encourage and diffuse the arts and sciences of Thailand while finding common ground in these domains shared by Thailand and her neighbours.

Though well established by the first quarter of the 20th century, the Siam Society did not truly have a permanent home until 1933 when it was quartered in the Wattana district of eastern Bangkok where it still remains today in Asoke Road. Once one of the capital's more tranquil backwaters, this part of the city has been considerably built-up in recent years, hence the Siam Society compound's status now as a green and shady oasis in a dusty and noisy concrete jungle.

■ **KAMTHIENG HOUSE BUILDING AND COLLECTION** The library, opened by the present Thai monarch King Bhumipol in 1962, is a few years older than the art collection. The latter, small and including some Buddhist art and ceramics, began being assembled in 1965 thanks in part to American financial support. More distinctive than the library and

▲ *Display of votive icons including Buddhist works of art on the house's ancestral shelf.*

general collection, however, is the Siam Society's Lanna dwelling, Kamthieng House, given to the institution in 1963 by a Lanna descendant of the house's original owner.

Reconstructed in Bangkok as part of the Siam Society complex, the house was launched as a Thai ethnological museum in 1966, its principal vocation to display the Lannas' beliefs, rituals and ideologies in relation to the natural world. Redesigned in 2001 to include traditional sound and visual portraits, the museum now juxtaposes contemporary displays, an authentic domestic setting, video and sound, the house thus offering an atmospheric, sensorily accurate and informative view of traditional Lanna life.

Built in 1848 by Mae (mother) Saed, a granddaughter of the Prince of Muang Chae, and until its move to Bangkok, lodged on stilts

▲ *Part of the museum complex, surrounded by its lush garden landscaped in Northern Thai style.*

▲ *View of woven rattan fishing and trapping equipment stored under the main house.*

on the banks of the Ping River in Chiang Mai, the well-preserved Northern Thai structure is one of the country's few remaining examples of traditional Lanna teak houses of such imposing size and pristine condition. Passed down matrilineally (from mother to oldest daughter), the dwelling came to belong to Mae Kamthieng, Mae Saed's granddaughter, hence its current name.

The house presents two components, the family's private area for sleeping, with a broad verandah, and a kitchen and granary area, the latter being one of the most authentic traditional Lanna kitchens surviving today. While the complex itself provides a fine and complete (considered complete because the granary, rice pounder and well are included in the structure as well as the living quarters and kitchen) example of mid-19th-century Northern Thai domestic architecture, it is further enhanced by informative and well-made multimedia exhibits.

The house is divided into five main exhibition spaces where music, cultural material (essentially domestic and agricultural utensils and textiles) and audio-visual narrative combine to recreate Northern Thai village life 150 years ago. The displays give particular weight to the Lannas' spiritual beliefs and their relationship with nature, as well as exposing the links forged between community and environment. The Lannas' code of conduct, established to govern relationships between people, spaces and spirits, is also explored.

The first exhibit, the **Music of Courtship**, greets the visitor as he approaches the verandah at the beginning of the tour. Here, *joi*

and *pin-pia* courtship music sets the mood for commentaries on the culturally important *aew-sao* courtship practice as well as the inner and outer household spaces accessible to outsiders according to clan membership.

Spirit Dance and **Family Lineage** concern protection and inheritance issues, which are documented in the house's main living space. Male tattoos and other Lanna symbols of protection are shown here. The house's matrilineal heritage is evoked by textile designs, the ancestral shelf, footage of a traditional spirit dance, and a video narrative of family history as told by a family elder.

The tour continues to the kitchen where **Old Lanna Cooking with Mae Champa** presents screenings of Mae Champa planning her menu, picking vegetables in her garden, and cooking Kaeng Khae Kob (Northern frog hot soup) in the very kitchen visitors are examining.

The fourth display, lodged on the ground floor of the main house (in effect beneath the

▲ *Display of domestic tools and tribal iconography inside the house.*

▲ *A loom and other weaving equipment displayed in the museum.*

house proper), is an animated short film *The Adventure of Tokto,* describing Lanna village life and architecture seen through the eyes of Tokto, a cartoon gecko. Designed to appeal principally to children, the film enables viewers to learn about the relationship between the house and the community, as well as see how Lanna houses are built. Bamboo traps and a functioning loom, among other domestic tools and implements, are shown in this part of the museum as well.

Calling the Rice Goddess, the fifth multimedia exhibit, is housed in the granary and serves to explain Northern rice culture through *naga* rain symbols, agricultural implements, lunar calendars, and ritual chants sung by Pho-nan Praphat, one of the few remaining Northern ritual masters, calling to the spirit of rice and buffalo.

As well as the ethnological museum, the Siam Society grounds, landscaped in Northern Thai style, also feature **Saengaroon House**, providing an example of Central Thailand's traditional architecture.

The non-profit Siam Society offers Bangkok residents a scholarly but wholly accessible menu of cultural activities covering a broad range of topics. The overseas visitor will enjoy the society's tranquil and leafy grounds and its unique ethnological museum, Kamthieng House, with its collection of Northern Thai agricultural and domestic items and well-designed multimedia displays.

ADDRESS
352–354 Sri Ayudhya Road,
Rajathevi
Bangkok 10400
Thailand

CONTACT INFORMATION
T: +66 2 2245 4934 or
2246 1775 / 6 ext. 229
F: +66 2 2247 2079 or
2245 0569

E: cpfoffl@ksc.th.com
W: www.suanpakkad.com

OPENING HOURS
9am–4pm daily.

ADMISSION
100 baht;
student 50 baht.

Admission charges support a
number of charities as well as
the museum's operation.

FACILITIES
Good shop by the
ticket office.

HOW TO GET THERE
Sky train: From Phyathai
Station turn right and walk
for about 3 minutes.

AROUND THE MUSEUM
The museum is located in a
commercial district.

Suan Pakkad Palace Museum

The Suan Pakkad Palace Museum, established by a Thai royal couple to house their collection, offers a fine combination of traditional Thai architecture and distinguished art and antiques.

■ **THE BUILDING** The Suan Pakkad Palace is the creation of Prince and Princess Chumbhot of Nakhon Sawan Province, Central Thailand. Conceived in 1952, the royal couple acquired 19th-century traditional timber houses on stilts from provincial Thailand (several of these belonged to the prince's great-great-grandfather), dismantled and then rebuilt them on the present Bangkok site, a former commercial vegetable garden (hence the palace's name, Suan Pakkad or Lettuce Farm).

Starting with a reception pavilion and working on one house at a time, the project took a number of years to come to fruition. After the prince's death in 1959, his wife took over, finally donating the complete complex and art collection she and her husband had decided to house there to the Chumbhot-Pantip Foundation that continues to run the museum to this day.

▲ The verandah of House 2, displaying assorted furniture and memorabilia including commemorative Buddhist fans and an elephant tusk gong.

The museum consists of four groups of traditional Thai houses connected by raised walkways, the complex including eight dwellings in total as well as the Lacquer Pavilion and a Royal Barge. Unlike the Jim Thompson House (see pp. 138–142) where architectural alterations were made to the original teak pavilions, here, the houses have been reconstructed in their initial form. They are characterised by their large windows promoting ventilation, sharply sloping double roofs and deep eaves that offer protection from the tropical rain and glaring sun, stilts that raise them from the ground, thus preventing the access of snakes and flood waters, and panelled teak construction.

The museum's garden setting, with its wide variety of plants (some of foreign origin, brought back by the princess from her travels) and lotus pond, is no less remarkable than the buildings it encloses. That the compound is surrounded by densely built-up and bustling Bangkok makes it all the more magical.

■ **THE COLLECTION** Most of the art on display belonged to Prince Chumbhot's ancestors. However, a group of Ban Chiang pottery has been added in recent years, considerably extending the collection's dateline backwards in time. Since the addition, pieces in the museum range in date from roughly 3600 BCE to the 20th century.

Though much the material is of Thai origin, a number of foreign-made objects are also shown, including a selection of fanciful

▲ A room inside House 3 where some Bencharong ceramics are on display.

17th-century French drawings of the Siamese court that will give the visitor an idea of just how exotic Thailand must have seemed to Europeans 400 years ago.

Eclectic in content, yet impressive in breadth and in the quality of some of its pieces, the collection is charmingly displayed in a rather ad hoc manner, the works well suited to the house they have been chosen for.

■ **THE HOUSES** A different guide for each house escorts visitors on their exploration.

On the ground floor of **House 1** is the **Prince Paribatra Music Room** where a group of old Thai musical instruments belonging the late HRH Prince Paribatra, the 33rd son of King Chulalongkorn, is displayed. Drums, xylophones, Thai three-stringed fiddles and gongs are shown here. Upstairs, several Buddha icons of different periods and Asian origin are displayed (Southeast Asian private collections are not rife with Gandharan Buddhas), underscoring the collectors' breadth of interest and knowledge. Beyond, several Khmer stone sculptures are shown, among others a splendid 7ᵗʰ-century torso of Uma that the princess acquired from Aranya Prathet on the Thai-Cambodian border.

House 2 and **House 5** display some examples of the prince and princess's family furniture and personal and decorative items of fairly recent vintage, much being from the Rattanakosin period or later.

Some selected examples of Bencharong enamel ware are showcased in **House 3**. Though the collection does not approach Jim Thompson's in either breadth or size, those who have no time for the Thompson house will get a good idea here of these ornate, hybrid Thai-Chinese ceramics.

House 4 is a combined intimate family temple and dining room where a number of Buddha icons, either painted on cloth, or three-dimensionally sculptural, are on display.

House 6 contains a good assortment of early Chinese and Thai ceramics. As well as Sung, Yuan and Ming vessels, Thai pieces from the 14ᵗʰ and 15ᵗʰ centuries found here include Sawankhalok wares from the Sukhothai period and others from Chiang Rai. Burmese and Khmer pottery, some ancient beads, and prehistoric flint tools figure here as well.

House 7 is home to the **Khon Museum**, where a group of colourful Khon dance and performance-related masks and puppets are well displayed and documented.

House 8 lodges the **Chumbhot-Pantip Centre of Arts** on its second and third floors. Here, Ban Chiang ceramics of different varieties, as well as ancient bronze jewellery, spearheads, arrowheads, beads and remains, all excavated at Ban Chiang, are shown. Good

▲ *View of the Lacquer Pavilion, surrounded by the museum's lush grounds.*

labelling and modern displays and lighting ensure the visitor comes away with a clear understanding of this fairly recently discovered ancient culture. On the second floor, see too the **Marsi Gallery** where temporary exhibitions are scheduled.

Away from the entrance and the principal cluster of houses is the **Lacquer Pavilion**. Dating to the 17ᵗʰ or 18ᵗʰ century and the only one of its kind known in Thailand, the pavilion was formerly located in the precinct of the Ban Kling Temple on the Chao Praya River between Ayutthaya and Bang Pa-in. Prince Chumbhot was granted permission by the monks to move the pavilion to his palace. In compensation, he built new pavilions on the temple grounds.

Now a composite of two buildings, the pavilion's outer walls display elaborately designed carved reliefs evoking mythical beasts of all genres while its interior is decorated entirely in gold lacquer on black. Though not in pristine condition (thus adding to their charm) the paintings are particularly fine and lively, depicting scenes from the life of Buddha and the *Ramayana* epic, mirroring day to day events in Thailand 200 years ago, and describing foreign visitors touring Ayutthaya, Thailand's capital from the mid-14ᵗʰ century to the late 18ᵗʰ century.

In its idyllic garden compound and boasting the unique Lacquer Pavilion that in itself justifies a trip to the museum, the Suan Pakkad Palace Museum is a delightful place in which to forget the pace and pressures of contemporary Bangkok.

Interior of the Lacquer Pavilion
Gilt on black lacquer ground | Late Ayutthaya – early Bangkok period, 17ᵗʰ–18ᵗʰ century

Transported from a temple outside Bangkok, the well-conserved pavilion was reconstructed on the museum grounds in the 1950s, outer corridors added to enlarge the original building. The pavilion's murals are exquisitely painted, providing an example of artistic virtuosity not much seen in lacquer art of later periods. In additon to its expected Buddhist and Hindu iconography, the pavilion offers insight into secular Thai life at the end of the 17ᵗʰ century with its realistic evocations of daily life.

ADDRESS
16 Rajavithee Road, Dusit
Bangkok 10300
Thailand

CONTACT INFORMATION
T: +66 2 6286 300 ext. 5121,
5127 or 5128
F: +66 2 6286 049

OPENING HOURS
9.30am–3.15pm daily.

ADMISSION
Foreigners 100 baht ;
Thais 75 baht
child, student, monks and
nuns 20 baht.

Tickets for the Grand Palace
include entry to the mansion.
Mandatory English guided
tours start every 30 minutes
and last an hour.

FACILITIES
Souvenir shop; small
refreshments stand;
food shop.

Thai dancing twice daily at
10.30am and 2pm.

HOW TO GET THERE
By river taxi and taxi or *tuk-tuk* from a pier north of the
Old City.

By taxi from the centre of
Bangkok.

AROUND THE MUSEUM
There are cafés and shops
in the area around the
Dusit Palace.

Vimanmek Mansion Museum

Surrounded on three sides by water, Bangkok's turn-of-the-last-century Vimanmek Mansion in the Dusit Palace complex is one of the city's most charming architectural sites.

■ **THE BUILDING** The mansion was constructed at the end of the 19th century for Thailand's great and much-loved King Chulalongkorn (Rama V, reigned 1868–1910) and was designed by the king's younger brother, Prince Narisra Nuvadtiwongse.

It is located close to the National Assembly in Bangkok's Dusit Garden, an area north of Bangkok's Old City, once suburban and occupied by orchards and paddy fields, that King Chulalongkorn purchased upon his return from Europe in 1897 in order to establish a garden setting for the construction of a summer residence. Vimanmek ('celestial' or more literally 'cloud' residence) Mansion was the first and largest of the king's palaces to be built in the Dusit Palace complex. Far less

formal than the Grand Palace, the house is made of golden teak on brick and cement at ground floor level and is thought to be the largest teak dwelling in the world.

The mansion was initially partially erected on Koh Sri Chang in the Gulf of Siam (off Chonburi) as Munthaturattanaroj Residence. In 1893, however, construction was halted due to France's blockade of the Gulf following a dispute over the control of Lao territories east of the Mekong. In 1900, the King ordered the house dismantled and reconstructed in Bangkok's Dusit compound.

King Chulalongkorn, famous for his reforming and modernising initiatives, was the first Thai monarch to visit Europe and upon his return at the end of the 19th century, was clearly as impressed by Western architectural trends as he was by Western political institutions and educational systems. Designed in a hybrid Belle Epoque-Victorian-influenced style, with lacy gingerbread fretwork adorning the eaves and balconies, Vimanmek Mansion, light-filled and whimsical even to a European eye, must have seemed very exotic to Thais at the beginning of the 20th century. Pretty as the house may be, however, it is also cool, with deep enclosed balconies surrounding it on all sides, thus providing ventilation while considerably blunting the effect of the dazzling Bangkok sun.

'L-shaped in plan, the main structure is built on three levels while the octagonal-shaped appendage at the end of the west

▲ *Vimanmek Mansion's grand wooden staircase ascending three floors.*

wing, the king's private quarters, comprises four floors, surrounded as well by their own enclosed cooling balconies. The two right-angled wings that constitute the building's 'L' shape are each 60 metres long and 20 metres high, all floors thus enjoying uncommonly high ceilings, promoting the cooling effect of air circulation. Most of the large, airy apartments lived in by the king, his consorts, children and friends boast water views as the house is bordered by *klongs* and an artificial lake known as the Jade Basin on three sides. A short covered pier, the house's most

▲ *View of the palace's Victorian-style covered pier from the Jade Basin.*

obviously Victorian feature with its stylised neo-Gothic columns and decorative, painted lattice-work balustrades, juts out from the king's octagonal wing into the Jade Basin.

King Chulalongkorn moved into his mansion in 1901 and lived there for five years until departing for another residence in the compound. After the king's death in 1910, the house was inhabited only periodically and indeed, from 1932 to 1982, was altogether vacant, the property used solely as a royal household storage depot. Fortunately, however, the house had been maintained in reasonably good repair over the years and was successfully restored and opened to the public as a museum by Queen Sirikit in 1982 on the occasion of Bangkok's bicentennial celebrations.

▲ **Gold cigarette box**
*with a likeness of
King Chulalongkorn
surrounded by diamonds*

■ **THE ROOMS AND COLLECTIONS** The visitor, who must be escorted by the mansion's well-informed guides, may access 31 of the palace's rooms and apartments, the latter set up as domestic spaces rather than as galleries in a museum. A guided tour lasts roughly an hour and should be complemented by an exploratory walk around the palace's lovely grounds.

When Queen Sirikit rediscovered **Vimanmek Mansion** in the early 1980s, much of King Chulalongkorn's and his entourage's original furniture, art and personal effects were still *in situ*. Thus, the royal dwelling has retained its period atmosphere, the king's octagonal four-storey quarters particularly well restored to their early 20th-century splendour.

The collection includes paintings, a grand piano in the king's sitting room, photographs, furniture, carpets, glass and crystal, silver, ivory, ceramics and assorted memorabilia, among other categories, belonging to King Chulalongkorn or other members of the royal

household, as well as some more recent additions. The objects and furniture are for the most part European in origin—Fabergé and Tiffany are some famous names to look out for—or if not, in European taste, though there are some Thai traditional crafts, particularly ceramics, dating to the Bangkok period as well. A small collection of Chinese blue and white porcelain spanning several dynasties is another feature, as is a music room where traditional Thai instruments are displayed along with ceramics in glass cases.

On the Dusit Palace grounds there are a further **14 galleries** or **royal residential halls** (mainly clustered on Vimanmek Mansion's right side as the visitor

approaches from the ticket office) that exhibit a wide variety of objects and works of art. Among the more interesting exhibits are a collection of Thai craft wares under the patronage of the SUPPORT Foundation, photographs of royal ceremonies, Sukhothai and Ayutthaya pottery salvaged from a shipwreck off the eastern coast of Thailand, Buddhist art, Ban Chiang culture artefacts, old textiles and clocks, and royal carriages.

Though not boasting an art collection rivalling that of the Jim Thompson House for example, the Vimanmek Mansion Museum in Bangkok's Dusit Palace compound should be on travellers' itineraries for its delicate and whimsical architecture, eclectic interiors and picturesque lakeside setting.

Because the museum remains the property of the Thai royal family, decorum in visitors' dress is required.

▲ *One of the palace's many Residential Halls displaying a collection of early 20th-century royal family photographic portraits.*

ADDRESS
Chiang Mai-Lampang
Super Highway
Chiang Mai Province 50300
Thailand

CONTACT INFORMATION
T: +66 53 221 308
F: +66 53 408 568

OPENING HOURS
9am–4pm daily;

closed on New Year's Day and
Song Kran.

ADMISSION
30 baht.

FACILITIES
Gift shop; parking.

AROUND THE MUSEUM
Though the museum is
somewhat outside the older

part of the city, 15th-century
Wat Chetet Yot is a few
minutes away on foot to
the west.

The Tha Nin Market to the
south is also of interest.

The Tribal Museum (see p.
159) is a few minutes away.

Chiang Mai National Museum

The main regional museum of the North, Chiang Mai National Museum provides a good introduction to Northern Thailand's ancient culture from pre-Neolithic times to the present with emphasis on the Lanna Kingdom.

■ **THE BUILDING** The museum building, located on the northern fringe of Chiang Mai beyond the old city, on a major thoroughfare leading out of town, has been recently expanded and renovated to include modern displays and technology. Opened in 1973, the purpose-built, white-washed and red-gabled museum building is designed in typical Thai style with a traditional, steeply pitched tiered Lanna rooftop. Elegant and airy with its large open-air entrance pavilions, the museum is surrounded by leafy grounds, the neighbouring hills visible in the distance. In the compound around the museum, two kilns dating to the 17th century or earlier are displayed.

■ **THE COLLECTION** The museum's collection is large and diverse, its Buddhist art (issuing principally from Chiang Mai's many important *wats*), ethnological material and Sawankhalok ceramics of great interest. Including around a million objects, the collection first began being assembled in the 1950s and was moved to its current location in 1973. See in particular an extraordinarily imposing, nearly two-metre-high bronze Buddha head with traces of gilding dated to the 14th or 15th century, an 18th-century inlaid and lacquered Buddha footprint on panel from Chiang Mai's Wat Phra Singh, and a

bronze U-Thong head of Buddha dated between the 12th and 15th centuries.

■ **THE GALLERIES** The collection is split into six thematic sections displayed on two floors. On the ground floor, beyond the three linked open-air entrance pavilions, is a large auditorium on the left side. On the right, and towards the rear of the museum, are three galleries devoted to the natural and cultural background of the Lanna Kingdom (Topic 1), the establishment of Chiang Mai up to the time of Burmese control (Topic 2), and Chiang Mai under the Kingdom of Siam after the Burmese had relinquished control of the city (Topic 3).

▲ **Face of Buddha**
Terracotta | Hariphunchai art, 12th–13th century | H: 19.8 cm

The three thematic galleries on the second floor cover the trade and economy of the Lanna Kingdom from the late 18th to the 20th century (Topic 4), social development in various public spheres (Topic 5), and the evolution of Lanna art style and the history of art in Thailand from the Dvaravati period to the present (Topic 6).

The largest gallery area on the ground floor, covering **Topic 1**, includes material documenting the geology, ecology, geography and prehistoric settlement of the

▶ **Lacquer offering vessel with lid**
Lanna, for royal use | Late 19th–early 20th century | H: 59 cm

North. In modern-day geographical terms, the area described as the Lanna Kingdom covers Thailand's eight Northern provinces of Chiang Mai, Lamphun, Lampang, Chiang Rai, Phayao, Phrae, Nan and Mae Hong Sen. The city of Chiang Mai, the region's dominant urban centre since its founding in 1296, is given particular attention in this section, text boards and photographic panels narrating its topography, mineral production and other natural features and resources.

Objects such as Neolithic stone tools, iron implements, bronze

▲ Ban Chiang pottery vessel
Ban Chiang, Udon Thani | Prehistoric, 1000–500 BCE | H: 30 cm

ornaments and ancient pottery tell the story of the area's prehistoric settlement. A number of regional sites and their finds are documented here. See in particular tools excavated from the Ban Wang Hai archaeological site in Lamphun Province. Later material in this gallery includes examples of Lua (a people of the North) costumes and bronze and silver ornaments. The section ends with the documentation of the Hariphunchai Kingdom, the first state created in the North in the 7th century, the Kingdom's introduction of Buddhism and Indian civilisation to the region, and the establishment of Chiang Mai. Objects shown here include Hariphunchai-style terracotta vessels and Buddhist icons.

To the right of this gallery is the area covering **Topic 2**, the History of the Lanna Kingdom from its founding at Chiang Mai by King Mingrai to its subjugation by Burma (1558–1769). See in particular from Wat Chiang Man—Chiang Mai's oldest temple built in the year of its establishment—an ancient inscribed stele charting the city's founding. The gallery features text panels and objects documenting this important time (many of the city's *wats* were built during this period), with emphasis placed on Chiang Mai's transformation into a dominant centre of Theravada Buddhism. Works here include jewellery, replicas of gold and silver thrones of the 16th to the 18th century, various periods' ceramics and glassware from Lanna, Sukhothai ceramics contemporary to Lanna wares, a few Chinese porcelain vessels, and bronze and gilt bronze Buddhas spanning the 14th to the 18th century. See sophisticated painted ceramics from the San Kamphaeng and Wiang Kalong kilns.

Topic 3 is covered in the gallery jutting out towards the rear of the museum. Here, Chiang Mai under the Kingdom of Siam is explored from the brief period spanning the final expulsion of the Burmese in 1774 to the re-establishment of the city in 1782. Exhibits here include rifles and swords of the era as well as paintings and dioramas depicting its warfare. Lanna's relationship with the Kingdom of Siam, of which it became a tributary at this time, is also explored through elaborate court furniture and ceremonial dress.

Above this gallery, on the second floor, is the area covering **Topic 4**, the trade and economy of Lanna from 1782 to 1939 when the kingdom formally joined the modern state

▲ Cast bronze head of Buddha | *Lanna | 15th–16th century | H: 178 cm*

▲ Sacred jacket
Pigment on cotton | Lanna | Late 19th century

Bangkok period are evident in many of the Lanna works, these outside sources of aesthetic and formal inspiration explained here. See in particular a large gilt bronze seated Buddha of the 13th to 15th century from Wat Phra Singha as well as some 12th- to 13th-century terracotta torsos of Buddha found locally. Later material includes several exquisite 18th- to 19th-century lacquered and inlaid Buddhist scripture boxes.

Well laid out and clearly labelled in Thai and English, the Chiang Mai National Museum collection, centering on the history and culture of Northern Thailand, provides a comprehensive introduction to the lesser known Lanna Kingdom and its rich and impressive artistic heritage.

of Thailand. The gallery charts the development of Chiang Mai as a centre of commerce in the 19th century, with merchandise arriving by land and water to the city's markets. Photographs, dioramas and objects elucidate road and rail expansion as well as the teak industry that was a major source of income for the area at the time.

Topic 5 is sociological in flavour, the gallery on the museum's east side examining the social development of public health, education, banking, agriculture and industry in the region during modern times. Photographs and examples of machinery and tools such as fish traps and looms underpin this section. Some domestic works of art such as betel boxes and food containers manufactured from lacquer and silver are shown here too.

The last gallery, the museum's largest, located on the west side of the second floor and covering **Topic 6**, is one of the museum's richest in works of art. Here are studied stylistic changes in Lanna art over eight centuries, and the history of art in Thailand from the Dvaravati period to the present. Many Buddhist icons from the apotheosis of the kingdom in the 14th century are presented, as well as revival pieces from the 19th century. Influences from neighbouring cultures such as the Dvaravati, Mon, Khmer, Burmese, Sukhothai, Ayutthaya and later that of the

Cast gilded bronze figure of seated Buddha
Lanna, Chiang Mai | 13th–15th century | H: 114 cm

Presented to the museum by Chiang Mai's Wat Phra Singha, this stately figure of Buddha is positioned in 'Subduing Mara' *mudra*. Though its dating is approximate, spanning two centuries overlapping both the Early Chiang Saen and Sukothai-influenced Late Chiang Saen, this Buddha is modelled in Early Chiang Saen style, the figure displaying clear Hariphunchai influence in its halo, leg position and garment.

ADDRESS
Ratchamangkla Park
Chotana Road, Muang
Chiang Mai 50300
Thailand

CONTACT INFORMATION
T/F: +66 53 210 872

OPENING HOURS
9am–4pm Mon–Fri;
closed on public holidays.

ADMISSION
Free; donations are welcome.

FACILITIES
No lift, wheelchair access
is difficult.

Guided tours on request.

Library; well-stocked shop
with crafts, photos and
ethnological recordings; NGO

coordination; parking.

The museum organises
tribal village stays that
are informative while also
respectful of the local culture
and customs.

HOW TO GET THERE
By taxi from the centre of
Chiang Mai.

AROUND THE MUSEUM
The Chiang Mai National
Museum (see pp. 156–158)
is a few minutes away
towards town.

Tribal Museum

Located on the northern fringe of Chiang Mai, the Tribal Museum offers a fine collection of tribal artefacts, clothing and domestic tools in an attractive leafy site.

■ **THE BUILDING** The museum was established in 1965 on the campus of Chiang Mai University and attached to the government-run Tribal Research Institute, Department of Public Welfare. In 2002, it came under the Ministry of Social Development and Human Security. It then moved from its cramped premises to its current location in 1997. Housed on the first floor of a modern four-storey pagoda-shaped structure overlooking a small lake in Ratchamangkla Park, the museum benefits from a luminous environment because of the sweeping windows encircling the building. A library and auditorium on the second floor, above the gallery, complete the museum's facilities.

■ **THE COLLECTION** Numbering over 1,000 objects of which roughly 600 are on permanent display, the collection was initially assembled in the early 1960s for study purposes at a time when Thailand's rapid modernisation and urbanisation began to threaten the Northern minority peoples' traditional way of life and as a result, their material culture. Documenting the nine principal ethnic tribes of Northern Thailand, the museum presents examples of their different material culture as well as photographs and text boards elucidating their varying customs, languages, belief systems and aesthetic expression.

▲ Member of the Karen, the largest tribal group in Thailand, and established mainly on the Thai-Myanmar border.

Assembled all together in one space, the objects and associated rituals and practices can thus be contrasted and compared, affording the visitor a good understanding of both tribal organisation and the nuances differentiating the peoples' beliefs and cultures. Visitors keen to explore the subject further can consult the Highland Ethnic Information Centre within the institute.

The tribes surveyed include the ethnic Karen, the largest group, the Yao, Akha, Hmong, Lahu, Lisu, Lua, H'tin and Khamu. And though the museum and research institute behind it look more particularly at these peoples within the context of Thailand, since some of the tribes reach across the Golden Triangle over the borders of China, Laos, Myanmar, Vietnam and Cambodia, much of the information gleaned here applies beyond Thailand.

Objects on view include costumes, ornaments and jewellery, domestic utensils such as pots, cooking tools and basketry, agricultural implements, hunting tools, drums and ceremonial stringed and wind musical instruments, as well as ritual paraphernalia.

The collection continues to grow with additional research and donations.

■ **THE GALLERY** The museum is housed in a large airy room partitioned at the sides, with

▲ Young members of the Khamu tribal group, originally of Lao origin but now established in Thailand.

objects grouped thematically according to function. Mannequins wearing each tribe's characteristic dress are displayed, sometimes in diorama form, performing a ritual or playing an instrument. Labelling in Thai and English is detailed and informative.

A straw-decorated 'spirit gate' of the type marking the entrance of Akha villages and designed to ward off evil is positioned at the entrance of the museum.

Though small, the Tribal Museum provides an excellent introduction to the hill peoples of Northern Thailand and the surrounding region. Often overlooked because of their minority status, the ethnic tribes of Southeast Asia, studied as a whole, offer some fascinating insights on migratory, cultural and linguistic patterns in this part of Asia. As modernity encroaches on these peoples' traditions, institutions such as the Tribal Museum will be of increasing value to the understanding of fast disappearing indigenous cultures.

ADDRESS
Sala Michai, Muang district, Nakhon Si Thammarat Province 80000 Thailand

CONTACT INFORMATION
T: +66 75 341 075

OPENING HOURS
9am–4pm Wed–Sun; closed on National Holidays.

ADMISSION
30 baht.

HOW TO GET THERE
By bus from the centre of town.

FACILITIES
Guided tours by appointment.

AROUND THE MUSEUM
Wat Suan Luang and Wat Phra Mahathat (8th century) are located south and north of the museum respectively, on Rachdamnern Road.

The Regional Office of Archaeology is on the same road, north of the museum.

Surviving stretches of the old city wall can be seen north of the museum towards the city centre.

Nakhon Si Thammarat National Museum

Located in southern Thailand, 250 kilometres north of the Malaysian border, the Nakhon Si Thammarat National Museum offers a good selection of early Southern Thai works of art in a well-appointed setting.

▪ **THE BUILDING** On the southern edge of town, housed in a 1970s building designed by the province's team of architects and engineers, the museum presents two floors of exhibition space. In 1996, an extension was constructed to accommodate offices and a special exhibition area. Both buildings are surrounded by an attractive garden boasting a variety of century-old trees and an ancient well dating to the late Ayutthaya or early Bangkok period.

▪ **THE COLLECTION** The provincial city of Nakhon Si Thammarat, often referred to simply

▲ **Bronze kettle drum**
Ban Ketkai, Mueang district, Nakhon Si Thammarat Province | Prehistoric period, c. 500 BCE | H: 48.5 cm, D: 81.5 cm.

as Nakhon, was once an important trading centre on the commercial route connecting China and India. Strategically situated looking east to the Gulf of Thailand and the South China Sea beyond, Nakhon's seaport, though later eclipsed, was of significance from ancient times until the 13th century when the powerful royal centres of Ayutthaya and Sukhothai came to the fore. Early archaeological remains found in the region around the city—so rich is the area archaeologically that even the museum grounds, when being surveyed for the building's foundation, yielded a number of pots and shards—attest to the area's well developed cultural and religious fabric. The museum's collection thus reflects Nakhon's past as a prosperous and cosmopolitan hub of commercial, political and religious power.

Further to a series of excavations undertaken around Nakhon in the mid-1960s that yielded large quantities of artistically and historically significant archaeological material, the museum was conceived in 1971 and opened three years later.

The collection features prehistoric and historic material. The prehistoric artefacts, exclusively of Southern Thai origin, date as far back as 4500 BCE and include stone tools for

gathering and hunting, baked clay vessels, and metal-age utensils, drums and ornaments.

The historic material is divided into two groups. The earlier pieces, acquired from Nakhon Si Thammarat and its vicinity and dating to a period running from approximately the 1st century BCE to the 1st century CE, confirm a cosmopolitan presence in the region, with a number of objects of foreign origin having been excavated including inscribed seals, gold ornaments, medals, pottery, rings, beads and other types of personal ornaments.

The later dated material, from the 5th to the 19th century, are of various types. They include works of art found in Southern Thailand; works of art from other Thai cultures and periods brought from the National Museum in Bangkok specifically for study and comparative purposes; ancient implements and works of art found in the region but of foreign manufacture; and finally, household utensils and objects of socio-anthropological significance discovered in the southern part of the country.

Another feature of the museum, unrelated to the institution's main archaeological thrust, but of local interest, is the room dedicated to the Buddhist patriarch Phra Rattanathatchamunee (1852–1934).

▲ **Stone tools resembling a xylophone**
Tambon Srakaeow, Sala district, Nakhon Si Thammarat | Prehistoric period, c. 1st century | L (longest piece): 73.5 cm

THE GALLERIES The collections are presented on two floors.

Along with a small theatre, three galleries are laid out on the lower floor.

The **Prehistory** section, to the right of the entrance hall, includes an assortment of stone objects all found in Nakhon Si Thammarat province. Among the tools are interesting oblong implements displaying cross-hatched incised lines that were used for extracting fibre from tree bark. An ancient stone xylophone-like artefact dating approximately to the 1st century is shown too, as are some stone bangles. Other types of items featured in this part of the museum are earthenware vessels with cord-imprinted decoration or tripod legs, bronze wares in the form of two poorly conserved *mahoratuek* drums (kettle drums of the Dong Son genre, rarely found in Thailand) dating to approximately 500 BCE, and assorted coloured and sometimes decorated glass and stone beads that were both locally made and imported.

Opposite the Prehistory section is the **Arts In Thailand** section comprising a small but

▲ **Bronze figure of Uma (Southern School)**
Brahman shrine, Mueang district, Nakhon Si Thammarat Province | 17th–18th century | H: 45.5 cm

intelligently assembled group of works and artefacts of differing periods and indigenous cultures that invite comparison with local material. Represented here are pieces from the Dvaravati, Srivijaya, Lopburi, Lanna, U-Thong, Sukhothai, Ayutthaya and Bangkok periods and schools.

The third gallery and largest on this floor is the **Arts Found In The South** section. Here, a broad array of objects worked in a variety of media is shown, most of religious inspiration and confirming early cultural development in the southern part of the kingdom. Text boards and exhaustive labelling elucidate the particular role Nakhon Si Thammarat and its vicinity played in the dissemination of Buddhism and Hinduism in Thailand as these ancient religions travelled eastwards from India and Sri Lanka to greater Southeast Asia.

Though many works of art from the Southern region exhibit typically Thai stylistic characteristics, a number, surprisingly, are closer to India in feeling. Particularly noteworthy here are not only the early Hindu-influenced icons of southern Thai art, such as a 5th–6th century, well-worn stone figure of Vishnu (reputedly the oldest Vishnu in

▲ **Stone figure of Vishnu (Southern School)**
Vishnu shrine, Mueang district, Nakhon Si Thammarat Province | 5th–6th century | H: 78 cm

Southeast Asia) that was found in the Mueang district of Nakhon Si Thammarat and is of South Indian artistic style, but far later material that also bears strong traces of South Indian influence. Examples here are a bronze Uma of the 17th or 18th century found at a Brahman shrine in the province and displaying a decidedly Indian aesthetic, and a large bronze figure of a Dancing Shiva of the same period, also found in the district and exhibiting an even more South Indian appearance.

The three galleries on the larger upper floor cover **Southern Domestic Utensils** (see some rubber extracting utensils that remind the visitor of the region's links with the rubber industry a century ago), textiles, decorative works of art from the late Bangkok period of no particular distinction, basketry and ceramics, and finally, Phra Rattanathatchamunee's room.

Though geographically somewhat removed from the better-known archaeological and cultural centres of Thailand, the Nakhon Si Thammarat National Museum is a well-presented institution providing information about cultural and artistic influences, most importantly from India, in pre-modern Thailand.

▲ **Bronze dancing Shiva (Southern School)**
Brahman shrine, Mueang district, Nakhon Si Thammarat Province, Chola dynasty style | 17th–18th century | H: 76 cm

ADDRESS
Technopolis
Rangsit-Nakorn Nayok Road
Klong 5, Klong Luang
Pathum Thani 12120
Thailand

CONTACT INFORMATION
T: +66 2 577 9999 ext 1803
F: +66 2 577 9900
W: www.nsm.or.th

OPENING HOURS
9.30am–5pm Tue–Sun.

ADMISSION
Adult 50 baht;
child and student free;
10 baht for science shows.

FACILITIES
Wheelchair access.
Free parking; café; shop.

HOW TO GET THERE
Bus: 1155 from Future Park in
Rangsit; 381, 1156, 25 or 44
along Rangsit-Nakhon Nayok
Road.

By car: From Bangkok take the
exit to Rangsit-Nakorn Nayok
Road and turn left after the
small bridge over Klong 5. The
Technopolis is on the right.

AROUND THE MUSEUM
Thammasat University and
Pathum Thani are a short
drive away.

National Science Museum

Housed in a spectacular, gravity-defying building beyond the airport just outside Bangkok, the National Science Museum is one of the best of its type in Southeast Asia.

▪ **THE BUILDING** Located in the Technopolis science complex at Pathum Thani, 50 minutes north of Bangkok, the Science Museum is the first in a series of museums to be opened under the mantle of Thailand's new National Science Museum Organisation. Being built on the same site are the Natural History Museum, the Ecology and Environment Museum and the Information Technology Museum.

As well as technologically sophisticated, user-friendly interactive displays, the National Science Museum offers some of the most distinctive and exciting contemporary architecture in Southeast Asia.

Launched to celebrate Queen Sirikit's 60th birthday in 1992, the institution's construction was completed in 1996 and the museum was officially opened to the public in 2000. The museum's design team was led by Thai architect Chalermchai Honark (at the time the Deputy Governor of the Thailand Institute of Scientific and Technological Research),

▲ *View of a gallery.*

▲ *View of the museum's façade.*

whose three corner-supported cube structure, while aesthetically seductive, provides a clear reference to scientific and technological achievement.

Though sited on Pathum Thani's Klong Luang (Canal Five), the locale's water feature aside, the museum is situated in a flat, barren landscape which serves to accentuate the building's powerful, almost surrealistic appearance against the vast Thai sky. The building's structure is made of rust-free, epoxy-coated girders and reinforced concrete. The outer cubes are clad in ceramic-covered steel plates that are low maintenance and have insulating properties that reduce the heat inside the building, an important feature in

Central Thailand's tropical heat. The building's ceramic façade appears to subtly change colour during the day according to the amount of light reflected on its surface.

▪ **THE DISPLAY** The exhibition space is contained in the inner cube section of the building, the latter's 45-metre height divided into six floors with a total display space of 10,000 square metres. The two other tilted cubes house offices and workshops covering an additional 8,000 square metres.

When building the museum, the government set a number of goals, all of which have been met. The most relevant of these for the visitor are that the museum meets international standards, encourages interactivity (with museum-goers making their own discoveries), is fun and exciting in design and content, furthers science education, and perhaps most interestingly, acts as a link between modern and traditional technology. All the displays here are exhaustively labelled in Thai and English.

The visitor enters the museum on the ground floor, accessing the **Reception** and **Introductory Area**. To the right of the ticketing and information booth is a large and well-stocked museum shop, and further on, a text panel introducing the pioneers of science over the last 200 years. For those interested in the building itself, a small area next to the central meeting point documents the museum, its approach to science, and its fascinating architectural design. A large

▲ *Optics explained in the Basic Science and Energy display.*

temporary exhibition gallery is positioned on the left of the entrance, and a smaller one at the rear, adjacent to the escalator. With comprehensive signs in Thai and English, the museum, despite its overwhelming size, is easy to navigate.

Visitors can access the museum's five upper floors by escalator or lift.

Level Two presents the **History of Science and Technology**. The gallery consists of two areas split into further sub-sections. These highlight the Origin of the Human Species and the Development of Science, the History of Science, the Vision of Great Scientists, and the Fragile Earth. They aim to review the impact of science on our lives and the environment in which we live. Interesting exhibits include a cast of Lucy, the fossilised human found in 1974 in Ethiopia, and considered the oldest known hominid genus Australopithecus. Lucy is surmounted by a wooden model of Leonardo da Vinci's design for a flying machine, and suspended above this is a life-size model of an astronaut repairing a satellite in space. In the Vision of Great Scientists section, look for a well-made interactive video featuring six great scientists and philosophers (Charles Darwin, Albert Einstein, René Descartes, Isaac Newton, Aristotle and Dmitri Mendeleyev) discussing their work and world views.

Level Three presents **Basic Science and Energy**, where the fundamentals of science and energy are introduced through interactive exhibits that allow experimentation. Subjects here are grouped into Mathematics, Light, Force and Motion, Sound, Electricity, Magnetism, Friction, Heat, Matter and Molecules, Power Tunnel, Cinema and Chemistry. A mini-theatre with a multi-vision projector system shows films featuring energy in action to emphasise the significance of power as a resource. The exhibits in all 12 sections are varied, instructive and well designed, showing that much thought has gone into their development. And because most of them are interactive, visitors with young children will do well to start their museum visit here. Children and adults alike will delight in the fun and hands-on exploration of basic concepts such as shadows, lenses, colour, echoes, sunlight, static, tides, gears, gravity, water and wind.

Level Four explores **Science and Technology in Thailand**. Here, the natural history, geology, ecology and geography of the country are investigated.

Level Five is devoted to **Science and Technology in Everyday Lives**. The gallery is divided into five sub-sections emphasising Body and Health, Communication and Transportation, Quality of Life (air, water and refuse management), Home and Office, and Visions of the Future. The Health section is one of the most interesting and features models of organs and a wealth of explanatory information supported by touch-screen displays. The Transportation exhibit is also rich in detail and well designed: the visitor with a penchant for planes and boats can easily spend an afternoon here.

The museum's **Level Six** display, **Traditional Technology**, goes back to Thailand once more, documenting Queen Sirikit's interest in reviving traditional technologies in impoverished rural enclaves. Some emphasis is placed on the Queen's role in the development of rural craft industries; the displays are informative and well-executed. Subjects covered include carving, pottery, metallurgy, wickerwork and textiles. The finished products, as well as the machinery used to make them, such as looms and pottery wheels, are shown here as well. A general Thai lifestyle exhibit marks the tour's end.

Though a little off the beaten track outside Bangkok, with its creative and well-designed interactive approach to science and technology, the National Science Museum is worth the journey.

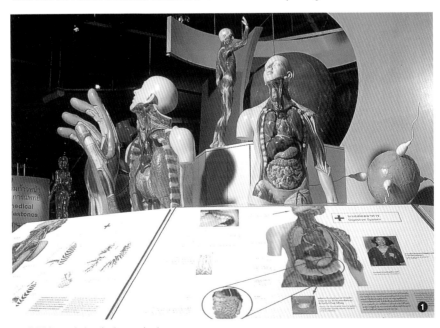

▲ *Exhibits exploring the human body.*

Vietnam ▶

ADDRESS
02 Tieu La 02, corner of Bach
Dang and Tran Phu Streets
Danang
Vietnam

CONTACT INFORMATION
T: +84 511 572 935
F: +84 511 887 635
E: btdn@vnn.vn

OPENING HOURS
7.30am–5.30 pm daily.

ADMISSION
Free.

FACILIITIES
Guided tours are available in
Vietnamese and English.

HOW TO GET THERE
On foot or by taxi from the
centre of town.

AROUND THE MUSEUM
There are bookshops and
cafés in the museum vicinity.

Museum of Cham Sculpture

Offering a unique and spectacular account of the brilliance of Vietnam's Cham civilisation, the Museum of Cham Sculpture in Danang, though somewhat off the beaten track, is well worth the detour.

■ **THE BUILDING** One of Vietnam's oldest museums, the largely open-air Museum of Cham Sculpture was founded in 1915 at the height of French colonial domination of Vietnam by the prestigious Ecole Française d'Extrème Orient. Located on the southeast side of Danang, on a little hill a stone's throw from the banks of the Han River, the museum complex, set in a well-maintained and bucolic garden, provides an outstanding environment for the presentation of stone sculpture.

The original museum, designed by French architects Delaval and Auclair on plans drawn up by scholar and conservator Henri Parmentier, is yet another East-West hybrid, the construction and basic structural form derived from European architectural tradition while the exterior borrows features from the Cham architectural repertoire. Here, elements essential to Cham structures, such as towers and temple adornments, are used as mere decorative devices, lending the building a graceful and romantic, if eclectic, appearance. The original design was vaguely reminiscent of classical Greek temple architecture and involved a rectangular stone plinth of Chamesque stepped design supporting multiple Cham-style columns upon which was placed a stone roof, the latter decorated with Cham-style turrets.

Extended in 1936 with the addition of two lateral wings, and having undergone some modernisation work in the 1990s, the museum and its pretty garden have nonetheless retained their early 20th-century charm. From 2005, a recently built annex, constructed in the same style as the original building, is to house newly discovered stone sculpture.

■ **THE COLLECTION** The ancient Hindu state of Champa is thought to have begun some time between the late 2nd and the 6th century. At its zenith, before the arrival of the Vietnamese, Cham civilisation pervaded the whole of Central Vietnam from the Hoanh Son region in the north to Phan Thiet in the south. Constant wars prompted the start of Cham decline from the 11th century, and in 1471 the ethnic Vietnamese captured and razed Vijaya, beheaded 40,000 people and deported 30,000 more, thus eclipsing the larger Hindu Cham kingdom and its great Hindu-Mahayana Buddhist sculptural legacy. Cham descendants, much diminished, struggled on until the early 19th century. A small Cham population still peoples Central Vietnam today.

As with Khmer civilisation, Cham civilisation had for centuries sunk into oblivion and it was only in the 19th century that the vestiges of its art were rediscovered and formal research into the lost civilisation began. The Museum of Cham Sculpture's origins coincide with and mirror this exciting period of rediscovery.

Though the museum's main building was erected in 1915 and construction only completed in 1919, the collection itself dates back to the late 19th century when French scholars and archaeologists (some laymen such as postal worker Camille Paris were also involved in the preservation of Cham heritage) were actively excavating and exploring Vietnam's central regions. In 1892, Charles Lemire brought an initial group of some 50 sculptures to Le Jardin de Tourane (Danang was known as 'Tourane' under the French) in Danang, the site of the later museum. The collection in the garden soon increased to 90 and in 1902 the French government decided to transfer these and other important Cham

▲ **Sandstone high relief of a four-armed goddess**
Chanh Lo style | 11th century | H: 164 cm

◄ **Sandstone figure of Dvarapala stamping on a bear**
Dong Duong style | 9th–10th centuries | H: 218 cm

cultural relics to Hanoi. The local authorities refused to allow this transfer, but the scattering and neglect of this recently found material was increasing and scholar Henri Parmentier, after whom the future museum would be named and who in 1919 wrote the museum's first catalogue, began lobbying for the establishment of a museum to conserve the growing Cham treasures. Danang, close to the old Champa capitals of Tra Kieu and Dong Duong as well as the sacred site of My Son, and the first home of the original Lemire sculptures displayed in its public gardens, was the confirmed choice, and a site was selected by the river in the very same Jardin de Tourane.

The history of the collection reflects 20th-century Vietnamese history. According to Parmentier's 1919 inventory, the collection included 160 pieces that provided a survey of Cham artistic achievement valuable for chronological and stylistic reference. Of these sculptures, Parmentier records well-apportioned representation from the major Cham sites, with My Son and Tra Kieu boasting the greatest number of pieces at 21 and 42 respectively. Roughly a dozen pieces each also originated from Khuong My, Phong Le, Ha Trung, Binh Dinh, Da Nghi and Chanh Lo. Thus, when the museum opened it already contained a superlative study collection. Over the next several decades, approximately a hundred new pieces were added, the majority in the Binh Dinh style from excavations at Thap Mam (Nghia Binh).

In 1946, however, at the beginning of the Indochina War, the museum and its library were looted. The stolen pieces were mostly recovered but two decades later, during the Vietnam War's 1968 Tet offensive, the museum was requisitioned for the use of South Vietnamese troops. Though the sites at Dong Duong and My Son suffered serious damage from American bombing, the museum, fortunately, was spared.

◄ **Detail of a sandstone high relief figure of a dancer from the 'Dancers' pedestal'**
Tra Kieu style | 10th century | H (figure): 63 cm, H (including pedestal): approximately 130 cm

Bronze figure of Tara
Dong Duong style, with original incrustation, 9th–10th century | H: 120 cm

This bronze figure of Tara, not part of the original early 20th-century group, was discovered in 1978. One of relatively few surviving and well-conserved early Cham bronzes, this figure is also one of the largest known to date. With its original incrustation in the eyes, finely cast form, realistic dress, severe facial features and elegantly modelled hands, the figure is considered a masterpiece of Cham art. Though fusing Chinese and Indian expression, the work moves beyond the two major Asian cultures to develop a wholly new aesthetic, confirming the originality of Cham art.

In 1996, museum staff discovered over 150 ancient fragments buried in the museum grounds. Currently housed in the garden, it is these pieces that will be moving to the new annex in 2005.

Containing the largest and most important collection of Cham art in the world, the museum currently boasts some 400 works of art (including the 1996 garden trove) from the central region of Quang Nam and the

▲ **Detail of a fully sculpted sandstone bust of Dvarapala**
Thap Mam style, 12th century | H: 107 cm

surrounding Danang provinces including My Son. Though the collection includes a few terracottas, the majority are sandstone reliefs, altars, full sculptures and architectural elements including lintels and ornamental corner pieces decorated with a full range of Hindu and Buddhist iconography.

■ **THE GALLERIES** Cham sculpture is characterised by its continuous process of change and renewal. Earlier examples tend to be stylised and not wholly individualised, while later works can be more naturalistic in their representation of form.

The museum's original ten galleries are well designed in terms of layout, the material arranged chronologically and in sections according to the part of the Cham kingdom where it was found, each room bearing the name of its material's locality of origin. The new annex's presentation has yet to be determined as this is being written. English labelling is succinct but the art speaks very much for itself. A thorough visit might well take a full day, the viewer paying particular attention to the difference between art from

the early period, spanning the 7th to the end of the 10th century and that of the second, spanning the 11th to the 15th century when Cham art, though still lively, began its gently progressive decline. From this period, see a 15th-century sandstone high relief of Shiva in Yang Mum style that is considered one of the last masterpieces of Cham stone art. Elaborately bejewelled (armlets, necklaces and bracelets) and crowned, its facial features highly worked and detailed, and its pose symmetrically frontal and stiff, this figure, for all its beauty, lacks the supple and sensuous subtlety of movement of earlier works.

At the time of writing, the gallery layout remained faithful to the original four-section plan, the visitor starting his tour in the eastern-most wing of the complex, **Hall 1**, where sculpture from the sacred site of **My Son** is displayed. Mostly dating from the 8th (see one of the earliest pieces, a stone stele dated to 717) to the 13th century, objects are largely sandstone but a few are terracotta. A central plinth recreates the powerful impact of My Son architecture as temple fragments are reassembled there. Free-standing sculpture and other smaller architectural fragments are displayed against the walls all around the room.

Leaving Hall 1, the visitor must skirt the east side of the building, following a narrow corridor that links up with **Hall 4** on the museum's south side where pieces from **Dong Duong** are displayed. From here, the tour progresses into the building's central axis to **Hall 3**, where an impressive number of works from **Tra Kieu** are shown. See here in particular the celebrated *Tra Kieu Dancer*, one of several similar female dancers carved in high relief on an imposing, three-dimensional sandstone architectural pediment. One of Cham art's best-known icons, the dancer, among others on a pedestal, entered the museum collection in 1918. She and the other women's facial features are exquisitely modelled to convey a mixture of serenity and ecstatic joy. Their expressive bodies are realistically and sensually curved in sacred dance, exhibiting supple, elegant movement and well-balanced

formal composition, the position of their legs echoing that of their arms, and their right or left wrist gently curving toward the ear in a sort of near caress. Intact save for the figures' missing feet, the relief is considered one of Cham art's greatest achievements.

The tour ends opposite Hall 1. On the western side of the museum is **Hall 2**, devoted to objects from **Thap Mam** and arranged in similar fashion to Hall 1, though here the central plinths are occupied by figurative sculpture rather than architectural remains.

Though lacking expansive explanation panels and other standard features of many modern museums in Southeast Asia, Danang's Museum of Cham Sculpture amply rewards the visitor with its spectacular art. Beyond the works' formal power, which can be appreciated without much explanation, Emmanuel Guillon's excellent *Cham Art—Treasures from the Danang Museum, Vietnam* is a worthwhile investment for understanding the art historical context of the pieces on view. Housing a unique collection that charts Cham sculptural achievement in uninterrupted sequence from the 7th to the 15th century in a lovely, bucolic setting, the Museum of Cham Sculpture should legitimately be the cultural centrepiece of any art, archaeology or ancient culture lover's visit to Vietnam.

▲ **Detail of a sandstone high relief figure of Shiva**
Yang Mum style, 15th century | H: 100 cm

ADDRESS
Contemporary Arts Center
621 La Thanh Road
Ba Dinh
Hanoi

CONTACT INFORMATION
T: +84 4 834 4927

OPENING HOURS
8am–11.30am, 2pm–5pm
daily.

FACILIITIES
Library.

Several rooms for artists with
two to four beds from US$7 to
US$9 per night.

HOW TO GET THERE
The CAC is a 15-minute taxi
ride from the centre of Hanoi
costing roughly US$3.

AROUND THE MUSEUM
There are plenty of small
shops, supermarkets, cafés
and hotels around the CAC.

Contemporary Arts Center

As well as showcasing the latest in Vietnamese contemporary practice, Hanoi's Contemporary Arts Center provides a forum for artistic exchange and a research facility for the better understanding of Vietnamese visual art.

■ **THE BUILDING** Located on the west side of Hanoi, a short taxi ride from the city centre, the Contemporary Arts Center (CAC) is housed in a recent three-storey building in a mixed residential and commercial neighbourhood. Covering 1,400 square metres of floor space, the CAC features an exhibition hall, a gallery, two art studios, a computer and graphic design room, a library and four well-equipped guest rooms for artists in residence.

■ **THE VOCATION** Further to *doi moi*, the state-led economic liberalisation of the late 1980s, Vietnam's long-repressed art scene exploded, leading to a surge of interest from outside Vietnam. As a result of this interest and foreign buyers' spending power, the Vietnamese art market developed at such a pace that Hanoi's two or three commercial art galleries of the early 1990s had mushroomed exponentially a decade later. However, the commodification of Vietnamese art naturally led to a swift decline in the quality of mainstream expression so that by the year 2000, disgust with the mediocrity of the

commercial art scene and its production of banal work was beginning to have an impact inside and outside the country. Partially as a reaction to this dilution of quality, the CAC was founded in 2000.

The CAC is not so much a museum with a static collection as a dynamic forum for the exchange and presentation of art information and visual expression. Opened with financial support from the Ford Foundation, the CAC is essentially run by artists. Established as an exhibition space for young practitioners of different genres, it also operates as a creation space where Vietnamese and foreign artists can experiment with all media, including installation art, video and performance practice. In the context of the material poverty of Vietnam, the CAC is particularly well-equipped technologically, owning a number of projectors, a digital camera and an etching machine, as well as other specialist art-making equipment and a library.

■ **EXHIBITIONS** Artists featured in past exhibitions include, among many others, Tran Khang Chuong, Dan Xuan Hoa, Dang Thi Khue, Ngo Van Cao, Nguyen Van Nghi, Le Lien, Tran Van My, Ha Khanh, Do Thi Ninh, Ly, Truc Son, Stephen Garret, Benjamin

◀ **Dang Xuan Hoa, Vietnam**
The new world – breaking news – the war | Oil on canvas | 2001 | Dimensions variable

▲ **Rodney Dickson, USA**
Close to Paradise | Mixed media | 2001 | 300 cm x 150 cm

Puah, Yoshiko Kanai, Thomas Beven, Una Walker, Rodney Dickson and Brian Avera.

Though technically not exactly a museum, Hanoi's well-appointed Contemporary Arts Center provides an unparalleled starting point for those wishing to further their knowledge of Vietnamese contemporary art beyond mainstream and commercial boundaries.

ADDRESS
1 Hoa Lo
Hoan Kiem, Hanoi
Vietnam

CONTACT INFORMATION
T: +84 4 824 6358 / 934 2253
F: +84 4 934 2317

OPENING HOURS
8am–11.30am,
1.30pm–5pm daily.

ADMISSION
10,000 dong.

HOW TO GET THERE
Taxi: The museum is a 5- to
10-minute taxi ride from the
centre of Hanoi.

AROUND THE MUSEUM
There are plenty of cafés,
restaurants and hotels in the
museum's vicinity.

Hoa Lo Prison Museum

Hanoi's Hoa Lo (Hell's Hole) Prison Museum, just west of Hoan Kiem Lake, provides an informative if harrowing view of Vietnam's political history over the last century.

■ **THE BUILDING** Dating back to 1896, Maison Centrale, as it was known then, was erected by the French colonial authorities to house common Vietnamese criminals. Of fairly basic European design and not particularly significant architecturally, the prison nevertheless soon distinguished itself as one of central Hanoi's most imposing structures. Though much of the stone prison and its compound were demolished over a decade ago to make way for a high-rise tower, a small corner of the prison's southeast side, including part of its original façade and main gate, were conserved. It now houses a museum.

■ **THE HISTORY** Hoa Lo always elicited fear in the local population. However, during the rise of Vietnamese nationalism—from the first decades of the 20th century to 1954 when Vietnam won its war of independence against France—an increasing number of political dissidents and revolutionary fighters began to join the numbers of common criminals held inside. As a result, Hoa Lo unwittingly played an important historical role as a breeding ground for nationalism and the political subversion that would result in France's expulsion from Vietnam. While incarcerated, nationalists not only exchanged information with other dissidents, they also reinforced the nationalist thinking of the less politically minded prisoners among them. Indeed, Hoa Lo's roster of prisoners corresponding to the years preceding liberation includes the names of many national heroes and those of men who would eventually run the

▲ American pilots freed by the North Vietnamese government on 12 February 1973.

North Vietnamese government in its fledgling days and beyond. Among the detainees who later rose to prominence were five future General Secretaries of the Vietnamese Communist Party—Nguyen Van Cu, Truong Chinh, Le Duan, Nguyen Van Linh and Do Muoi.

Hoa Lo was an infamous landmark during Vietnam's French period, with male and female prisoners for years enduring physical torture and appalling conditions including chains and tiny cells. It was during the Vietnam War, however, that the prison gained an international reputation. Known to the Americans as the Hanoi Hilton, Hoa Lo is of wider historical significance because between 1964 and 1973, about a hundred pilots, shot down over Hanoi, were housed there as prisoners-of-war before they were freed by the North Vietnamese government. Two of these pilots went on to gain prominence in American public service—Senator John McCain, and Pete Peterson, Vietnam's first US ambassador.

■ **THE DISPLAY** Though small, the museum's remaining cells and key pieces of museum

paraphernalia aptly evoke the prison's atmosphere at the end of the colonial period when Hoa Lo was a hotbed of dissent.

In **Rooms 1 and 2**, an aerial photograph and a well-made scale model give a good idea of the prison's original design and features. Visitors may visit **cell 'E'**, where the French kept male inmates, and view a display featuring Vietnamese prisoners' belongings such as bowls, spoons and blankets. In an **inner courtyard**, an imposing stone wall and a French-period guillotine provide a forbidding testament to the prison's history. A less harrowing experience follows with a visit to a section of the **underground sewer pipe** in front of camp 'J', through which 100 local prisoners escaped Hoa Lo in March 1945.

Part of Vietnam's complex and violent 20th-century history, Hoa Lo Prison Museum offers a potent reminder of the ugly aspects of colonisation and war that many wandering the café-dotted streets of Hanoi may have forgotten.

▲ A section of the underground sewer pipe through which 100 political prisoners escaped in 1945.

ADDRESS
19 Ngoc Ha Street
Ba Dinh, Hanoi
Vietnam

CONTACT INFORMATION
T: +84 4 846 3757
F: +84 4 843 9837
E: bthochiminh@hn.vnn.vn

OPENING HOURS
8am–11.30am, 2pm–4pm
Tue–Thu, Sat–Sun;
8am–11.30am Mon, Fri.

ADMISSION
5,000 dong.

FACILITIES
Wheelchair access.

Documentaries are available
in English and French.

A bookshop, souvenir shop
and café are located on the
museum's premises.

HOW TO GET THERE
Taxi: The museum is a
10-minute taxi ride from Hoan
Kiem Lake.

AROUND THE MUSEUM
One Pillar Pagoda is a short
walk east.

The Ho Chi Minh Mausoleum is
north of the museum.

There are plenty of cafés in
the area.

Ho Chi Minh Museum

Built in 1990 to commemorate President Ho Chi Minh's 100th birthday, this Hanoi landmark is as much a symbol of 20th-century Vietnamese history as it is a valuable source of historical information.

▪ **THE BUILDING** The museum is located west of Hoan Kiem Lake in Ba Dinh, a short walk south of the modest house on stilts in which Ho Chi Minh lived from 1954 until the end of his life. More importantly, however, Ba Dinh is where Ho Chi Minh read the Declaration of Independence and announced the founding of the Democratic Republic of Vietnam on 2 September 1945.

Nearly 20 metres in height, the monumental white building, designed by Russian architect Garon Isakovich resembles a lotus in shape and symbolises the noble and modest life of Vietnam's great leader. Combining traditional design characteristics and modern technological features, it was, when built, one of the best-equipped public buildings in Vietnam.

Three storeys high and covering about 13,000 square metres of floor space, the museum includes a library, an auditorium and an archive containing over 150,000 documents relating to Vietnam's recent political history.

▪ **THE COLLECTION** The main exhibition area is located on the third floor and occupies 4,000 square metres. Here, over 2,000 documents, consisting essentially of books, photographs and newspaper clippings, follow Ho Chi Minh's career from his early days as a revolutionary fighter in the war against the French, to the founding of the Vietnamese Communist Party in 1930, Ho Chi Minh's

▲ *President Ho Chi Minh after the success of the anti-French war, 1954.*

declaration of independence in 1945 and the struggle that followed, partition in 1954 and the subsequent Vietnam War, and finally his death in 1969. As well as his speeches and ideological tracts (see the important *Le Procès de la Colonisation Française* of 1925), the leader's literary works, such as *Prison Diary*, written while in detention in Southern China, are on display. The museum also documents key historic world events linked to Vietnamese statehood. The material, mostly in Vietnamese, also appears in French, English, Chinese and Russian. Those keen not to miss anything may enlist the help of a local guide who will translate the foreign language text.

▪ **THE GALLERIES** Following the building's lotus theme, the exhibition galleries are arranged in a petal-style configuration. The vast and imposing **First Hall** forms the gallery's centre and contains a large bronze statue of the great leader. This space is surrounded by **Galleries A, B, C, D, E and G**, where the Vietnamese people's struggles and victories of the 20th century are documented. Beyond these sections, a surrounding belt displays material related to Ho Chi Minh's life. Finally, the gallery's outermost areas focus on the landmark events of world history that influenced Ho Chi Minh's revolutionary activities.

The galleries devoted to Ho are organised around eight themes: Ho Chi Minh's youth and

initial patriotic and revolutionary activities (1890–1911), the President affirms the path of the Vietnamese revolution (1911–1920), the President struggles to apply Lenin's line on national and colonial questions (1920–1924), the President founds the Party of the Vietnamese Working Class (1924–1930), President Ho founds the Republic (1930–1945), President Ho faces French colonial aggression (1945–1954), the fight against US aggression (1954–1969), and following the path charted by President Ho.

Several **Special Subject Halls** examine particular themes such as fascism and the Soviet Revolution, while temporary politically flavoured exhibitions are organised every year.

The Ho Chi Minh Museum in Hanoi, overseeing the country's other 12 Ho Chi Minh museums, including the one in Ho Chi Minh City, is doubtless the best of its genre to be found in Vietnam.

▲ *Inaugural ceremony of the Ho Chi Minh Museum on 19 May 1990.*

ADDRESS
1A Trang Tien Street
Hoan Kiem District, Hanoi
Vietnam

CONTACT iNFORMATION
T: +84 4 825 3518 / 824 1384
F: +84 4 825 2853

OPENING HOURS
8am–11.30am,
1.30pm–4.30pm Tue–Sun;

closed on Tet holiday.

ADMISSION
Adult 15,000 dong;
child (under 16) 8,000 dong;
surcharge for use of camera
or video.

FACILITIES
The 2nd floor is not accessible
to wheelchairs as there are
no lifts.

Guided tours in foreign
languages are available by
appointment.

HOW TO GET THERE
On foot, or by cyclo or taxi.

AROUND THE MUSEUM
Located in central Hanoi, the
museum is just a short walk
from the Hotel Metropole and
the Opera House.

There are plenty of shops,
restaurants and cafés around
the museum.

National Museum of Vietnamese History

Housed in an elegant and well-kept colonial building set in attractive shaded gardens, the National Museum of Vietnamese History provides an excellent introduction to Vietnam's complex history and culture.

■ **THE BUILDING** The National Museum of Vietnamese History is located in the area of Hanoi that was first ceded to the French by the Vietnamese in 1874.

One of Hanoi's most distinctive and aesthetically pleasing colonial edifices, the centrally located museum was designed by French architect Ernest Hebrard in 1926 in a hybrid style that marries Western concepts of space with Eastern decorative devices. The building, completed in 1932 and originally named the East Art Museum—French residents of Hanoi at the time also referred to it as Musée Louis Finot, after the French scientist who supported the city's prestigious Ecole Française d'Extrême Orient's (EFEO) research—was purpose-built as an Asian art museum to be run under the auspices of EFEO. The EFEO emblem is still visible on the upper part of the façade's octagonal tower.

The building combines classical Western architectural features such as a galleried, octagonal entrance rotunda and an elongated façade with distinctive tropical attributes including a deep, covered entrance porch, shaded balconies running the length of the building which afford protection from the sun and monsoonal rains, and double walls for ventilation. The building also exhibits an interest in indigenous taste with its octagonal windows, lattice-decorated balustrades and decorated triple-eaves.

Unique in Hanoi for its East-West style, the museum was initially conceived to house a general collection of Asian and Indo-Chinese antiques, but now presents a full spectrum of Vietnamese cultural objects.

■ **THE COLLECTION** Between 1945 and final liberation in 1954, the museum's fate was rather uncertain, its administration passing from the French to the Vietnamese and back to the French again. The institution only shifted definitively to Vietnamese hands when the French withdrew from Vietnam and partition between the North and South was instituted in 1954. At this time, the collections, already impressive, expanded to focus more exclusively on Vietnamese material. The museum was reopened to the public in 1958.

Now, the museum houses around 7,000 objects ranging from Stone Age tools collected from 50 sites around the country, to highly ornate Nguyen dynasty furniture of the late 19th century, and the mandatory Ho Chi Minh paraphenalia.

▲ **Stone mortar and pestle**
Hoa Binh culture, Hoa Binh Province | c. 8000 BCE | D: approximately 35 cm

■ **THE GALLERIES** As one enters the pleasantly green museum compound, the ticket office, gift shop and a small café are to the right, bordering Pham Ngu Lao Street. The grounds are worth exploring, and while admiring the elegant building's exterior, visitors will come across the remains of Hanoi's old city gate, dating back to 1805 and positioned on the right side of the museum. Another work of art, located on the left side of the façade, is a stele of the 3rd century discovered in Khanh Hoa province known as the Vo Canh epitaph and thought to be the oldest surviving piece of this type in Indochina. The garden also features other stone and terracotta sculpture from the Ly, Tran, Le Mac and Nguyen dynasties spanning the 11th to the 19th century.

▲ *View of the museum's elegant octagonal rotunda seen from the entrance gate.*

Housed on two floors and covering over 2,200 square metres, the galleries are laid out in chronological sequence. Upon passing the octagonal vestibule, visitors will first see Neolithic material in a room to the right. The **Hoa Binh and Bac Son cultures** (circa 500,000–2000 BCE) are well represented here with tools for hunting and domestic use along with innumerable pottery shards and fossils excavated all around Vietnam.

A highlight of the museum is its collection of bronze works of art from the **Dong Son culture** (circa 500 BCE–300 CE). Located on the first floor, beyond the vestibule, the Dong Son items are numerous and varied, featuring tools, weapons, domestic objects, jewellery and musical instruments. Among the items on display are several large drums for which the Dong Son culture is probably most famous. These drums, widely distributed around mainland Southeast Asia, a symbol of wealth and power, were used for ceremonies and rituals. The examples here are worth looking at in detail as they are finely cast and represent significant technical and artistic achievement at a time when some argue Southeast Asia could not yet boast any true artistic culture (this point seems increasingly debatable as historians find out more about the ancient peoples of Southeast Asia).

Though there is some speculation as to the origin of the lost wax technique in Vietnam, and though Han dynasty style may have influenced late Dong Son, there is no doubt as to the originality of the culture's aesthetics. The central star or sun motif on some drums, and the animal, bird and frog motifs on others are iconographies quite unique to Vietnam. See a large and well-conserved Ngoc Lu drum (circa 500 BCE) from the Binh Luc district.

Other wares from the same period are also displayed here including a number of

decorated bronze axe heads and utilitarian objects made of bamboo, glass and wood. Vessels and implements manufactured from stone, horn and animal tooth are also interesting.

Early Vietnamese ceramics, much sought-after in the auction rooms of Europe these days, are displayed towards the middle and end of the gallery. Spanning the 11th to the 19th century, the collection is representative of all periods and types of wares from subtle early celadons, reminiscent of Chinese Yuan wares, to enamel overglaze and blue and white wares of the 16th century. Some Chinese Han dynasty funerary ceramics from Southern China are also represented here.

The museum's second and top floor is home to larger **Nguyen dynasty** material of the 19th century. Forming a circle around the rotunda balustrade are the collection's **Cham pieces** (Champa, like Dong Son, is another of Vietnam's original and artistically spectacular indigenous cultures), well lit and displayed so that they can generally be seen from at least three vantage points. Though the museum's stone sculpture cannot rival the collection in Danang, those pressed for time but interested in Cham art will be rewarded here. Look for a niche boasting a lively full-relief sandstone figure of a dancing Shiva from the 12th century found in Binh Dinh province. A series of photographs depicting Cham temples and sites in Central Vietnam provides useful references to the sculpture, particularly when the labelling is in Vietnamese only.

At the rear of the gallery, the museum houses a good collection of **18th to early 20th**

▲ **Stone relief of dancing Shiva**
Cham, Mam Temple, Binh Dinh Province | Late 12th century | H: 118 cm

century art. A complete set of ornate ceremonial bronze bells from the Nguyen dynasty, quite different from their Chinese equivalent, is worth noting, as is a small group of very elaborate gilt and lacquered furniture from roughly the same period that gives the visitor a good idea of the opulence of the elite in pre-colonial Vietnam. Since replaced by a replica, a star piece of this section was an impressive gilt and lacquered wooden statue of Avalokiteshvara dated to 1656 from But Thap Pagoda in Bac Ninh Province. Those interested in this style and period may ask the curators if they may view the real thing.

Indeed, though the great majority of pieces in the museum are original, a few copies are present as well and should not be entirely dismissed as they are often interesting for reference purposes.

Housed in one of Hanoi's most beguiling colonial buildings, the National Museum of Vietnamese History provides a good starting point for visitors wishing to come to grips with Vietnam's cultural history. A return visit to view one of several annual temporary exhibitions is also recommended.

▲ **Cast bronze drum**
Dong Son culture, Ngoc Lu, Ha Nam Province | c. 500 BCE | H: 63 cm, D: 79 cm

▲ **Top view of a cast bronze drum, rubbing** | *Dong Son culture, Ngoc Lu, Ha Nam Province | 500–400 BCE | D: 79cm*

ADDRESS
66 Nguyen Thai Hoc Street
Ba Dinh District, Hanoi
Vietnam

CONTACT DETAILS
T: +84 4 823 3084 / 733 2131
F: +84 4 734 1427

OPENING HOURS
8.30am–5pm Tue,
Thu–Fri, Sun;

8.30am–9pm Wed, Sat;
closed Mon.

ADMISSION
10,000 dong

FACILITIES
Radio Tourguide System;
guided tours are available
in Vietnamese, English
and French.

Documentation centre
(including video, photo
archive and library);
auditorium; conference hall.

A restaurant and museum
shop are located on the
museum's grounds.

AROUND THE MUSEUM
The museum is located in
the centre of Hanoi near

the historic Temple of
Literature, an 11th-century
Confucian temple.

There are many cafés
and restaurants in the
museum's vicinity.

Vietnam Fine Arts Museum

Located in a graceful colonial building, the Vietnam Fine Arts Museum provides a comprehensive survey of Vietnamese fine and decorative art from pre-Christian times to the present in a pretty garden setting.

▪ **THE BUILDING** Originally a Catholic dormitory reserved exclusively for the daughters of French Indochina officials who had left their provincial estates to attend school in Hanoi, the then Dortoire de Famille Jeanne d'Arc was built in 1937. An eclectic mix of Art Deco, tropical and Eastern architectural characteristics, the structure features a three-storey, streamlined Classical façade typical of French-designed Hanoi Deco, large shuttered windows necessary for air circulation in the humid climate, a high-ceilinged shaded gallery, and generic 'Oriental' upturned eaves that were added when the building was transformed from Western dormitory to Vietnamese museum. A strikingly grand circular staircase, visible as one enters the museum, lends the interior a faded glamour particularly evocative of 1930s Hanoi.

▪ **THE COLLECTION** Established in 1962 by the Vietnamese state, the museum's collection was assembled in four years, the Vietnam Fine Arts Museum opening to the public in 1966.

Though undoubtedly a survey museum, the emphasis of the collection is skewed toward the 20th century. Indeed, in view of Vietnam's 20th-century history of civil war, partition and war with America, followed by extreme economic hardship until *doi moi's* economic reforms in the late 1980s, the museum's comprehensive selection of outstanding objects must be viewed as an achievement in itself.

The collection, labelled in Vietnamese, English and French, is divided into six sections including ancient and prehistoric art, art from the early 11th to the 19th century (including pieces from the Ly, Tran, Early Le, Mac, Restored Le, Tay Son and Nguyen dynasties), 20th-century painting and sculpture, folk art, applied decorative art and 11th- to 20th-century ceramics.

With the collection numbering nearly 20,000 works, the museum rotates its holdings roughly twice a year, showing approximately 2,000 pieces at a time.

▲ **Tran Van Can**
Little Thuy's Portrait | Oil on canvas | 1943 | 58 x 44 cm

▲ **Tran Van Can**
Young Girl Washing Her Hair | Woodcut on paper | 1940 | 34 x 22 cm

▪ **THE GALLERIES** The galleries occupy the building's three floors and basement and are set out so that the rooms on the ground floor cover Vietnamese art from ancient times until the 20th century, those on the second are dedicated to folk art, and those on the third to 20th-century art of all genres. Ceramics are housed in the basement and 20th-century sculpture is displayed in the corridors of the museum's second and third levels.

Proceeding chronologically, the institution's earliest material is presented in **Room 1**. Stone, bronze and some Iron Age tools, weapons, musical instruments, household utensils and jewellery from North, Central and South Vietnam are displayed, bronze drums from the Dong Son culture a focal point here. Still on the ground floor, **Rooms 2, 3 and 4** include fewer exhibits and focus on art from the 11th to the 19th century, the period covering the Ly dynasty to the Nguyen period. After a millennium of Chinese rule in the 10th century (this explains the 11th century cut-off), Buddhism took hold in Vietnam while the first independent dynasties were founded in the North. During Viet culture's flowering in the North, the art of Champa blossomed in the South, allowing Imperial and Buddhist architecture to flourish and thus facilitating the growth in importance of painting and sculpture. The Ly dynasty stone works (see a large 11th-century stone figure of a seated Buddha) in these galleries warrant the closest attention here.

Rooms 5 and 6 feature Vietnamese art spanning the 15th to the early 18th century, a period coinciding with the early Le, Mac, Restored Le and Tay Son dynasties. By this time, war and the eclipsing of the Southern Cham had provoked the decline of the previous period's monumental art, which was replaced by an artistic expression of smaller scale. The Viet style grew closer to that of the Chinese in the North, a more decorative artistic language emerged, and a definite folk genre came to the fore. A variety of objects are worth looking at here including a large stone stele, carved stone animals, and several figures of Buddha worked in clay, metal, lacquered wood or stone. A 16th-century carved lacquered wood figure of Guanyin stands out in particular.

Rooms 7 and 8 are the last two on the ground floor and contain works from the short-lived Tay Son and Nguyen dynasties, the latter being the last of Vietnam's independent dynasties. A distinctive mid-17th-century lacquered wood Buddha with 'a thousand eyes and arms' dominates this part of the gallery.

▲ **Guanyin** | *Carved and lacquered wood on an ornate pedestal* | *16th century* | *H: 320 cm*

Those interested in Southeast Asian folk cultures will enjoy the museum's second floor, entirely devoted to many sophisticated folk works characterised by their relationship to communal living, clan ancestor worship, religious festivals, and folk hero devotion.

Here, the visitor will find fine older examples of the charming and expressive woodblock prints that continue to be produced today during Tet, Vietnam's Lunar New Year period. Though some can still be purchased in Hanoi's many shops selling tribal material, the

Nguyen Phan Chanh
On The Way to Rice Fields | Ink on silk | 1937 | 48 x 87 cm

Nguyen Phan Chanh (1892–1984) is considered one of Vietnam's most important 20th-century painters. Though favouring the traditional Asian medium of ink on silk, the artist was an early exponent of Modernism to which he gave thoroughly indigenous characteristics. Though he remained faithful to Vietnamese themes and iconography, his depictions of Vietnam's people evoked in either rural landscapes or domestic settings are never romanticised, exuding instead dignity and a subtle lyricism. Formally his painting is neither Chinese nor Western in feeling; his frieze-like compositions, sometimes assembled on the diagonal, and stains of limpid organic colour—browns, ambers, bottle-greens, nile-blues—are original to the artist and thus served to define a new Vietnamese artistic vernacular in the 20th century.

museum is a good place to see top-notch examples. Shamanistic wooden sculpture made by members of ethnic minorities and traditional water puppets are also on display in these galleries.

The museum's last floor is given over to 20th-century painting. **Rooms 9, 10 and 11** explore the first half of the century, stopping with the departure of the French and formal independence in 1954. Paintings produced by the first wave of Vietnamese graduates from the 1925 French-established Ecole des Beaux-Arts de l'Indochine are included here and followers of Vietnamese Modernism from this era will find some 100 works by the masters of the period. See in particular a 1937 painting by Nguyen Phan Chanh (1892–1984) depicting peasants leading a water buffalo. Resplendent despite its poor condition, the painting is modern in both its frieze-like composition and the unsentimental rendering of its traditional content, confirming the artist as one of the period's most important painters and, a pioneer of indigenous Modernism.

While painting from 1930 to 1945 showed either Romantic or Realistic tendencies, painting from 1945 to 1954 reflected a shift in orientation toward the patriotism and nationalism that fuelled the war of resistance against the French. Many artists were also fighters and their works often evoke themes of revolutionary struggle.

Works dating from after the Dien Bien Phu victory of 1954 are arranged according to their media: lacquer, silk, paper and oil.

Rooms 12, 13, 14, 15, 16 and 17 contain works in lacquer, the old traditional medium having been resurrected in the 1920s and put to new use in the service of two-dimensional fine art. Over 100 lacquer-on-panel works are housed here, perhaps the most splendid a huge 1939 lacquer screen with a gold background by Vietnam's lacquer pioneer of the 1930s and undoubtedly the country's most famous modern lacquer artist Nguyen

Gia Tri. From 1955 to 1963 lacquer experienced a boom with other outstanding artists such as Nguyen Van Binh, Le Quoc Loc, Nguyen Van Que and Nguyen Van Ty emerging.

Rooms 18, 19 and 20 house paintings on silk. Silk is a traditional Eastern medium and an interest in ink on silk was revived in 1930s Vietnam. Nguyen Phan Chanh was this medium's most accomplished proponent. See in particular *Washing Vegetables in the Pond* of 1931 and *On The Way to Rice Fields* of 1937, where the artist's subtle earth tones, pared-down compositions and peasant themes combine to produce an art of quiet beauty and dignity that has come to define Vietnamese Modernism. Other well-known painters on silk shown here are Le Van De, Nguyen Tuong Lan, Luong Xuan Nhi, Mai Trung Thu and Le Pho. After the August Revolution of 1945 and especially since Vietnam's reunification in 1975, silk art evolved, light and shade and a more vivid palette being introduced.

Rooms 21, 22 and 23 contain work on paper, including gouache, drawings and woodblock prints while oil painting in Western style can be found in **Room 24**. Here, the

▲ **Duong Dang Can**
Earth Love and Tree Perfume | *Carved wood* | *1928* | *H: 118 cm*

medium is explored from its introduction to Vietnam in the late 19th century (see in this gallery several of Vietnam's first oil paintings by Le Van Mien dating to the 1890s), through to its popularity in the 1920s when it became integral to Vietnamese expression, and ending in works from the last decade.

Intelligently organised, Room 24 provides a survey of the various currents in 20th-century oil painting from Romanticism, to Realism (1925–1945), Revolutionary Realism, Socialist Realism (1945–1980), Impressionism, Expressionism, Abstractionism and Surrealism (from 1980 to date). Artists represented here include To Ngoc Van, Nguyen Do Cung, Bui Xuan Phai, Nguyen Sang and Nguyen Tu Nghiem among many others. Though the museum purports to examine Vietnamese painting in the 1990s, this section is less strong, failing in particular to include Hanoi artists such as Nguyen Minh Thanh, Nguyen Van Cuong, Truong Tan and Vu Dan Tan who, post-*doi moi*, broke with Vietnamese painting's modernist and decorative tradition and took their critical view of their country's socio-political conditions to the world beyond.

Rooms 25, 26 and 27, with over 600 exhibits, are devoted to Vietnamese handicrafts. Here, objects have been chosen to highlight their technical virtuosity as well as their beauty. Utilitarian and sophisticated examples of basketry, tools and clothing show the cultural identity of each ethnic group in the Vietnamese community. Folk art follows in **Rooms 28, 29 and 30**. Religious and festival pictures as well as wooden sculpture including masks and funerary statues are featured here.

The last galleries, **Rooms 31, 32, 33, 34, 35, 36 and 37**, located in the museum's

basement, are filled with nearly 450 ceramic pieces, the visitor able to trace the development of ceramic art in Vietnam from the 11th century to the present day. From the early celadon ware of the Ly dynasty (11th–12th centuries), to ceramics decorated with brown floral motifs of the Tran dynasty (12th–14th centuries), to ceramics featuring blue floral designs of the Early Le, Mac and restored Le dynasties (14th–17th centuries), the visitor moves seamlessly through Vietnam's ceramic art history to contemporary wares.

The Vietnam Fine Arts Museum's comprehensive and well-labelled collection can be absorbed over a day as a survey of Vietnamese culture from the Iron Age to the present, or alternatively, viewed selectively according to the visitor's special interests. Though the highlights of the museum are probably its ceramics and 20th-century painting sections, those with little time for more specifically focused museums such as the Vietnam Museum of Ethnology (see pp. 180–181) or the Museum of Cham Sculpture in Danang (see pp. 166–170) would do well to spend more time here.

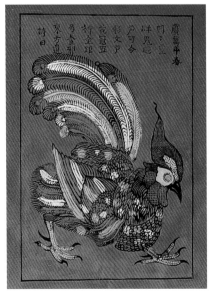

▲ **Kim Hoang**
Rooster | *Ha Tay Province* | *Ink and pigment on paper* | *20th century* | *37.5 x 25 cm*

▲ **Nguyen Van Binh**
Bamboo and Banana Trees | *Lacquer* | *1958* | *67 x 100 cm*

ADDRESS
Duong Nguyen Van Huyen
Cau Giay District, Hanoi
Vietnam

CONTACT INFORMATION
T: +84 4 756 2193
F: +84 4 836 0351
E: vme18@hn.vnn.vn

OPENING HOURS
8.30am–5.30pm Tue–Sun;
closed Tet holiday.

ADMISSION
10,000 dong.

FACILITIES
Wheelchair access.

Guided tours are available in
Vietnamese, French
and English.

Documentation centre; video,
music and photo archive;
auditorium.

HOW TO GET THERE
Taxi: The museum is in the
Cau Gay district, a 20-minute
taxi ride from the city centre.

AROUND THE MUSEUM
A restaurant offering Asian
and Western cuisine is
located on the grounds.

The museum shop is well
stocked with reference
material and a wide variety of
craft items produced by
ethnic communities.

Vietnam Museum of Ethnology

Housed in an attractive, contemporary building, the Vietnam Museum of Ethnology is both a research centre and museum documenting the cultural heritage of Vietnam's ethnic groups through their dress, music and artefacts.

■ **THE BUILDING** On the western outskirts of Hanoi, the museum's semi-circular, two-storey building was designed by Vietnamese Tay minority architect Ha Duc Linh, who was inspired by the elegant shape of ancient Vietnamese Dong Son culture bronze drums. French architect Veronique Dollfus was responsible for the museum's interior, in collaboration with a team from the Musée de l'Homme in Paris. Inaugurated in 1997, the museum's striking Modernist structure is the perfect foil for the tribal houses reconstructed in the museum's grounds.

A granite bridge leads from the compound's main gate to the exhibition building, creating a feeling reminiscent of ascending a ladder to reach a house on stilts—a type of housing still popular in many areas of Vietnam and associated with numerous

▲ *Bahnar communal house in the compound.*

ethnic cultures. Upon entering the museum, the visitor will notice an 'S' shape arranged on the granite floor in dark tiles. This emblem symbolises the Vietnamese coastline, the earth a dark colour and the ocean in light grey.

Incorporating exhibition space, a research centre, library, technical laboratory, offices and an auditorium, the museum building covers around 2,500 square metres of floor space.

The galleries flow seamlessly into one another, the building's vaguely snail-like form both organic and rational in feeling.

■ **THE COLLECTION** Over the centuries, more than 50 Vietnamese ethnic groups have created, modified and maintained their own rich and varied cultural heritage. The Vietnam Museum of Ethnology presents a wide variety of objects for each ethnic group, effectively splitting its collection into 54 sub-collections, one for each tribal culture represented. The huge diversity of cultures is reflected by the broad mix of artefacts. These range from important ceremonial textiles and jewellery to more mundane material such as knives, baskets, pipes, musical instruments, fishing paraphernalia, agricultural tools and floor mats. Because of the wide variety and differing levels of sophistication in agricultural practices, linguistic traditions, religious beliefs and economic models, the objects are necessarily shown in the context of how they relate to each group's culture and daily life, thus increasing the understanding of the general public and specialist alike.

Currently standing at around 20,000 tribal artefacts, the collection also includes a large body of photographic and audio-visual material. Only recently started, the museum holdings continue to grow through donation, purchase and excavation. Well-labelled in Vietnamese, English and French, the ethnological objects on display are generally contextualised by a wide range of media tools such as dioramas, film and photographs.

■ **THE GALLERIES** The museum offers both indoor and outdoor exhibition sites.

Visitors access the museum on the ground floor and proceed first through the **Introductory Gallery** where Vietnam's general historical and cultural periods are presented and a large coloured map shows the distribution of ethnic groups according to language and their affinity for settlement according to geographic elevation. Through audiotapes, the visitor can listen to an individual from each of the five ethnic language families: Austro-Asiatic, Hmong-Yao, Thai-Kadai, Sino-Tibetan and Austronesian.

Moving clockwise to the right, visitors then enter the **Viet or Kinh Gallery**. Representing Vietnam's majority culture which covers 87 per cent of the population, this space is devoted to illustrating main Viet activities involving trade and production, with weaving, selling and shopping chosen as examples. Key objects here include a series of water puppets, a form of popular entertainment in Northern Vietnam, woodblock prints traditionally produced to celebrate Tet (the Vietnamese Lunar New Year), pottery of various genres, bronze ware and carved wooden objects including animal forms.

Behind the Viet section and to the right are the Muong, Tho and Chut ethnic group displays. Characterised by their intense valley cultivation of wet rice and their hunting skills, the **Muong** are represented here by rice baskets and hunting paraphernalia. In addition, a diorama recreates a Muong funerary ceremony and is shown in tandem with video footage documenting a real ceremony.

The **Tho** ethnic group display includes a number of smaller groups characterised by objects associated with their hemp-weaving skills. The **Chut** are few, totalling some 3,000 people living in small, dispersed groups in both the highlands and the lowlands. Objects in their section highlight their hunting-gathering abilities.

On the floor above, the **Tay-Thai** and **Kadai** ethnic group displays are introduced, the most interesting here being the reconstructed, full-size, Black Thai house on stilts from North Vietnam that visitors can walk through. Cloth figures are shown weaving and grinding meal inside the house while traditional artefacts associated with Black Thai life are displayed in cases along the walls. A video depicting a Tay shamanistic ritual is also of interest. Of the materials linked to these groups, the finely made brocade blankets and utilitarian baskets are among the most appealing.

To the left of this section visitors will find a grouping of **Hmong-Yao**, **Tibeto-Burma**, **San Diu** and **Ngai** objects representing these tribes, including batik decoration, wooden furniture, Hmong cotton, silk and hemp clothing, and Pathen household utensils, basketry and clothing.

Further on, a portion of the gallery is devoted to the **Tibeto-Burman** language group. Sophisticated basketry and embroidered clothing figure here.

The **Mon-Khmer** are next with more basketry, some examples exquisite and beautifully conserved. Their weaving is distinctive as well, often beaded and more delicate in appearance than that of other groups.

The **Austronesian** language group, to the right, is represented by musical instruments, tools, furniture, basketry and weaving.

At the end of the gallery the Cham, Hoa and Khmer ethnic groups are represented—the **Cham** by religious objects, textiles, carts and pottery, the **Hoa** with depictions of wedding ceremonies and lion dances, and the **Khmer** with religious objects, manuscripts, clothes, silk dyeing processes and farming tools. Coexisting closely with the Viet people in South Vietnam, these three groups have largely influenced Vietnamese culture and so it is surprising to find a rather small gallery devoted to their culture.

The galleries are not equal in size, their square footage reflecting the amount of material the museum owns as well as the ethnic groups' proportionate importance in the country as a whole. No more than 700 objects from the permanent collection are on display at one time—relatively few in relation to the whole—thus preventing visitors from feeling overwhelmed and allowing better concentration on the works' form as well as function. Rotated regularly, the objects are displayed in such a way that they can be appreciated on aesthetic, formal and technical levels, but also so that, with the help of photographs and documentary video, they tell a story. Unlike in many ethnology museums, the balance between art and education is nicely achieved

▲ **Cotton and silk embroidered tunic**
Yao Quan Trang, Yen Son, Tuyen Quang, Yao

here, the visitor leaving stimulated by beauty and also more aware of Vietnam's ethnic composition. The different collections are displayed according to language groups and territories, and most of the objects presented here are original.

As interesting as the collections shown indoors is the **outdoor museum** which displays some examples of ethnic houses around the compound. Visitors can currently view an Ede long house, a Tay stilt house, a Yao house half on stilts and half on the ground, a Hmong house with a *pomu* wood roof, a Viet house with a tiled roof, a Giarai tomb, Cham houses and a Bahnar communal house. Trees indigenous to the areas represented by the houses have been planted nearby thus lending more authenticity to the concept.

Not far from Hanoi and in a remarkable setting, the Vietnam Museum of Ethnology sheds light on many fascinating but lesser known Southeast Asian ethnic populations. As with all Vietnamese, the lives and cultures of these populations are changing very quickly with the country's burgeoning modernisation and urbanisation. The museum thus plays a very important role in documenting these cultures as they change, for the benefit of later generations.

▲ **Women's cotton dress with appliqué decoration**
Meo Vac, Ha Giang, Flowered Lolo people

ADDRESS
2 Nguyen Binh Khiem Street
District 1, Ho Chi Minh City
Vietnam

CONTACT INFORMATION
T: +84 8 829 8146 / 0268
F: +84 8 825 8784
E: btlsvntphcm_hoa@
hcm.vnn.vn

OPENING HOURS
8am—11am, 1.30pm—4pm
Mon—Sat;
8.30am—4pm Sun and
holidays.

ADMISSION
US$1.

FACILITIES
Guided tours are available in
Vietnamese, French, English
and Mandarin.

HOW TO GET THERE
By taxi or cyclo.

AROUND THE MUSEUM
The zoo is a stone's throw
away from the museum in the
Botanical Gardens.

There are plenty of cafés in
the neighbourhood.

The Museum of Vietnamese History

Dominating the northwest corner of Ho Chi Minh City's Botanical Gardens and housed in a purpose-built colonial exhibition building, The Museum of Vietnamese History offers a good collection spanning the period from prehistory to 1930.

■ **THE BUILDING** Set in a shady garden, the museum was inaugurated in 1929 as the Musée Blanchard de la Bosse, built and run by the French. At that time, the institution featured a broad collection of works of art from various parts of Asia. After the French withdrawal and subsequent partition, the museum was renamed the Saigon National Museum in 1956. In 1979, four years after South Vietnam had fallen to the communists and the country was reunified, the museum was launched again under its present name,

and its collection's focus shifted to highlight Vietnamese material.

With its long façade, central cupola marking the entrance, and rear quadrangle galleries surrounding a courtyard, the museum is clearly of European structural design. However, the museum's pagoda-like tiered dome, platform elevation, sloping overhanging eaves, and decorative lattice work framing the façade lend the building an Eastern grace of undeniable charm. The building continues to function very well as a museum despite its age and change of identity over the years.

■ **THE COLLECTION** Much of the collection was assembled in the 1920s by French academics of the Société des Etudes Indochinoises. It spans prehistory to 1930, the year the Vietnamese Communist Party was formed. Like its sister museum in Hanoi (see pp. 174–175), Ho Chi Minh City's Museum of Vietnamese History boasts a representative collection of Neolithic wares, Dong Son bronzes, Vietnamese ceramics and Cham stone sculpture, the latter probably second only to Danang. Roughly half the museum is devoted to the nation as a whole while the rest of the collection focuses specifically on Southern Vietnamese groups such as the Oc-Eo, the Ben Nghe Saigon and various local hill tribes. Chen-la, Funan and the Khmer are also represented. A selection of ancient pan-Asian pottery, including Han dynasty Chinese ceramics is featured as well, and several

▲ **Ceramic plate**
Chu Dau | Le dynasty, 15ᵗʰ century | D: 35 cm

cannons from 19ᵗʰ-century Hue are displayed in the garden. The collection of Ho Chi Minh memorabilia, however, is small.

■ **THE GALLERIES** The collection is distributed in the galleries more or less chronologically, with visitors starting on the left side of the cupola and working their way around the inner courtyard in a clockwise direction. The **Primitive Gallery**, to the left of the main entrance, houses axe heads, pestles and other Neolithic tools of the Hoa Binh culture. Next, a small space holds bronzes of the **Dong Son culture** as well as some contemporary beads and pots, circa 500—100 BCE. The works in the next gallery are less clearly defined chronologically and include 6ᵗʰ- and 7ᵗʰ-century ceramics as well as 1ˢᵗ-century bronzes.

▲ **Ceramic wine pot**
With applied decoration | Bat Trang | Nguyen dynasty, 19ᵗʰ century | H: 22.5 cm

The subsequent five galleries follow Vietnam's dynastic history. **Gallery 4** is devoted to the **Ly dynasty** with a mixture of media spanning the 1st to the 12th century. Next are objects dating from the 13th and 14th centuries of the **Tran dynasty**. **Gallery 6**, one of the museum's largest, houses a variety of works dating to the **Le dynasty**. Look out in particular for a pair of cast bronze unicorns from the 17th century as well as ceramics exhibiting various glaze techniques and styles. The **Tay Son dynasty** gallery at the rear of the museum is small, as is the **Nguyen dynasty** gallery to its right—rather surprising considering the wealth of Nguyen material still available in Vietnam. Here, decorative domestic objects are displayed, including richly embroidered ceremonial silk robes in Chinese style from the court at Hue, 19th-century ceramics with overlaid applied decoration on a crackled ground, characteristically Vietnamese rather than Qing in style, and elaborate carved wood furniture that would once have graced the homes of Vietnam's elite.

Gallery 9, opposite Gallery 6, on the other side of the inner courtyard, contains an assortment of pan-Asian ceramics of mixed origin and date. Visitors will see Khmer, Chinese, Japanese and Siamese vessels in particular here. A Khmer pottery vase of the 12th century, an elegant 19th-century Kakiemon vase from Japan, an 18th-century Qing porcelain wine cup from Fukien and a 15th-century Sawankhalok glazed dish from Thailand are a few of the examples on display.

Galleries 10 to 13, to the right of the central cupola, are devoted more specifically to the art and

▲ **Terracotta lotus-shaped pedestal**
Hanoi | Ly dynasty, late 11th–early 12th century | D: 56.7 cm

▲ **Wooden figure of Amitabha**
Ho Chi Minh City | 19th century | H: 188 cm

culture of South Vietnam. In **Gallery 10**, works from the Oc-Eo culture of ancient Funan spanning the 1st to the 6th centuries are displayed. Several ill-conserved but striking wooden Buddhas are shown here, as is, interestingly, a Roman gold coin of the 2nd century which testifies to Funan's importance as a trading centre two millennia ago. Beyond is **Gallery 11**, housing stone sculpture from the Mekong Delta. A large, 7th- to 8th-century sandstone *linga* from Long An province and a sandstone figure of Surya of the same period are displayed here.

Gallery 12, though small, is one of the museum's most exciting, featuring the art of Champa and related works. Highlights include some fine Cham sandstone works of sculpture and a rare, early, and well-conserved bronze Buddha from the 4th-century found in Quang Nam Province. Beautifully cast, with crisp details, perfect proportions and a subtly expressive countenance, this Buddha alone justifies a trip to the museum.

The large **Gallery 13** contains utilitarian craft ware of South Vietnam's ethnic minorities including those of the Mon-Khmer speaking groups. Basketry, household vessels and domestic tools predominate here.

Gallery 14, adjacent to the inner courtyard and Gallery 6, houses a small collection of Khmer religious stone sculpture. Beyond this section, having returned to the central cupola area, **Gallery 15** contains Buddhas from around Asia, dominated by a large, giltwood seated Buddha from 19th-century Saigon. Diverse and well-presented in an attractive

Bronze figure of Buddha
Quang Nam Province | 4th century | H: 120 cm

Housed in the Cham section of the museum, this superb Buddha was found in Quang Nam Province, an area of Vietnam largely known for the carved stone temple architecture, religious icons and architectural elements associated with the great Cham sites at My Son, Dong Duong and Tra Kieu. Though Cham sites have survived and much stone sculpture has made its way into Vietnam's public collections, related bronze art of the period, Cham or otherwise, remains rare and of historic importance.

and functional architectural setting, the collection of Ho Chi Minh City's Museum of Vietnamese History offers a well-appointed introduction to the vagaries and complexities of Vietnam's culture and past as well as a fairly broad selection of South Vietnamese material that is quite unique to the museum.

ADDRESS
149 Tran Phu Street
Hoi An
Vietnam

CONTACT INFORMATION
T: +84 510 862 367
F: +84 510 861 779
E: ttqlbtdt@dng.vnn.vn

OPENING HOURS
7am–5pm daily.

ADMISSION
US$5 for five Hoi An sites.

FACILITIES
Guided tours are available.

HOW TO GET THERE
On foot from the centre
of town.

AROUND THE MUSEUM
Other specialist museums in
Hoi An include the Museum of

Trade Ceramics (see p. 185),
the Museum of the Revolution
and the Museum of History
and Culture.

There are plenty of galleries,
restaurants and cafés around
the museum.

Museum of Sa Huynh Culture

One of Hoi An's several specialist museums, the Museum of Sa Huynh Culture, housed in an early 20th-century Chinese-style shophouse, offers a small but unique collection of objects documenting this ancient culture.

▪ **HOI AN** Formerly known as Faifo, the ancient port town of Hoi An, located on the banks of the Thu Bon River, lies 30 kilometres down the Vietnamese coast from Danang. Operating as one of the Champa Kingdom's most important trading centres from the 2nd to the 15th century, the town's port expanded further to accommodate international trade in the 15th and 16th centuries, experiencing its commercial zenith in the 17th and 18th centuries when it was one of the busiest ports in Southeast Asia. At this time, Hoi An served as the gateway to Cochinchina for Japanese, Chinese, Southeast Asian, European and even American traders.

Due to its status as a centre of trade, cosmopolitan 17th-century Hoi An was also an important point of dissemination for Christianity and Buddhism.

Hoi An's fortunes changed radically when, in the 19th century, the Thu Bon River, until then able to accommodate sea vessels, became impossible to navigate due to the accumulation of silt, leaving Danang to take over as central Vietnam's most important port.

Today, Hoi An is a pleasantly small-scale provincial town yet to be overcome by the thrust towards modernisation that characterises other Vietnamese urban centres. Though settled in successive waves by Japanese and Chinese traders, French missionaries, and the Dutch Verenigde Oostindische Compagnie (VOC) in the 17th century, Chinese architecture and overall cultural atmosphere dominate the town.

▪ **THE BUILDING** Located in Hoi An's old town and housing not one but two museums, the Museum of Sa Huynh Culture on the ground floor and the Museum of the Revolution on the upper floor, the building occupies the corner

▲ **Funerary urn**
Pottery | An Bang, Hoi An | c. 1st century | H: 120 cm, D: 55 cm

plot of a row of shophouses which present a generically Chinese style prevalent throughout Southeast Asia. Though the precise date of construction is uncertain, with its flat roof and symmetrically columned, balcony-shaded façade designed to deflect heat and tropical rain, the building would be equally at home in provincial Java, Bangkok's Chinatown, Malaysia or Singapore.

▪ **THE COLLECTION** Established in the mid-1990s, the Museum of Sa Huynh Culture is one of Hoi An's most recent museums. The collection of 216 artefacts originates from excavations of roughly 50 Sa Huynh sites, mainly along the river or ocean, discovered in the early 1990s. The culture is related to Vietnam's Dong Son civilisation and the objects on display in the museum are around 2,000 years old.

The collection consists essentially of large pottery vessels such as funerary urns and their contents which include beads and other items of jewellery.

See in particular a pair of pale green jade earrings found at the bottom of a burial urn at the Hau Xa I site in Hoi An Town as well as a collection of multi-coloured agate beads found at the Hau Xa II site, also in Hoi An Town.

A small, compactly presented institution, amounting to only a few display cases, the Museum of Sa Huynh Culture is nonetheless worth discovering for its unique material elucidating one of Southeast Asia's many obscure but fascinating ancient cultures.

ADDRESS
80 Tran Phu Street
Hoi An
Vietnam

CONTACT INFORMATION
T: +84 510 862 367
F: +84 510 861 779
E: ttqlbtdt@dng.vnn.vn

OPENING HOURS
7am–5pm daily.

ADMISSION
US$5 for five Hoi An sites.

FACILITIES
Guided tours are available.

HOW TO GET THERE
On foot from the centre
of town.

AROUND THE MUSEUM
Other specialist museums in
Hoi An include the Museum of
the Revolution, the Museum
of Sa Huynh Culture (see p.
184) and the Museum of
History and Culture.

There are plenty of galleries,
restaurants and cafés around
the museum.

Museum of Trade Ceramics

Located in a converted house a few doors down from two other specialist museums, the Museum of Trade Ceramics assembles ceramics from around Asia that document Hoi An's rich mercantile history.

■ **THE BUILDING** The museum, opened in 1995, is housed in a renovated, two-storey, Chinese-style house. Retaining many of its original features, including its teak floors, inner staircase and interior beamed structure, the century-old house, with its tiled roof, balcony-shaded façade and pleasant inner courtyard is characteristic of the late 19th-century Chinese architecture of Southeast Asia. Though Hoi An is an ancient and cosmopolitan town, little of its varied 15th- to 18th-century architecture has survived due to its destruction during the Tay Son Rebellion that began in 1773. Thus, most remaining old buildings date to the late 19th-century and beyond, and are either French colonial or Chinese in style.

■ **THE COLLECTION** The collection numbers some 430 ceramic vessels spanning the 8th to 19th century. Of Vietnamese, Japanese, Chinese, Thai and even Middle Eastern manufacture, the wares, of variable quality and condition, would all have been traded through Hoi An from the 15th to the 19th century and thus attest to the port's cosmopolitanism and stature as a place of exchange.

Though Vietnamese ceramics were not traded in as much volume as their contemporary Chinese or Thai wares, as early as the 14th century they nonetheless made their way to the furthest reaches of Southeast and North Asia. According to information in the museum, some Annamese pieces have even been traced to Egypt. A number of good blue and white examples displayed in the museum come from a shipwreck off Cham Island, near Hoi An, and date back to the 15th century. Reasonably well conserved, these ceramics underscore the overall quality of some Vietnamese export porcelain.

From the 15th century onwards, the most widely traded ceramics were Chinese, with both mass market and high quality wares much sought after in both the East and West. Though finer vessels and plates were frequently commissioned and thus expensive and rare, the ubiquitous export wares of the 18th century made their way to every corner of the globe. The museum boasts a number of Chinese trade vessels, some from the Jingdezhen kilns.

Japanese trade ceramics are also well represented here. Seventeenth-century Japan was an active provider of blue and white ware to Southeast Asia and beyond, and Hoi An at the time was an important port for the diffusion of these vessels. However, by the second half of the 17th century, the Japanese trade ban had taken effect and Japanese ceramics were eclipsed by their contemporary Chinese equivalents. See some good examples of 17th-century blue and white Hizen plates from Japan.

A small but very stimulating museum, Hoi An's Museum of Trade Ceramics sheds much light on the dynamism and centrality of Vietnam as a strategic Asian trading hub in pre-colonial days.

▲ **Middle Eastern pottery shard**
*Found in Hoi An |
9th–10th century*

▲ **Japanese underglaze blue plate**
*Hizen, found in Hoi An | 17th
century | D: 22.3 cm*

Vietnamese underglaze blue ceramic bowl

Chu Dau, from a shipwreck off Cham Island, Hoi An | 15th century | H: 8.2 cm, D: 13.2 cm

Though not as well distributed as Chinese Ming dynasty ceramics of the same period, 15th-century Annamese wares were nonetheless produced in large quantities for dissemination around Asia. Unlike much 'sloppy' Chinese export ware, this piece is well potted and nicely painted despite its status as an 'export' piece.

ADDRESS
3 Le Truc Street
Hue
Vietnam

CONTACT INFORMATION
T: +84 54 524 429
F: +84 54 526 083
E: hue-mcc@dng.vnn.vn

OPENING HOURS
6.30am–5pm Tue–Sun.

ADMISSION
30,000 dong.

FACILITIES
An idyllic garden.

HOW TO GET THERE
Taxi: The museum is a
5-minute taxi ride from the
centre of town.

AROUND THE MUSEUM
There are many cafés and
shops in the centre of Hue.

Hue Museum of Royal Fine Arts

Located in an elegant Nguyen dynasty palace, the Hue Museum of Royal Fine Arts assembles a varied collection of antiques that paint a vivid picture of court and commoner life under the Nguyen.

▪ **THE BUILDING** The museum is housed in the Long An Palace built by the third Nguyen dynasty Emperor Thieu Tri (1841–1847) at the end of his reign in 1845. The Nguyen dynasty (1802–1945) was Vietnam's last imperial dynasty and Hue was its imperial capital and cultural centre until it was replaced by Hanoi which became the capital of French Indochina in 1902 and the capital of North Vietnam in 1954.

The palace, dismantled in 1909 and rebuilt on its present site, is a stone's throw from Hue's Imperial City. Built in Chinese architectural style, the palace consists of a single pavilion with a raised sloping roof fronted by slim support columns. The rich, wooden beamed interior is elaborately carved and inlaid with precious materials (floral and foliate motifs, animal masks and auspicious

characters being the most frequently used), the building's luxurious and exotic elements combined with its refined architectural lines echoing the splendour and confidence of Hue in the middle of the 19th century. Elegant and filled with light due to the presence of openings on all sides, the palace also aptly reflected the power and wealth of a Vietnamese state unified from Yunnan to the Gulf of Siam in the decades just before the French attacks that would lead to Vietnam's colonisation.

Set in a quiet and seductively atmospheric garden that even today seems oddly undisturbed by Vietnam's recent decades of violence and turmoil, Long An Palace and its green surroundings are without a doubt as attractive as the household objects and works of art they contain.

▪ **THE COLLECTION** Though the Nguyen dynasty still officially had several decades to its name, its demise was already effective with the fall of Emperor Tu-Duc in 1883. Thus, in 1913 in Hue, the Association des Amis du Vieux Hué was founded by local art and history lovers with the mission of gradually collecting

▲ **Porcelain jar decorated in underglaze 'Hue Blue'**
Nguyen dynasty, reign of Minh Mang (1820–1840) | H: 54.5 cm

court-associated antiques. Thousands of objects dating from the 16th to the 19th century, along with some Cham pieces were gradually assembled. In the early 20th century, the most readily available works were of relatively recent Nguyen vintage and included royal ceremonial articles as well as utilitarian ones. These on the whole form the basis of today's museum.

The Musée Khai Dinh (Khai Dinh was the second last Nguyen emperor) was thus established in 1923 under French patronage and at the time was one of the largest museums in Indochina. The institution changed names several times after this, becoming the Museum of Antiques in the late 1940s, then, after the North-South partition, the Hue Museum in 1958, finally becoming the Hue Museum of Royal Fine Arts in 1995.

The Nguyen dynasty marked the first time in Vietnamese history that the country was fully unified from north to south. The imperial court was rich, and as a result, an abundance of precious objects—works of art of all kinds and specially made household items—were accumulated in Hue. By the middle of the 20th century, however, French colonisation,

▲ *View of a central gallery in the Museum of Royal Fine Arts.*

the country's creeping modernisation, and important socio-political developments (the socialism that had come about partly as a reaction to colonialism) combined to trigger the end of dynastic control in Vietnam, with the last Nguyen emperor, Bao Dai, abdicating in 1945. Despite, and indeed probably as a result of the demise of the Nguyen, the museum and its royal collection continued to solicit the interest of art lovers and remaining French expatriates alike. Unfortunately, the decades that followed Bao Dai's abdication were fraught with turmoil. The war with the French, which ended with independence and partition in 1954, and the subsequent Vietnam War which brought more violence just a decade later, succeeded in either destroying or dispersing significant elements of Hue's very impressive architectural legacy and its many material treasures, some of which had been conserved in the museum. The 1968 Tet Offensive, an important battle of the Vietnam War, was responsible for the destruction of much of the old imperial city.

■ **THE DISPLAY** Today, several thousand objects from the original collection remain, displayed more or less according to category

▲ **Cast bronze incense burner**
Late Nguyen dynasty, early 1920s | H: 43 cm | Commissioned as a gift for the 12th Nguyen sovereign King Khai Dinh's 40th birthday in 1924

and medium within the vast palace and its alcoves. Bronze ware, including ancient rifles, bells, cannons (the latter exhibited in the garden), huge basins, incense burners and vases dating from the 16th to the 20th century; ceramics of 16th- to early 20th-century manufacture from Vietnam, China, England, France and Japan; some gifts to the court from foreign dignitaries; pictures on glass, marble and stone; glassware; Nguyen dynasty books made of bronze or silk; an impressive collection of royal garments (see the well preserved, opulent and vividly coloured and embroidered silk ceremonial and audience robes belonging to various 19th-century emperors and consorts), as well as other 19th- to 20th-century textiles; Nguyen furniture including ornately carved, lacquered and gilded tables and chairs, some in dark precious hardwood inlaid with mother-of-pearl; a diminutive throne made for the eleventh Nguyen king, Duy Tan, upon his accession at age seven; an intricately decorated bed that is an odd juxtaposition of late 19th century French 'Tous les Louis' style and ornate Vietnamese-taste decoration; a collection of musical instruments; decorative gilded trees studded with colourful semi-precious stone flowers and leaves; and household objects used by various Nguyen emperors and their

▲ **Royal robe**
Silk, embroidered with gilt metal thread | Nguyen dynasty, 19th century | H: 110 cm

imperial households are some of the many marvels assembled here.

Despite the segregation of the objects and the fact that the rooms are not set up to reflect their use as they might have appeared when they were lived in before the palace became a museum, the visitor will have no trouble conjuring up an accurate idea of the palace as it might have looked when furnished and inhabited some 150 years ago.

The Museum of Royal Fine Arts in Hue presents an eclectic but representative collection of mainly 19th-century court material that vividly evokes Hue's court life in the old capital's last decades before dynastic Vietnam's terminal decline. Seemingly untouched by the events of the last century, this atmospheric museum should be on all Hue intineraries.

▲ **Royal throne**
Carved gilded and lacquered wood | Nguyen dynasty, early 20th century | H: 94.2 cm

Other Spaces ▶

Other Spaces

BRUNEI

Bandar Seri Begawan
BUBONGAN DUA BELAS

ADDRESS Jalan Residency, Bandar Seri Begawan, BS 8110

CONTACT T: +673 2 226 937 • E: bmconsv@brunet.bn

OPENING HOURS 9am–5pm Sat–Thu, 9am–11.30am, 2.30pm–5pm Fri

The 1907-built former residence of the British High Commissioner houses a documentary exhibition examining the relationship between Brunei and the United Kingdom from the 19th century.

Bandar Seri Begawan
MALAY TECHNOLOGY MUSEUM

ADDRESS Jalan Kota Batu, Bandar Seri Begawan, BD 1510

CONTACT T: +673 2 244 545 • E: bmethno@brunet.bn

OPENING HOURS 9.30am–5pm Sat–Thu, 9am–11.30am, 2.30pm–5pm Fri

Various traditional technologies and handicrafts are examined here. The museum is sponsored by the Shell petroleum group.

Bandar Seri Begawan
ROYAL REGALIA BUILDING

ADDRESS Jalan Sultan, Bandar Seri Begawan, BS 8811

CONTACT T: +673 2 238 358 • E: bmexhib@brunet.bn

OPENING HOURS 9am–5pm daily

Situated in the heart of the capital, this large domed building houses an impressive display of the Sultanate's royal regalia.

Tutong
MERIMBUN HERITAGE PARK

ADDRESS 24 km from Tutong town, Tutong District, TH 1349

CONTACT T: +673 4 261 179 • E: bmddir@brunet.bn

OPENING HOURS 9am–4pm Sat–Thu, 9am–11.30am, 2pm–4pm Fri

A peaceful and not overly developed natural history park and nature trail located roughly an hour-and-a-half's drive from the capital.

CAMBODIA

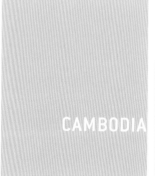

Phnom Penh
THE ELEPHANT PLACE

ADDRESS Royal Palace, Preah Sothearuos Boulevard, Sangkat Cheychumnah, Khan Daun Penh, Phnom Penh

CONTACT T: +855 23 223 724 • E: domrei@online.com.kh

OPENING HOURS 7.30am–11am, 2pm–5pm daily; closed on public holidays

Housed in an 1892 pavilion in Wat Preah Keo Morokat, this small museum presents objects related to royal ceremonies involving elephants.

Phnom Penh
REYUM INSTITUTE OF ARTS AND CULTURE

ADDRESS 47, Street 178, Phnom Penh

CONTACT T: +855 23 217 149 • E: reyum@camnet.com.kh • W: www.reyum.org

OPENING HOURS 8am–6pm daily

A non-profit NGO located near the National Museum, Reyum is a mixed exhibition space showing non-commercial contemporary art.

▼ *Bas-reliefs of devata.*

Siem Reap
CONSERVATION D'ANGKOR

ADDRESS Just off the main road to Angkor, 1 km from the Grand Hotel, Siem Reap

CONTACT T: +855 23 725 747 / 217 645 / 8

OPENING HOURS By invitation of the Ministry of Culture and Fine Arts only

Though not a museum, it is worth getting an official invitation to the repository where 'loose' Angkorian sculptures are housed and restored.

INDONESIA

Bandung
MUSEUM GEOLOGI BANDUNG

ADDRESS 57 Jalan Diponegoro, Bandung 40122, West Java

CONTACT T: +62 22 720 3205 • E: grdc@grdc.esdm.go.id • W: www.grdc.esdm.go.id/museum

OPENING HOURS 9am–3pm Sat–Thu; closed on public holidays

This large geological museum founded in 1929 has a good collection of rocks, fossils, skulls and minerals.

Cirebon
CIREBON KRATON MUSEUM

ADDRESS Museum Kraton Kasepuhan, 37 Jalan Kasepuhan, Cirebon, Java

OPENING HOURS 9am–4pm daily

This small, private museum is housed in the architecturally distinguished 15th-century Cirebon Kraton. The museum boasts a varied collection of old batik pieces, decorative works of art, and craftware.

Jakarta
BALAI SENI RUPA & MUSEUM KERAMIK

ADDRESS Fatahillah Square, Jalan Pintu Besar Utara 27, Jakarta 11110

CONTACT T: +62 21 690 7062

OPENING HOURS 9am–2pm Tue & Thu, 9am–11am Fri, 9am–1pm Sat, 9am–3pm Sun

This museum in the centre of Jakarta features Indonesian collector and dignitary Adam Malik's collection of ceramics and porcelain of various periods and types.

Jakarta
INDONESIA NATIONAL GALLERY

ADDRESS 14 Jalan Medan Merdeka Timur, Jakarta 10110

CONTACT T: +62 21 3483 3954 / 5 • E: galnas@indosat.net.id • W: www.gni.or.id

OPENING HOURS 10am–4pm Tue–Sun

This museum is an off-shoot of the National Museum and contains the national painting collection. The gallery is also involved in contemporary art exhibitions.

Jakarta
WAYANG MUSEUM

ADDRESS West side of Fatahillah Square, Jalan Pintu Besar Utara 27, Jakarta 11110

CONTACT T: +62 21 692 9560

OPENING HOURS 9am–3pm Tue, Thu & Sun, 9am–4.30pm Fri

This museum in central Jakarta features the finest and largest display of *wayang* puppets in Indonesia. Puppets from other parts of Southeast Asia are included as well.

Magelang
| WIDAYAT MUSEUM

ADDRESS 32 Jalan Letnan Tukiyat, Sawitan, Mungkid, Magelang 56511, Central Java

CONTACT T: +62 293 788 251 •
E: museum@widayat.com •
W: www.widayat.com

OPENING HOURS 9am–4pm Tue–Sun

A short distance from Borobodur, the Widayat Museum was established to commemorate the Javanese Modernist painter Widayat (1923–2002).

Mojokerto
| MUSEUM TROWULAN

ADDRESS 141–143 Jalan Majapahit, Trowulan, Mojokerto 61362, East Java

CONTACT T: +62 32 149 5515 •
E: bp3-jatim@indo.net.id

OPENING HOURS 7am–4pm Sat–Thu, 7am–11am, 1pm–4pm Fri

Founded in 1926, the museum is a repository of some of the architectural and religious archaeological finds from the Majapahit site at Trowulan, East Java.

Yogyakarta
| CEMETI ART HOUSE

ADDRESS 41 Jalan D.I. Panjaitan, Yogyakarta 55143

CONTACT T: +62 274 371 015 •
E: cemetiah@indosat.net •
W: www.cemetiarthouse.com

OPENING HOURS 9am–2pm Tue–Sun

A veteran of the contemporary art scene in Yogyakarta, Cemeti functions as both an exhibition centre and a meeting place for artists. The Cemeti Foundation is a short distance away.

Yogyakarta
| GALERI BENDA

ADDRESS 62A Jalan Kemetiran Kidul, Yogyakarta 55272

CONTACT T: +62 274 512 010 •
E: benda@angelfire.com

OPENING HOURS 9am–5pm Mon–Sat

Cooperative-style art gallery featuring the work of contemporary artists from both Indonesia and abroad. Installations, new media art and painting are featured.

Yogyakarta
| KEDAI KEBUN FORUM

ADDRESS 3 Jalan Tirtodipuran, Yogyakarta 55143

CONTACT T: +62 274 376 114 •
E: kkforum@indosat.net.id

OPENING HOURS 11am–11pm Wed–Mon

An off-shoot of the attractive courtyard restaurant of the same name, the space features small exhibitions of Indonesian contemporary art while performances take place upstairs.

Yogyakarta
| VIA VIA CAFÉ

ADDRESS 24B Jalan Prawirotaman, Yogyakarta 55153

CONTACT T: +62 274 386 557 •
E: viavia@yogya.wasantara.net.id •
W: www.viaviacafe.com/noflash/yogyae.htm

OPENING HOURS 7.30am–11pm daily

A small but attractive café/restaurant in the heart of Yogyakarta where contemporary art by young Indonesians is displayed and sometimes sold.

MALAYSIA

Kedah
| LEMBAH BUJANG ARCHAEOLOGICAL MUSEUM

ADDRESS Lembah Bujang 08400, Merbok, Bedung, Kedah Darulaman

CONTACT T: +60 4 481 1236 •
E: zulkifli@jma.gov.my •
W: www.jma.gov.my

OPENING HOURS 9am–4pm daily; closed on the first day of Hari Raya Aidilfitri and Hari Raya Aidiladha

This museum is associated with the Bujang Valley Hindu-Buddhist site.

▼ *Ornamental bead panel of male guardian figures.*

Kuala Lumpur
| PUCUK REBUNG ROYAL GALLERY MUSEUM

ADDRESS Lot 302-A, Level 3, Ampang Mall, Suria KLCC, Kuala Lumpur

CONTACT T: +60 3 382 0769 •
E: prebung@maxiginet.my

OPENING HOURS 10.30am–8.30pm Sun–Thu, 10.30am–9.30pm Fri–Sat

A museum-style space attached to the high-end commercial gallery of the same name. Tribal art, textiles, metalware and more are shown.

Kuala Lumpur
| ROYAL MALAYSIA AIR FORCE MUSEUM

ADDRESS Jalan Lapangan Terbang Sungai Besi, 50460 Kuala Lumpur

CONTACT T: +60 3 2141 1133 •
E: nazriaziz@hotmail.com •
W: www.gtitec.com.my/af_museum

OPENING HOURS 8am–4.30pm Mon–Thu, 9am–5pm Sat, Sun and public holidays

Located just outside Kuala Lumpur, this museum houses 18 aircraft as well as related material.

Kuala Lumpur
| SPACEKRAFT

ADDRESS 1595 Jalan Jiran 10, Happy Garden, 58200 Kuala Lumpur

CONTACT T: +60 16 374 5848 •
E: king@spacekraft.net •
W: www.spacekraft.net

OPENING HOURS 9am–6pm daily

An artist-run space, Spacekraft was established as an alternative avenue enabling young and radical Malaysian cultural and art workers to showcase their works to the general public.

Penang
| CHEONG FATT TZE MANSION

ADDRESS 14 Leith Street, 10200 Penang

CONTACT T: +60 4 262 0006 •
E: cftm@tm.net.my •
W: www.cheongfatttzemansion.com

OPENING HOURS 11am–3pm daily

A restored century-old Chinese courtyard house, the Cheong Fatt Tze Mansion, though operating as a boutique hotel, is worth a visit for its impeccable and faithful restoration.

▲ *Scottish ironworks from the foundry of Walter Macfarlanes.*

Perak
| GEOLOGICAL MUSEUM

ADDRESS Jalan Sultan Azlan Shah, Peti Surat 1015, 30820 Ipoh, Perak

CONTACT T: +60 5 545 7644 / 85 •
E: pasmj@gsmipoh.po.my •
W: www.jmg.gov.my

OPENING HOURS 9am–6pm daily; closed every first and third Sat of the month and during Hari Raya Aidilfitri and Aidiladha

Minerals, rocks and fossils are displayed in this Perak state museum. There are also workshops and a laboratory on site.

Sabah
| SABAH STATE MUSEUM

ADDRESS Jalan Muzium, 88000 Kota Kinabalu, Sabah

CONTACT T: +60 88 253 199 / 255 033 / 215 563 • E: jmuzium@tm.net.my •
W: www.mzm.sabah.gov.my

OPENING HOURS 9am–5pm daily; closed on 1ˢᵗ May

A large modern museum showing Sabah's ethnological, zoological, botanical, geological, and archaeological material, as well as ceramics.

MYANMAR

Bagan
BAGAN ARCHAEOLOGICAL MUSEUM

ADDRESS Bagan Pyataik Lanson, Bagan

CONTACT T: +95 62 70 271

OPENING HOURS 9am–4pm Tue–Sun; closed on public holidays

A large museum featuring Buddhist and other sculpture from some of Bagan's temples, as well as scale models and floor plans of the Bagan monuments. See the Myazedi Pillar in particular.

Mandalay
LACQUERWARE MUSEUM

ADDRESS Next to Aye Yar Hotel, Bagan, Nyaung U Township, Mandalay Division

OPENING HOURS 10am–4pm Mon–Fri; closed in April and on public holidays

A small but compact specialist museum annexed to the National Lacquerware Institute in Bagan. The museum showcases mainly 19th-century and later pieces of both secular and religious function.

Sittway
RAKHINE STATE CULTURAL MUSEUM

ADDRESS 70 Main Road and Yetwin Road, Sittway, Rakhine State

OPENING HOURS 10am–3.30pm Tue–Sun

This museum, housed in a large modern building, presents Rakhine cultural material, including traditional dress, musical instruments, coins, Buddhist art, paintings, weaving equipment, models of stone inscriptions and 62 types of hair knots.

Taunggyi
SHAN STATE CULTURAL MUSEUM

ADDRESS Bogyoke Aung San Road and Eintawshay Road, Taunggyi

OPENING HOURS 9.30am–3.30pm Tue–Sun; closed on public holidays

Located in a modern, purpose-built building, the museum features cultural objects such as swords, fans and furniture belonging to Shan leaders, as well as paintings, coins and traditional costumes.

Yangon
BAGYOKE AUNG SAN MUSEUM

ADDRESS 15 Boyoke Museum Lane, Bahan Township, Yangon

CONTACT T: +95 1 550 600

OPENING HOURS 10am–3.30pm Tue–Sun

Housed in the 1920s villa where Aung San lived with his wife until he was assassinated, the museum assembles a collection of personal memorabilia, photographs and personal effects belonging to the Burmese leader.

THE PHILIPPINES

Makati City
TOTAL GALLERY ALLIANCE FRANÇAISE

ADDRESS 209 Nicanor Garcia Street, Bel-Air II, Makati City

CONTACT T: +63 2 895 7585 / 441 • E: info@alliance.ph • W: www.alliance.ph

OPENING HOURS 8am–8.15pm Mon, Tue & Thu, 8am–9.30pm Wed, 8am–2pm Fri, 8am–5pm Sat, 1.30pm–5pm Sun

The Alliance organises a dynamic calendar of art exhibitions featuring the work of local and international artists.

Manila
COCONUT PALACE

ADDRESS CCP Complex, Roxas Boulevard, Manila 1000

CONTACT T: +63 2 832 1898 • E: cocopalace@pacific.net.ph

OPENING HOURS 9am–11.30am, 1pm–4.30pm Tue–Sun

This charming/kitsch place, built to accommodate a visiting dignitary during the Marcos era, was designed to incorporate Filipino coconuts into the furniture, lighting and wall panels.

Manila
KANLUNGAN NG SINING GALLERY

ADDRESS T.M. Kalaw Street, Rizal Park, Manila

CONTACT T: +63 2 587 411

OPENING HOURS 10am–5pm Tue–Sun

Located in the heart of Rizal Park, this Artists' Haven is housed in a 5000-square-metre space that accommodates working art practitioners and exhibitions of all kinds.

Quezon City
BIG SKY MIND (ARTISTS' PROJECTS FOUNDATION)

ADDRESS 70, 18th Avenue, Murphy, Cubao, Quezon City 1109

CONTACT T: +63 2 421 2125 • E: info@bigskymind.org • W: www.bigskymind.org

OPENING HOURS 1pm–5pm Tue, Thu or by appointment

A dynamic cooperative-style foundation that welcomes all types of art initiatives.

Quezon City
GOETHE INSTITUT

ADDRESS 687 Aurora Boulevard, Quezon City

CONTACT T: +63 2 722 4673 • E: goethepr@pacific.net.ph • W: www.goethe.de/so/map/

OPENING HOURS 8am–6pm Mon–Fri

The Goethe Institut in Manila offers a broad spectrum of activities and events, including visual art exhibitions that present works of both local and international artists.

SINGAPORE

Singapore
SG PRIVATE BANKING GALLERY, ALLIANCE FRANÇAISE

ADDRESS 4th Floor, 1 Sarkies Road, Singapore 258130

CONTACT T: +65 6737 8422 • E: syap@alliancefrancaise.org.sg • W: www.alliancefrancaise.org.sg

OPENING HOURS 9am–7.30pm Mon–Fri, 8.30am–3.30pm Sat

A gallery on the top floor shows a broad selection of international art.

Singapore
THE ARTS HOUSE AT THE OLD PARLIAMENT

ADDRESS 1 Old Parliament Lane, Singapore 179429

CONTACT T: +65 6332 6900 • E: enquiries@toph.com.sg • W: www.theartshouse.com.sg

OPENING HOURS 10am–12am Mon–Fri, 10am–2am Sat, 10am–10pm Sun; closed on Christmas Day and Chinese New Year

Located in a renovated colonial building along the Singapore River, this space boasts a café and an exhibition space.

Singapore
CIVIL DEFENCE HERITAGE GALLERY

ADDRESS Central Fire Station, 62 Hill Street, Singapore 179367

CONTACT T: +65 6332 2996 • E: subandi_somo@scdf.gov.sg • W: www.scdf.gov.sg/heritage/index.htm

OPENING HOURS 10am–5pm Tue–Sun

Housed in the charming, restored early 20th-century Central Fire Station, this gallery highlights the island's civil defence heritage.

Singapore
EARL LU GALLERY

ADDRESS LASALLE-SIA College of the Arts, 90 Goodman Road, Singapore 439053

CONTACT T: +65 6344 4300 / 6340 9102 / 116 • E: earllugallery@lasallesia.edu.sg • W: www.lasallesia.edu.sg/secondary.html

OPENING HOURS 10am–6pm daily

Earl Lu Gallery, attached to Singapore's LASALLE-SIA arts college, is devoted to the organisation and exhibition of international contemporary art with an emphasis on the visual arts of Asia.

Singapore
JENDELA VISUAL ART SPACE

ADDRESS Esplanade – Theatres on the Bay, Level 2, Esplanade Mall, 8 Raffles Avenue, Singapore 039802

CONTACT T: +65 6828 8222 • W: www.esplanade.com

OPENING HOURS 10am–8pm daily

A curved gallery with a sea view, Jendela presents contemporary art of all kinds. The Tunnel and Foyer are other art spaces in the complex.

Singapore
THE NUS MUSEUMS

ADDRESS National University of Singapore, 50 Kent Ridge Crescent, Singapore 119279

CONTACT T: +65 6874 4617 • W: www.nus.edu.sg/museums

OPENING HOURS 9am–5pm Mon–Sat

The art and archaeology of ancient China, Chinese brush painting, Indian stone art, contemporary Singaporean works and historical documents are all shown in this large, state-of-the-art museum at NUS.

Singapore
PLASTIQUE KINETIC WORMS

ADDRESS 61 Kerbau Road, Singapore 219185

CONTACT T: +65 6292 7783 • E: admin@pkworms.org.sg • W: www.pkworms.org.sg

OPENING HOURS 11am–7pm Tue–Sat

A cooperative space formed in 1998, Plastique Kinetic Worms assembles a dynamic group of contemporary Singaporean artists in Little India.

▼ *Lichtenstein's 'Six Brushstrokes'.*

Singapore
ROY LICHTENSTEIN SCULPTURE PLAZA

ADDRESS Millenia Singapore, Temasek Avenue, Singapore 039192

OPENING HOURS Open daily

The Millenia Singapore development houses one of the finest and largest corporate art collections in the region. A highlight is Roy Lichtenstein's last commissioned masterpiece which consists of six, large, colourful brushstroke sculptures.

Singapore
SCULPTURE SQUARE

ADDRESS 155 Middle Road, Singapore 188977

CONTACT T: +65 6333 1055 • E: arts@sculpturesq.com.sg • W: www.sculpturesq.com.sg

OPENING HOURS 11am–6pm Mon–Fri, 12pm–6pm Sat–Sun

Set in an old church surrounded by an attractive garden, Sculpture Square is a contemporary art space showing principally 3D art by regional artists, with a focus on modern practices.

▲ *The Sculpture Square gallery.*

Singapore
SINGAPORE TYLER PRINT INSTITUTE (STPI)

ADDRESS 41 Robertson Quay, Singapore 238236

CONTACT T: +65 6336 3663 • E: stpi@stpi.com.sg • W: www.stpi.com.sg

OPENING HOURS 10am–6pm Tue–Fri, 10am–8pm Sat

With one of the most sophisticated presses in Asia, STPI sponsors printmaking and exhibitions involving work on paper.

Singapore
THE SUBSTATION

ADDRESS 45 Armenian Street, Singapore 179936

CONTACT T: +65 6337 7535 • E: admin@substation.org • W: www.substation.org

OPENING HOURS 11am–9pm daily; closed on public holidays

Launched in 1990, The Substation is a multicultural and multi-disciplinary arts centre. Conferences, exhibitions and theatre all take place here.

THAILAND

Bangkok
ABOUT CAFÉ & STUDIO

ADDRESS 402–408 Maitrichit Road, Pomprab, Bangkok 10100

CONTACT T: +66 2 639 8057 • E: aara@yipintsoi.com • W: www.yipintsoi.com/ffaara/

OPENING HOURS 10am–9pm Wed–Sun

An informal space in Bangkok's Chinatown showing cutting-edge contemporary practice from Thailand and beyond. AARA is also involved in curating other exhibitions in Thailand.

Bangkok
ALLIANCE FRANÇAISE

ADDRESS 29 South Sathorn Road, Bangkok 10120

CONTACT T: +66 2 670 4200 • E: bangkok@alliance-francaise.or.th • W: www.alliance-francaise.or.th/

OPENING HOURS 8am–6.30pm Mon–Fri, 8.30am–5pm Sat, 8.30am–12.30pm Sun

The gallery at the Alliance Française often shows exciting contemporary art of all kinds, including installation art and new technology practices from Thailand and beyond.

Bangkok
THE ART GALLERY OF THE FACULTY OF PAINTING, SCULPTURE AND GRAPHIC ARTS

ADDRESS Silpakorn University, Wang Tha Phra, 31 Na Phra Lan Road, Bangkok 10200

CONTACT T: +66 2 221 0820 / 1 / 225 8991 • E: monrudeep@hotmail.com • W: www.rama9art.org/gallery/artgallery/

OPENING HOURS 9.30am–4.30pm Mon–Sat

A variety of predominantly Thai art is displayed here.

Bangkok
BANGKOK UNIVERSITY ART GALLERY

ADDRESS 3rd Floor, Building 9, Kluanamtai Campus, Bangkok University, Rama IV Road, Klong-toey, Bangkok 10110

CONTACT T: +66 2 350 3626 • E: Bugartgallery@bu.ac.th • W: www.rama9art.org/gallery/bkkuni/

OPENING HOURS 9.30am–7pm Tue–Sat

This is one of Bangkok's more interesting alternative art spaces, featuring contemporary Thai art.

Bangkok
CHULALONGKORN UNIVERSITY ART CENTRE

ADDRESS 7th Floor, Centre of Academic Resources, 254 Phya Thai Road, Patumwan, Bangkok 10330

CONTACT T: +66 2 215 0871 / 3 / 5 • E: info@chula.ac.th • W: www.chula.ac.th/arts/index_en.html

OPENING HOURS 10am–7pm Mon–Fri, 9am–4pm Sat

An important venue for experimental and other Thai art.

Bangkok
EAT ME ART RESTAURANT/GALLERY

ADDRESS 20 metres off Convent Road Silom in Soi Pipat 2, Bangkok 10500

CONTACT T: +66 2 238 0931 •
E: eatmeconvent@hotmail.com •
W: www.hgallerybkk.com

OPENING HOURS 6pm–1am daily

A pleasant and informal eatery in central Bangkok where contemporary Thai art is displayed in a gallery above the restaurant.

Bangkok
GOETHE INSTITUT BANGKOK

ADDRESS 18/1 Soi Goethe, Sathorn 1, Bangkok 10120

CONTACT T: +66 2 287 0942 / 4 •
E: goetheth@loxinfo.co.th •
W: www.goethe.de/bangkok

OPENING HOURS 9am–7pm Mon–Fri, 9am–2.30pm Sat

A good art space showing various types of contemporary and modern art from Thailand and beyond.

Bangkok
JAPAN CULTURAL CENTRE, BANGKOK

ADDRESS 10th Floor, Serm-Mit Tower, Sukhumvit 21 (Asoke), Bangkok

CONTACT T: +66 2 260 8560 / 4 •
E: jccadmin@jfbkk.or.th •
W: www.jfbkk.or.th

OPENING HOURS 9am–12pm, 1.30pm–5pm Mon–Fri

A well-appointed space in the Sukhumvit area where different kinds of visual practices are featured.

Bangkok
THE JIM THOMPSON HOUSE ART CENTRE

ADDRESS 6 Soi Kasemsan 2, Rama I Road (opposite the National Stadium), Bangkok 10330

CONTACT T: +66 2 632 8100 ext. 373 •
E: pr@jimthompson.com •
W: www.jimthompsonhouse.org

OPENING HOURS 9am–5pm daily

This is one of Bangkok's most recently opened non-commercial private exhibition venues, set in the elegant Jim Thompson House compound.

Bangkok
THE KUAN YIN MUSEUM

ADDRESS 104 Solid Group Building Pattanakarn, 40 Pattanakarn Road, Suanluang, Bangkok 10250

CONTACT T: +66 2 321 0048 / 50 / 322 2431 / 4

OPENING HOURS 10am–5.30pm Mon–Sat

A privately-owned museum that specialises in Buddhist art from Thailand and throughout the Buddhist world. All periods and cultures are represented here.

Bangkok
MISIEM'S SCULPTURE GARDEN

ADDRESS 38/9 Puthamonthon Sai 7, Nakornpatom, Bangkok

CONTACT T: +66 2 639 8056 / 7 •
E: aara@yipintsoi.com •
W: www.yipintsoi.com/ffaara/

OPENING HOURS 9am–5pm Fri–Sun

Attractive sculpture garden located roughly an hour's drive out of Bangkok and featuring the work of Thai pioneer artist Misiem Yipintsoi.

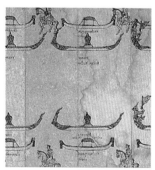

▼ *Manuscript on Royal Barge Processions.*

Bangkok
NATIONAL MUSEUM OF ROYAL BARGES

ADDRESS Bangkok Noi Canal, near Arun Ammarin Bridge, Bangkok 10700

CONTACT T: +66 2 424 0004

OPENING HOURS 9am–5pm daily; closed on 31 Dec, 1 Jan and 12–14 Apr

Located on the Bangkok Noi klong off the Chao Praya river and near the Royal Palace, this national museum assembles royal barges dating from the 18th century and later.

Bangkok
PROJECT 304

ADDRESS Royal Park Condo 41/16, Room 307, Soi Sailom 1, Phaholyothin 8 Road, Phayathai, Bangkok 10400

CONTACT T: +66 2 616 8272 •
E: project304@yahoo.com •
W: www.geocities.com/SoHo/Square/5334/

Project 304 was founded to support contemporary artistic activities through exhibitions as well as media events, such as the Bangkok Experimental Film Festival.

Bangkok
THE QUEEN'S GALLERY

ADDRESS 101 Rajdamnern Klang Boaworrniwet, Pranakorn, Bangkok 10200

CONTACT T: +66 2 281 5360 / 1 ext. 518 / 523 • E: tqg.art@ksc.th.com •
W: www.rama9art.org/gallery/queen/

OPENING HOURS 10am–7pm Sun–Tue, Thu–Sat

Initiated to honour Thailand's queen, this non-profit gallery aims to promote current Thai art of various kinds. Its affiliation to the royal family ensures its popularity with the Thai public.

Bangkok
SILPAKORN UNIVERSITY ART GALLERY

ADDRESS 31 Nah Pha Road, Bangkok 10200

CONTACT T: +66 2 221 3841 •
E: vichoke@su.ac.th •
W: www.rama9art.org/artisan/museum4/mus4.html

OPENING HOURS 9am–7pm Mon–Fri, 9am–4pm Sat

Art gallery of Thailand's foremost art university showing all types of work.

Bangkok
TADU CONTEMPORARY ART

ADDRESS 99/2 Tiam Ruam Mit Road, Barcelona Motors Building (BMW Car Showroom), Huaykwang, Bangkok 10310

CONTACT T: +66 2 645 2473 •
E: taduart@loxinfo.co.th • W: www.tadu.net

OPENING HOURS 10.30am–6.30pm Mon–Sat

Contemporary art space where Thai visual art, performances, workshops and talks are presented.

Chiang Mai
CHIANG MAI UNIVERSITY ART MUSEUM

ADDRESS Faculty of Fine Arts, 239 Huey Kaew Road, Chiang Mai 50200

CONTACT T: +66 53 211 724 •
E: pongdej@chiangmai.ac.th •
W: www.cmu-museum.org

This large and fairly new museum is developing a reputation as one of the country's most cutting-edge contemporary Thai art spaces.

Kamphaeng Phet
KAMPHAENG PHET NATIONAL MUSEUM

ADDRESS 174 Pin-Damri Road, Muang District, Kamphaeng Phet 62000

CONTACT T: +66 55 711 570

OPENING HOURS 9am–4pm Wed–Sun; closed on public holidays

An eclectic collection of early works of art, as well as geographical and ecological materials are kept in this museum. See in particular the large bronze 16th-century Shiva.

Nakhon Pathom
PHRA PATHOM CHEDI NATIONAL MUSEUM

ADDRESS Khwa Phra Road, Muang District, Nakhon Pathom

CONTACT T: +66 34 242 500

OPENING HOURS 9am–12pm, 1pm–4pm Wed–Sun; closed on public holidays

An old collection that has continued to grow and is now housed in a recently refurbished museum building. See here excellent stone sculpture of the Dvaravati culture.

▲ *Carved limestone dharmacakra found in Nakhon Pathom.*

Nakhon Ratchasima
MAHA WIRAWONG NATIONAL MUSEUM

ADDRESS Ratchadamnoen Road, Muang District, Nakhon Ratchasima 30000

CONTACT T: +66 44 242 950

OPENING HOURS 9am–4pm Wed–Sun; closed on public holidays

This museum displays artefacts found in Nakhon Ratchasima. Some of the interesting objects include lintels, fragments of Khmer architecture and images of Hindu gods.

▼ *Ayutthaya-style bronze garuda.*

Phra Nakhon Si Ayutthaya
CHAO SAM PHRAYA NATIONAL MUSEUM

ADDRESS Rotchana Road, Pratuchai, Phra Nakhon Si Ayutthaya 13000

CONTACT T: +66 35 241 587

OPENING HOURS 9am–4pm Wed–Sun; closed on public holidays

The gallery displays artefacts found during the excavation and restoration of the ancient ruins in Ayutthaya. Buddhist relics, golden treasures and other works of art are shown.

Prachinburi
PRACHINBURI NATIONAL MUSEUM

ADDRESS Prachin Anusorn Road, Muang District, Prachinburi 25000

CONTACT T: +66 37 211 586

OPENING HOURS 9am–4pm daily

An excellent archaeological museum in a modern building housing works of art of the Dvaravati period, Khmer-style Lopburi bronze objects found at Muang Si Mahosot in Prachinburi province, as well as assorted ceramics.

Songkhla
SONGKHLA NATIONAL MUSEUM

ADDRESS Vichianchom Road, Bo Yang, Songkhla 90000

CONTACT T: +66 74 311 728 • W: www.thailandmuseum.com

OPENING HOURS 6am–4pm Wed–Sun

Though somewhat off the beaten track, this museum is worth seeking for its good collection of ancient religious art and the charming 19th-century building in which it is housed.

Sukhothai
RAMKHAMHAENG NATIONAL MUSEUM

ADDRESS Muang Kao Sub-district, Muang District, Sukhothai Province

CONTACT T: +66 55 612 167 W: www.thailandmuseum.com

OPENING HOURS 9am–4pm daily

A good museum to visit in tandem with exploring the ruins in Sukhothai. Includes explicatory panels, some Buddhist art from the site and a reproduction of Ramkhamhaeng's stele.

▼ *Prehistoric baked clay pot.*

Udon Thani
BAN CHIANG NATIONAL MUSEUM

ADDRESS Ban Chiang, Nong Han District, Udon Thani 41320

CONTACT T: +66 42 261 351

OPENING HOURS 9am–4pm Wed–Sun; closed on public holidays

This museum at the most important prehistoric site in the northeastern region displays painted pottery, as well as bronze and iron implements of the Ban Chiang culture.

VIETNAM

Hanoi
L'ESPACE, CENTRE CULTUREL FRANÇAIS

ADDRESS 24 rue Trang Tien, Hanoi

CONTACT T: +84 4 936 2164 • E: Contact@espace-ccfhanoi.org • W: www.ambafrance-vn.org

OPENING HOURS 8am–9pm Mon–Sat

Recently moved, the space remains in an easily accessible part of Hanoi and shows and curates a variety of visual art from Vietnam and other countries.

Hanoi
GOETHE INSTITUT ART GALLERY

ADDRESS 56-58, Nguyen Thai Hoc, Ba Dinh, Hanoi

CONTACT T: +84 4 734 2251 / 2 / 3 • E: gihanoi-il@fpt.vn • W: www.goethe.de/hanoi

OPENING HOURS 6am–4pm Wed–Sun

Located in central Hanoi, this art gallery is one of the city's most dynamic contemporary art spaces, showing all forms of practice.

Hanoi
NHA SAN DUC

ADDRESS Phuong Cong Vi, Ba Dinh District, Hanoi

CONTACT T: +84 4 762 5452

Located in what was until a few years ago a pastoral suburb of Hanoi (the area is now being steadily built up), Nha San Duc is the creation of members of Hanoi's community of practitioners of the contemporary non-mainstream genre. Visual art, poetry and performances are hosted here.

Hanoi
RYLLEGA GALLERY

ADDRESS Trang Tien Street, Hoan Kiem District, Hanoi

CONTACT E: ryllega@yahoo.com • W: www.ryllega.com

A relatively new addition to the Hanoi contemporary non-mainstream art scene, Ryllega is located in the city centre. A broad variety of practices can be seen here, and the space provides a good opportunity to meet local artists who congregate at the gallery.

Hanoi
SALON NATASHA

ADDRESS 30 Hang Bong, Hanoi

CONTACT T: +84 4 826 1378 • E: natasha@artsalonnatasha.com • W: www.artsalonnatasha.com

OPENING HOURS 9am–7pm daily

Salon Natasha is Hanoi's best independent non-mainstream commercial art space and has forged a reputation for its curated exhibitions featuring innovative work. It is also the studio of celebrated artist Vu Dan Tan.

Ho Chi Minh City
BLUE SPACE

ADDRESS Le Thi Hong Gam, District 1, Ho Chi Minh City

CONTACT E: blu.space@hcm.vnn.vn • W: www.bluespaceart.com

Another fairly recently established gallery, Blue Space features innovative work for exhibition as well as for sale. Well-presented, the space is a good place to meet the less commercially-oriented members of Ho Chi Minh City's art world.

Ho Chi Minh City
MAI'S GALLERY

ADDRESS 16 Nguyen Hue, District 1, Ho Chi Minh City

CONTACT E: mai_gallery@hotmail.com

Though this is a commercial art gallery that supports itself through commercial exhibitions, Mai's Gallery shows good quality visual practice from around Vietnam and can be relied upon to present innovative work by the country's most interesting up-and-coming artists.

Glossary

Abhaya hasta: gesture of blessing and encouragement in Hinduism and Buddhism.

Annas: former Indian monetary denomination worth 1/16th of a rupee.

Appliqué: decorative technique used in sewing whereby smaller pieces of cloth are stitched onto a larger textile to form a pattern.

Ardhanari: aspect of Hindu god Shiva representing both masculinity and femininity.

Art Deco: architectural and decorative art style of the 1920s–1930s characterised by linear, stylised and geometric forms.

Avalokiteshvara: Bodhisattva and the central force of creation in Buddhism.

Ayutthaya: Thai royal capital from the 14th to the 18th century which was sacked by the Burmese in the mid 18th century, leading to the founding of the Chakri dynasty at Bangkok in 1782.

Bagan: previously Pagan, an ancient religious site in Myanmar where many of the remaining temples date to the 11th, 12th and 13th century.

Bagor: traditional Balinese cloth.

Bahay na bato: Philippines, stone house.

Bale: Bali, ceremonial pavilion.

Ban Chiang: prehistoric archaeological site in the Northern Thai province of Udon Thani and name of the Bronze Age culture discovered there, thought to be one of Southeast Asia's first indigenously-developed Bronze Age cultures.

Bangkok period: the period (1767–1932) began with the fall of Ayutthaya and ended with constitutional monarchy in 1932. The Bangkok and Rattanakosin periods are often assimilated.

Barangay: Philippines, municipal district.

Baroque: referring to a European architectural and art historical style of the 17th century characterised by organic, complex and dynamic forms. Also used to describe a generically ornate style.

Beji: Bali, royal bath.

Bencharong: defines Chinese polychrome enamel ceramics made for the Thai market from the 18th century.

Bhumisparca mudra: Buddhist gesture of calling the earth to witness.

Blanc de chine: type of white Chinese porcelain with a brilliant, glassy glaze manufactured under the Ming dynasty.

Blue and white: a 'blue and white' ceramic vessel's white porcelain body decorated with underglaze blue pigment which is then fired.

Bodhisattva: one who has achieved enlightenment, or an enlightened being who forgoes nirvana for the human world to help mortals attain enlightenment.

Bodegones: Philippines, still-life paintings.

Bodhi Tree: often used as a symbol of the Buddha because it is under this sacred tree that Buddha achieved enlightenment.

Buddhist triad: the Buddha at the centre, flanked by the bodhisattvas Prajnaparamita and Avolokiteshvara.

Candi bentar: form of Balinese gate, split.

Candi kurung: form of Balinese gate, covered.

Champa: Hindu-Buddhist culture and empire that flourished in present day Vietnam from the 2nd and 6th century to the 15th century.

Chiaroscuro: refers to the contrasting evocation of light and shadow in painting or drawing.

Crackled glaze / ware or craquelure: deliberate or accidental hairline cracking of a ceramic glaze.

Dayak: tribal people of Borneo.

Dhamasala: assembly hall.

Dhammapala: one of the Buddha's early disciples.

Dong Son: Bronze Age culture of Northern Vietnam thought to be one of the earliest sophisticated Bronze cultures to have evolved indigenously in Southeast Asia. Also a specific archaeological site in Northern Vietnam.

Doric: classical order of Greek architecture, often referring generically to columns of a simple style.

Durga: Indian female goddess responsible for slaying the demon Mahisa.

Dvaravati period: also known as the Mon period, extended from the 6th to the 11th century in Thailand.

Dwarapala: Indonesia, guardian of temples.

Gamelan: Indonesia, percussion orchestra.

Ganesha: son of Hindu gods Shiva and Parvati. Ganesha is the god of prophecy, always represented by an elephant's head.

Gedung: Bali, enclosed pavilion.

Geringsing: warp and weft tie-dyed textile or double *ikat*.

Harihara: Hindu deity combining Vishnu (Hari) and Shiva (Hara).

Haripunchai: modern Northern Thai city of Lamphun. The city was founded in the 7th century by Mon immigrants from the Dvaravati kingdom.

Hasta Kosala Kosali: book of Balinese building principles.

Hor trai: Thailand, library for conserving sacred scriptures in a monastery.

Ijuk: black fibre of the jaka palm tree.

Ikat: complex traditional Southeast Asian textile manufacturing technique involving tie-dyeing the yarn before weaving to create patterns. Also refers to the textile itself.

Impasto: thickly applied paint, usually on canvas.

Iwan: the principal arch of a mosque.

Jaba: Bali, front courtyard of a temple.

Jaba tengah: Bali, central courtyard of a temple.

Jataka / Vessantara Jataka: refers to the 547 stories narrating the lives of Buddha (three additional stories in Burma), each story illustrating one of the Buddha's virtues.

Jeroan: Bali, back courtyard of a temple.

Kala: refers to a mask combining human and lion-esque features. Seen in Majahapit art and representing time, life-giving powers, death and prosperity.

Kamcheng: Peranakan, covered vessel for food.

Kamphaeng Phet: garrison city north of Sukhothai, built in the 14th century, that has given its name to a style of religious art made at the time in and around the city.

Kendi: a water vessel with a bulbous body and thin neck.

Klong: Thai, canal.

Koftgari: Indian metalware technique involving inlay and the ornamental juxtaposition of gold and steel.

Koh: Thai, island.

Kufic: angular early Arabic script used for architectural inscriptions and copying the Qur'an.

Kufi banaie: form of Kufic script.

Linga: a phallic form symbolising Shiva.

Lopburi: city in Central Thailand that was an important outpost during the Khmer period of influence. Also refers to the Khmer-influenced school of art of Central Thailand that was active from the 10th to the 13th century.

Mahabharata: one of two ancient Hindu morality epics (*also see Ramayana*).

Mahjong: Chinese game.

Mamluk: refers to a dynasty that ruled Egypt, Arabia, Syria and Iraq from the 13th to the early 16th century.

Mara: embodies evil, tempter of Buddha.

Mudra: Hindu-Buddhist iconography referring primarily to the Buddha's sacred symbolic hand gesture. Some of the most common *mudra* are *Abhaya mudra*, *Bhumisparca mudra* and *Dhyana mudra*.

Naga: sacred snake of Hindu-Buddhist mythology.

Narayana: Vishnu as the creator of life.

Nielloware: metalware decorating technique involving the application of a dark metal amalgam to surface etching to create patterns.

Orang Asli: indigenous tribal peoples of peninsular Malaysia.

Orang Ulu: upriver tribal peoples of Borneo.

Overglaze: technique referring to enamels applied to a ceramic vessel which has already been glazed and fired.

Palladian: referring to Italian Renaissance architect Andrea Palladio whose sober, pared-down and symmetrical style revived and reinterpreted the classical architecture of the ancient world.

Panchatantra: collection of Indian fables relating to animals.

Parvati: one of Shiva's consorts.

Pita Maha: Balinese artists' association of the 1930s.

Plain of Jars: plain in central Laos that is home to roughly 300 ancient stone jars thought to be funerary urns.

Prada: gold leaf applied to textile.

Prajnaparamita: Buddhist goddess of transcendental wisdom.

Pura: Bali, temple.

Pusaka: Indonesia, heirloom with a sacred connotation.

Pyu: early Indianised people of Burma.

Ramayana: one of two ancient Hindu epics adapted to local culture in many parts of Southeast Asia (*also see Mahabharata*).

Rattanakosin period: this period began with the founding of the Chakri dynasty at Bangkok in 1782 and is still ongoing, King Bhumiphol the current regent.

Repoussé: metalsmithing technique that creates relief on the metal's surface as the sheet is worked from below.

Rococo: style of art and architecture that originated in 18th-century France and is characterised by elaborate, florid and asymmetric ornamentation. Also used to refer generically to a pretty and heavily decorated style.

Samsui women: (lit. 'mountains and water') refers to female immigrants from the Samsui district of Southern China who fled economic hardship or arranged marriages at home and sought labour-intensive jobs (construction site work for example) in Singapore to maintain their independence.

Sawankhalok: type of celadon ware produced in Si Satchanalai, Central Thailand in the 14th and 15th century.

Shiva: or Siva, the destroyer or creator, one of the gods of the Hindu trinity.

Soi: Thai, alley or road.

Songket: Indonesia, weaving technique. Songket usually incorporate gold or other metallic threads as supplementary weft.

Srivijaya: Hindu-Buddhist empire that spanned the southern reaches of Southeast Asia from Sumatra to South Thailand from the 8th to the 13th century.

Stele: an upright stone slab decorated with figurative relief carvings or an inscription.

Stupa: domed structure housing Buddhist relics. A symbol of Buddha's enlightenment.

Sukhothai: seat of the first independent Thai kingdom that began in the mid 13th century. It was eclipsed by Ayutthaya in the 14th century. Also refers to Thai art of the Sukhothai period.

Suriya: Hindu god of the sun.

Tantri Kamandaka: collection of Javanese fables relating to animals.

Tree of Life: ancient Middle Eastern pre-Islamic symbol representing divine creation.

Tuk-tuk: open, motorised vehicle common in Thailand.

Ukiran: fine woodcarving in Malaysia and Indonesia.

Uma: one of Shiva's consorts.

Undagi: expert of Balinese architecture.

U-Thong style: refers to a Thai artistic style of the 12th–15th century that absorbed competing influences.

Vasudeva: Hindu god and father of Krishna.

Vishnu: the protector, one of the gods of the Hindu trinity.

Warung: Indonesia, small food stall.

Wat: Thailand, Buddhist temple complex.

Wenchang: Chinese god of literature.

Wheel of law: Buddhist symbol representing the fundamental teachings of Buddha.

'White Rajahs': refers to three generations of Englishmen who were the political leaders of Sarawak in the 19th and 20th century.

Bibliography

The Asian Civilisations Museum A–Z Guide, Asian Civilisations Museum, Singapore, 2003.

Arts of Asia, Singapore Edition, Vol. 32, no. 6, Nov–Dec 2002.

Carpenter, Bruce W., *Emilio Ambron – An Italian Artist in Bali*, Archipelago Press, Singapore, 2001.

Chandler, David et al., *In Search of Southeast Asia – A Modern History*, University of Hawaii Press, 1987.

Colayco, Tina (ed.), *Museum Treasures of Southeast Asia*, The ASEAN Committee on Culture and Information and ArtPostAsia Ptd Ltd., Singapore, 2002.

Couteau, Jean, *Museum Puri Lukisan*, Ratna Wartha Foundation, Ubud, Indonesia, 1999.

Dermawan, Agus T. and Wright, Astri, *Hendra Gunawan – A Great Modern Indonesian Painter*, Archipelago Press, Singapore, 2001.

Di Crocco, James V. et al., *Treasures from The National Museum Bangkok*, National Museum Volunteers, Bangkok, 1995.

Dumarçay, Jacques and Smithies, Michael, *Cultural Sites of Burma, Thailand and Cambodia*, Oxford University Press, Singapore, 1995.

Girard-Geslan, Maud et al., *L'Art de L'Asie du Sud-Est*, Citadelles & Mazenod, Paris, 1994.

Guillon, Emmanuel, *Cham Art Treasures from the Da Nang Museum*, Vietnam, River Books Ltd., Bangkok, 2001.

Haks, Leo and Maris, Guus, *Lexicon of Foreign Artists who Visualized Indonesia (1600–1950)*, Archipelago Press, Singapore, 1995.

Hall, D.G.E., *A History of Southeast Asia*, Macmillan Press Ltd., London, 1994.

Kelly, Kristin, *The Extraordinary Museums of Southeast Asia*, Harry N. Abrams Inc., New York, 2001.

Khoo, C.M. James (ed.), *Art & Archaeology of Fu Nan – Pre-Khmer Kingdom of the Lower Mekong Valley*, Orchid Press, Bangkok, 2003.

Lewis, Paul and Elaine, *Peoples of the Golden Triangle – Six Tribes in Thailand*, Thames and Hudson, London, 1998.

Liu, Gretchen, *One Hundred Years of the National Museum – Singapore 1887–1987*, National Museum, Singapore, 1987.

Manh Phuc (ed.), *Bui Xuan Phai (1920–1988)*, Truong Hanh, Hanoi, 1997.

Michell, George, *Hindu Art and Architecture*, Thames and Hudson, London, 2000.

Miksic, John and Simon, Richard (eds.), *Art of Indonesia – Pusaka, From the Collections of the National Museum*, Periplus Editions, Singapore, 1998.

Neka, Suteja, *The Development of Painting in Bali*, Yayasan Dharma Seni Museum Neka, Ubud, Indonesia, 1989.

Nguyen, Quan, *Traditions and Acculturation, Uncorked Soul: Contemporary Art from Vietnam*, Plum Blossoms Ltd., Hong Kong, 1991.

Rawson, Philip, *The Art of Southeast Asia*, Thames and Hudson, London, 1995.

Tarling, Nicholas (ed.), *The Cambridge History of Southeast Asia*, Cambridge University Press, Cambridge, 1999.

Warren, William and Beurdeley, Jean-Michel, *Jim Thompson: The House on The Klong*, Archipelago Press, Singapore, 2002.

Warren, William, *The Prasart Museum Treasures of Thailand*, Ibis Books, Singapore, 1990.

Woodward, Jr Hiram W., *The Sacred Sculpture of Thailand: The Alexander B. Griswold Collection – The Walters Art Gallery*, Thames and Hudson, London, 1997.

Vietnam Museum of Ethnology, Vietnam Museum of Ethnology, Ho Chi Minh City, 1998.

Picture Credits

BRUNEI
Brunei Museum: 13, 14–17

CAMBODIA
National Museum of Cambodia: front cover (figure of Shiva and Uma), 8, 20–21, 23–24
The Royal Palace's Silver Pagoda: 19 (top), 25
Tuol Sleng Genocide Museum: 19 (centre), 26–27

INDONESIA
A. Blanco Renaissance Museum: 35
Agung Rai Museum of Art: 29 (below), 36–37
Jakarta History Museum: 43
Le Mayeur Museum: 31
Museum Bali: 32–33
Museum Prabu Geusan Ulun: 49
Museum Puri Lukisan: 38–39
Museum Semarajaya and Kertha Gosa: 34 (top)
Museum Seni Lukis Affandi: 50
National Museum: 6, 29 (top), 44 (top and centre left)
Neka Art Musuem: 29 (centre), 40–41
Purbakala Archaeological Museum: 30
Ullen Sentalu Museum: 51

LAOS
Champasak Provincial Museum: 56
Lao National Museum: 53 (centre and below), 57 (top and below)
Luang Prabang National Museum: 53 (top), 54–55

MALAYSIA
Baba Nyonya Heritage Museum: 78
Islamic Arts Museum Malaysia: 5, 59 (top and centre), 60–61
Labuan Maritime Museum: 75 (top)
Melaka Sultanate Palace Museum: 79
Museum and Art Gallery, Penang: 80 (centre and below), 81
National Art Gallery: 66–67
National History Museum: 68 (below), 69
National Museum: 70–71
Orang Asli Museum: 72
Perak State Museum: 82–83
Petronas Gallery: 73 (centre and below)
Sarawak State Museum: 59 (below), 76–77

MYANMAR
National Museum of Myanmar: 86 (top)

THE PHILIPPINES
Ateneo Art Gallery: 110–111
Ayala Museum: 93
Bahay Tsinoy: Museum of Chinese in Philippine Life: 94–95
Cultural Center of the Philippines: 91 (below), 106–107
Jorge B. Vargas Museum and Filipiniana Research Center: 112–113
Lopez Memorial Museum: 108 (centre and below), 109
Metropolitan Museum of Manila: 91 (centre), 96–98
Museo Pambata: 99 (centre and below)
Museum of Philippine Political History: 91 (top), 100–101
National Museum of the Philippines: 102 (top)
University of San Carlos Museum: 92
University of Santo Tomas Museum of Arts and Sciences: 104 (centre and below), 105

SINGAPORE
Asian Civilisations Museum (Armenian Street): 115 (below), 117 (top left and below)
Asian Civilisations Museum (Empress Place): 2, 118–122
The Changi Museum: 123 (centre and below)
Raffles Hotel Museum: 124 (centre and below), 125
Singapore Art Museum: 126–129
Singapore History Museum: 115 (top), 130–133, back cover (dome)
Singapore Philatelic Museum: 115 (centre), 134–135

THAILAND
Chiang Mai National Museum: 137 (below), 156–158
Nakhon Si Thammarat National Museum: 160–161
National Art Gallery: 143
National Museum Bangkok: 3, 144–147
National Science Museum: 137 (centre), 162–163
The Siam Society and Kamthieng House Museum: 150–151
Suan Pakkad Palace Museum: 152–153
Tribal Museum: 159
Vimanmek Mansion Museum: 154–155

VIETNAM
Contemporary Arts Centre: 171
Hoa Lo Prison Museum: 172
Ho Chi Minh Museum: 173
Hue Museum of Royal Fine Arts: 186
Museum of Cham Sculpture: 167 (top), 206–207

Museum of Sa Huynh Culture: 184
Museum of Trade Ceramics: 185
The Museum of Vietnamese History: 182–183
National Museum of Vietnamese History: 174–175
Vietnam Fine Arts Museum: 165 (centre), 176–179
Vietnam Museum of Ethnology: 165 (below), 180–181

OTHERS
Ban Chiang National Museum: 195 (below)
Carpenter, Bruce W., *Emilion Ambron: An Italian Artist in Bali*, Archipelago Press, Singapore, 2001: 34 (below)
Chao Sam Phraya National Museum: 195 (top)
Cheong Fatt Tze Mansion: 191 (below)
Frenchie Cristogratin: 116 (top)
Martin Cross: 65, 68 (top), 74 (top)
Department of Museums and Antiquities, Malaysia: 75 (centre and below), 80 (top)
Goh Seng Chong: 74 (below)
Roy Lichtenstein: 193 (top)
Magsaysay Ho, Anita, *Anita Magsaysay-Ho, An Artist's Memoirs*, Archipelago Press, Singapore, 2000: 109 (top)
Museum Treasures of Southeast Asia, The ASEAN Committee on Culture and Information, Malaysia, 2002: 57 (centre), 85, 86 (below), 87–89, 102 (centre and below), 103
National Archives of Singapore: 116 (below), 117 (top right)
Photobank/Tettoni, Cassio and Associate Pte Ltd: 34 (centre)
Pucuk Rebung Royal Gallery Museum: 191 (top)
Royal Barges, The Fine Arts Department, Thailand, 1996: 194 (top)
Sculpture Square: 193 (below)
Sin Kam Cheong: 123 (top), 124 (top)
Ravi John Smith 73 (top)
Somchai Warasart and Phra Pathom Chedi National Museum: 194 (below)
George C. Tapan: 99 (top), 104 (top), 108 (top)
Luca Invernizzi Tettoni: 10, 19 (below), 22, 137 (top), 138–142, 148-149, 165 (top), 166, 167 (below), 168–170, 190
Treasures of the National Museum, Buku Antar Bangsa, Singapore, 1997: 44 (centre right), 45–48
Nanok Tunarno: 42

Index

Note: Numbers in italic refer to illustrations

A

Abad, Pacita 97, *98*
aborigines 72, 83
    Also see tribal artefacts
aboriginal art 67, 72, 82, 83
About Café & Studio, Thailand 193
Abueva, Napoleon 108, 111, 112
Adams, Ansel 67
Affandi 41, 50
    Also see Museum Seni Lukis Affandi
Affandi Foundation 50
Aga Khan Award 50
Aguinaldo, Emilio 101
Aguinaldo, Lee 110
Agung Rai Museum of Art 36
Agung Sukawati, Tjokorda Gde 38
Albano, Ray 109
Alliance Française, Thailand 193
Ambarawa Railway Museum 42
Ambron, Emilio 34, *34*
Amorsolo, Fernando 93, 105, 108–109,
    110, 113
Amorsolo, Pablo 105
Ampa field 17
ancestor worship 47
ancestral altar 117
Ang Kiukok 109, 110
Angkor art 23
    Also see pre-Angkor *and* post-Angkor
Anglo-Burmese wars 86
Anglo-Dutch Treaty 69
animal money 65
    Also see tin ingot
Annamese blue and white wares 16, 146,
    175, 185, *185*
annas stamp *134*, 135
anthropology 102
Apin, Muchtar 50
Apollo 17 mission 54
aquarium 75
Aquinas, St Thomas 104
Aquino, Corazon 101
archaeological artefacts 45, 56, 57, 70, 92,
    93, 102, 103, 108, 109, 133, 145, 146
architectural styles 32, 56, 63, 68, 70, 73,
    76, 79, 80, 82, 118, 134, 174, 176
Arcilla, Ros 111
Ardena, Pedro 96
Ardhanari 139
Ariff, Abdullah 67
ARMA *see* Agung Rai Museum of Art
Art Gallery of The Faculty of Painting,
    Sculpture and Graphic Arts, Thailand 193
Art Gallery, Brunei 14

Art Nouveau 78
Arts House at The Old Parliament, The,
    Singapore 192
Asian Civilisations Education Space 122
Asian Civilisations Museum
    (Armenian Street) 116–117, 118, 126,
    134
    (Empress Place) 118–122, *118*, 126
Ateneo Art Gallery 110–111
Avalokiteshvara 175
Aviado, Virgillio 111
Aw Boon Haw 131
Ayala Foundation 93
Ayala Museum 93
Ayutthaya 146, 149
Azidin, Raja 67
Aziz, Abdul 41

B

Ba Dinh 173
baba nyonya *see* Peranakan
Baba Nyonya Heritage Museum 78
Bac Ninh 175
Bac Son culture 175
Bagan Archaeological Museum, Myanmar
    192
Bagyoke Aung San Museum, Myanmar 192
Bahay Tsinoy 94–95
Balai Seni Rupa & Museum Keramik,
    Indonesia 190
bale (pavilion) 32, 33
Ban Chiang National Museum, Thailand 195
Ban Chiang wares 145, *145*, 152, 153, 155,
    157
Bangko Sentral ng Pilipinas (BSP) collection
    96
Bangkok Museum *see* National Museum
    Bangkok
Bangkok University Art Gallery, Thailand 193
barter 65, 79, 94, 96
basketry 47, 56, 72, 77, 83
Baskin, Leonard 110
Batak 120
Batanes Archaeological Project 103
Batavian Society 9
Batavian Society of Arts and Sciences *see*
    Institute of Indonesian Culture
bath sites 30, 32
'batik renaissance' 50
Bayan 100
Bayon style *8*, 23, *24*, 140
beadwork 30, 65, 77, 79, 89, 94, 102, 116
Bedil, Dewa Putu 40, 41
bees' wax 16
beji (baths) 32
Benavides, Miguel de 104

Bencharong *141*, 146, *152*, 153
Benpres Building 108
betel nut chewing 16, 92, 94, 117
Bhirasri, Silpa 143
Big Sky Mind (Artists' Projects Foundation),
    The Philippines 192
Binh Dinh 169
Binokasih coronation 49
birth-related rituals 16
bisect stamp cover *134*, 135
blanc de Chine 121, *121*
Blanco, Antonio 35
Blanco, Mario 35
Blanco Renaissance Museum, Indonesia 35
blown glass *17*
blowpipes 72
Blue Space, Vietnam 195
blue and white wares *see* Annamese,
    Japanese *and* Ming
boat building and models 77, 82, 93, 103
Boat Quay 118
Boghosian, Varujan 110
Boisselier, Jean 21
Bondoc, Jesus 110
Bonifacio, Andres 101
Bonnet, Rudolf 37, 38, 40, 41, *41*
books, rare ancient 49, 94, 112
Boonma, Montien 143
botany 103
    Also see natural history
Brahman art 146
brassware 16
British colonisation 44, 68, 69, 74, 81, 86,
    87, 124
British East India Company 80, 81, 135
    Also see Straits Settlements
British North Borneo (Chartered) Company
    69
British Residential System 69
Bronze Age 30, 89
bronze works *14*, *20*, 23, 30, 47, 48, 56, 63,
    64, 89, 140, *146*, 147, *147*, 161
Brooke dynasty 69, *77*
Brooke, Sir Charles 76
Brunei Arts & Handicrafts Training Centre
    14
Brunei Museum 14–17
Brunei Museums (cultural body) 14
Brunei Sultanate 16
Bubongan Dua Belas, Brunei 14, 190
Buddha images 30, 86, *87*, 89, *89*, 118,
    140, *140*, 141, *142*, 145, 146, *146*, 147,
    157, 158, *158*, *183*
Buddha Phra Buddhasihing 144
    Maitreya (Gold Buddha) 25, 54, 55, *55*
    Emerald 25

Buddhism and Buddhist art 23, 24, 25, 30,
    54, 55, 57, 68, *69*, 86, *89*, 119, 121, 145
Budi, Made 41
Buhid Mangyans 92
Bui Xuan Phai (1920–1988) *129*
Bumi Kaler Building 49
burial artefacts *see* funerary
Burnham, Daniel 102
But Thap Pagoda 175

C

C.P.G. Architects 126
Cabrera, Ben 97, *98*
calligraphy 15, 63, 121, *122*
camphor 16, 79
candi (Balinese gates) 32
cannons 16, 82, 83, *83*, 100
canoes, dugout 83
Capili, Arsenio 113
Carillon University 112
Castrillo, Eduardo 111
cave paintings 86, 89
celadon 15
Cemeti Art House, Indonesia 191
ceramics, 14, 15, *15*, 17, 45, 48, 54, 57, 63,
    64, 71, 73, 78, 82, 83, 94, 95, 105, 116,
    140, *141*, 142, 145, 175, *176*, 179
    glazed 14, *14*, 15
    underglaze 15, *17*, 44, 45, 62
    ceremonial wares 47
Cham art 138, 145, *167*–170, 175, 181, 182,
    183
Champasak Provincial Museum 56
Chang Fee-Ming 41
Changi Airport, Singapore 135
Changi Chapel 123
Changi Gaol 123
Changi Murals 123
Changi Museum, Singapore 123
Changi Quilts 123
Chanh Lo 169
Chao Sam Phraya National Museum,
    Thailand 195
Chea Thay Seng 21
Chen, Georgette 67
Cheong Fatt Tze Mansion, Malaysia 191
Cheong Lai Tong 70
Cheong Soo Pieng 67
Cheung Yee 111
Chiang Mai 156, 157–158
Chiang Mai National Museum 156–158
Chiang Mai University Art Museum, Thailand
    194
Chihuly, Dale 126
Chin, Edmond 120
Choeung Ek extermination camp 26

choppers 30
Chulalongkorn University Art Centre, Thailand 193
circumcision ritual 16
Cirebon Kraton Museum, Indonesia 190
Civil Defence Heritage Gallery, Singapore 192
Classical style 45, 47, 100
clay pots 30
Co, Charlie 97
Coconut Palace, The Philippines 106, 192
Coen, Governor General Jan Pieterzoon 43
coins see numismatic relics
Colegio de Nuestra Señora del Santisimo Rosario 104
Colegio de Santo Tomas 104–105
communist insurgence 69, 71, 74
Conservation d'Angkor, Cambodia 190
construction, without nails 139
Contemplacion, Flor 97, 98
contemporary art 126–127, 143
Contemporary Arts Center, Vietnam 171
costumes 63–64, 71, 72, 80, 81, 82, 83, 87, 92, 99, 119, 131, 146
    wedding 51, 56
cotton 79, 94
court culture 50
Couteau, Dr Jean 39
Covarrubias, Miguel 37
Cristobal, Bonifacio 113
Cultural Center of the Philippines 106–107
currency see numismatic relics
cyber art 128

D
Da Nghi 169
Dan Xuan Hoa 171
Danang 167, 168, 170, 175
dance forms and ceremonies 33, 36, 71
Dayak 120
de Ayala y Montojo, Fernando Zóbel 93, 110, 111
de Flines, E.W. van Orsoy 45
de Foutereau, Alex 54, 55
de Jesus Nakpil, Felipe 112
de la Cruz, Filemon 111
de la Rosa, Fabian 105, 110, 112
decorative art 54, 63, 176
Delacroix, Eugène 110
Department of Aboriginal Affairs 72
Dhammapala 142
Diliman Campus 112, 113
dioramas 70, 71, 74, 93, 94, 95, 132, 145
Djirna, Made 37
Domingo, Damian 93
Dong Duong 169, 170

Dong Son culture 47, 54, 68, 175, *175*, 177, 180, 182, 184
Dortoire de Famille Jeanne d'Arc 176
drums 174, 175
    Also see Dong Son culture
Dullah 41
Dupont, Pierre 21
Durga 23, *23*
Dutch colonisation 42, 44, 48, 65, 69, 74
Dutch East India Company 42, 43, 45
Dvarapala 47, *166*, 170, 171
Dvaravati School 142, *142*, 146, 147

E
Earl Lu Gallery, Singapore 193
early trade see trade relations
East Art Museum see National Museum of Vietnamese History
Eastern and Oriental Hotel 124, 125
Eat Me Art Restaurant/Gallery, Thailand 194
Ecole Francaise d' Extrême-Orient (EFEO) 167, 174
Edades, Victorio 106, 107, 113
EDSA Revolution 101, 106
Eduardo Ah Tay 95
Elephant Place, Cambodia 190
elephant statuary 44, 54, 57
Elks Club Building 99
embroidery 70, 116
Emerald Buddha 25
Emergency, The (1948–1960) 69, 74
Empress Place 118
enamel ware 45, 175
Endaya, Imelda Cajipe 111
'Enemies of Angkar' 26
erhu 71
Esplanade arts complex, Singapore *135*
Estrada, Joseph Ejercito 101
ethnic communities 80, 89, 133, 135
ethnography 34, 45, 70, 92, 102, 105, 120
ethnological material 47, 48, 76, 83, 92, 93, 102, 104, 107, 119
Europeans, arrival of the 16, 45
ewer 14, *14*, 15, *15*

F
Fang Lijun 127
Farquhar Botanical and Zoological Drawings *131*, 132, *132*
Farquhar, William 132
Fatahillah Park 43
Fer, Anna 97, *98*, 111
Fernandez, Egai 111
festivities, ethnic 71, 119
Filipinas Foundation Inc 93
first day covers see philately exhibits

fish traps 77
flora and fauna see natural history
Flores, Simon 113
folk art 89, 176, 177, 179
Folk Arts Theater, Philippines 106
Fort Canning Hill 130, 132, 133
Fort Canning Rise 134
Francisco, Carlos 'Botong' 105, 109, 113
French colonisation, Indochina 9, 20, 57, 167, 173, 174
frescoes, religious 25
    Also see murals
Friend, Donald 37, 41
Friendship Bridge 56
funerary relics 30, 87, 89, 92, 92, 97, 102, 103, 105
furniture 78, 81, 87, 96, 116, 117, 141, 145, 147

G
Galeri Benda, Indonesia 191
Galeri Petronas see Petronas Gallery
gamelan orchestra 38, 47, 49
Gamelan Building 49
games, traditional 16, 77
Ganesha 57, 57, 119, *119*
Gedung Buleleng 32, 33
Gedung Gajah 44
Gedung Karangasem 32, 33
Gedung Tabanan 32, 33
Gedung Timur 33
genocide 26–27
Geological Museum, Malaysia 191
gerinsing ceremonial cloth 32
gerobag (traditional cart) 50
Giteau, Madeleine 21
glass collection 15, 63, 64, 79, 94, 126, 128
Goethe-Institut Art Gallery, Vietnam 195
Goethe-Institut Bangkok, Thailand 194
Goethe-Institut, The Philippines 192
Goh Geok Khim 132
goldware 47, 79, 89, 94, 96–97, 98, 103, 142, 145, 146, 175
Gold Buddha see Buddha Maitreya
Golden Palace, Laos 54
Gonzales, Ben 111
Goya, Francisco 110
Grand Palace, Bangkok 144
Groslier, George 20
Grundler, Curt 32
Guanyin (goddess of mercy) 121, 148, *177*
Gunawan, Hendra 50, 128

H
Ha Trung 169

Hai Bo 127
Halong Bay 129
Han dynasty (205 BCE–220 CE) 45
hand axes 30
Hang Tuah *and* Hang Jebat 79
Hanoi 174
Haribitak, Fua 143
Harihara 21, 23, 47, *147*
Haw Par Jade 131
hawker culture, Penang 81
Hebrard, Ernest 174
Hechanova, Lamberto 111
Hickley Collection 121
Hidalgo, Felix Resurreccion 96, *97*, 108, 109, 113
Hindu art and relics 20, 21, 22, 23, 30, 47, 119
Hmong 120
Ho Chi Minh Museum 173
Ho Kham, Laos see Golden Palace
Hoa Binh culture 175
Hoa Lo Prison Museum 172
Hofilena, Presentacion 108
Hofker, Willem 37, 41
Hong Zhu An 127, *127*
hornbill 76, 77
Hotel Majestic 66
How Kok Hoe 70
howdah 145
Huang Zhou 127
Hue Museum of Royal Fine Arts 186–187
Hugo, Victor 108
human skulls 66
hunting tools 72

I
I Gusti Ketut Gde 32
I Gusti Ketut Kobot 40
I Gusti Ketut Rai 32
I Gusti Nyoman Lempad 37, *37*, 38, 39, 41, *41*
I Ketut Boko 39
I Ketut Budiana 41
I Ketut Gelgel 39
I Ketut Murtika 39
I Ketut Soki 39
I Made Sukada 39
I Wayan Bendi 41
Ida Bagus Gelgel 39
Ida Bagus Made 37
Ida Bagus Made Kembeng 39
Ida Bagus Nyana 38
Ida Bagus Nyoman Rai 41
Ida Bagus Rai 40
Ida Bagus Togog 41
Ida Dewa Agung Jambe 34

Ifugao 103
ikat 33, 47, 120
Imao, Abdulmari 111
independence
   Burma 87
   Indochina 57
   Indonesia 45, 128
   Malaysia 69, 135
   Singapore 125
   Vietnam 172, 173
Indochina War 169
Indonesia National Gallery, Indonesia 190
Inovero, Reynaldo 100
Institute of Indonesian Culture 44, 45, 48
Insular Museum of Ethnology *see* National
   Museum of the Philippines
International Style 110
iron ware 30
Isakovich, Garon 173
Iskandar, Popo 50
Islamic art and influence 14, 45, 63, 69,
   119, 121, *133*
Islamic Arts Museum Malaysia 60–64
Issares Rajanusorn 144, 145, 148, 149
ivory 89
iwan (front portal of mosque) 60–61

J
jaba (courtyard) 32
Jabatan Hal Ehwal Orang Asli see Orang Asli
   Museum
Jade Basin 154, *154*, 155
Jakarta History Museum 43
'Jalong Buddha' 69
Japan Cultural Centre, Bangkok, Thailand
   194
Japanese blue and white wares 185
Japanese occupation 42, 43, 69, 80, 95,
   101, 104, 112, 123, 133, 135
Jayavarman VII 8, 24, *24*
Jendela Visual Art Space, Singapore 193
jewellery 15, *15*, 25, 30, 47, 48, 56, 63, 64,
   80, 81, 83, 89, 92, 93, 98, 102, 103,
   116, 119, 120, 132, *133*, 145.
   tribal 47, 72, *72*
   Also see regalia
Jim Thompson House 138–142, 152
Jim Thompson House Art Centre, Thailand
   194
Jingdezhen porcelain ware 15, *117*
Johor-Riau Empire 69
Jorge B. Vargas Museum & Filipiniana
   Research Center, The Philippines
   112–113
Joya, Jose 107, *107*, 109, 110

K
Kaisa-Angelo King Heritage Center 94
kamcheng 117
Kamphaeng Phet 147, 149
Kamphaeng Phet National Museum,
   Thailand 194
Kamthieng House Museum 150–151

Kanbawathadi Palace 87
Kanlungan ng Sining Gallery, The
   Philippines 192
Karalama 121, 122
Karen 120
Kataas taasang Katipinan ng mga anak ng
   Bayan (*also* Katipunan) 100
Kebyar Seni 38
Kedai Kebun Forum, Indonesia 191
kendi 15, 48
kenyalang 76
   Also see hornbill
Kertha Gosa 34
kettledrums 47
Khmer art 20–25, 56, *139*, 140, 142, 145,
   147
Khmer Rouge (1975–1979) 20–21, 25,
   26–27
Khuong My 169
kiblah (direction of Mecca) 63
King Bhumipol 143, 150
King Chulalongkorn (1868–1910) 44, 143,
   144, 145, 148, 154, 155
King Mindon 87
King Mongkut 144
King Norodom 25
King Rama I 144
King Rama VI 143
King Sasavangvong 54
King Sihanouk 25
King Thibaw 86, 87
Kipling, Rudyard 125
kite flying 16, *70*
Klong Saen Saep 138, 141, 142
Koke, Robert 41
Kokoschka, Oscar 110
Kollwitz, Käthe 110
Koppelman, Chaime 110
kris (*also* keris) 49, 69, 71, *71* 80, 83, 98,
   100
Kuan Yin Museum, Thailand 194
Kuching *77*
kufi banaie 60
Kumpulan Senireka Sdn Bhd 60
Kunavichayanont, Sutee *126*, 143
Kuvera 47

L
L'Espace, Centre Culturel Français, Vietnam
   195
La Liga Foundation 100
Labuan Maritime Museum 75
lacquer art *87*, 89, 144, 153, *153*, *156*, *175*
Lacquerware Museum, Myanmar 192
Lai Nam Thong wares 146
Lan Xang Period 57
land reclamation 124
Lanna 146, *147*, 148, 150–151, *157*–158
Lao National Museum 57
Lao Revolutionary Museum *see* Lao
   National Museum
Lao-Japan Bridge *see* Friendship Bridge
Laurel, Jose P 101

Laya, Dr Jaime C. 96
Le dynasty 174, 176, 177, 179, 183
Le Mayeur de Merprès, Adrien-Jean 31, *37*
Le Mayeur Museum 31
Lebuh Acheh Mosque 80
Legaspi, Cesar 109, 110, 113
Lembah Bujang Archaeological Museum,
   Malaysia 191
Lemire, Charles 167, 168, 170, 175
Leper, Dewa Nyoman 39
Leper King 24
Lertchaiprasert, Kamin 143
life cycle 16
Lim, Alfred 99
Limbang gold hoard 16
Lim-Yuson, Nina 99
linga 32, 33
liquefied natural gas 17
Liu Xiaodong 127
Lluch, Julie *97*, 111
Locsin Jr, Leandro V 93, *106*, 112
Long Bar 124
Long Jaafar Cannon *83*
longhouse *77*
Lopburi School *139*, 145, 146, *146*, 147, 148
Lopez, Benito 108
Lopez, Eugenio 108
Lopez, Robbie 109
Lopez Memorial Museum 108–109
Lorenzo, Diosdado 113
Low, H. Brooke 76
Low, Sir Hugh 82
Luang Prabang National Museum 54–55
Luna y Novicio, Juan 93, 96, 108, 109, 113
Luz, Arturo 107, 109, 110, 111, 112, 113
Ly dynasty 174, 176, 177, 179, 183
Ly Vou Ong 21

M
Mac dynasty 174, 176, 177, 179, 183
Macapagal, Diosdado P 101
Macapagal-Arroyo, Gloria 101
Maceda, Dr Marcelino 92
Magsaysay, Ramon F. 101
Magsaysay-Ho, Anita 109, 110, 113
Maha Wirawong National Museum, Thailand
   195
Mahabharata epic 40
Mai's Gallery, Vietnam 195
Maison Centrale *see* Hoa Lo Prison Museum
Majapahit Empire 16, 132
Malay Technology Museum, Brunei 14, 16,
   190
Malayan Union 69
Malolos Republic 100
Mamanuas 92
Mamluk style 14, 16
mamuli ornaments 120
Manansala, Vicente 105, *107*, 109, 110, 112,
   113
Manet, Edouard 110
Manila Film Center 106
Mansaka 92

Manunggul Cave 103
manuscripts, ancient 49, 63, 87, *87*, 112,
   122, 147
maps, ancient 94, 108, 109
Maranao 103
Marcelo, Ildefonso 112
Marcos, Ferdinand E. 101
Marcos, Imelda 107
maritime relics *see* shipwrecks
marriage rituals 16, 72, 81, 116, *116*, 117
martial law 101
Marxism 57
masks 33, 47, 72, 77, *77*, 83, 98, 103, *118*,
   120
Mataram Kingdom 51
Maybank Numismatic Museum 65
McCallum, Henry 130
McNair, J.F. A. 118
Medalla, David Cortez 110
Megalithic tools 68
Meier, Theo 37, 41
Mekong Valley 57
Melaka Sultanate 65, 69, *74*
Melaka Sultanate Palace Museum 79
Memmi, Lippo 97
Menara Maybank 65
Merimbun Heritage Park, Brunei 14, 190
metal age 102
metalware 15, 47, 63, 64, 105
Metropolitan Museum of Manila 96–98
mihrab (prayer niche) 63
minbar (pulpit) 63
Ming blue and white 15, 109, 140, 185
   Also see Annamese *and* Japanese
Ming dynasty (1368–1644) 45
Mir Sharuddin, Dato' Mir Shariman 66
Misiem's Sculpture Garden, Thailand 194
mo-aqali script *see* kufi banaie
Modernism 14, 39, 50, 66, 86, 106, 107,
   109, 110, 112, 129, 143
Mohidin, Abdul Latiff 67, *67*, 73
Monsani, Roberto 60
Monti, Francesco 104
moon rocks 54
MOPA 107
mother-of-pearl inlay 78, 79, 94, 146
Mouhot, Henri 21
Mountain Railway Tours 42, *42*
Mughal art 15, 63
murals 34, *34*, 38, 39, *54*, 55, 70, 89, 123,
   144
   Also see frescoes
Musée Albert Sarraut 20
Musée Louis Finot *see* National Museum of
   Vietnamese History
Museo ng Kalinangang Pilipino (Museum of
   Philippine Humanities) 106
Museo Pambata 99
Museum & Art Gallery, Penang 80–81
Museum Bali 32
Museum Geologi Bandung, Indonesia 190
Museum Nasional *see* National Museum,
   Indonesia

Museum of Arts and Sciences. The
　Philippines 104—105
Museum of Cham Sculpture, Vietnam
　167—170, 179
Museum of Chinese in Philippine Life
　94—95
Museum of Philippine Art (MOPA) 107
Museum of Philippine Humanities 106
Museum of Philippine Political History
　100—101
Museum of Sa Huynh Culture, Vietnam 184
Museum of the Aboriginal People of
　Peninsular Malaysia see Orang Asli
　Museum
Museum of Trade Ceramics, Vietnam 185
Museum of Vietnamese History, Ho Chi
　Minh 182—183
Museum Prabu Geusan Ulun, Indonesia 49
Museum Puri Lukisan, Indonesia 38—39
Museum Semarajaya, Indonesia 34
Museum Seni Lukis Affandi, Indonesia 50
Museum Trowulan, Indonesia 51
musical instruments 54, 57, 71, 72, 77, 77,
　83, 86, 89, 105, 107, 119, 122, 145
Muzium Negara, Malaysia see National
　Museum
My Son 169, 170, 183

N

Nakhon Si Thammarat National Museum,
　Thailand 160
Nang Ngales 39
Nang Ramis 39
Nath, Vann 27
National Archive of Brunei Darussalam 14
National Art Gallery, Malaysia 66—67
National Art Gallery, Thailand 143
National Gallery, Indonesia 45
National Historical Institute, The Philippines
　100
National History Museum, Malaysia 68—70
National Museum Bangkok 144—147, 148
National Museum Building, Singapore 130
National Museum of Malaysia 131
National Museum of Myanmar 86—89
National Museum of Royal Barges, Thailand
　194
National Museum of the Filipino People 102,
　103
National Museum of the Philippines
　102—103
National Museum of Vietnamese History,
　Vietnam 174—175
National Museum, Cambodia 20—24
National Museum, Indonesia 44—48
National Museum, Malaysia 70—71
National Museum, Singapore 126
National Science Museum, Thailand 162—163
nationalism 69
natural history 17, 70, 71, 77, 82, 83, 89,
　92, 102, 104, 105, 131, 132, 135
Natural History and Commerce see National
　Museum of the Philippines

Navarro, J. Elizalde 109
Nederlandsch Indische Spoorweg
　Maatschappij 42
Negano, Paul 41
Negritos 72, 92
Neka, Suteja 40
Neka Art Museum 40—41
neo-Classical art 44, 78, 102
Neolithic tools 16, 30, 68, 175
ngengong 72
Ngoc Lu drum 174
Nguyen dynasty 174, 175, 177, 183, 186
Nguyen Phan Chanh 178, 178, 179
Nguyen Sang 129
Nguyen Tu Nghiem 129
Nha San Duc, Vietnam 195
Ni Pollok 31, 31
Ni Rongji 35
Nias 120
Norman, A.C. 68
numismatic relics 45, 48, 49, 63, 65, 69,
　71, 92, 105, 112, 147
NUS Museum, Singapore 131
nyonya baba see Peranakan

O

Ocampo, Galo 105
Ocampo, Hernando R. 109, 110, 113
oil and petroleum, discovery of 17, 79
Old Batavia Museum see Jakarta History
　Museum
Old Congress Building 102
opium 79
Orang Asli Museum 72
　Also see aborigines and aboriginal art
Orlina, Ramon 111
Osman, Ahmad Fuad 67
Osmena, Sergio 101
Ottoman Syria 63, 64

P

PAG see Philippine Art Gallery
paintings 31, 33, 36—37, 36, 37, 39, 40, 40,
　61, 63, 63, 73, 89, 94, 97, 97, 98, 105,
　108—109, 110, 112, 128, 131, 132, 140,
　140, 142, 143, 176
Pakse 56
Palace of the Front see National Museum
　Bangkok
Palawan 103
Paleolithic discoveries 30
Pali manuscript 87, 87
　Also see manuscripts
panels, inscribed 17
Pangeran (Prince) Sugih 49
Pangeran Kornel 49
Pangkor Treaty 68, 69
Pardo, Jose 113
Parian 94—95
Paris World's Fair 45
Parmentier, Henry 169
Parsons, William 99
Parvati 32, 45

Paterno, Pa 96
Paua, Jose Ignacio 95
pearls 79, 94
Penang Free School 80
pensol 72
people power 93, 101
Perak State Museum 82—83
Peranakan culture 78, 81, 81, 116—117
Peranakan Museum see Asian Civilisations
　Museum (Armenian Street)
performing art exhibits 89, 119
　Also see dance, musical instruments
　and theatrical
Petroliam Nasional Berhad 73
Petronas Gallery 73
Petronas Twin Towers 73
Phaosavasdi, Kamol 143
Philately 147
philately exhibits 112, 134—135
Philippine Art Gallery 110
Philippine Center for Trade and Exhibitions
　106
Philippine Cultural Heritage Institute 100
Philippine International Convention Center
　106
Philippine Library and Museum see
　National Museum of the Philippines
Phong Le 169
photographs, old 41, 73, 117
Phra Pathom Chedi National Museum,
　Thailand 194
Phunsombatlert, Bundith 143
Picasso, Pablo 110
Pilapil, Impy 111
Pita Maha painting society (1936—1942)
　37, 38, 39
Piyadasa, Redza 67
Plain of Jars 57
Plastique Kinetic Worms, Singapore 193
Pol Pot 26
porcelain 15, 78, 79, 81, 94, 94, 104, 117,
　117, 140, 141
Portuguese occupation and influence 16,
　65, 69, 74, 79
post-Angkor art 24, 56
postcards see philately exhibits
pottery 30, 66, 89, 94, 96, 97, 103, 145,
　184, 185
Prabang 54
Prachinburi National Museum, Thailand 195
prada 33
Prajnaparamita 47
Prasart Museum 144, 148—149
Praset Andet style 21, 23
pre-Angkor art 21, 23, 23, 142
prehistoric tools 16, 23, 34, 43, 45, 57, 68,
　89, 93, 94, 103, 144, 148
Prei Khmeng style 23
Prince Sisavang Vatthana 54, 55
prints 73, 94, 110, 131, 142
Product Design and Development Center,
　Philippines 106
Project 304, Thailand 194

Proto Malay 72
Proto-Historic tools 68
pua kumbu 120
Pucuk Rebung Royal Gallery Museum,
　Malaysia 191
Pulau Labuan 75
puppets 149
pura (temple) 32
Purbakala Archaeological Museum 30
puri (palace) 32
Purugganan, Ricarte 113
pusaka (sacred heirloom) 48
Pusaka Building 49
Pyu period and relics 87, 87, 88

Q

Qi Baishi 127
Qi Gong 127
Qing dynasty 61, 78, 81, 132, 140
Queen Sirikit 155, 162, 163
Queen's Gallery, Thailand 194
Quezon, Manuel L. 101
Qur'an relics 15, 16, 60, 61, 61, 63, 121, 122

R

Raffles, Sir Stamford 9, 44, 118, 131, 132
Raffles Hotel Museum 124—125
Raffles Museum and Library 118, 130, 131
Rahmann, Rudolph 92
railway coach 42
rainforest 71, 77, 99
Rakhine State Cultural Museum 192
Ramayana epic 25, 40, 55
Ramkhamhaeng National Museum,
　Thailand 195
Ramos, Fidel V. 101
Rasdjarmrearnsook, Araya 143
Ratna Wartha see Yayasan Ratna Wartha
rattan 16
Rattanakosin art 147, 148, 149
Rauschenberg, Robert 67
Red Palace, Bangkok 144, 145, 148, 149
regalia 25, 49, 54, 55, 86, 145, 146, 187,
　187
religious art 47, 57, 61, 89, 92, 93,
　105—106, 119, 141, 146, 147
repoussé 47
Reyum Institute of Arts and Culture,
　Cambodia 190
rice planting, wet 79
rickshaws 83
Rijn, Rembrandt van 110
Riverside Point 132
Rivertales 133
Rizal Library 110
Rodriguez, Manuel 111
Roxas, Manuel A. 101
Roy Lichtenstein Sculpture Plaza,
　Singapore 193
Royal Asiatic Society 132
Royal Malaysia Air Force Museum, Malaysia
　191
Royal Malaysian Police Museum 74

Royal Palace, Cambodia 25
Royal Regalia Building, Brunei 14, 190
Ruang Pameran Lukisan. Indonesia 33
Ruano, Roque 104
Ruiz, Jose Tence 111
Ryllega Gallery, Vietnam 195

S

Sabah State Museum, Malaysia 191
sago 16
Saguil, Nena 109
Salazar, Pedro 96
Saleh, Raden 36, 37
Salon Natasha, Vietnam 195
SAM see Singapore Art Museum
Sama d'laut 103
samsui 131
San Miguel, General Luciano 100
sandalwood 16
sandstone 21, 22, 23, 24, 119, 166, 167,
    168, 170
Sanpitak, Pinaree 143
Sanso, Juvena 109, 111
Santos, Pablo Beanse 97, 111
Sarawak State Museum 76–77
sarcophagi 30, 30
Sari Oneng Parakan Salak 49, 49
Sarkies brothers 124, 125
sarong 47
Sarraut, Albert 20
Sawankhalok 147
    wares 153, 156
science, ancient knowledge of 122, 162–163
sculpture 39, 54, 56, 73, 83, 94, 97, 109,
    110, 111, 112, 119, 126, 131, 140, 142,
    142, 144, 146, 147, 176
Sculpture Square, Singapore 193
seashells see shell ornaments
See, Professor Chinben 94
Sejarah Melayu (Malay Annals) 79
Selangor Museum 70
Seni, Kebyar 38
Senoi 72
Sepi, Valeriu 123
Seria oilfield 17
Seven Heavenly Bodies 61
SG Private Banking, Alliance Française,
    Singapore 192
Shah Jahan, Emperor 63
Shahn, Ben 110
Shan State Cultural Museum, Myanmar 192
shark's fin 94
shell ornaments 102, 104, 105
ship cloth 48
shipwrecks 15, 17, 71, 75
Shiva 22, 32, 45, 47, 47, 139, 140, 170, 171,
    175
Shwe Dagon Pagoda 86
Siam Society 150
silk 79, 94, 138
Silpa Bhirasri Memorial Gallery 143
Silpakorn University Art Gallery, Thailand 194
Silver Pagoda, Cambodia 25

silverware 48, 89, 116, 117, 120
Singapore Art Museum 118, 126–129
Singapore Gin Sling 124
Singapore History Museum 118, 126,
    130–133
Singapore Philatelic Museum 134–135
Singapore Post Office 134
Singapore River 133
Singapore Stone 132
Singapore Tyler Print Institute (STPI),
    Singapore 193
Sitthiket, Vasan 143
Smit, Arie 37, 41
Smith, Captain Robert 80, 81
Sobrat, Anak Agung Gede 37, 40, 41
social customs 16
Soedarsono, Srihadi 41
songket 33, 47
Songkhla National Museum, Thailand 195
Sonnega, Auke 37
Soriano, Lazaro 111
Spacekraft, Malaysia 191
Spanish colonisation 92, 93, 95, 96, 100,
    105
Sparke, Robert 80
spices 45, 79
Spies, Walter 37, 38, 40
Srimanganti Building. Indonesia 49
Srivijaya art 45, 142, 146, 147
St Joseph's Institution, Singapore 126
St Xavier's Institution, Malaysia 80
stamps, postage see philately exhibits
stele 45, 88, 121, 145, 146, 174
Stone Age 174
stoneware 15, 23, 30, 47, 48, 56, 68, 89,
    119, 121
Straits Settlements 134, 135
Straits-born Chinese see Peranakan culture
Su Xinping 127
Suan Pakkad Palace Museum 152–153
Subanen 103
Substation, Singapore 134, 193
Sud, Aupam 67
Sudjojono 41, 50
Sugai 111
Sukhothai 146, 147
Sultan Bolkiah 14
Sultan Mansor Shah (1459–1477) 69, 79
Sultan Muzaffar Shah (1564–1570) 65, 69,
    71, 79
Sultan Zainul Abidin II 63
SUPPORT Foundation, Thailand 155
Suriya 142
Swettenham, Sir Frank 67

T

Tabuena, Romeo 109
Tadu Contemporary Art, Thailand 194
Taiping 82, 83
Taiping Prison 82
Tamnak Daeng 144, 145, 148, 149
Tan Kim Seng Altar Table 117
Tan, Royston 133

Tang Da Wu 127
Tang dynasty 121
Tantisook, Sawadi 143
Tantri Kamandaka cycle 39
Tanumaja, Dalem Adipati 49
Tao Nan School 116
Tay Son 176, 177
Temple of the Emerald Buddha see Silver
    Pagoda
terracotta 174
Tet (Vietnamese Lunar New Year) 177, 181
textiles 33, 45, 47, 48, 54, 56, 63–64, 73,
    83, 116, 120, 145, 146
Thai Silk Company 140
Thanateeranon, Jakraphun 143
That Mak Mo 55
The Museum of Vietnamese History,
    182–183
theatrical paraphernalia 36, 57
Thit Tanh 55
Thompson, Jim 138–142
    Also see Jim Thompson House
tin mines 82, 83
    ingot 65
Tok Panjang 117
Tolentino, Guillermo 112
Tomlinson and Lermit Architects 134
top spinning 16
topeng dance 33
    Also see dance forms
tortoise shell 16, 94
Total Gallery Alliance Française, The
    Philippines 192
Toulouse-Lautrec, Henri 110
Tourane 167, 168, 170, 175
Tra Kieu 169, 170, 183
trade relations 15, 16, 45, 65, 68, 81, 92,
    93, 94–95, 103, 105, 116, 119
Tran culture 174, 176, 177, 179, 183
Tran Van Can 176
'Trapunto' 98
Tree of Life 61
tribal artefacts 47, 56, 57, 79, 89, 92, 107,
    120–121, 180–181
Tribal Museum, Thailand 159
Tsinoy culture 94
Tunku Abdul Rahman 66
Tuol Sleng Genocide Museum, Cambodia
    26–27

U

Ullen Sentalu Museum 51
Uma 22, 142, 161, 161
umbrellas, ceremonial 49
University Carillon 112
University of San Carlos Museum 92
University of Santo Tomas Museum of Arts
    and Sciences, The Philippines 104–105
University of the Philippines 112, 113

V

Vargas, Jorge B. 112, 113, 113
Verenigde Oostindische Compagnie (VOC)

see Dutch East India Company
Via Via Café, Indonesia 191
Vietnam Fine Arts Museum 176–179
Vietnam Museum of Ethnology 179, 180–181
Vietnam War 57, 169, 172, 173, 176, 187
Vietnam Fine Arts Museum 176–179
Vietnamese Communist Party 173
Vietnamese nationalism 172
Vigil, Ramon Martinez 104
Vijaya 167
Villarosa, Rogelio 94
Villasenor, Vincente 96
Vimanmek Mansion Museum 154–158
Vishnu 23, 23, 24, 140
Vishnu-Vasudeva-Narayana 20, 23
Vo Canh epitaph 174
Vongsakul, Prasart 148

W

Wang Na see National Museum Bangkok
Warren, Stanley 123
Wat Buddhaisawan 144, 145
Wat Pho 144, 149
Wat Phou 56
Wat Preah Kaeo Morokat, Cambodia see
    Silver Pagoda
Wat Suthat 149
Wat Yai Suwannaram 149
wax technique 175
Wayang Museum, Indonesia 190
weaponry 47, 49, 63, 69, 71, 74, 77, 79, 83,
    92, 100, 105, 107, 119, 146
weaving 138
wedding rituals see marriage rituals
Wedyadiningrat, Dr Samuel Haryono 51
Weld, Frederick 131
Wenchang statuary 121, 121
'White Rajahs' 9, 76
Widayat Museum, Indonesia 41, 191
Widjaja, Anton Kustia 41
Wija, Ida Bagus 41
Wong Hoy Chong 67
woodcarving 47, 63, 64, 76, 77, 79, 89, 92,
    103, 146
World War II 38, 42, 43, 45, 70, 75, 87, 95,
    99, 113, 124, 133, 135
Wray, Leonard Junior 82

X

Xu Beihong 127

Y

Yamashita, General Tomoyuki 101
Yao 120
Yayasan Ratna Wartha 39
'year zero' 26
Yimsiri, Kien 143
Yipintsoi, Misiem 143
Yong Mun Seng 67
Yoshida, Masaji 111
Young Artists 39, 41
Yu Youren 127

Acknowledgements

THE PUBLISHER WOULD LIKE TO THANK:

BRUNEI:

Awang Haji Matasim bin Haji Jibah, Director, Museums Department, Brunei Museum

Pengiran Haji Mohd Yamin bin PSJ Pengiran Haji Abd Momin, Curator of Exhibitions / Manager of Royal Regalia, Brunei Museum

Dayang Fauziah binti A. Habib, Head of Information Technology Section, Brunei Museum

Rafeah Haji Ahmad, Information Technology Section, Brunei Museum

CAMBODIA:

Françoise Alves, French Embassy of Cambodia

Khun Samen, Director of the National Museum of Phnom Penh

Hab Touch, Deputy Director, National Museum of Phnom Penh

Rhys Butler, Curator, National Museum of Phnom Penh

Bertrand Porte, Curator, National Museum of Phnom Penh / EFEO

Melanie Eastburn, National Museum of Phnom Penh

Sotha Bou, Deputy Director of Conservation Department, Ministry of the Royal Palace

Chum Ngoeun, Ministry of the Royal Palace

Chey Sopheara, Director, Tuol Sleng Genocide Museum

INDONESIA:

Anak Agung Asrama, Director, Agung Rai Museum of Art

Sudono, Director, Ambarawa Railway Museum

Mario Blanco, Manager, The Blanco Renaissance Museum

Tinia Budiati, Director, Jakarta History Museum

Ketut Mantara Gandhi, Le Mayeur Musem

Dr I Ketut Narya, Director, Museum Bali

Anak Angung Ngurah Muning, Curator, Museum Puri Lukisan

Ida Bagus Wisnaya, Director, Museum Semarajaya

Dr Endgang Sri Hardiati, Director, National Museum

Pande Wayan Suteja Neka, Founder and Director, Neka Art Museum

Garrett Kam, Curator, Neka Art Museum

Maya Sujatmiko, Director, Prabu Geusan Ulun

Made Kusuma Jaya, Purbakala Archaeological Museum

Juki Affandi, Director, Seni Lukis Affandi Museum

Yenny Haryono, Director, Ullen Sentalu

LAOS:

Jean-André Viala, Directeur Adjoint du Centre Culturel et de Coopération Linguistique

Bounlap, Director, Champasak Museum

Phengsavan Vongchandy, Director, Lao National Museum

Bronwyn Campbell, Curator, Lao National Museum

Bounhom Chanthamat, Deputy Director, Department of Museums and Archaeology, Ministry of Information and Culture

Vanpheng Keopannha, Curator, Royal Palace Museum

Khamnoy Manivong, Director, Wat Phra Keo

MALAYSIA:

Loh-Lim Lin Lee, Cheong Fatt Tse Mansion

Chan Kim Lay, Director, Baba Nyonya Heritage Museum

Dato' Dr Haji Adi Bin Taha, Director General, Department of Museums and Antiquities

Janet Tee, Information Resources Division, Head of Public Relations, Department of Museums and Antiquities

Dianne Buerger, Editions Didier Millet (Kuala Lumpur)

Michel-Louis Pasquir, French Embassy of Malaysia

Corinne Amraoui, French Embassy of Malaysia

Zainol Abidin bin Ahmad Shariff, Director, Galeri Petronas

Shahnaz Said, Curator, Galeri Petronas

Norminshah Hamzah, Marketing & Communication, Galeri Petronas

Adline Abdul Ghani, Assistant Curator, Islamic Art Museum Malaysia

Mohmd Shawali Badi, Director, Labuan Maritime Museum

Amirsham Abdul Aziz, Director, Maybank Numismatic Museum

Mohd Nasruddin Abd. Rahman, Curator, Melaka Sultanate Palace Museum

Koo Boo Chia, Director, Museum and Art Gallery of Penang

Wairah Marzuki, Director, National Art Gallery

Zanita Anuar, Director of R&D Department, National Art Gallery

Mohd Khazrul bin Sharuddin, Assistant Curator, Documentation Unit, National Art Gallery

Sitti Rabia binti Abd Rahman, National History Museum

Khalid Syed Ali, Department of Museums and Antiquities, National Museum

Asmawi Mohd Yunos, Curator Assistant, Orang Asli Museum

Tuan Hahi Zainal Abidin bin Jamaludin, Curator, Perak State Museum

Henry Bong, Managing Director, Pucuk Rebung Royal Gallery Museum

Terence Tay, Pucuk Rebung Royal Gallery Museum

Supt. Haji Halal Haji Ismail, Curator, Royal Malaysian Police Museum

MYANMAR:

Jean Hourcade, Conseiller Culturel, French Embassy of Myanmar

Tin Maung Oo, Frang • Tours

Daw Nu Mra Zan, Director, National Museum of Myanmar

THE PHILIPPINES:

Ramon E. S. Lerma, Curator, Ateneo Art Gallery

Joel de Leon, Assistant Curator, Ateneo Art Gallery

Florina H. Capistrano-Baker, Director, Ayala Museum

Christy Monastrial, Ayala Museum

Teresita Ang See, Bahay Tsinoy: Museum of Chinese in Philippine Life

Lisa Alcayde, Bahay Tsinoy: Museum of Chinese in Philippine Life

Mila Blanquera, Director, Coconut Palace

Sid Gomez Hildawa, Department Manager, Visual, Literary and Media Arts Department, Cultural Center of the Philippines

Pilipino Mitzie J. Icasiano, Cultural Center of the Philippines

Franck Hébert, Counselor for Cooperation and Cultural Affairs, French Embassy of the Philippines

Ricardo L. Punzalan, Museum Archivist, Jorge B. Vargas Museum and Filipiniana Research Center

Yeyey Cruz, Curatorial Consultant, Lopez Museum

Victorino Manolo, Director, Metropolitan Museum of Manila

Elvira T. Arafol, Exhibitions Department, Metropolitan Museum of Manila

Madonna B. del Mundo, Executive Director, Museo Pambata

Ludovico Badoy, Executive Director, National Historical Institute

Romel Aquino, National Historical Institute

Corazon S. Alvina, Director IV, National Museum of the Philippines

Elenita D.V. Alba, Curator, Chief of Education Division, National Museum of the Philippines

Marlene Samson, Curator, University of San Carlos Museum

Fr Isidro Abaño, Director, University of Santo Tomas Museum of Arts and Sciences

Clarissa Avendaño, Assistant Director, University of Santo Tomas Museum of Arts and Sciences

Maita Oebanda, Documentation Assistant, University of Santo Tomas Museum of Arts and Sciences

SINGAPORE:

Randall Ee, Assistant Curator, Asian Civilisations Museum (Armenian Street)

Kenson Kwok, Director, Asian Civilisations Museum (Empress Place)

Jeya Thurai, Director, The Changi Museum

Simon Goh, Manager, The Changi Museum

Kwok Kian Chow, Director, Singapore Art Museum

Suenne Megan Tan, Manager, Communications, Singapore Art Museum

Ahmad Mashadi, Senior Curator, Singapore Art Museum

Lee Chor Lin, Director, Singapore History Museum

Tresnawati Prihadi, General Manager, Singapore Philatelic Museum

Jocelyn Lee, Education & Public Communication Officer, Singapore Philatelic Museum

THAILAND:

Thomas Baude, Director, Alliance Française of Chiang Mai

Siranee, Alliance Française of Chiang Mai

Dianne Josse, Cultural Attaché, French Embassy of Thailand

Saiwimon Wongjarin, Curator, Chiang Mai Contemporary Art Museum

Wiset Phetpradab, Museum Director, Chiang Mai National Museum

Eric Booth, Director, Jim Thompson House

Phongthorn Wongkietkachorn, Head of Curatorial Section, Art Gallery National Museum

Somchai Na Nakhonphanom, Director, National Museum

Napatr Vacharapimolmas, Public Relations, National Science Museum

Charlermchai Honark, President, National Science Museum

Prasart Vongsakul, Prasart Museum

Anuwat, Manager, Prasart Museum

Kanitha Kasinau-Bol, Siam Society and Kamthieng House

Albert Paravi Wongchirachai, Siam Society and Kamthieng House

Naris Srisawang, The Siam Society and Kamthieng House Museum

Nipa Lachroj, Tribal Museum

Watcharakitti Watcharothai, Assistant Lord Chamberlain Vimanmek Mansion Museum

VIETNAM:

Mme Do Thi Minh Nguyet, Chargée de Mission, Ambassade de France

M. Bruno Asseray, Attaché Culturel, Directeur, L'Espace— Centre Culturel Français de Hanoi, Centre Culturel et de Coopération auprès de l'Ambassade de France au Vietnam

Quyen, Artist, Contemporary Art Center

Le Phuong Lan, Contemporary Art Center

Dr Nguyen Thi Don, Director, Hoa Lo Prison Museum

Dinh Cong Chinh, Hoa Lo Prison Museum

Nguyen Thi Tinh, Director, Ho Chi Minh Museum

Dr Tran Duc Anh Son, Director, Hue Museum of Royal Fine Arts

Ha Phuoc Mai, Director, Museum of Cham Sculpture

Phan Van Canh, Deputy Director, Museum of Cham Sculpture

Tran Thuy Diem, Curator, Museum of Cham Sculpture

La Thi Thanh Thuy, International Relations Officer, Museum of Ethnology

Tran Anh, Director Museum of Trade Ceramics

Trenh The Hoa, Director, The Museum of Vietnamese History

Ms Dao, The Museum of Vietnamese History

Dr Pham Quoc Quan, Director, National Museum of Vietnamese History

Dao Minh Nguyet, Deputy Head of Division for Exhibition, Vietnam Fine Arts Museum

Lan, Vietnam Fine Art Association

AND ALSO:

Ratna Amatsarie

Martin Cross

New Bee Yong

Hélène Ratier

Sim Kam Cheong

George C. Tapan

THE AUTHOR WOULD LIKE TO THANK:

Arahmaiani

Danielle Becker

Isabelle Blot

Jacqueline Cheah

Natasha Kraevskaia

Kenson Kwok

Lee Chor Lin

Mok Kim Chuan

Jean-Louis Morisot

Jennifer Potter

Pinaree Sanpitak